Children's Spaces

For Sarah and Hamish

Children's Spaces

Mark Dudek

ELSEVIER

AMSTERDAM • BOSTON • HEIDELBERG • LONDON • NEW YORK • OXFORD
PARIS • SAN DIEGO • SAN FRANCISCO • SINGAPORE • SYDNEY • TOKYO
Architectural Press is an imprint of Elsevier

Architectural
Press

Architectural Press
An imprint of Elsevier
Linacre House, Jordan Hill, Oxford OX2 8DP
30 Corporate Drive, Burlington, MA 01803

First published 2005

British Library Cataloguing in Publication Data
A catalogue record for this book is available from the British Library

ISBN 0 7506 54260

For information on all Architectural Press
publications visit our website at architecturalpress.com

Typeset by Charon Tec Pvt. Ltd, Chennai, India
Website: http://www.charontec.com
Printed and bound in Great Britain

Contents

Contents

Introduction

This is a book about children, for children. However, I suspect it will not be read by many children. Rather, it attempts to provide a framework, a forum within which their views and sensibilities may be better interpreted by adult voices. By encouraging them to describe their worlds in relation to the physical spaces within which they spend much of their time, we can see and understand more clearly their child-centric view.

I have therefore invited people to contribute chapters on the basis of their work as designers of children's spaces or in the context of their academic work in the area of contemporary childhood studies. Each contributor has in common a sympathy for children and how their lives are shaped by physical and bureaucratic structures, such as nurseries, schools and play parks, which helps to create the material culture of childhood.

However, I do not forget that children are increasingly dependent on new technology, not just for educational purposes in the school, but also for leisure and social interaction at home. This also defines their 'space' as much as the streets and fields in and around our cities might have done for children in former times. Viewed in this way, the architecture of the computer and the television may be just as important to them as the architecture of the classroom or the playground.

Most important is the recognition that children need to be observed and listened to in order for their priorities to be understood within a complex urban environment. Each contributor has this priority in mind, acting as an interpreter of their subtle needs and aspirations, often outside the traditional educational and economic conventions. The end result is, I hope, a diverse range of perspectives which will provide a vision for the future, largely defined by children themselves.

The chapters

Childhood is sometimes described as a state of mind. It is also a distinct physical and mental phase which is experienced between ages one and a half to 16. Although it is debatable when childhood actually ceases and adulthood becomes a reality, for the purposes of this collection, our definition of childhood is broadly determined by these age criteria. Within this framework three sections emerge which order the chapters in this book: firstly, the child in early years; secondly, the child in school; and thirdly, the child in the city. Each theme is linked and interconnected, with the chapters ordered chronologically and loosely linked by a thematic narrative.

Chapter 1 is an introduction to some of the main issues around listening to young children in an effort to take on board their views within the design process. Alison Clark has helped to develop a methodological framework, called the Mosaic approach, for listening to young people about the important details of their daily lives. She is concerned that those details and architectural features which young children really need, are not taken for granted by the adults who are creating them. She argues that only by listening to young children can we can begin to understand how important this iconography is to them. The methodology relates specifically to young children, however, many aspects of the approach are equally valid if applied to listening with older children.

Michael Laris is a designer of playground equipment for children of all ages which is widely recognized for its quality and style. In Chapter 2 he describes his approach to designing and most importantly evolving the equipment to better suit the needs of its users. He does this by observing children playing in the environments he has helped to create. This gives a fascinating perspective on the way children play. Through this two key criteria emerge, firstly, the need for flexibility, so that children can follow their own personal imaginative intentions and are not dictated to by overly descriptive imagery; play is rarely a straightforward appropriation of adult pre-conceptions. Secondly, there is a need to consider the details to which children's minds and bodies can relate. The equipment must strike a balance between safety in use and the need to challenge the child to explore the limits of their physical dexterity. He describes the conceptual thinking which goes into his work, elevating a piece of climbing equipment to part of a psychological landscape of play and experimentation which extends development opportunities for those who use it.

In Chapter 3, Bruce Jilk presents a radical view of contemporary education which, he argues, is outdated and does not meet the needs of the modern world. Instead of providing for a world of individuals operating within a wider urban environment, schools have become internalized ghettos of childhood, cut off from the communities they are supposed to serve, centrally administered in a 'one size fits all' ethos. He describes an alternative strategy he helped to devise which has been used to develop a new school in Reykjavik, where a whole range of factors such as politics, society, environment and economics have been brought into the discussion about the shape of the new school, its architecture and its curriculum. By engaging with the community, the process moulds the school to its individual needs, recognizing it as a unique community in its own right.

Eleanor Nicholson was a schools inspector in California before her recent retirement. She describes a more enlightened approach to school design in Chapter 4. Drawing upon her discussions with staff and students over many years she explains how important the environment is in complementing the educational and social support of the pedagogy. She cites a number of key examples of good school design, which values the needs of children and forms a lasting impression on the users. In her view it is important because the environment sends out messages about how children are valued. One historical example is of particular interest because it gauges the views of alumni and the positive effects the environment had in forming and shaping their lives fifty years ago.

Nicholson describes the classrooms at a well-loved school in Winnetka, Illinois as being 'humane and democratic' because simple needs are respected, with classrooms having access to the garden, en-suite WCs and enough space to enable teaching to take place in a number of different forms. This allows schools to deal with special needs within an increasingly individualized society.

In Chapter 5, John Edwards illustrates the intensive integration of activities and functions within the framework of this single room, the primary school classroom, where children aged 5 to 11 years spend most of their time. Based on observation of children and their teachers in 40 or so existing classrooms, Edwards listens to children and observes the way in which they use their spaces. His research represents a significant contribution to our understanding of the way in which classrooms operate. Here, the views of teachers are particularly enlightening as they comment on the shortcomings of their own teaching spaces. In search for a common language, his work sets out to translate the misunderstandings which often occur when architects try to talk about education and when educationalists try to discuss architecture and space. The chapter is an ideal briefing tool for designers and architects embarking on the construction of new or refurbished classrooms.

In Chapter 6, architect and academic Prue Chiles describes her work on a research-orientated building project initiated by the UK government to explore new educational ideas. She designed one of Sheffield's 'Classrooms of the Future', where the needs of children were established as the priority from the outset, often at the expense of a more mundane health and safety agenda. Her approach incorporates a process of deep consultation with the end users, and an overtly child-centred attitude to design, which encapsulates the key principles of designing the inside–outside classroom; a true landscape for childhood. Her report includes a commentary on some of the difficulties encountered when she tried to 'jump outside the box' and develop new innovative educational ideas.

The view that children's perceptions of space are different to those of adults is the central premise of Chapter 7. Ben Koralek and Maurice Mitchell illustrate a range of initiatives which has been implemented within the UK over the past ten years, intended to include pupils in the design processes. These initiatives have helped to transform the perceptions of those who have participated. In the second part of Chapter 7 the authors describe important case studies where school students have actually worked with designers on real school projects. Although full of childlike fantasy, there are some remarkably grounded ideas to transform existing and new school environments and to make them more appropriate for the present and future generations who will be expected to use them. The authors argue that as huge amounts of investment flow into the state education system (within the UK), the need to get it right has never been more critical.

Creating a landscape for physical exploration was a concept I understood very clearly as being of tremendous value for young children, through my own design work. But what about older children?[1] What additional factors, whether they are environmental, technological or pedagogical, come into play as children grow and develop?

Over the age of seven, children may begin to explore landscapes in a less physical way, nevertheless the extent to which the environment encourages play and enquiry can have a similar cognitive benefit. As the physical dimension of younger years play gives way to a more intellectual independent engagement during the teenage years, the importance of fantasy and imagination should not be overlooked. Older children still need to explore new and challenging 'metaphorical landscapes'.

We can include new digital culture as part of these 'landscapes'. Other social landscapes also need to be considered. For example when people can sit together in school and share lunch, this can have tremendous social benefits especially when linked to a healthy eating regime. The sustainability agenda can and should become an essential part of the experience of school architecture, so that students pick up important messages about their environment reinforced through explicit architectural expression.

Architecture can, and should, go beyond the merely functional. The richer and more stylish it is, the more likely it is to turn older children onto education and learning, and perhaps most importantly encourage meaningful social interactions. However, we are not concerned here exclusively with school buildings. Although there is no other activity which occupies as much of a child's life as that involved in attending school, other aspects of children's time impacts on their development. In this respect we felt we needed to consider the home environment. We must remember that the context of the school is its community – urban, suburban or rural.

Computer games also play an increasingly important role in the lives of children at home. Many young people playing games with realistic animated landscapes, which can be explored, spend significant amounts of time hunched over a computer console. In Chapter 8 I will describe some of these games and assess their effect on the contemporary culture of childhood. Other aspects of digital culture are also informing the lives of our children. New educational strategies at schools place ICT at the heart of the process. To a certain extent this too is a generational issue. At least as adults we have, during the course of our lives, accumulated direct experiences for ourselves (largely without the aid of computers) and hence have a perspective formed alongside the virtual realm. Increasingly, however, our children's experiences of the world are effectively second-hand, communicated through a voracious electronic landscape, detached from the real physical landscapes of earlier childhood experience.

Continuing this theme in Chapter 9, Helen Penn describes how confined children are today, restricted by a health and safety agenda, which emphasizes the need for constant adult surveillance at the expense of independent play and exploration. Arguably, there has never been so much control imposed upon children as there is today. This is tending to diminish the quality and

Illust C
Children playing in the street (Hulton Getty: reproduced with permission).
Play streets. Young boys playing cricket in London's East End, 1929. In streets like these, motor cars were almost unknown, pavements made a firm playing surface, and lamp posts were excellent wickets or goal posts.

scope for independent imaginative play, and the uses children had previously for chance play in 'found' (mainly) urban places around the city, and in previous centuries, within the surrounding countryside. Today, most children are simply never permitted the freedom to explore the areas around their home freely. Less freedom is creating a generation of children over-anxious about their external environment. A survey indicates that in 1989, 62 per cent of primary-age children walked to school. A decade later it was only 54 per cent.[2] There is growing concern that youngsters are losing their connection with the natural environment because they have limited opportunities to play and learn outside controlled zones like the home or the school.

As Penn asserts in Chapter 9, it is a widely held view amongst many commentators and parents that health and safety legislation relating to children's environments is limiting their capacity for free imaginative play. In Chapter 10, Judith and John Hicks take these concerns and place them in the context of a modern world which must legislate for risks and hazards, as never before. They describe

the basic principles which designers must adhere to and place these into a historical context. They explain the basic rules for evaluating safety and developing good design strategies for children's play parks. They go some way towards defining exactly what 'child friendly' means and set out the rules which ensure that the environment complies with the legislation. They will argue that whilst children's safety must always be paramount, this is by no means incompatible with the provision of well-designed imaginative play spaces that encourage both independence and collaboration.

In Chapter 11, Susan Herrington describes the approach to procuring a new schoolyard in a suburb of Vancouver. The schoolyard is intended to provide a centre for the wider community in general as well as a safe but stimulating area for school pupils. A recent international design competition run by the author attracted 270 submissions from throughout the world. They were challenged to create an interactive sustainable environment which would help to put adventure back into play and learning. This chapter will describe the concept behind the original competition brief and outline some of the author's concerns about the external environment around the school, and the messages it sends to children about their place in a fragile world.

Most of the contributors are also parents with a wealth of practical experience regarding the well-being of their own children. Catherine Burke is no exception and she explores a concern for many parents at present; that is the quality of food our children consume both at home, in the urban environment and at school. Chapter 9 explains the pivotal role food should play within the educational curriculum and the physical shape of the school itself. Certainly when visiting most Italian childcare centres where lunchtime is usually a pure gastronomic pleasure, organized almost as a ritualistic event, one is starkly reminded of how our own fast food culture has diminished our children physically and socially. She has visited a number of inspiring international examples of what is currently happening in the edible landscape of schools. She reports on her findings.

It will be apparent from this brief description that the views expressed are largely consistent with the principle that in the modern world, children should be seen AND heard. As editor I would like to complete this introduction with a summary of two concerns which have emerged over the past decade from my own personal experiences both as a designer of children's environments and as a parent. Both concerns relate to the nature of education and care. One is my view that education (within the UK) is failing many of our children because it does not match the needs of individual children closely enough; secondly, that children benefit from an environment which challenges them to adopt independent behaviour from the earliest years. Both of these views are illustrated by examples of what I consider to be excellent innovative design for children which also has considerable benefits for the wider community.

1. Education in the UK: small is beautiful

In the UK, daycare remains the preserve of two social types, each at opposite ends of the wealth divide. Firstly, for the children of relatively well-to-do working parents who can afford to pay for private and very expensive daycare; secondly, it is reserved for children of the non-working poor, who benefit from free daycare through services like Sure Start, who provide targeted, fully subsidized family provision directed towards the poorest communities in Britain.

Daycare is not available for the majority of lower to middle class children simply because it is unaffordable.[3] Parents of these children continue to go out to work. What happens to their children before they are admitted to mainstream school aged 4? The reality is they are ferried around between friends, neighbours and relatives, they attend shoddy part-time facilities in church halls, or part-time sessions in mainstream school nurseries. Through this experience they may feel marginalized and uncared for, as they learn to survive in a regime where they understand that parents simply cannot cope with their need for love and nurturing, which only time and space can provide. In a society where a market place for labour consumes people's time voraciously and dictates that parents work long hours, young children pay their own price. The allocation of wealth in these Anglo-American societies is largely based on non communal anti-social values.

However, from the age of five (or in some cases aged four), children spend much of their time in school. Primary school is a good experience for many children. Up to the age of 8 or 9, most of these young people will behave well and work harmoniously within a nurturing setting. Further up the education line, just when children have found their feet, they have to move on, to a secondary school. For the most part, they and their parents will get another stark reminder of the market place which prevails in education. If their parents can afford it, some lucky children will be taken out of the state sector at the age of eight or eleven and sent to private schools. There, class sizes will be small, with specialist support for those who need it and perhaps most importantly, a good quality environment. Alternatively, parents may be lucky enough to find themselves living in a middle class area with a good local school, which maintains its standards by selecting children who fit the middle class profile. What happens to the remainder? They will almost certainly experience extremely poor education because it will be carried out in old run-down buildings with poor facilities in class sizes which are too large to cater for diverse social and educational needs. In an environment which one teacher describes as 'continuous low level insubordination', the minority of bullies will be allowed to hold sway over the majority of students and thus establish an anti-education culture. This drowns out the needs and aspirations of those receptive students who want to have a decent education. Children in these places will dwindle their class time away, until they come out at the other end with half an education. Another teacher puts it more emotively:

> ... in my own school what finally makes me break down and cry is the quiet child who sits through all the abuse and sexual garbage littered throughout every lesson and break, six hours a day, five days a week, and comes to me at the end of the lesson and says: 'What was that X squared, miss?' He is the one I have flashbacks remembering at two in the morning.[4]

As an architect working solely in the education field (and therefore someone who visits lots of schools and talks to many teachers), my perception is that modern education is fine for students of above average self-motivation and self-discipline, but it damns the rest. It also damns the teachers. A recent report on secondary school teachers in the UK indicates that they are spending so much time dealing with worsening pupil behaviour that they are battling to 'be allowed to teach'.[5] This independent report shows how fundamental rights of teachers within the UK are being ignored, as they are forced to work in cramped, overcrowded environments full of abuse and threatening pupil behaviour. How often teachers are criticized for poor performance yet the most basic architectural function, that of having enough space within the teaching environment to fulfil their task, for example, is denied to them. Many schools do not even provide staff with office space to carry out

lesson preparation. As for more sophisticated lifestyle props, such as gyms for use at lunchtimes, these are unheard of; yet consider many contemporary office buildings which provide such facilities as part of a sophisticated support system to retain and promote the well-being of their staff. Today schools still rely on a conveyor belt approach to education, in a world which is geared towards the individual.

Many of our political leaders lecture us about creating a market in education based on 'choice' as being the way to go. Yet for the majority there is still simply no choice. Aged 11, children look in vain for hope in these chaotic places and for many there is very little hope to find. There is simply not enough specialist care and attention being spent on the state education system to reach those children who really need support, for their benefit and for the well-being of society as a whole. The real needs of children, and in particular their parents, are largely ignored in all of this, and the new replacement buildings for education which are coming on stream within the UK seem to be at best peripheral, at worse reinforcing of the status quo. This is a pessimistic view admittedly, however it feels like an accurate one from where I am observing.

I wish to emphasize here that I am no collectivist willing to sacrifice his own family wealth to the education and well-being of other people's children through higher taxation. Like most other people brought up in the new global market place, my motivations are in the main selfish. I am lucky enough to be able to send my children to private education or in the case of the youngest child, to a religious well-funded selective school with good facilities where respect for teachers is enforced. The onus is placed on parents to ensure their children comply with rules and discipline. Feckless parents will be found out, and their children will be dumped out of the school to return to the local comprehensive. Everyone understands the rules; break them and you are out. However, through the misty memory of my former liberal past, I still regret that much of the mainstream education system is highly flawed, with little compensatory funding for schools with educational disadvantages. These schools, particularly at secondary level, are failing our children and those teachers who must put up with challenging and disruptive behaviour. What is the main problem?

It would appear that education is playing to a tune of bygone times. Education within the UK, in its basic structure, has hardly changed since the nineteenth century; it is largely conducted in class sizes of around thirty students, organized in a hierarchical form, with children all in age-related 'squads'. Yet society has changed. For example, the relatively recent transformation of communications technology makes the world a far more intimate place, yet at the same time one which is incredibly complex and in many ways chaotic. In his seminal book on children's digital culture, Douglas Rushkoff puts it in somewhat extreme terms:

> *... The degree of change experienced by the past three generations rivals that of a species in mutation. Today's 'screenager' – the child born into a culture mediated by the television and computer is interacting with his world in at least as dramatically altered a fashion from his grandfather as the first sighted creature did from his blind ancestors ....* [6]

There are many other aspects of children's material culture which have altered out of recognition. However there is little new educational practice which truly reflects this seismic shift. Even recent initiatives such as the UK Government's 'Schools for the Future' document, shows little real innovation taking place.[7] It is full of colourful images wrapped up in seductive computer graphics which tend to disguise the reality of the architectural structures described. For example, the projects featured maintain the closed classroom format, each one accessed from a long dangerous corridor. And it is an understandable outcome reflecting a centralized educational curriculum which has barely changed in a century. For example Richard Aldrich compared the new National Curriculum introduced in 1988 to the old Board of Education regulations issued to state secondary schools in 1904:

> *... There is such a striking similarity between these two lists that it appears that one was simply copied from the other, although the term 'modern foreign language' in the 1987 excludes Latin which featured prominently in the secondary school curricula of 1904 .... Thus in essence the proposed national curriculum in so far as it is expressed in terms of core and foundation subjects, appears as a reassertion of the basic grammar school curriculum devised at the beginning of the twentieth century by such men as Robert Morant and James Headlam .... This curriculum is now extended to primary and comprehensive secondary schools ....* [8]

Thus a dumb, boring, rigid, educational conformity dictates the main architectural straight-jacket for all new school buildings within the state sector. School buildings are for the most part antiquated, or in the case of new schools, of fairly shoddy quality. As a result, schools do not inspire their people; they are always constrained by limited budgets and lesson plans which carve the student's day up into arbitrary snapshots, so that each student can get round and get their bit of art, maths and english, etc. To quote again from Rushkoff: 'If like immature children, we steadfastly maintain our allegiance to the sinking, obsolete institutions of the past, then we will certainly go down with the ship.'[9]

Today, what makes a good school is the people, the structures and the ethos that they promote through their care for the individual, and his or her individual needs. Part of John Edward's research in Chapter 3 illustrates the reality of how little time teachers spend with children on individual tuition in a class of thirty (approximately 45 seconds per pupil per lesson).

A good building will help to raise standards generally, however, it will not change the condition of those unruly students who for whatever reason feel bored and alienated from education, and in many ways, from polite society as a whole. Their behaviour is learned and mimicked from a combination of too much trash culture, poor parenting and lack of discipline and mutual respect shown in society as a whole. It is the role of education to win these people round in order that they can play an active and fulfilling role in society. Part of the need for this is to prevent them from

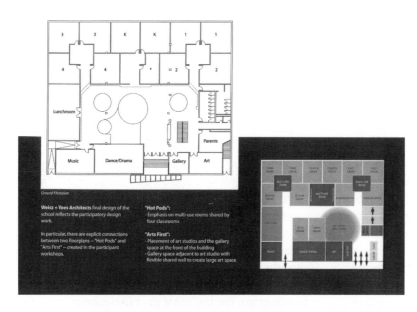

Ground Floorplan

Weisz + Yoes Architects final design of the school reflects the participatory design work.

In particular, there are explicit connections between two floorplans -- "Hot Pods" and "Arts First" -- created in the participant workshops.

"Hot Pods":
- Emphasis on multi-use rooms shared by four classrooms

"Arts First":
- Placement of art studios and the gallery space at the front of the building
- Gallery space adjacent to art studio with flexible shared wall to create large art space

Illust D

(a) Floor plan shows a number of spatial ideas which emerged from the participatory process including Hot Pods, multi-use rooms shared by four classrooms, and Arts First, positioning art studios and the gallery space at the front of the building. Gallery space adjacent to the art studio with moveable wall panels to create flexible art spaces.

(b) Architects Weisz and Yoes' photocollage shows the school's entrance. Children will literally take to the street as the school utilizes the dead end street as a playground. The former factory building now has a colourful new façade.

(c) Internal views with retractable 'up and over' walls to provide a fully flexible environment. Published from Adam Lubanski material.

December 9, 2002

FINAL DESIGN:

Weisz + Yoes Architects design development work: photocollage shows the school's entrance. Children will literally take to the street as the school utilizes the dead-end street as a playground.

CONCLUSION

The challenge to site and design a school in an old factory for a unique arts-based elementary school required a combination of participation by educational professionals, people familiar with the community, real estate consultants, design professionals, and participatory design facilitators to mediate the process.

The building chosen represented a particular challenge. In all of the other potential sites, the building envelope was much smaller, and the location of the windows would have determined the location of the classrooms. Working with a large floorplate and forced to rely on clerestory skylights, Bronx Arts had much greater flexibility in determining the floor layout.

The participatory design process led by Sam Schwartz LLC allowed the Bronx Arts' staff and board to develop their educational philosophy into a workable plan. Their initial floorplans enabled collaboration between multiple classes, flexible spaces for small group work, prominence for the arts-oriented spaced, and a large-scale community gathering space.

Weisz + Yoes Architects, committed participants in the participatory design process, applied their technical expertise to the work of the Bronx Arts board, staff, and future parents. They expanded upon the initial concepts with new ideas, such as the office mezzanine and the sustainable design elements.

An initial review of the participatory design process reveals some critical points:
- the full-day session devoted to discussion, viewing of precedents, and formation of design guidelines formed the basis of the final design
- the willingness of the participants to embrace architectural concepts and explore new media enabled the transformation of educational ideas into spatial designs;
- the fluid transition from design workshop to architect's drawing board came about because of the commitment of the architects to the process and their relationship with the facilitator

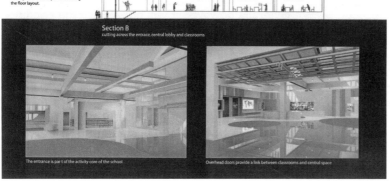

Section B
cutting across the entrance, central lobby and classrooms

The entrance is part of the activity core of the school

Overhead doors provide a link between classrooms and central space

jeopardizing the education of others. Education must go further, it must be better, it must be innovative, it must in some localities spend more of our money to compensate for poor social conditions and most importantly, it must be local.

In the Netherlands, a debate emerged from the beginning of the 1990s as to how best to address the issues facing schools in areas of high economic and social disadvantage. So-called compensatory funding, directed towards areas of high migration from the 1960s had not really worked and it was recognized that a less centralized more municipally based system would better address the particular needs of each locality.

An Educational Opportunity Policy was launched in February 2000 which directed funding towards the grass roots. Part of the deal meant that municipalities had to confer with school governing bodies to draw up an action plan to realize a coherent compensatory policy. However, specific research in each school became the starting point for this planning. By asking the right questions they endeavoured to identify the real problems which required solutions. A mirror was held up to the schools through dialogue based not just on inspection evidence, but also on pupil and teacher interviews, classroom consultations and other supplementary data.

This is a real turnaround in policy, and recognizes that society is more dynamic than ever, repeatedly subject to major changes. The approach offers an evolving process which is not set from the centre, rather it grows organically from the community itself. '… With the school as the

Illust D (Extended caption)

Innovation in the design and procurement of schools. Bronx School for the Arts is a public charter elementary school that opened in the South Bronx last year. The school is founded on the principle that arts education is critical to human development and learning and is the creation of a grass roots team of educators, parents and community residents. Bronx Arts is located in the Hunts Point area, a growing community surrounded by an industrial neighbourhood.

The selection of the school site was particularly important. A number of criteria were established including its location in the heart of the community and its proximity to the school's partner, Bronx Arts Community. Also, space for a pre-school was required, a single-storey building for accessibility, large column spacing for flexibility and the potential for some outdoor play space. Therefore a former factory building was selected which was robust enough for conversion rather than demolition.

A deep participatory process included parents, children and community residents all coordinated by the developers, Civic Builders, and the architects, Weisz and Yoes Architects.

They came up with the following community design guidelines:

- achieve a balance between order and spontaneity
- emphasize spillover spaces for small groups
- cluster classrooms to share multi-use spaces for small group work
- produce flexible spaces driven by an openness to change and opportunities to partner
- create spaces that allow teachers to function as professionals and support parents as partners in education
- display artworks throughout the school including privileged spaces for gallery shows, 'free' spaces for kids to design and display spaces for teachers, community members and artists
- incorporate the community experiences into a coherent approach to the school facility
- provide colorful light-filled playful and textural experiences
- promote the healthy development of children.

The process has enabled an interesting mix of public and private finance to create a small-scale facility right at the heart of the community with a walk in off the street feel. This is also a very economical project to build and maintain and most importantly the stakeholders have had a genuine say in its shape and development. Currently, people are much more aggressive in defining the places where they live, their locality. This is an example where the local community took the initiative – the scheme is both site-specific and user-specific. It develops connections with the surrounding community, has a sense of arrival and is inherently secure, yet welcoming. It provides a variety of individual and group learning places which encourage connections across age divides.

starting point, and choosing concrete objectives, there are guidelines for the actions that schools can take. Leaving the choice with the schools emphasizes their autonomy and uniqueness. There is after all, no universal recipe for tackling educational disadvantage.'[10] Our extended caption on the Bronx School for the Arts in New York is a case study which recognizes the need for schools to grow out of the local community rather than sitting beside it, closed, separate and autonomous.

2. Metaphors for play: innovation and risk

Ten years ago I visited an exciting new children's daycare centre in Souest, Netherlands. I observed that if children were allowed, they would spend as much time as they could outdoors, in any kind of weather. I noticed that in this particular setting, even when children were not allowed to go outdoors, they still sought to utilize the whole of the interior environment. They would, if permitted, explore linen cupboards, climb stairs (or any type of feature which enabled this to occur), set up games in corners and niche areas, and mount stairs to access high level walkways. All of these features were fundamental to the architectural experience at Souest. This determination to explore is, I surmized, an essential ingredient for learning and healthy social development.

What this design succeeded in doing was to create situations which afforded children a sense of adventure where they could test their mental and physical coordination with a strong illusion of their own independence. I noticed how children were engaged in their own self-generated activities, played out in different corners and areas of their daycare 'landscape'. I concluded, that for young children in particular, there was no perceptual difference between an exterior landscape and an interior landscape. Indeed, children would relate to both in similar ways if allowed.

Perhaps the key dimension of this was the process of listening and hearing the views of

children which had largely dictated the framework of its architectural development. For Venhoeven, the children's voices were what he needed to hear loudest. Ultimately children's needs dictated the form of that labyrinthine, multi dimensional environment to create a really child-centred design. This, in my experience, is a rare and inspiring convergence of educational and architectural wisdom.

The architect had deliberately diminished what he considered to be an overpowering health and safety agenda which threatened to stifle imaginative creativity with layers of bureaucracy and restrictions. By and large, most children's environments, nurseries and schools are predicated around a narrow health and safety agenda limited by cost constraints. New and existing nurseries and childcare centres are generally of a very poor quality compared to most other public buildings. Small buildings with small budgets do not usually allow adequate resources to be devoted to areas such as developing a meaningful strategy for consultation with the end users within the design process. As a consequence, these buildings are often designed to a lowest common denominator. In the worst cases they adopt a quaint adult perception of what children's architecture should be; this then is 'bolted onto' the building as something of an after-thought, perhaps with the use of very explicit childlike references such as teddy bear door handles or decorations which are over elaborate, or perhaps by utilizing strident primary colours which are aesthetically poor. All this does for children is to patronize them and to make them feel as small as they obviously are. Children, young or old, know good design when they see it. They are aware of quality. This is particularly so for the older age ranges where they want to be seen on stylish play equipment.

Elsewhere, beyond the confines of the childcare centre or the school, an urban environment has evolved which offers only moderate benefits to modern childhood. Looking back it seems that little has changed. In *The Theory of Loose Parts*, Simon Nicholson (1971), son of artist Ben Nicholson and sculptor Barbara Hepworth, wrote an article about the importance of creativity for children

Illust A
The childcare centre at Souest, Netherlands designed by Ton Venhoeven. A challenging 'landscape' for early years' play and learning. The children perform gleefully for my camera, running up and down this stepped ramp, with the adult carer relaxed and impassive. Today health and safety guidance coming from most education authorities in the UK would ban such a potentially hazardous feature. (Photos: Mark Dudek.)

participating in play schemes. He called his article 'How NOT to Cheat Children – The Theory of Loose Parts'. In it he made a number of key observations regarding the lack of involvement children have with the design of their spaces. Although published thirty years ago, it remains a cogent reminder of the importance of young people's participation in the design process, and in the scope they have to modify or change their spaces subsequently.

One particularly interesting section of his piece is worth repeating here:

In any environment, both the degree of inventiveness and creativity, and the possibility of discovery are directly linked to the number and

Illust B

(a) The main entrance atrium has high quality graphics; images of every student personalize the space.

Extended caption

The Bexley Academy, a new secondary school designed by Foster and Partners. It is an environment which treats children with respect. Walk through the doors of Bexley and the interior immediately feels more like a corporate headquarters than a school. From the entrance and reception desk, visitors have views into a large top-lit atrium space and beyond to the restaurants, meeting rooms and classes, many of which take place in open-plan areas. Even traditional closed classrooms are highly glazed to make the activities transparent and visible. Each classroom appears to be filled with flat screen Apple Macs with teachers standing at interactive white boards. These buildings are lavishly appointed particularly in information and communication technology.

Illust B

(b) The teaching atrium with an art lesson taking place outside the confines of a traditional classroom.

Extended caption (*contd.*)

The scheme is organized around three top-lit, glazed courtyards, each with a different functional theme; there is the entrance business court (designed like a mock trading floor), a technology court and an art court. Users are constantly aware of the whole school community simply because they can see what everyone else is doing. No hiding behind the bicycle sheds here.

According to the lead architect, Spencer de Grey, the scheme sponsors took some lessons from the architect's own office layout, which consists of open-plan working areas with discrete bays off the main spaces to provide for quieter more contemplative activities. 'The main emphasis is on transparency to create a different slant on the normal educational experience,' he says.

That 'different slant' is conditioned by the fact that city academies depend on business for an element of their financial support. They receive preferential public funding in return for concentrating on a particular curriculum, so supporting a key plank of the UK government's education strategy – specialism in vocational subject areas. (All photos by Nigel Young, Foster & Partners.)

kind of variables in it … it does not require much imagination to realize that most environments that do not work (i.e. do not work in terms of human interaction and involvement) such as schools, playgrounds, hospitals, day-care centers, international airports, art galleries and museums, do not do so because they do not meet the 'loose parts' requirement; instead, they are clean, static and impossible to play around with. What has happened is that adults in the form of professional artists, architects, landscape architects, and planners have all the fun playing with their own materials, concepts and planning alternatives, and then builders have had all the fun building environments out of real materials; and thus has all the fun and creativity been stolen; children and adults and the community have been cheated and the educational-cultural system makes sure that they hold the belief that this is right. How many schools have there been with chain link and black-top playground where there has been a spontaneous revolution by students to dig it up and produce a humane environment instead of a prison.[11]

His polemical thesis reminds us of the arid scaleless school buildings which many of this generation's parents grew up in. A lot of these sites are still in use today and in Chapter 5 Ben Koralek and Maurice Mitchell describe how they worked with children and architect students incorporating their joint thinking into a scheme to adapt a number of Victorian Board School spaces to make them fit and inspiring places for modern education. This chapter, which is central to our publication, reminds us of the need to interact with children as much as to instruct them. The best form of architecture for education is the result of an informed dialogue between teachers and children, where children feel that they can have an active involvement in the decisions which shape their lives. The architecture is the third dimension, which creates the whole.

My aim with this book therefore is to stimulate more debate about education and its context, buildings and processes which take place there through the views of children. The contributors are drawn from a range of disciplines which are not specifically architectural. As a consequence, language and general terms of reference are not always consistent with the overall architectural theme. However, through this inter-disciplinary approach, I hope to encourage better understanding of key issues which contribute towards the landscapes of childhood. What I am clear about is that the current education dictates, upon which many school buildings and dedicated children's landscapes are predicated, are not fit for the twenty-first century.

Each one of our contributors has been asked to consider the evolving nature of children's culture and the environments within which it is currently being played out. Children spend a great deal of their waking lives in daycare facilities and at school, as parents are often engrossed in wall-to-wall work. This places an emphasis for architects and planners to consider the needs of children in a new

light. Arguably, the children's environment must be conceived of as a 'world within a world'; it should be a special place with all the aspects that make the environment a rich landscape for exploration and play. And this ideal should apply well beyond the nursery.

In the childcare centre he designed in Souest, architect Ton Venhoeven had deliberately incorporated ramps, terraces and level changes which encouraged children to climb and explore, just as they would in a natural landscape; indeed Venhoeven explained that his inspiration for that interior had been his own childhood play area, a wild rambling garden around his house which had a large wooden boat marooned there, a long-term restoration project for his father. As a child, Ton played in it, around it, and underneath it.

Although the boat never actually made it back to the water, it fulfilled a crucial childhood fantasy. When he was subsequently commissioned to design a new daycare centre within an existing building, the architect drew on some of his boyhood experiences. He designed a boat form as a recognizable part of the children's play area at Souest, to create a more dramatic space for children to explore. This transfer of his childhood experience had created a rich 'interior landscape', establishing what child psychologist Harry Heft called affordances, the possibility for children to test and develop their physical and social skills through the specific architectural features on offer.[12]

Venhoeven's initial inspiration developed into a whole host of affordances, which tested health and safety requirements to the limit. Because of that, the landscape was extremely rich and challenging, not just for children but also for the teachers and carers who used the new building. It has, over the years, become a positive benefit to everyone involved, in particular for the children who attended during their formative years. It is an environment which trusts children.

It is my strongly held view that most children do not really differentiate between the interior and the exterior of a building. To most, the landscape is simply there to be explored in its own terms, as and when it is available to them. The freer they are of adult supervision and the richer the landscape for exploration, the more benefit that environment will have for them in developmental terms (until a painful fall adjusts their adventurous spirit). That is why the digital environment of the internet holds such attractions for older children. It is relatively free of adult control and supervision.

The best landscapes enhance development for all children. The best form of learning takes place within an integrated environment of architecture, technology and teaching, which comes together seamlessly. If it engages the child, it will enhance their learning and their social development in equal measure. The landscapes of childhood are everywhere, however, today they are no longer freely available to children. As a result the real needs of children for freedom and adventure in their own worlds are censored. We must somehow give this back to them.

Mark Dudek, June 2004

Notes

1 The Pocket Oxford Dictionary describes a child as 'a young human being'. Our definition of a child covers the age range 0–16, recognizing the reliance most teenagers have to their parents, even when the relationship they have may be poor.

2 Stranger Danger Drive Harms Kids, the *Observer*, 24 May 2004.

3 Daycare is a full-time care and education which enables parents to attend full-time work during the child's early years. It provides structured play which is intended to support the child in its own personal development and unlike part-time sessional nursery or crèche, it requires a purpose-made environment rich in stimulation and sensory pleasures.

4 *Private Eye Magazine*, London, no. 1105, 30 April, p. 14.

5 *A Life in Secondary Teaching: Finding Time for Learning*, commissioned by the National Union of Teachers from independent researchers John MacBeath and Maurice Galton, Cambridge University Faculty of Education.

6 ibid, p. 3

7 Schools for the Future, Department for Education and Skills, 2004.

8 Aldrich R. (1998). The National Curriculum: an historical perspective. In (D. Lawton and C. Chitty eds) *The National Curriculum*, Institute of Education, London.

9 ibid, p. 8

10 From OECD Forum on Schooling for Tomorrow, Futuroscope, Poitiers, France, 12–14 February 2003, Document No 07. The report provides information note for Netherlands for the Forum session on Building an Operational Toolbox for Innovation, Forward Thinking and School System Change.

11 'How NOT to Cheat on Children – The Theory of Loose Parts' by Simon Nicholson published in *Landscape Architecture*, October 1971, pp. 30–34.

12 For example, Heft cites a smooth flat surface, which affords or encourages walking and running while a soft spongy surface affords lying down and relaxing. Heft, H. (1988) 'Affordances of children's environments: a functional approach to environmental description', *Children's environment quarterly*, vol. 5, no. 3, pp. 29–37.

Mark Dudek has two children. He lives and works in London. He has written and broadcast on many aspects of school and pre-school architecture. The second edition of *Kindergarten Architecture* was published in September 2000 (SPON). Other recent publications include *Building for Young Children* published by the National Early Years Network and *Architecture of Schools – The New Learning Environments* published by the Architectural Press in 2001.

He has also been involved in the design of numerous educational facilities. With his architectural practice Mark Dudek Associates, he recently completed the Windham Early Years Excellence Centre in Richmond upon Thames, UK. He is currently working on a range of education projects including new buildings for the National Day Nurseries Association in Grantham and Birmingham, UK. He has designed and supervised the construction of one of the Government pilot projects 'Classrooms of the Future' at Yewlands Secondary School in Sheffield and is working on a new 'eco nursery' for a rural community in South West Ireland.

The editor has lectured all over the world including a recent series of AIA talks in Michigan, USA. He has been a keynote speaker at many conferences organized by groups such as Surestart, The Daycare Trust, the National Early Years Network, National Day Nurseries Association, The Regional Childcare Working Group, South West Ireland, NIPPA (promoting quality care in Northern Ireland) and CABE (the UK Commission for Architecture and the Built Environment). He presented a paper at the conference 'Exploring the Material Culture of Childhood' at the University of California, Berkeley in May 2003 and was a keynote speaker at the conference 'Spaces and Places' for children organized by Canterbury Christ Church University College in 2004. He is a Research Fellow at the University of Sheffield and a CABE Enabler.

1

Talking and listening to children

Alison Clark

Editor's introduction

'In my cave listening to music. It's magic music from my magic radio.'

This was one response from 3-year-old Gary about his favourite place in the nursery. The statement was one of many insights given by a group of young children, about their views and experiences of everyday life in their early childhood institution. It was recorded during a recent research project implemented by the author.

There is an increasing interest in listening to children and the importance of children's participation when making important decisions about their lives. Central to this is the need for children's views to be heard regarding the form and shape of their own physical world. These views are particularly important in relation to the design of the childcare centre, a space within which many children in full daycare will spend much of their formative years.

Listening to young children (in this context, defined as the under fives), holds particular challenges for the architectural community, who often find their design process to be confined by limited budgets and health and safety frameworks. These constraints can limit the quality of the environment, and make it less suitable for young children. In addition, the restricted framework within which architects now work makes innovative new practice within the early years built environment, increasingly difficult. Considering this is a relatively new building type for the UK, this is regrettable. The new generation of Family and Childcare Centres, many of which are adopting an interesting mixed economy of public and private finance, has a duty to explore the architectural needs of its community through a deeper, more considered process of consultation with the users.[1]

This chapter explores the development of a methodological framework, the Mosaic approach, for listening to young children about important details of their daily lives. The author looks in particular at how this methodology can help designers to reflect on young children's experience of place and architecture and enhance their understanding of exactly who children are, in relation to the worlds they inhabit.

Of particular importance within the design of childcare environments are the details. Often these important features enable them to relate successfully to their environment so that it becomes not just a home from home but also a place of exploration, discovery and developing environmental awareness. Young children in Alison Clark's study described the spaces in a variety of ways; for example, their associations with people and past events, with objects, activities, routines, access, and other crucial factors, which defined their daily lives. Some were merely functional, others sensory and others symbolic.

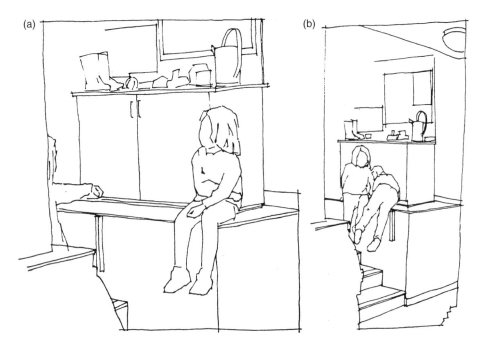

Figure 1.1
Children using a ledge in a Sheffield daycare facility (from observational studies by Simon Pryce): (a) A child sitting on the ledge is spotted by her friend; (b) The friend climbs along the ledge to take up the position now being vacated by the first child. (By permission of the editor, Mark Dudek, from *Building for Young Children* published by the National Children's Bureau, London.)

They were insights, which added a crucial dimension to the conventional adult view of what constitutes a place. These observations can be a vital support for a deeper understanding of children's needs within the environment, and a way for architects and designers to construct an alternative set of priorities to the current, somewhat standardized criteria which do not take into account the particularities of the users and their local context. As Alison Clark points out, it is an alternative to the adult view of environment; where the designer can start with the child's view, their local knowledge, their attention to detail and particular visual and sensory quirkiness, a much more child-orientated architecture may emerge. This, in my experience as an architect, has been a particularly useful approach at an early stage when taking the brief.

Theoretical underpinnings of the participatory approach

There were three main theoretical starting points for this research approach, each based on notions of competency. Firstly, I acknowledged the importance of the ideas expressed in the emerging sociology of childhood. This supports the view of children as 'beings not becomings'. In other words, their views are not to be ignored because of their status as young people subservient to adult carers. Rather they are to be valued and listened to as authentic individuals in their own right functioning within a democratic community.

Childhood is viewed as one of a number of authentic structures within society, as quoted from Qvortrup et al.[3] '…children have their own activities and their own time and their own space'. This proved to be a useful theoretical beginning for this study, acknowledging that children have important perspectives to contribute about their lives in early childhood institutions and elsewhere within the urban environment. This view of competency is in contrast to other research models, which can exclude the voices of children:

> *Children are often denied the right to speak for themselves either because they are held as incompetent in making judgments or because they are thought of as unreliable witnesses about their own lives.*[3]

Instead, this study views children as 'experts in their own lives' and especially in the understandings

SPACE AVAILABLE   HOTEL   CHAINS   EXPRESSWAY JUNCTIONS   INTERCOM   INTERCONTINENTAL RESERVATIONS AUTOMOBILES   TOURIST VILLAGES   MEZZANINES   SUBWAYS   PANORAMIC RESTAURANTS   EMAIL   OVERPASSES CAFETERIAS   AUTOMATIC BATHROOMS   TELEPHONE CARDS   FAST-FOOD ESTABLISHMENTS   PASSING LANES   RAMPS FREIGHT ELEVATORS   PNEUMATIC MAIL   PARKING MACHINES   SHOPPING MALLS   DUTY-FREE AREAS   ELEVATORS EXPRESSWAY TOLL BOOTHS   VIACARD   EUROPASS   JUNCTIONS   PRIORITY LANES   VIDEOTEL   FAX   RECREATION CENTERS   TELECOM NETWORKS   FALSE CEILINGS   PARTITION PANELS   EMERGENCY LANES   INDUSTRIAL ZONES CHANNELS   24-HOUR WEATHER REPORTS   OPTIC FIBER COILS   AIR-BORNE TRANSMISSION   UNDERPASSES   GAS STATIONS   HOT BEVERAGE MACHINES   SNACK MACHINES   CHEWING GUM MACHINES   PROPHYLACTIC DISPENSERS TOOTHBRUSH WITH TOOTHPASTE DISPENSERS   CIGARETTE MACHINES   TOYS IN PLASTIC BALLS DISPENSERS   STAMP MACHINES   COIN AND TOKEN MACHINES   SLOT MACHINES   EXACT TIME   CUSTOMS BORDERS   VIDEOGAMES MISSING PERSONS ADS   DIGITAL CONSOLES   INTERCOMS   BLEEPERS   DETECTORS   MODEMS   QUALITY CONTROL PANORAMIC POINTS   CLOSED-CIRCUIT TV CAMERAS   AIRPLANES   ALARM SYSTEMS   S.O.S. BOXES   ISLAND CONNEC-TIONS   PUBLIC BATHS   OFFICIAL INAUGURATIONS   ORGANIC CULTIVATION   SERVICE STATIONS   REST AREAS INTERNATIONAL REPORTING   WAITING ROOMS   ATM MACHINES   ROWS OF SUPERMARKET BUGGIES   DISTANCES BETWEEN AIRPORT AND DOWNTOWN   AUTOGRILL CHECK-OUT   FIRE ESCAPES   JET LAG   EMERGENCY EXITS   SLEEP-ING CARS   UNDERGROUND PARKING LOTS   WAITING AT TRAFFIC LIGHTS   TRAFFIC JAMS   EMERGENCY ROOM OPERATING ROOMS   INTERCITY TRAINS   DOCTOR'S OFFICES   OPTIMIZATION OF SERVICES   COPYRIGHT   BANK ACCOUNTS   CREDIT CARDS   TELEPHONE EXCHANGES   FLIGHT PATHS   OPERATOR-ASSISTED TELEPHONE CALLS MUZAK WHILE WAITING FOR EXTENSION CONNECTIONS   CONFERENCE ROOMS   AUTOMATIC TICKET MACHINES   MAG-NETIC CARDS   TELEPHONE WAKE-UP SERVICE   DATE CHANGE LINE   WEIGH SCALES WITH HOROSCOPE   ACCESS CODES ANSWERING MACHINES   BUS STOPS   BICYCLE PATHS   ENTER THE EXACT AMOUNT   TRAVEL AGENCIES   NO PARKING INVOICE OR CASH RECEIPT?   NEWS AGENCY   PHOTO: IMAGE BANK   SATELLITE CONNECTIONS   STOCK EXCHANGE LISTINGS   TELESELECTION   EMERGENCY SERVICE   NEW YEAR'S EVE   NUMBERED SEATS   SPECIAL MAINTENANCE STATION CANOPIES   INFORMATION DESK   UNLIMITED MILEAGE   CORRIDORS   FITNESS CENTERS   ADVERTISING SPACE TRAFFIC DIVIDERS   24-HOUR SERVICE   CLAIMS OFFICE   DIVIDER PANELS   WORKSTATIONS   PEDESTRIAN CROSSINGS REMOTE MEDICAL TREATMENT   TV NEWS   FREE TIME   MINI-VANS   DRINK INCLUDED IN TICKET PRICE   TRAIN RESERVATIONS   RADIO-TAXI   EXPRESS TRAIN SURCHARGE   ADVANCE LIST   COLD BUFFET   STUDIO APARTMENTS FOLDING SEATS   RAILROAD CROSSINGS   INFORMATION OFFICE   CATALOGUE AVAILABLE   REVOLVING DOORS   GRAPH PAPER   STOCK TRANSACTIONS   TREASURY BONDS   SPERM BANK   ARTIFICIAL INSEMINATION   D.O.C.   VISTA POINT BUMP   PLASTIC SURGERY   ALLERGIC PHENOMENA   CUSTOMS BORDERS   INTERNET   PRESS RELEASE   CLOSING TIME DISCOUNT STORE   COMPLETE CHECK-UP   WHEEL ALIGNMENT   SATELLITE CONNECTIONS   SUPERCONDUCTORS WEATHER CHANNEL   SPACE TRASH   INCINERATORS   TERRITORIAL WATERS LIMIT   CONTROL TOWER   CNN   LEAVE A MESSAGE AFTER THE TONE   PASS CHECK-IN   ELECTRONIC SPEED CONTROL   PICTURE POST CARDS   PAVEMENT SIGNS BEING REPAINTED   CONTROLLED ATMOSPHERE   SPEED TRAP   LANDING RUNWAYS   BIRTH CONTROL   CLUB MEDITERRANEE   FREE TICKETS   AIR CONDITIONING   WORKS IN PROGRESS   PRESS RELEASES   TIMETABLES   CHECK POINTS   FREIGHT YARD   CARD NOT ENABLED   DOUBLE CLICK   NORTH BARRIER   SYSTEM ERROR   CLONING   FM   CB VESUVIUS   MAGNETIC FIELD   SCALE 1:100,000   HIGH VOLTAGE   NON-NUCLEAR COMMUNITY   PROTECTED AREAS COUNTDOWN   INDUSTRIAL WAREHOUSES   NON-RESIDENT RENTAL   FREE POST CARD   DISPLAY UNITS   FOR RENT   AIR CORRIDORS   SATELLITE CITIES   AUTHORIZATION   FROM-TO   LUNCH BREAK   DOGS ON LEASHES   SMOKING SECTION X-RATED   PASSIVE EXERCISE   FREE VACATION   UNPAID WORK   PRESS CONFERENCE   DISCOTHEQUES   EMERGENCY SWITCH   TAKE-OFF AND LANDING STRIPS   SHORT WAVES   NAVIGATION ROUTES   BANK CREDIT   FLIGHT SIMULATOR PUBLIC WINDOW   FOREIGN EXCHANGE   EMERGENCY LANES   APPROVED SYSTEMS   HIGH BEAM HEADLIGHTS   TAXIS TRAFFIC CIRCLES   UNUSED AREAS   DIFFERENTIATED WASTE COLLECTION   STREET CLEANING   METER READING TELEPHONE COUNTER   PEDESTRIAN ZONES   GENEROUS FINANCING   QUARTZ CHRONOGRAPHS   MICROPROCESSORS DIETARY SUPPLEMENTS   ANTIDEPRESSANT DRUGS   SOCIAL CENTERS   RAILROAD CARS   UNLEADED GAS   CONTAINER SHIPS   INTERCHANGES   INTERPORTS   NO ACCESS   ELECTRONIC ALARM SYSTEMS   CLAUSTROPHOBIA   STRUCTURAL VIBRATIONS   RESEARCH LABORATORY   HUMAN GUINEA PIGS   GENETIC MANIPULATION   COMMERCIAL COLONIZA-TION   PLASTIC BAGS   RECYCLABLE PLASTIC   WEB PAGES   SIMULTANEOUS INTERPRETING   SAFETY EXIT   RECYCLING RANDOM ACCESS MEMORY   TURBO   ONLY CHILDREN   DEMOGRAPHIC CONTROL   ULTRASOUND   G7   LEGAL SIZE BUSINESS CARD   MUSICAL SAMPLES   DEPOSITS FOR CONTAINERS   SOFT SHOULDER   ROADSIDE   COST ESTIMATES TOUR OPERATORS   CENSORSHIP   PREFABRICATED BUILDINGS   DIGITAL THERMOMETERS   HIGH SPEED   PLAY-GROUNDS   STOP: STATION AHEAD   HAVE A GOOD JOURNEY WITH VIACARD   COIN-OPERATED BINOCULARS   PANO-RAMIC VIEWS   PRODUCTION SCHEDULES   STAND-BY   SHOP WINDOWS   COMPANY GIFTS   GREENHOUSES   PARTITION WALLS   FENCES   CONTAINMENT WALLS   SHUTTLES   EVERYTHING INCLUDED   BEEPS   EMERGENCY BRAKE   TURN-KEY   SUPPLEMENTARY LEVIES   OBLITERATION   SELF-DESTRUCTION   END OF THE LINE   EJECT   BANKS   DAMS   PAUSE RECEPTION DESK   SKELETONS OF BUILDINGS   ARMS MANUFACTURERS   BUILDING SITES   RADAR COVERAGE   SUB-URBAN SUBDIVISIONS   DECORATIVE SHEET METAL   REMOTE CONTROLLED MISSILES   HEAT-SEEKING MISSILES   PEAK HOURS   JET LAG   HANGOVER   SEWAGE SYSTEMS   FREE ADS   COFFEE TABLE MAGAZINES   PHOTO ID   CHARTER FLIGHTS   ON LINE   DATA BANKS   ATLANTIC CROSSINGS   INSTRUMENT NAVIGATION   CARPET BOMBING   HELLO? CAMOUFLAGE   CHEMICAL INDUSTRIES   PHARMACOLOGICAL RESEARCH   LOCAL ANESTHETIC   URBAN WASTE COLLEC-TION   TWO SECONDS   PANTONE SCALE   TYPOGRAPHICAL SETTINGS   POST OFFICES   CRUISING SPEED   CONTROL SYSTEMS   LIGHT POLLUTION   ADVANCED CONCEPTS   BASEMENTS   ACOUSTIC INSULATION   BAGGAGE DEPOSIT RAISED FLOORING   MARKET SURVEYS   CABLE TENSIONERS   MHZ   CONTAINERS   UNMARKED POLICE CARS   TUG-BOATS   DOWNTOWN   PIAZZA DUOMO   HANGING GARDENS   RIVER BARGES   SEMI-TRAILERS   INTERNATIONAL EXPRESS COURIER   INTERMODAL TERMINAL   RAILROAD CONVOYS   CISTERNS   SILOS   CARGO CENTER   GOODS STORAGE   AUTOMATED WAREHOUSES   GOODS HANDLING AREAS   ROAD TRANSPORT   STATION PARKING   EMBAR-KATION POINT   CONVEYOR BELTS   CRANES   INTERNATIONAL ARRIVALS   WATERWAYS   ACCESS RAMP   SELF-BEARING STRUCTURES   PASSENGER DE-BOARDING   DANGEROUS CURVE   MEDICINS SANS FRONTIERES   ENVIRONMENTAL RECOVERY   DEFORESTATION   FAST REWIND   MASTER MIXERS   COMPATIBLE INTERFACES   OPTICAL READER   POST BOX NUMBERS   INSPECTION WELL   TIME ALMOST UP   ALUMINUM WINDOW FRAMES   PESTICIDES   BIRD-WATCHING WILDLIFE DOCUMENTARIES   ELECTRONIC WINDOW SHADES   MAKEUP   SATELLITES   LED   RENTALS   COLUMNS OF MERCURY   CORE BORING   APPROVED SYSTEMS   HIGH DEFINITION   LOW RESOLUTION   NOISE POLLUTION   ORGAN-IZED TOURS   MAGNETIC SUPPORTS   WOULD YOU LIKE THE TRANSACTION SLIP?   MULTIPROCESSORS   UNDO   SLOW-MOVING VEHICLES   FULL IMMERSION   INSURANCE POLICIES   YIELD RIGHT OF WAY   PRECAUTIONS   WAITING LIST MEMBERS ONLY   DELIVERY   SPEED ELECTRONICALLY CONTROLLED   GENERATION GAPS   PROGRAMMING TIME SLOTS RATINGS   NO PARKING ANY TIME   OFFICE HOURS   HAPPY HOUR   SLOGANS   PRESS OFFICE   REC   MUTE   CLEARANCE SALES   BREAKWATERS   NIGHTSTICKS   ACCESS LANES   HEAT SEEKING   POWER GENERATION   PLOTTER   BACK-GROUND NOISE   BY FAX

Figure 1.2
Architecturally the Reggio concept goes beyond the limits of the building, rather it is a worldwide urban concept, Luca Pancrazzi, 'Space Available', 1990–1997. Mixed media, variable dimensions. Reproduced with permission of the Domus Academy Research Centre, Via Savona, 97 20144 Milan. Tel +39 2 47719155. Originally in *Children Spaces Relations*. Published by Reggio Children, Piazza della Vittoria, 6 42100, Reggio Emilia, tel +39 522 455416.

and insights they may offer regarding space and the environment.[4]

Secondly, I looked to Participatory Appraisal to see how an existing methodology developed to empower adults in communities in the majority of the world could be applied to young children. The concept of 'voice' was important here. These tools have been designed to give voice to those who are disempowered. In an international development context these methods acknowledge that local people are the ones best equipped to know about the lives lived in their own places.

Inevitably there have been some challenges as to whether these techniques have been used to bring about effective change. However, as a theoretical starting point this view of competency was of interest to those I consulted with at the formative stages of this study. It was the assumed competency, which led to the development of imaginative methods that enabled often-illiterate adults to communicate their local knowledge within Participatory Appraisal methods. This same trigger has been the spur for developing the Mosaic approach with young children.

Thirdly, my background in early years education led me to consider notions of competency and young children, referring to pedagogical frameworks in their totality. The pre-schools of Reggio Emilia, a region in Northern Italy, have strongly influenced this study. The theoretical framework for these early childhood institutions, established by Loris Malaguzzi in the 1940s, is one of the 'competent child' working within a rich and supportive childcare environment.

Educators in Reggio refer to an image of the child as a 'rich child' who is strong, competent and active. This view is reflected in the architecture of Reggios' childcare centres and in the child-friendly city itself. The relationships, the routines and the pedagogy, all speak of an integrated approach to designing the architecture. Learning is seen as a collaborative process in which adults and children search for meanings together: 'We construct the meaning of school as a place which plays an active role in the children's search for meaning and our own search for meaning, shared meanings'.[5] In this regard the architecture is a fundamental element of this knowledge and search for social cohesion within the city and the spectacularly successful welfare of young children in Reggio.

The Study

The study took place between January 1999 and June 2000 at an early childhood institution, which was part of a multi-agency childcare network or community campus.[6] This exploratory study on listening to young children was part of a wider evaluation of the campus, which includes an early childhood centre, a parents' centre and a homeless families project. The main focus of the study was two key groups within the early childhood centre: children aged 3–4 years in the kindergarten and children under two in the nursery. Pilot work was carried out with refugee children attending the homeless families project. I will explore here the research carried out with a group of eight children in the kindergarten group. The children used the term 'nursery' to refer to their institution. I will therefore use 'nursery' to refer to a more complex early years model in the following account.

Developing the Mosaic approach

The focus of the development phase of this study was to find methodologies which played to young children's strengths rather than weaknesses. This ruled out certain traditional methods such as written interview schedules. I wanted to find ways of harnessing young children's creativity and physical engagement with their world. Such methods would acknowledge what Malaguzzi described as the 'hundred languages of children': the verbal and non-verbal ways in which young children communicate their feelings.[7]

The approach developed as a multi-method model. It was important to include a range of methods in order to allow children with different abilities and interests to take part. A multi-method approach also enabled traditional tools of observation and interviewing to contribute to the overall picture or 'mosaic'. There was also the added benefit for triangulation of the findings across the different methodologies. The various methods used were implemented as follows:

- *Observation*: narrative accounts of children's progress through the day.
- *Child conferencing*: a short structured interview schedule conducted one-to-one or in a group.
- *Using cameras*: children using single use cameras to take photographs of 'important things'.
- *Tours*: tours of the site directed and recorded by the children.
- *Map-making*: 2d-representations of the site using children's own photographs and drawings.
- *Interviews*: informal interviews with staff and parents.

The first tool used in the sequence was observation. I chose to use narrative accounts based on written descriptions of episodes of a child's play. The use of learning stories in evaluation in the New Zealand early years programme, Te Whaariki, was an important influence here (Ministry of Education, 1996). I used two questions as the basis for my observations: 'Do you listen to me?' and 'What is it like for me to be here?'.

This form of observation allowed me in as the 'inexpert' who is there to listen and learn from the children. This form of participant ethnographic observation is similar to the technique used by Corsaro (1985, 1997) to reveal details of the lives of pre-school children.[8] Observation is an important part of listening, but it still relies on an adult perspective on children's lives. I was also interested in pursuing participatory ways in which young children can convey their views and experiences.

Child conferencing provided a space for including formal conversations with children about their early childhood institution. This structured interview is based on a schedule developed by the Centre for Language in Primary Education in the 1980s. The questions I used were adapted from the interview schedule used by the head of the nursery. The fourteen open questions ask children why they come to their nursery, what they enjoy doing or dislike or find hard. Some questions focus on important people, places and activities. There is the opportunity for children to add other information they think the interviewer should know about their institution. I carried out the child conferencing with a group of children in the nursery twice over a four-month period. The children were able to listen to their previous responses, reflect on any changes and add new comments. However not all children were interested in talking in this formal way. I then adapted the child conferencing to be conducted 'on the move' so children could take me to places they spoke of.

Cameras provided a participatory tool through which the young children could communicate. Walker refers to the 'silent voice of the camera'.[9] A number of recent studies have incorporated the use of cameras with older children.[10] This silent tool also appears to have potential for use with young children. I was interested in exploring their competency using a camera, as they would be representing not just objects, but also the context of that object, in other words, the space itself. The Daycare Trust in 1998 carried out a similar form of camera consultation, where children photographed their 'favourite things'. I extended this approach to see if young children could provide a more in-depth view of life in the nursery using the 'voice' of the camera. I asked children to take photographs of what was important in the nursery. Single use cameras proved a useful tool for this age group as the children could be given freedom with the cameras without causing adult anxiety about expensive equipment. The children expressed pride in the photographs they had taken. Children who have seen adults taking photographs and pored over family albums know that photographs are valued in the 'adult world'. This is not always the case with children's own drawings and paintings. The cameras gave the children a powerful new language. They were given their own set of the photographs. The second set was used by the children to select photographs to make their own individual books about the nursery.

Tours and map-making emerged from the use of the cameras. I was interested in finding ways of gathering young children's experiences which were best suited to their natural ways of communicating. This called out for an active approach. Tours are a participatory technique, similar to the idea of 'transect walks' which have been used in International Development programmes for people to convey their knowledge of their immediate surroundings.[11] The physicality and mobility of this technique means that it lends itself to being used by young children. Neighbourhood walks have also been used to involve children in environmental planning.[12] Langsted (1994) describes a similar approach in the BASUN Project, a comparative study of the daily lives of young children in five Nordic countries, where each 5-year-old took the researcher on a 'sightseeing trip of his or her daily life'.

Following Langsted's model, I used issues of time and space to help structure the walking interview. Working with children individually, in pairs or threes, I asked the children to take me on a tour of their nursery, beginning with where they entered in the morning. The children then gave a running commentary on what happened next, whom they met and which rooms they went into (or didn't have access to). Children were in charge of the tour and how it was recorded. This involved the children taking photographs of important places and people, and making sound recordings of the tours using a small tape recorder with a clip mike.

Map-making was developed as a way for children to bring together the material they had gathered from the tours. Hart also describes the use of child-made maps:

> The method can provide valuable insight for others into children's everyday environment because it is based on the features they consider important, and hence can lead to good discussion about aspects of their lives that might not so easily emerge in words.[13]

Children's photographs provided the bridge between the children's physical experiences of their environment and the two-dimensional nature of the map. The maps proved to be an interesting talking point for other children who had not been involved in the tours. Thus the mapping exercise led to more opportunities for talking and listening to a wider group of children about their nursery, through the visual language of their maps.

Interviews with staff and parents were developed as an important part of understanding young children's lives in this place. Accounts from those who know the personalities and daily routines of the individual children need to sit alongside the other participatory tools in the Mosaic approach in order to build a more detailed understanding of young children's experiences. The interview schedule was similar to the questions used in the child conferencing but the emphasis was on adults' perceptions of everyday experience rather than first hand accounts from the children. These interviews were particularly valuable when using the Mosaic approach with pre-verbal children.

Stages in the Mosaic approach

The first stage is where children and adults gather the documentation; the second stage is piecing together information for dialogue, reflection and interpretation.

The focus in stage one is gathering information led by the children using the tools described above. Each tool can be used in isolation. However the strength of this approach is in drawing together the different methodologies through discussion. Stage two focuses on this interpretation: staff and parents now listen to the children's own perspectives. This use of documentation has drawn on the process developed in the pre-schools of Reggio Emilia, which Rinaldi has described as 'visible listening'. Listening is not limited to a two-way conversation between one adult and a child. Child conferencing is one of the pieces in the jigsaw which provides this documentation, but equal worth is given to children's photographs, narrative accounts from observations, recordings of tours, maps and recordings of role play. Discussions included both formal and informal exchanges between children and adults, planned and unplanned. One formal exchange of ideas, based on the documentation, took place between parents, the children and the researcher. This took the form of a planned meeting to explore the material gathered including children's responses to the child conferencing, the researchers' narrative accounts from observation, and children's photographs and maps.

A formal discussion was also held at a stage meeting, using documentation gathered by one 3-year-old as the basis for reflection and interpretation. Informal exchanges also took place between the children who had been directly involved in the study and other children in the nursery. This was mirrored by conversations with staff who had not taken part but who had become aware of the children's enthusiasm for the project.

In the following sections I will explore what the material gathered revealed about young children's experience of place.

A Sense of Place?

An important aspect of young children's lives is their physical engagement with their environment. The classic study by Hart (1979)[14] into children's experience of place is relevant here. This was a two-year ethnographic study of the everyday experiences of the locality conducted with children living in New England. His creative responses to recording children's intimate knowledge of their area have been of interest to me in this study. Hart discusses children's experience of place in terms of their place knowledge, place values and feelings and place use. In a similar way to Hart, I wanted to find out about children's knowledge and feelings about their everyday environment.

Constructing meanings: place use

The young children in this study defined the spaces according to their associations with people and past events, with objects, activities, routines and access.

During a child-led tour the children stop at a door and look in.

Researcher: What's this room?
Clare: It's the Parents' Room – where people have their leaving parties.
Researcher: Can we go in here?
Clare: Yep, we can go in there.

Clare, in this account, demonstrates how the meaning she gave to the Parents' Room was closely linked to her memories of past uses of the room for farewells. Other rooms were associated with the adults whom children regularly saw working in those spaces. The office was linked to the member of staff who was there when the children arrived in the morning and who was the first adult they met in the nursery each day. Two of the children had younger siblings in the nursery. The tours of important places and subsequent map-making revealed the spaces where siblings 'lived' as significant parts of the nursery for older children.

Objects

Children also associated rooms with certain objects or toys which they could play with in those spaces, as can be seen in the following excerpt from a child-led tour.

Gary: There are some toys over there and books. Where are the toys gone? Here they are. Let's get them down. Can you get down the truck with the hook?

Figure 1.3
An important place in the Windham Early Years Centre. Sylvia the administrator in her office linked directly to the entrance. She is the first person children meet in the morning, her presence is an important constant throughout the year. (Photo: Mark Dudek.)

In this example, a layer of meaning was given to this room by the particular toy he liked playing with there. My observations have also shown that another inside space in the nursery was associated with the large, soft toy dog, which had been named by the children and lived in the carpeted area of the classroom.

Activities

There were specific spaces in the nursery in which children used the activities experienced there to describe them. One important space was the music room. This was a multi-purpose space, which was the largest gathering point in the nursery. It had low windows allowing an open view of the courtyard and garden.

This room was described as the 'dancing room' and 'the listening room' as well as the music room. Most children included this room in their tours and took photographs of the room in use and when empty. This room was also associated with past uses. At one point it had been filled with small plastic balls, making it a giant ball pool. This was remembered with affection. It served as an example of the complex layering of experiences, which children could recall when revisiting a space.

Routines

Children also added meanings to spaces by the personal routines which took place there. The 'fruit place' was the phrase used by most of the group for the space in the conservatory where they had their mid-morning snack. The conservatory was a corridor space between the classrooms and the courtyard. It had several functions, including storage for children's coats and hats, as well as housing display areas and bookshelves. My observation has reinforced this space as an important one for the children. 'Fruit time' was a relaxed time when an adult would sit with the children, chatting and listening to them whilst they prepared the fruit. In the following excerpt from a child-led tour the children are sitting in the Orange room during the tour.

Meryl: We eat our dinners and then (ssh, I want to talk) I play in here. I eat my dinner. I get a knife and fork and when we've finished we having pudding and cake and custard and then we wash our hands and then we have a partner and then we play outside.

There was a wealth of detail given by children about place use in this way. Children's ability to talk about the meanings they gave to a place seemed to be enhanced by talking in the place itself. Hart found working with older children that 'place expeditions' elicited far more details about children's experiences than traditional methods alone. This is particularly valuable when there is an existing spatial experience to make reference to, prior to

the design of a new building, no matter how poor the quality of the existing provision may be.

Access

Spaces also acquired significance according to whether the children had access to the space or not. Children remarked that the staff room was a place they could not go into and were keen to photograph it on their tours. The kitchen was another space known to be out of bounds but signalled as important. Access was also controlled by adults according to age of the child. The Orange room (described by Meryl earlier) was a place where 4-year-olds had their lunch. Each key group in the kindergarten section of the nursery had 3–4-year-olds together so these children would eat lunch separately according to age. Meryl had lunch in the Orange room, but Gaby being 3 had lunch in the conservatory. Gaby described on the tour how much she wanted to be old enough to go to the Orange room saying 'I can't wait to get big.'

This example supports Sibley's view that children's experience of place is closely associated with issues of power.[15] Adults' demarcation of place use by age led to a differentiation of experience for the children in the group.

Gaby's comment leads me on to the question of children's place feelings and values, which are at times difficult to separate from knowledge about place use.

Constructing meanings: place feelings and values

Hart describes children's experience of place feelings and values in terms of preferences and fears. I will use these categories to examine children's feelings about places in the nursery. The following excerpt is from a child conference about favourite places.

Researcher: Where is your favourite place in the nursery?
Clare: Outside and inside and having fruit time.
Laura: On the bikes.
Gary: Going in my cave, near the big dark trees [July]. In my cave listening to music. It's magic music from my magic radio [November].
John: The garden. I roll in the green rollers.

Gaby: Inside – the fruit place. We always do singing there.

Mark: I live in here [classroom] so my mummy knows where I am. I like playing with the sharks.

Children's preferences ranged from personal spaces of imagination or safety to social places linked to activities as discussed above. Gary was unusual, at the age of 3, in being able to speak about his imaginary space. A traditional interview might however have left me baffled about this secret place. I took the decision to conduct the child conferencing with these boys on the move. I became a 'walking interview' (4) or as Hart described it, a 'place expedition'. The boys took me outside and showed me the 'cave'. It was not a hidden corner as I had imagined but a curved bench on the grass in the play area. My observations had indicated that this was a public social place where children gathered with each other or with an adult. Gary's description shows the imaginative meanings children can give to familiar objects and illustrates Hart's descriptions of children's personal or phenomenal landscapes.[14]

Social spaces

Children identified several key sites in the nursery which were focal points for being with their peers and sometimes also with adults. The 'fruit place' was a shared space for children and adults to interact together, as discussed earlier. The curved bench in the garden was another meeting place. This indicates how the same object or space held different meanings for individuals within the group. Gary's 'cave' represented a significant social space for another child, Cary. She took a photograph of the bench and included it in her set of important photos. It represented for her the place where she used to sit with Molly, her key worker, who had recently left on maternity leave. The memories associated with the space still gave this part of the nursery meaning for Cary.

The large sandpit was a central feature of the outside play area and acted as a focus for social interaction. Children in the study took photographs of the sand and the toys and the features linked to the sandpit, a wooden bridge over the sand and a large canopy.

Another preferred social space was the climbing frame, tunnel and slide. This piece of play equipment featured in many of the children's photographs. Some children made carefully framed shots of the slide or the tunnel. Others chose this play equipment as a background against which to photograph friends. The photographs were then used as significant places on their maps.

Private spaces

Children in the study also valued places with a degree of privacy where they had the ability to regulate social interaction.[16] There were few spaces indoors or outdoors where the children could exercise this control. One such space was behind the shed at the far corner of the garden. I had observed that some children would go to this corner to play before being asked to move away by an adult. It was one of the few places in the nursery where children were out of sight. It did not appear from my observations to be a space used exclusively by boys. However, in the group I was working with, it was Gary and John who identified this space as important. Gary selected the photographs he took of the shed to include on his map of the nursery.

The tunnel was another child-only space. It was small enough for children to regulate who used this equipment. Several children in the group chose to take close-up photographs of the tunnel. Laura and Clare both included these photographs in their books of the nursery. The tunnel serves as another example of the multiple meanings given to places: the tunnel as private space as well as social space. The tunnel was also a raised space, which was above the heads of the children. Corsaro discusses the importance of raised spaces for control. The height of the climbing frame and tunnel resulted in a useful vantage point for the children.

Individual landmarks

In addition to the shared spaces which held meaning for children in the group, this study also revealed a complex web of individual traces or landmarks.[17] These landmarks ranged from objects and photographs to people, which summed up what was important about the nursery for different children. Younger siblings acted as landmarks for two of the children in the group. The child-led tours indicated that their morning routine of taking their brother and sister to their place in the nursery was a significant part of the day. Gary and Meryl took photographs of their siblings, including personal objects such as their siblings' mattresses, towels and pegs.

Photographs displayed around the building also acted as individual markers. The staff photographs near the entrance hall proved to be an interesting example. The photographs were on a large display board which showed all the members of staff. Cary asked to have her own photograph taken on the tour and placed beside her previous key worker's photograph. This was the same child who associated the curved bench with previous conversations with this significant adult.

Photographs also provided links to past activities and events enjoyed by the children. Clare remarked on a display of photographs taken on a recent outing to a train station and she took a photograph of the display.

Children's own work also acted as personal landmarks around the nursery. Children leading me on the tour were quick to point out any of their work on the walls. They also stopped to show me their portfolios. These carefully presented folders held examples of their own work that the children had chosen with their key workers since joining the nursery. Children took photographs of memorable paintings and drawings in portfolios. These personal details or 'traces' of the children's own work appeared to have great significance in developing place identity as well as self-identity: 'the history of who I am in this place'.

Place fears

The young children in my study were given direct as well as indirect opportunities to express negative feelings about places in the nursery. This can be seen in the following excerpts from a child conference.

Researcher: Which part of the nursery don't you like?
Clare: The staff room 'cos they have their lunch break.
Laura: I don't like the boys.

Gary: That building there and the bridge.
John: Where 'x' did a poo.
Gaby: Nowhere.

The direct question in the child conferencing led to a range of responses. Children interpreted this question in a broader way than I had anticipated. Children's negative feelings towards places included frustration. The tours and children's photographs had clarified the views expressed by some of the children in the child conferencing that the staff room was out of bounds. This underlined their interpretations of the nursery as a place where different hierarchies operated between adults and children.

One of the children in the group expressed what appeared to be fear rather than discomfort or frustration. These negative feelings were associated with a past incident involving another child whom we did not like. John mentioned this incident several times during the child conferencing. His key worker confirmed that he was aware that John had found this disturbing. It was like a negative marker, which affected John's feelings about the space in the past and the present.

Discussion

The Mosaic approach offers a framework for listening to young children, which reflects the complexities of their everyday lives. This complexity does not fit well with easily measured targets and standards. At the time of undertaking the study, one approach to gathering the views of young users was by using stickers with 'smiley' faces and 'sad' faces to express preferences. This shorthand may be useful on occasions but there is a limit to such a simplified approach. Children are not in charge of the questions but only, in a limited way, of the answers. This seems to be an adaptation of a consumer model of gathering views designed for adults – a top down approach. The Mosaic approach is one attempt to turn this upside down and begin from young children's strengths – their local knowledge, their attention to detail, and their visual as well as verbal communication skills.

The use of participatory methods with young children has opened up more ways of communicating. This contradicts the myth that researchers and practitioners need to simplify their approaches with young children. This exploratory study has shown that there is a need to think differently and be flexible, but not to oversimplify. I learned this lesson early on in the study when describing to the children how to use the cameras. I explained the procedure for using the viewfinder, the flash button and how to wind on the film. I added a comment about keeping the camera still 'otherwise you'll get a wobbly picture'. One of the girls then disappeared with her camera. When I caught up with her she was taking a photograph of the sandpit while moving the camera gently from side to side. When I asked her what she was doing she replied: 'I'm taking a wobbly photo'.

Participatory tools such as the cameras and the tours allowed the children to set more of the questions as well as provide answers. The issue of contact with siblings was one such question. The child conferencing did not reveal any details about this aspect of some of the children's lives in the nursery. It only became apparent when the children walked me to their siblings' rooms. The participatory nature of the tools meant that they acted as mediators between me as researcher and the children as informants.[18] It was, I found, the process of using the various methodologies, which increased my understanding of the children's lives.

The notion of 'interpretation' raises an interesting difference between some research and practice perspectives on listening to children. Within the research paradigm of the sociology of childhood there is an acknowledgement of need for interpretation to construct meanings. There is also recognition that the research task is not limited to unearthing one 'true' meaning. This seems to differ from some understandings of children's participation, where the task is seen as extracting children's views as untainted by adult 'interference' as possible. I have tried in the Mosaic approach to set up a platform where children are given many different opportunities to express their views and experiences and then to be part of the interpretation – this search for meanings. This seems to be of particular importance when working with young children who are in the

process of establishing their identities and place identities. Throughout the study the children were involved in discussing, reflecting on and reassessing what it was like to be in their nursery.

It's not so much a matter of eliciting children's preformed ideas and opinions, it's much more a question of enabling them to explore the ways in which they perceive the world and communicate their ideas in a way that is meaningful to them.[19]

This view of listening, as part of an ongoing exploration of the world, presents a challenge to the designers of children's daycare centres. The outcomes will be open ended and open to interpretation. This calls for a redefinition of listening, away from a one-off event to meet a prescribed target, towards an acknowledgement of listening as an active process of communication involving hearing, interpreting and constructing meanings. The effective process will provide significant rewards to architects who are prepared to listen.

Early years practitioners are in the best position to listen to the young children in their care. There is a danger in the target-driven climate of education design that there is little time to notice young children's own agendas, feelings and experience. There may be a place for a framework such as the Mosaic approach to help practitioners concentrate on the small details of the children's lives around them. A number of staff could work, for example, with a group of children, using this approach as part of their induction. There may also be children within a group who could benefit from the opportunities for communication offered by the different tools. One of the shyest children in this study took great pleasure in taking me on tour and in using the camera. Her key worker remarked on how keen she was to talk about her photographs.

There appears to be practical application for using the Mosaic approach to change the environment. As discussed above, this study revealed a detailed picture of children's knowledge of place use and their place preferences and fears. Children could be involved in recording their feelings about an existing space. Older children in a setting (3–4-year-olds) could be involved in recording pre-verbal children's use of the space. This could inform future decisions about changes to the indoor and outdoor environment.[20] However, the greatest challenge within the context of this publication would be for architects to become engaged in this in-depth discussion with children at design stage. It provokes the important question, who really is the client? My answer would be, the children, together with the early years practitioners.

Conclusion

This small exploratory study set out to develop an imaginative framework for listening to young children. It has involved moving across disciplines and blending methods. The emphasis has been on the use of multiple methods, including the traditional tools of observation and interviewing, but also investigating the use of participatory methods with children under 5. The suggestion from this study, subsequent training sessions and feedback, is that the Mosaic approach offers new possibilities for furthering our understanding of the complexities of the everyday lives of older as well as younger children.

However, the information gained from children within the framework of this short study, illustrates a fascinating range of features which could be incorporated in to the architect's thinking in terms of detail design, and in the distribution of specific rooms within the framework of the client's schedule of accommodation. For example, children talked of the importance of specific rooms within the centre where special activities took place, such as the music and dancing room. This suggests that children should be permitted time beyond the confines of their homebase. Meeting spaces and defined 'landmarks' are important. The bench next to the sandpit was viewed as an important social space, and the landmark of a display board in the conservatory was important in developing place identity and enhanced meanings for the children. It is clear that these lessons can have real immediacy for architects developing new strategies for the design of childcare centre architecture. Children see the centre as their world, and very much a landscape of play and discovery.

Notes

1 Daycare Trust (1998). *Listening to children. Young children's views on childcare: a guide for parents.* London: Daycare Trust.

2 The editor's experience in designing childcare centres for a number of different clients within both the public and private sector is always structured around strict age groupings. Homebase areas are created which confine babies, toddlers, 3–4-year-olds and 4–5-year-olds into separate, largely autonomous, homebase areas. Children of different ages are usually prevented from having much to do with each other except in more innovative settings such as some Montessori nurseries, which establish family groups of mixed ages.

3 Qvortrup, J., Bardy, M., Sgritta, G. and Wintersberger, H. (eds) (1994). *Childhood Matters.* Vienna: European Centre.

4 Langsted, O. (1994). 'Looking at quality from the child's perspective.' In P. Moss and A. Pence, (eds) *Valuing Quality in Early Childhood Services: new approaches to defining quality.* London: Paul Chapman.

5 Rinaldi, C. (1999). Paper presented in Reggio Emilia, Italy. April 1999.

6 Clark, A. and Moss, P. (2001). *Listening to Young Children: the Mosaic Approach.* London: National Children's Bureau.

7 Edwards, C., Gandini, L. and Foreman, G. (eds) (1998). *The Hundred Languages of Children: the Reggio Emilia approach to early childhood education,* 2nd edn. Norwood, NJ: Ablex.

8 Corsaro, W. (1985). *Friendship and Peer Culture in the Early Years.* Norwood, NJ: Ablex and Corsaro, W. (1997). *The Sociology of Childhood.* Thousand Oaks, CA: Pineforge Press.

9 Walker, R (1993). 'Finding a voice for the researcher: using photographs in evaluation and research', in M. Schratz (ed) *Qualitative Voices in Educational Research.* London: Falmer Press.

10 Smith, F. and Barker, J. (1999). From Ninja Turtles to the Spice Girls: children's participation in the development of out of school play environments. *Built Environment,* **25** (1), 35–46.

Smith, F. and Barker, J. (2002). Contested spaces. *Childhood*, **7** (3), 315–333.

11 Hart, R. (1997). *Children's Experience of Place*. New York: Irvington Publishers. Hart, R. (1997). *Children's Participation*. London: UNICEF and Earthscan.

12 Adams, E. and Ingham, S. (1998). *Changing Places: children's participation in the environmental planning*. London: Children's Society.

13 Hart, R. (1997). p. 165.

14 Hart, R. (1979). 12–13.

15 Sibley, D. (1995). 'Families and domestic routines: constructing the boundaries of childhood' in S. Pile and N. Thrift (eds), *Mapping the Subject: geographies of cultural transformation*. London: Routledge.

16 Altman, I. (1975). *The Environment and Social Behaviour*. Monterey, CA: Brooks/Cole.

17 Weinstein, C. (1987). 'Designing pre-school classrooms to support development: research and reflection', in C. Weinstein and T. David (eds) *Spaces for Children: the built environment and child development*. New York, Plenum. Trancik, A. and Evans, G. (1995). 'Places fit for Children: competency in the design of daycare centre environments'. *Children's Environments*, **12** (3), 311–319.

18 Christensen, P. and James, A. (eds) (2000). *Research with Children*. London: Falmer Press.

19 Tolfree, D. and Woodhead, M. (1999). Tapping a key resource. *Early Childhood Matters*, **91**, 19–23.

20 This has been explored in Clark, A. and Moss, P. (2005) *Spaces to Play: More Listening to Young Children using the Mosaic Approach*. London: National Children's Bureau.

Alison Clark is a Research Officer at the Institute of Education, University of London. Her research interests focus on young children's participation. Her work has included a research and development project funded by the Joseph Rowntree Foundation on listening to young children. She has recently completed a pilot project involving young children in the designing of an outdoor play area. She is engaged on a three year project to bring architects, early years practitioners and young children to plan, design and change indoor and outdoor environments.

Figure 1.4
The author Alison Clark standing at the entrance to the University Daycare centre in Berkeley, California. This is an old building dating back to the 1960s, however, it is intimate in scale and uses light and colour to create memorable child-friendly areas. The simple pergola roof structure with coloured corrugated roof panels welcomes parents and children with its soft warm lighting. (Photo: Mark Dudek.)

Acknowledgements

This chapter is an edited version of a chapter published in *The Reality of Research with Children and Young People*, edited by Vicky Lewis et al. (2004) published by Sage in association with the Open University and is reproduced with permission.

2

Designing for play

Michael Laris

Editor's introduction

As I write, another child has been murdered on a London street. He was robbed for his mobile phone then stabbed by a gang of older boys. In the light of urban crime such as this, it is important to consider the environmental quality afforded to children living in the city. Play parks, dedicated children's areas within the city, are practical because they can be controlled and therefore made safe. However, children will only use them if they are stimulated and engaged by what they find there. Designing effective environments for play must be in tune with the contemporary culture of childhood.

Michael Laris works for Kompan, a manufacturer of contemporary play equipment which has been widely recognized for its quality and style, a factor which is particularly important for older children. However the author conceives his designs in a totality, recognizing that play equipment is only one aspect of the playground environment. In this chapter he describes the conceptual thinking which goes into his work, elevating a piece of climbing equipment to part of a psychological landscape of play and experimentation which extends developmental possibilities for those who use it.

Laris starts his piece with a relatively simple question 'what is design?' and in particular, 'how do children use these places which are essentially adult visions of childhood needs?'. In order to answer this he adopts research-based methods, observing children as they use play spaces, particularly the spaces he has designed. This information helps him to modify and transform those spaces so that they are more in line with childhood aspirations. Change and evolution are fundamental aspects of his vision, and the novelty this affords is an essential dynamic in the definition of his thinking.

This then provides a crucial insight into the realities of a top designer who sees through the eyes of a child. This perspective is laced with fun and wry humour, this attitude being an essential part of the designing for play. Laris also has a wider perspective which recognizes that we are only another layer between past and future; we build upon the past and set the framework for the future. In an urban environment which is often confined and limited by dangers, nothing could be more important than designing for play.

Introduction

Design is primarily about use – imagining, inventing, drawing and forming things that are useful to others. It is a complex developmental process that starts with a vision and ends with a product. In order to design successfully, one must understand the user and reconcile all aspects of the user's relationship to the forthcoming product. When working on the design of playground equipment, many contrasting needs come into play. The safe

Figure 2.1
Almost anything can be used for play, even church steps in Granada, Spain. (Photos: Michael Laris.)

functioning of the equipment is particularly important, yet the equipment must also be challenging to the user. It must also fulfil the demands of a manufactured industrial product, being attractive, robust, and affordable, and most importantly, it must appeal to the user in a deeper, more intangible way than most adult products. It must excite the child's imagination and create a sense of magic.

For the past seven years, I have worked as a playground equipment designer. My role has been to invent new play items for the outdoor environment. I find this profession highly rewarding because it brings together two delightful and inspiring subjects, children and play, and also because throughout the past seven years I have been fortunate enough to be able to include my own children in my daily work. In fact, they have been the experts, the test pilots, and my toughest critics. Through them I have been able to enter the child's world, and design things for play that I otherwise could not have.

Understanding the concept of usability, i.e. making something that has a specific function to be used by a unique group of people, is essential when designing playground equipment. In theory, this task should not be that difficult, as play has few boundaries and children can use almost anything for play. The designer's task should thus be to discover why some things work well and to optimize these characteristics. To do so requires

the utilization of a design process wherein factors such as play value, safety, accessibility, product life span, and methods of production are considered from the very start and integrated into the final design.

In the following pages I will explain in greater depth the factors of this design development process and open a discussion around the role of the designer. I will also illustrate my approach to design with two play products currently on the market, explaining the sources of my inspiration and describing key design principles that support the child's developmental growth and ultimately enable the child to take ownership of the product. Throughout this chapter, I wish to focus on the users – the children – and there is no better way of doing this than by beginning with a story about them.

Castle or ship?

Most adults, I imagine, recognize the form in Plate 1 and interpret it as a children's castle. We assume it is a castle because of the turrets and battlements, the archway, perhaps the choice of vibrant colours and, although it is not visible here, the drawbridge at the front entrance. This product had been available in another version for many years before it was revised to incorporate new accessibility standards. As part of the development process, the new updated castle was manufactured, installed and then tested. As I stood alongside it making observations during the play evaluation, three boys came running over and entered the castle through the main entrance, under the arch. The first boy ran up onto the upper platforms. The second hid below in the 'dungeon' area. The third stopped at the portal, took hold of a lever arm, placed there so that children could pretend to lift the drawbridge, and shouted, 'anchors up, we're sailing!'

Sailing? My new castle, sailing? Here I learned an important lesson – it is not the designer who decides how a thing will ultimately be used. It is the children who decide. In this case the boys needed a ship in order to carry on the game they were playing. The explicit castle references were of no relevance to the narrative of their play at that moment, so instead, the castle became a ship. This observation made clear to me the crucial need for designs which are less obvious, more abstract, and include a diversity of shapes and materials so that they are open to a wide range of imaginative interpretations – interpretations made by the children themselves.

Children are constantly trying out new things. Their world is a novel experience and investigating and experimenting with things is their natural way of being. It is not, as sometimes thought, a haphazard way of being. On the contrary, children over two years of age are well skilled at recognizing their own physical limitations and are usually able to grade the difficulty of the task they face, taking on only those risks that they feel equipped to handle.

They are also critical observers, watching and listening to older or more experienced children and adults. When they have gathered an appropriate level of knowledge about something that intrigues them, they will try it out. This brings them new knowledge about their physical and mental dexterity, which they will apply immediately to their subsequent cycle of play. In very general terms, this is what children are doing when they play. They observe others, try it out for themselves, analyse what happened, adjust their actions, and try again. Children are creative inventors because they can progress through this process intuitively, largely unencumbered by the inhibitions many adults have.

Inventors vs translators

The photos in Figure 2.2 and Plate 2 were taken in Barcelona at Güell Park, an important historical piece of landscape architecture designed by the great master Antonio Gaudi. It has a complex yet abstract spatial quality, with interesting shapes and textures that reflect color and light. On a recent visit there, I met a group of children who were not so taken by Gaudi's masterwork but were however fascinated by an old crooked tree they found there. They climbed onto it, sat on it, and explored its form; they hid behind it and played chase around it. For the hour of their visit the tree became a centre of magical activity, the focus of the children's developing narrative play. At last, the whole class sat and ate lunch on and around this tree. The children used it as a 'bench-table-climber-balance-beam', a functional invention which emerged simply through their spirited interaction with its strange sensuous shape. This was just an old tree, however, it was located within a context that enabled the children to transform its meaning to meet their particular play needs. The children immediately projected their own imaginative interpretation onto the setting, taking temporary ownership, and

Figure 2.2
An old belt crooked tree … a wonderful tree, in Güell Park, Barcelona. (Photos: Michael Laris.)

giving it many new uses. One imagines Gaudi would have approved.

If children are the inventors, what then is the designer's role? Designers are the translators. They are the ones who can give form to something that will meet the diverse imaginative needs of children's developing personalities. Simply stated, designers translate an imaginative idea into a tangible form, with colours and materiality that can be freely enjoyed by the child.

Clearly, the practical side of creativity, developing imaginative ideas into practical proposals, is something that children do not do very well. In my experience, when children are asked what they would like in their playground, they usually refer to something they have seen elsewhere, or something they know well, though usually requesting a taller, bigger, or faster version of it. Yet children are good at doing new things and therefore I have found it worthwhile to enter into a dialogue with them, not so much a verbal conversation, but rather a dialogue of action (by the child) and our own reflective observation.

Being a designer is in itself a learning process. It therefore mirrors the children's pattern of play. Often by simply watching children at play an idea forms in the designer's imagination. An initial sketch for a new play item can then be drawn or modelled. From scale models, a full size functional model can be constructed and children can then test this model. Observations of children using the functional model provide new information that can be used as the basis for alterations. Then, the improved model is tested again. This goes on again and again until the design meets all the specified criteria.

The product in Figure 2.3 went through a design developmental process as just described. The initial design was inspired by observations of older children who were using traditional slides just as much to climb up, as they were to slide down. The designers made a curving tube-like form that children could slide down like a banister or climb up like a leaning tree trunk. Children were then invited to test the functional model. Observations of their play suggested certain modifications; side handholds were added to use when climbing up, and a rocking effect was designed to mimic the movement of a log rolling in water. This made the activity more challenging yet almost paradoxically increased the safety and usability of the product. The equipment could be installed horizontally and used as a rocking balance beam as well as a slide and a climbing frame. The product's sensuous quality was important from the start so that children would not be deterred from having full body contact with its surfaces. This is especially significant for children with low levels of physical or visual ability. Overall the product succeeds because it provides diverse play possibilities, meets the needs of children in several age groups and levels

Figure 2.3
Slide down, climb up, balance across. (Photos: Kompan.)

of ability, is safe yet challenging, and is enjoyed by many.

Design origins

The previous example expressed the importance of maintaining a dialogue between the users and the designer and though I stated earlier that it is the children who are the inventors and the designers the translators, in fact the design development process is more complex than that.

Initially, most design projects begin in outline form, described in a project programme. This programme usually includes a list of pragmatic criteria, a budget, and a time frame. A programme for a new play activity might incorporate criteria for its size, age group, material, sales price, and level of customization. Such a programme is just the beginning of the project and no matter how detailed the programme is, it does not generate new ideas on its own. These must come from a thought generated by an inspired moment. We all have ideas and we all know that they come to us at the most unlikely of times. Where exactly they come from is hard to say, but I find that it is usually when I am relaxed and away from work, yet still immersed, albeit subconsciously, in the problem of invention.

Briefly, the work of the design profession can be divided into three major groups, ranging from innovation, to evolution, to formation. Innovation implies an entirely new symbiosis of form and function, whereby the user now has the ability to make use of a function previously unknown. Evolution describes advances made to a known function, whereas formation is about giving a new form to an existing function. As a designer of children's play equipment, I am most interested in the first two areas of design – innovation and evolution – because it is within these areas that new functions are developed and where involvement with the users is critical.

But, what brings about innovation? In my experience, no idea is created by one independent thought or vision. Rather, innovation and evolution are the outcome of a web of ideas and inputs. Some

are what I would call pragmatic decisions, others are wholly intuitive. However, functional ideas are deeply connected to the time and place in which the design is conceived. In other words, an innovative idea is the product of a unique synthesis of people, places, need, and the time at which it is developed. From this synthesis, new ideas arise in many different ways.

One such way is via a 'break-through' – when an idea seems to come unexpectedly and out of the blue. In my experience, break-throughs seem to come most often when I am doing something that does not require my full attention and when my mind is allowed to float and make chance connections with disparate thoughts. Recently I met a film writer and producer who agreed with this theory and confided in me that for a long period of time his best ideas came when he was vacuuming. He was vacuuming until his carpets wore thin. Then one day that ceased to be a source of inspiration, instead his ideas began coming to him while he was in the shower. I told him that oddly enough, my best ideas are also inspired while showering or at times when biking. The editor, Mark Dudek, finds the best time for thinking is when he is jogging. Ideas seem to emerge in the most unusual moments, not always in time for deadlines, but most often when the mind and body are relaxed.

After the initial idea, many months of development work are required; with designers usually working in collaboration, 'ping-ponging' ideas back and forth. Often it is chance happenings within the process that lead to the best designs. A colleague once told me how a mistake led to one of his best designs. He was working with a partner who lived in another city. They were developing a new wood-burning stove, sending drawings back and forth by e-mail. At one point the partner wrote that he was very pleased to see the latest changes that the other had made and he could see that the modifications made to the stove would greatly improve its efficiency. My colleague responded that he had not drawn it with these intended modifications. In fact, his partner had misread the drawing. They developed the 'error' and it significantly improved their earlier idea. Generally, the richer the process, the more chance there is for the unexpected to occur.

A multitude of factors

An initial idea, whether it comes from a breakthrough, by mistake, or by following a specified design development method, is just the beginning of the design development process. In the case of playground equipment, a multitude of factors beyond form and function must be considered if the product is to be a success. One of the most important practical criteria is that the product must be safe.

There are strict safety codes in place in North America and in Europe. The North America safety codes for play equipment are defined by ASTM (American Standards for Tests and Measurements) and in Europe by EN 1176. These standards are intended to prevent unforeseen risks and hazardous situations, for example, a hole size in which a child could get their head stuck or a configuration where a string from a child's jacket hood could get caught.

Preventing hazardous situations is mandatory in relation to the design of playground equipment and no one would argue otherwise, yet there is a hot debate as how best to do this. The safety standards in general describe things in two dimensions, for example, barrier railings shall be a minimum of 800 mm high, and that there shall be no hole larger than 8 mm in diameter or no smaller than 25 mm in diameter. However, playground design is becoming more spatially complex and often the standards do not keep pace as new concepts emerge. The safety standards are based on what has already been designed and can be inappropriate when applied to new innovations. This situation adds an extra challenge, and entails ongoing debate with safety specialists. Thus when designing new play equipment it is necessary to have a safety specialist involved in the design process from the very start.

Another important issue when considering safety is risk management. This is the term used to describe one's ability to assess and manage any risk and thus avoid a dangerous situation. Being safe is

about preventing hazards, not about preventing risk, for risk is always present. Viewed as a fundamental part of a child's development it is essential that each child has the opportunity to experience situations where the risk level is appropriate to their skill level. This way a child can evaluate potential dangers and learn to manage similar situations as they occur. More and more often we see caregivers who follow their child around the playground with one hand under the child at all times (refer to editor's introduction). This is an inappropriate form of protection. If a child does not have the opportunity to tumble, fall, and experience accidents and occasional pain, they will miss an invaluable stage in their development. As a consequence of an overprotective environment, the child might grow to be shy of physical activity, or clumsy, or possibly even accident prone as they have not had the vital experience that is a necessary part of growing up.

A challenging yet hazard-free playground is the ideal 'safe haven' for children to test themselves, to learn about risk and the limitations of their own abilities, both physically and socially. With these skills in place, children have a foundation upon which to build, giving them the confidence to overcome all kinds of new challenges in the future.

A second essential factor when designing playground equipment is accessibility. For all play areas in the United States, US law requires compliance with the Americans with Disabilities Act Accessible Guidelines (ADAAG). In The United Kingdom, the DDA guidelines (Disability Discrimination Act) are now in place and other similar standards are in various levels of implementation across Europe. These standards seek to ensure equal access for all users. The ADAAG, which is the most detailed of the accessible standards, outlines requirements for both ground level accessibility (ramps and paths), as well as elevated accessibility (access to upper platforms in play structures). This second requirement adds great challenges to the design development process and opens yet another debate concerning the relationship between access and safety for all users.

Forming the ADAAG for play areas was a long and difficult process. Once complete, my fellow colleagues (designer Lani Wollwage and child development specialist Karin Müller) and I were commissioned by the US Access Board to explain the guidelines in a user-friendly booklet.[1] In general I believe that the guidelines are a reasonable compromise of many varying viewpoints; however one issue that is still unresolved in my mind is the potential increase in hazards when adding a ramp to a play structure.

A ramp provides greater access to elevated platforms but this access cannot be limited to a specific group. Access is made available for users of wheelchairs, as well as bikes, mopeds, skateboards, and two-year-olds. It is clear why children riding bikes should not be allowed up on the play structure, however the issue concerning two-year-olds might not be so obvious. Safety standards permit more challenging activities for older children so that play items can be designed to meet their developmental needs and skill levels. Before ramps were an issue, designers and safety experts made sure that a play structure was designed such that, in order to reach the upper platforms, a child had to have a given level of ability, a skill level that would ensure that the child could also navigate the more challenging activities found higher up. However, ramps provide an easy access to all children regardless of age or skill level. This means that two-, three-, or four-year-olds can easily access the upper platforms and once there, find activities that they are not yet experienced enough to handle. Fortunately, in some cases, the ADAAG allows exceptions to ramps and I encourage the profession to use these exceptions as well as to develop new equally accessible alternatives.

Other factors affecting the design development process include: engineering, production, sales, and installation. With regards to engineering, the product must be able to stand at least 10 years in all climates and weather conditions, and under heavy use and abuse, which may sometimes border on vandalism, and be virtually maintenance-free. To comply with contemporary production values, the product must be able to be manufactured, packed, and dispatched around the world at a reasonable price, using environmentally sustainable materials and methods of production. It is also important that the product appeals to the buyer, the adults paying for it, whilst being appropriate and attractive to the end user, the children. These two criteria are often in conflict – especially with regards to colour.

Finally, to meet installation requirements, the product must be able to be easily installed, for example by parent groups with no previous experience, and if necessary, be able to be quickly and simply repaired.

One way to insure that all of these factors are addressed and integrated throughout the design process is to assemble a team of specialists, which from the very outset, have the experience to contribute ideas, negotiate compromises, make decisions, and take action to make the product development process work on all levels. In the years that I have been working as a playground designer, I have been fortunate to be part of such a team and in the next section I will introduce two products that were designed by the Kompan Design Team and developed by Kompan's International Product Development department. I will also describe the design development process behind them, and touch on some personal sources of inspiration.

Product one – the long story

The two products that I will discuss here, the Minkar and the Supernova, were developed as part of a product series called Galaxy and, in my opinion, each product holds a significant place in the history of playground equipment. As lead designer of this design process, I shall do my best to remain objective as I describe these two products and the concepts behind them.

As I mentioned in the opening page, it is crucial to understand the user group and in the case of the following two products, the target group is the 6- to 12-year-olds i.e. primary school age children. These children have already mastered the basics of climbing and balancing and require more complex spatial arrangements to further develop their skills.

The first product that I will describe began with an idea that came to me late one night when I was sketching ideas for the second development phase

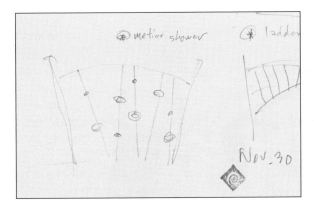

Figure 2.4
Meteor Shower – the first step towards Minkar – an initial sketch and a 1:1 model. (Sketch and photo: Michael Laris.)

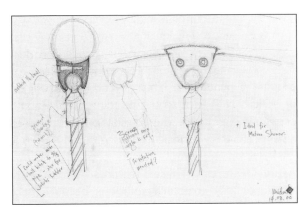

Figure 2.5
A small plate is welded to the beam and two identical half parts capsulate a ball at the end of the rope or support pole. (Sketch: Michael Laris; Photos: Kompan.)

of Galaxy. It was a simple idea of hanging a series of ropes down from a curving beam and attaching various objects to them, so that children could climb through them, rather like Tarzan swinging through the vines of the jungle. Since the product series was called Galaxy, I decided to call this play activity the Meteor Shower as the objects attached to the rope seem to float in space.

After the initial concept was drawn, a 1:10 scale model was quickly made. These models are important tools in the initial phase of design because it is much easier for the development team to discuss relevant issues when handling a model than it is when looking at a set of sketches. The sketching phase, therefore, is very short. On

the other hand, literally hundreds of models are made that go through a strict process of evaluation based on three key criteria: play value, safety, and engineering.

In the case of the Meteor Shower, few changes were required to approve its play value and its safety. The more difficult discussions related to engineering and shipping. Due to their length, the long curved beams posed a transportation problem. On this issue, a compromise was eventually reached, balancing transportability issues against the play value of having a longer beam.

Developing an engineering solution that met the wishes of the design team proved to be more difficult. The challenge was how to attach the ropes

Figure 2.6
Minkar is a constellation of activities with the Meter Shower in the middle. (CAD drawing by Kompan.)

to the beam, allowing for multiple and flexible usage, without piercing the beam's top surface. The design required this flexible solution because the ropes needed to be attached at various angles to the beam in order to achieve optimal play value. The top surface of the beam needed to remain smooth, as it was clear that children would be climbing there and a protrusion, no matter how minimal, would disturb play patterns and compromise safety. Ultimately, the design team came up with a solution whereby the ropes where attached to the bottom of the beam as shown – a solution that met the need for play value, and most importantly in this case, for strength and safety.

The 'Accessible' significance of galaxy

As the design development process continued, the Meteor Shower was linked to other newly designed activities forming the Minkar Constellation. The concept of linking one ground level accessible play to another, in a series, was an innovation in playground design. The design team called this solution a 'Ground Level Composite Play Structure' and at the time of its development, this was, I believe, unique in the industry.[2] Since then it has become the inspiration for many other playground

equipment producers. This ground level concept has special relevance to the ongoing debate about accessibility and it is the foundation upon which the entire Galaxy series complies with the ADAAG. Galaxy achieves compliance by providing several unique features. These features differ from traditional play structure solutions because here the child is not required to overcome structural barriers, such as ramps or stairs, in order to play. On the contrary, the Galaxy activities come down to the ground, presenting play opportunities directly in front of any child, and inviting the child to engage in play at any point. Thus play is immediate and instantly accessible.

Another significant feature of the Galaxy products is the concept of repetition. For example, when a special component is placed at a higher level, an equal component is placed at ground level. As such the focus of play is not necessarily about reaching the highest point and as such a wider range of children can take part. A third key feature of Galaxy is the intentional transparency of the design, which makes for easy visual and vocal communication between children, and between children and their caregivers. In this way Galaxy differs from the traditional composite play structures where play often takes place on upper

Figure 2.7
Labyrinths from East Asia, North America, and Europe. (Drawings: Michael Laris.)

platforms hidden behind safety barrier screens. In addition, Galaxy is built up around a concept called 'Activity to Activity', meaning that there are no platforms, walls, steps, or other components that cannot be used as part of the activity of play. Instead, it is deliberately designed so that one play component is directly linked to the next in a complex sequence. Connection joints are rubber coated so that they facilitate children in their natural tendency to do things in their own way and climb in unintended directions around the equipment.

The result of the combination of these design features is that the Galaxy activities are accessible to all participants regardless of whether they have the ability or desire to leave behind their mobility device, caregiver, parents, or their friends.

Spaces and qualities of inspiration

With the key factors of safety, engineering, production, and accessibility in place, the emphasis for the development of Minkar could again be placed on design and play value and in order to go into more depth here, I will first touch on two areas of inspiration that are important to me.

Since my time as a student of architecture, I have been fascinated by the qualities of two types of conceptual space, the labyrinth and the café. The labyrinth has specific qualities that are elementary to its form. A labyrinth is not a maze. A maze has shortcuts, dead-ends, and possibly more than one solution to its puzzle. In contrast, a labyrinth consists of a single path, spiralling inward to its centre point. There is only one way in, which is the same way out.

The labyrinth is a constructed journey, which because of its physical qualities promotes contemplative thought, and supports personal development. Throughout history and in many cultures around the world, the labyrinth has symbolized the notion of rebirth. The idea being, that by travelling in and back out, one has grown, changed, been renewed and transformed. I use the word *transform* purposefully as it implies a change in form and this is appropriate when discussing design. The type of change is not brought about by manipulation, distortion, or mutation. Transformation is closer to the kind of change that a caterpillar goes through in order to become a butterfly; its essence emerges as part of a natural organic process. The labyrinth is designed specifically to bring about a transformation of spiritual dimension. When designing playground equipment, the labyrinth reminds me of how a space can help a child along their own path of personal development.

The second point of reference for me is the café. The café space that I have in mind is Linnea's Café, my favourite from my college days, though there are many cafés with similar qualities and most of us are familiar with such interiors. A café is remarkably different from the concept of the labyrinth. Cafés are social spaces, containers, which are used for much more than sharing a cup of coffee. Though there is nothing exceptional about Linnea's furnishings – shelves with games and books, a mess of tables and chairs, and an alcove by the window – it is a space where you can watch the world unfold. In itself, the alcove provides a space for quiet contemplation, for meeting friends, for live music or for a serious game of chess. The same space has many uses and it is transformed time and again when tables and chairs are moved around and people sit alone or together in groups. It is a fluid space that transforms in tune with the users and as a result they feel a sense of ownership of the space.

Where the labyrinth is a fixed form, the café is fluid. Comparing the two, it is clear that the relationship between time and space is fundamentally different. The labyrinth is predictable, stable, ordered, introverted, and has a sense of universality about it. The café is social, unpredictable, constantly changing, chaotic, extroverted, and has a 'make it your own' quality about it. When setting out to design playground equipment I am inspired to balance these contrasting qualities – changeable yet stable, personal yet social. To reiterate, these qualities can, on the one hand, transform the user, and on the other, they can be transformed by the user. This encapsulates the balance that was sought in the design of the Galaxy series.

Furthermore, in any design it is important to incorporate two additional characteristics – what we call affordance and holding power. Affordance is the quality a product can have that makes it immediately draw the interest of children. Holding power is the quality that encourages the child to maintain interest after the initial novelty has dissipated. For example, the Galaxy's abstract, sculptural quality gives it a sense of wonder and sparks enquiry within the child. However, it takes more than an interesting visual appearance to maintain holding power. To invest the equipment with holding power, a number of different principles that cause the product to transform the user, and allow it to be transformed by the user, were considered.

The application of transformation

Three principles that were significant during the design of the Minkar were agility, flexibility and proprioception. These three are built into Minkar and take discreet effect, stimulating and supporting the child's natural urge towards self-development. It is important to note that the children are not consciously setting out to train their sense of agility, flexibility, or proprioception. Like the visitor to the labyrinth, they are simply transformed by the space within which they find themselves.

In this context, agility is the ability to recognize and respond to new and changing situations as they

Figure 2.8
Manoeuvring through Minkar helps to develop a child's sense of agility, flexibility and proprioception. (Photos: Kompan.)

arise. This quality is crucial and enables each adult to negotiate complex situations; it is a skill we depend on throughout our lives and an important aspect of our survival mechanism. From the beginning, we reach out, we crawl, we balance across objects in our environment, we walk, we run, and we cycle, learning to negotiate our way between obstacles. Playing is part of this training and prepares us for more complex physical and intellectual activities that come later in life, for example, activities such as navigating a highly trafficked road or moving through a busy airport. Such tasks require us to quickly analyse a situation, make a plan, and take action. If something interrupts us, we must re-plan and continue with an adjusted plan. Without these negotiating skills developed in childhood such tasks would be daunting and therefore it is crucial that we develop agility in our physical relationship to space, as well as in our intellectual endeavours and in our social relations.

For younger children, setting out to walk or crawl along a balance beam is a simple yet challenging task. Creating a challenge for the older age groups requires a more diverse landscape, one that is designed to include different shapes, sizes, and materials. One of the ideas behind Minkar was to provide a route for agility training, a path that transformed along its course. In order for the child to get from one side to the other, they would have to climb up, down and sideways.

Components were designed to wobble and rock, adding new and intriguing challenges. Because the many climbing ropes hang all the way down to the ground, children tend to be interrupted in their play strategies because other children can easily enter the climbing route at any point. This situation requires the children to adjust their plan, quickly making a new strategy.

This process is a form of mental flexibility, however physical flexibility is also important. In a digital age we observe that people (adults and children) spend more and more time in sedentary activities, and this makes maintaining physical flexibility all the more critical. Stimulating one's major joints, such as ankles, hips, shoulders, wrists and neck and generally stretching muscles, is important to maintain smooth bodily movement. The more flexible one is, the less likely it is that one will get hurt when being physically active during the day or when participating in the various leisure and sports activities, which add health and social value to our lives.

When children have to reach and stretch beyond their known capabilities, they develop and improve their skills. In the Minkar, various components are placed a good distance from one another, which challenges the children to go beyond their present skill level. The use of rope creates a situation where the child's arm and leg joints are constantly stimulated as they adjust to the natural movement in the rope. To move from one rope to the next

Figure 2.9
Up, down, over, under, in-between, upside down, and in the middle of it all. (Photo (a): Michael Laris; (b) and (c): Kompan.)

demands gripping power and upper body strength, additional important physical qualities to the basics of crawling, walking, running.

Proprioception is the knowledge and understanding of one's own body in space and this is something children learn through experience: How big am I? Can I fit under the bed? Can I reach something if I stretch? Older children have established their basic spatial understanding and therefore naturally seek out greater spatial complexity. They like to experience their bodies in all kinds of positions: up, down, over, under, in-between, and upside down. This over-under-between movement is especially apparent on the right-hand side of the Minkar, where three playshells are hung one above the other. Moving through this spatially complex arrangement of curving forms, enhances a child's perception of their own body and its relationship to the things around them. Spatial complexity is also present in the left-hand side, where children can climb over, under, or around each other — or just relax and watch the others at play.

These three *transforming* principles — agility, flexibility, and proprioception — can be built into any space for children so that development of these essential skills just happens as children naturally do what they do.

Designing the quality of *transformability* into playground equipment is perhaps more challenging. A café is a private sheltered environment. Tables and chairs can be moved around without causing safety hazards. There is no real threat of vandalism and the micro-climate can be controlled reasonably well. On a public playground these stable conditions do not apply. Yet, the ability of the children to transform their environment is crucial in maintaining the child's interest and making the product relevant for many uses over a long period of time.

Three of the principles that allow children to transform a play item to suit their needs are multi-functional activities, colour variation, and moving parts.

Multi-functional activities are those activities designed to provide a diverse range of play possibilities and thus they may be used in more than one way. A typical slide, for example, has one main function — for children to slide down. Children also climb up slides, but this is generally not intended; there are no added details to support this form of use safely. The Minkar includes a variety of materials and types of assembly. There are three large curving plastic playshells, there is a twisted steel ladder, there is a suspended climbing plate with rubber cleats, and there are ropes with disk-shaped objects attached in different sizes and colours, some that turn and some that do not. The largest disk is wide enough for children to sit on, and from it a child can rest or watch the others. These components provide for a more varied range of climbing experiences, as well as places to meet and hang out. What is important is that diversity of form, material, and spatial arrangement is provided and the use is not limited or proscribed. Children invent different ways in which the equipment is utilized as they transform it to meet their needs.

Colour variation is the intentional inclusion of different colours, which are placed deliberately around the product. One way in which colour variation was achieved in Minkar was by making the disks several different colours. The production department would have preferred all of them to be the same colour as this would be easier to manufacture. However, the added play value that colour variation provides made it worth doing. When different colours are carefully chosen and precisely placed in the design, many additional play opportunities become possible.

Children may choose their favourite disk, just as in a café, adults may repeatedly select their favourite table. A variety of colours clearly distinguishes one part from another and allows children to make up their own rules when engaged in play. It is common that groups of children will agree on a rule where a colour is a key factor, indeed a catalyst in their game. For example they will say, 'let's climb through the ropes, but this time, no touching the green ones'. The colour variation affects the pattern of use in a way that encourages decision and rule codification. The children also do this when playing chase and catch. They will commonly use a particular component distinguished by colour

Figure 2.10
Up or down the pole like a nut on a bolt.
(Photo (a): Kompan; Photo (b): Michael
Laris.)

to establish a 'free' or 'safe' zone. Colour variation is also used on the various climbing cleats so that children can design their own colour-coded route. This may seem relatively insignificant to adults, but it is an important level of detail, which increases play value tremendously. Colour variation instigates invention and promotes opportunities for imaginative play, and in my opinion rarely should the use of colour be based merely on aesthetics.

The concept of moving parts is central to making a product transformable because it enables children a degree of control. Here they can modify the equipment so that patterns of play can evolve over time; this supports the natural instincts of children and is therefore one of the best kinds of play. Minkar is limited when it comes to moving parts. Although the ropes, the playshells, and even the climbing plate can sway, which is a significant feature, I do not consider them to be true moving parts. However, another Galaxy product, the Propus, is equipped with authentic moving parts. A triangular pod is mounted on a stainless steel pole and can be twisted up or down like a nut on a bolt. Children use the pod to sit on, spin downwards on, or as footholds when climbing through the equipment. Because the pod can be moved, children have the opportunity to decide their own individual path or choose for themselves how high up they wish to sit. Another benefit of moving parts is the promotion of a sense of ownership. For example, a child might arrive at the playground to find the pods turned all the way to the ground and half covered by the sand or bark surfacing. Or the

pods might be twisted all the way up to the top, where they are hard to reach. In a situation like this the child recognizes that others have been there using the pods, and the child now has the choice to adapt them to his or her own needs, or leave them where they are. By altering the form of the play equipment the child takes ownership of the space, similar to what adults do in a café when they move chairs around to form an arrangement suitable to their group size. Play items that can move bring added value to the playground. Such products are usually difficult to develop and more expensive, however, the result is well worth it.

Product two – a short story

Having described the principles of agility, flexibility, and proprioception, and explained the importance of multi-functional activities, colour variation, and moving parts, I finally wish to illustrate one of the best pieces of play equipment with which I have been involved, the Supernova. Here, Claus Isaksen of the design team succeeded in integrating some of the functions of a traditional merry-go-round with the movement and excitement to be found in skateboarding. The result is a product with a unique function, which includes all six of these key principles.

The concept of Supernova is one big moving part. It is a 30 cm wide 'huggable' ring (2 cm in diameter) that spins around on a 10 degree tilt. It is multi-functional as it can be used in many ways by a

Figure 2.11
The Supernova is one big moving part. (Top left photo: Michael Laris; other photos: Kompan.)

single child or by a group of children. The younger children usually sit or lie on it and push each other in turns. I have also seen children using it in their games of chase where they keep their captives held in the centre of the ring. Older children use the Supernova for high-level competitive games, dancing back and forth, trying to force each other off, seeing who can stay on the longest. Because the Supernova is tilted, simply standing and balancing on the Supernova develops agility and stimulates flexibility. As children crawl under it, hop over it, and spring across it, they train their sense of proprioception.

There are seven coloured connection bands around the Supernova; one green rather than orange like the other six. There are several reasons for this. If all the bands were the same colour, it would be difficult to keep count of the number of rotations the Supernova makes. This numerical understanding is very important when competing with oneself or with others. The green band can also be used as a pointer. At times, children stand in

a ring around the Supernova and spin it to see to whom the green ring points, deciding whose turn it is next. All ages, including adults, use it as a moving bench on which to sit and socialize.

The Supernova transforms the children because it stimulates the development of agility, proprioception, and flexibility. It can also be transformed by the children, as they make choices as to how they will use it, what its function will be, and what the different colours will mean in the context of their game.

Conclusion

Throughout this chapter, I have focused on industrially manufactured play items because, in my view, such items can provide better play opportunities than natural elements, when used within controlled urban environments. These industrial products have the benefit of being designed and produced by a team of experts who ensure critical factors such as safety, accessibility, play value, and durability are optimized through good design. In addition, crucially important details can be designed into each product, details that support the growth of specific areas of children's development such as agility, proprioception, flexibility, ownership, imagination, invention, social awareness, and joy.

Yet despite all this, these products should be only one constituent part of the offer made to children within a well-designed play area. To be successful and fulfil the criteria that I consider important, the playground environment must be rich and diverse. A few other possible ingredients are: child-scaled features that replicate natural elements such as hills, valleys, and trees for climbing, complemented by natural additions such as grassed areas, cultivation zones, areas for sand and water play, and functional features such as sun shades. Most important is to create diverse landscapes for children that are made up of spaces designed in proportion to a child's own size and developmental stage, spaces that are safe and inviting, spaces where all children can take part, spaces that inspire invention and wonder.

Special thanks to KOMPAN A/S and the Galaxy Connect Design Team (John Frank and Philip Laris) and to Milo Myers and Daniel Lee.

Notes

1   *A Guide to the ADA Accessibility Guidelines for Play areas*, US Architectural and Transportation Barriers Compliance Board, May 2001.

2   The Galaxy series was first released in 1998 and won the Danish Industrial Design Prize and the Japanese Good Design Award in 1999, the US Industrial Excellence Award in 1999 and 2002 and the Independent Living Design Award – an English award presented to exceptional design solutions that create an environment of inclusion between handicapped and non-handicapped children – in 2001, and the GaLaBau Innovations Medal in 2002.

Michael Laris was born in California and studied architecture at the State University before designing a number of experimental architectural projects. He worked in England and Denmark as a residential architect, educator and researcher. Since 1997, he has worked as a designer with Kompan A/S, an international playground equipment manufacturer based in Denmark. During this time he has co-authored a design guide for the ADA Accessibility Guidelines for Play Areas and led the design team on the Kompan Galaxy play equipment range, which has won a number of awards including the US Industrial Excellence Award (1999 and 2002).

He is a keen amateur musician and is proud of his role as lead singer and rhythm guitarist with The Batos. He has two sons and lives in Denmark.

3

Place making and change in learning environments

Bruce A Jilk

Editor's introduction

Mass education originally mirrored society's view that its main role was to control and discipline children in order to create pliant citizens who would fit into the new industrialized world; in short, education was to create factory fodder for mass production. Arguably, the physical form of most school buildings has barely changed since mass education was first established in its basic form at the beginning of the twentieth century.

Here, the author posits a radical view on this antiquated system. In a post-industrial world, an educational straight-jacket is no longer an appropriate model, since by its very nature it tends to diminish the prevalent cultural tendency within society, that of individualism. The effects of this approach to education create disaffected students who are more chaotic and less disciplined, partly as a result of the educational conformity they are forced to endure.

Individualism can inevitably be read on two levels; firstly, a somewhat negative 'do whatever you like' attitude, which flies in the face of the obvious need for discipline and self-control within society as a whole. We all recognize that personal creativity can only develop within the disciplined learner. However, it is clear that for many students who are disciplined, the standard educational format within most state-sponsored education systems excludes the possibility for that individual to grow and develop in their own way. Everything is far too confined and limited. As a consequence, education becomes stultified and boring.

However, it is possible to design environments which expand the possibilities for learning, and the author develops his argument along these lines. He illustrates his polemic with a case study, which is conceived along radically inclusive lines. The Ingunnarskoli in Reykjavik adopts a 'bottom up' approach (as opposed to a top down approach) where the priorities are established by the community, rather than a pre-determined set of standardized educational guidelines such as the Area Guidelines for Schools.

Introduction

Imagine expanding the possibilities for learning. Having more places where learners are engaged, enthusiastic, and motivated. These characteristics are often found in kindergarten, yet they disappear in the later grades. Our current approach to learning compared to what learning is possible, parallels the relationship of the narrow band of visible light to the rest of the electromagnetic spectrum; the possibilities that we cannot see are immense.

There are numerous reasons why we do not expand the possibilities for learning. These include policy, traditions, and pre-determined standards or guidelines which supposedly answer all the questions, yet in reality allow little scope for creativity and innovation. The common thread to all of these reasons is resistance to change itself. The built infrastructure is often identified as being particularly difficult to change. However, when we accept that learning is not limited to a classroom, we realize we can also learn in a closet, a café, or a cathedral. We need to understand why we have put the current limits on our designs of the learning environments. Although learning environments have often been built with some physical flexibility, their basic design concepts are structured around a very narrow interpretation 'school'. It is possible, however, to design settings for education that do indeed expand the possibilities for learning.

The challenge

To do this we must abandon practically everything we know about today's school facilities. Twentieth-century school building design has been driven by two primary philosophies. First, the core-building block of the educationist's philosophy is reflected in the classroom: one teacher who has the knowledge ready to disseminate to a group of learners. This goes back to the Greek civilization when a teacher (who then was the primary source of knowledge) needed about thirty students to make a living. This core concept was further shaped by the Fordist mentality (industrial, assembly line efficiencies) predominant in the first half of the twentieth century, when mass education became a reality in the USA and other developed nations. Second, also from the first half of the twentieth century, is the philosophy of modernist architecture. Often described as 'Form Follows Function', the idea is to fit the shape and form of the building exactly to its educationist's efficiency needs. The reality is that a school's design is always shaped by additional, non-functional issues. These include the architect's

aesthetic, the community's image, and the client's politics.

This approach was further shaped by the military, particularly during World War II in the first half of the twentieth century. Military planners needed to use their resources very quickly and efficiently. Therefore, they developed the facility planning processes that are the basis of today's educational/architectural programming approach. Both the process and the content for school design were focused on functional efficiency. This ethos naturally led to greater specialization for nearly every classroom, laboratory and room in the building. Each had a dedicated function which left little scope for alternative uses. This positivistic approach continues to dominate the school agenda, where most other building types have become far less proscriptive.

As educators and architects designed schools that were highly demanding from a functional perspective, it became apparent that the buildings needed to allow for some activities that did not fit the primary function. This resulted in a number of 'flexibility' strategies. The more tightly the design fits the function, the more flexibility was called for. Attempts at maximizing flexibility often resulted in school designs that no longer provided the learner with a sense of place. As we enter into the twenty-first century the world of education is exploring an expanding variety of new learning strategies based on research on how we learn. The functionalist's approach is increasingly limiting and is being called into question. School facilities begin to be unsupportive of multiple effective learning strategies.

To provide environments that do support expanding the possibilities for learning a new approach is required. One concept is to frame the problem around the idea of contingency. The definition of contingency used here is 'that which is dependent on conditions or occurrences not yet established'. Actually integrating contingency concepts into the design of learning and learning environments is a necessity. To be sustainable we must simultaneously design for greater longevity and increased flexibility of use. Economics and public policy are pressuring educators toward changes in their approach to learning while communities expect a long-term return on their investment in schools. In order to make these investments, the facility, and learning itself, sustainable we must implement new design strategies. This will result in facilities that are not only durable but will also accommodate numerous use patterns (including non-educational use). Schools must not only be designed for their first life, but also for their second, third and even fourth life. I will now explore these new strategies as they apply to the classroom, the whole school, and the community.

The purpose

There are limited resources in society, so the objective of an efficient education (a quantity measure) is certainly valid. But that by itself falls short of the goal of a good education. This education also needs to be effective, which is a quality measure. Certainly the design of learning environments should be responsive to supporting effective education. Although most people would agree with this, in practice this has not been the case. The form may follow the function, but this by itself is also insufficient. Our efficiency- or 'outcome'-driven learning environments become barriers to expanding the possibilities for learning and the creativity of learning.

Creativity is used here in the broadest sense, an aspect of human behaviour that encompasses more than the creativity of an artist or a composer. To form a word as you speak, to imagine an image in your mind, or to recognize the smell of a flower takes a creative action in the mind. Even in sports, to hit a ball is acting creatively. In learning, one formulates thoughts in the mind that did not exist there before. Learning is a creative action.

In order to insure discipline and behaviour control, creativity is designed out of schools. The physical space is created on the principle of surveillance by those in control, the teachers. The environment becomes a barrier to those actions which are not predetermined. The users are told what to do to take noncreative action. This

is often done in the name of safety and security. These concerns are important, but it is possible to achieve this without resorting to a prison-like, barrier-impregnated atmosphere. The key to doing this is for the architect to share the 'authority' in the design with the learners and their teachers.

The purpose is to enable learner creativity. The learning setting needs to engage the learner. This is why the wilderness is such a powerful place. When you are in the wilderness, it is out of necessity that you think creatively in order to take action. Schools do the opposite. There are no decisions to be made. Everything is predetermined. The building sends the message 'Learner, do this but not that'. Schools are over-designed; they leave no active role for the learner. To design a place where learning is the goal, but in reality is one that obstructs learning, is a crime.

Flexibility, typically done as a reaction to the limits of efficiency, does offer some opportunity for engaging the users in taking some creative action. However, the experience has been that folding partitions, demountable walls or other major room configurations require efforts that overwhelm the users and therefore go unchanged. This is probably because the changes are insignificant. The alternative approach proposed here is to build all major spaces as permanent, but incomplete.

The concepts

Like the twentieth century, the twenty-first century school building design is also driven by two primary philosophies of education and architecture. However, these philosophies have changed from those of the last hundred years. These shifts in philosophies are appropriate because they reflect the new primary context of today's civilization, culture and ecology.

From the educationist's world, an approach to learning is indeed a hybrid stemming from two learning theories, one focused on culture and the other on ecology. This hybrid has recently been articulated as 'Critical Pedagogy of Place'. As such, it is the synthesis of 'critical pedagogy' and 'place-based education'. Both are concerned about the space or geography of learning.

Critical pedagogy speaks to learners taking action based on their situation. Pre-requisite to this is reading the context they find themselves in. This requires learners to understand the social, political, and economic forces surrounding them. It is the cultural dimension. This includes recognizing and dislodging dominant ideas, which is called 'decolonization'. It is a process of reading the world through taking it apart.

Place-based education, as the name suggests, is focused on the place where the learners find themselves. The idea is that citizens need to understand the complexities about the places they inhabit in order to have some direct bearing on their well-being. This is the ecological aspect. This learning to live well where you find yourself, most often in a place that has been previously exploited, is called 'reinhabitation'. It is a process of understanding and taking action through putting things together.

A 'Critical Pedagogy of Place' suggests a learner who is creative.

To complete this new, twenty-first century formula for creating new learning environments is an architectural philosophy that addresses not spaces so much as their relationships. This approach is in alignment with the learning theory of 'Critical Pedagogy of Place'. The learning concept of taking it apart and putting it together becomes a metaphor for design. The key to understanding this shift in approach revolves around the concept of authority in architecture. In schools designed in the Modernist era, the author of the designed environment is solely the architect (as an agent of the client). The user has no role other than being passive within the environment. However, in moving from considering learners as passive recipients to active players in their learning experience, the objective becomes one of engaging them in their situation (which includes the environment). To do this they must also become authors of their environment. Authority becomes shared between the producer (architect) and the consumer (learner).

This is consistent with the purpose of developing creative learners. Rather than an environment where all actions are predetermined, the goal is a setting that engages the learner by a design that requires them to participate in that environment. These places are incomplete without the user's involvement. These building are not experienced all at once, but rather piece by piece, in moments separated by gaps in space, time, and climate. It is these gaps or relationships that become the focus of the design.

This strategy of designing relationships, such that it requires the creative engagement of the user to complete the setting, has recently been identified as the 'Montage of Gaps'. A montage is a composite of juxtaposed elements. In this design approach these elements are the gaps of space, time, and climate. This theory also builds on some other late twentieth-century architectural theories including the idea of uselessness and the architecture of disjunction.

The concept of uselessness in architecture is the idea of rejecting determinism about the future use of space. Uselessness in space suggests users who display mental, bodily, and physical creativity. This also connects directly to the concept of contingency because the space use is not yet established. Together these concepts have significant implications for programming. The functional designs of last century's schools were driven by intense investigations to determine what functions to design to. This led to extensive programming tasks which helped to determine the educational curriculum. Today this can be seen as a futile exercise (as currently practiced). The programme or use is established, not through numerous meetings prior to design, but rather by the user, as appropriate in an interactive place after construction.

An architecture of disjunction concerns spaces, events, and movements and their separation. As a user experiences such fragmented situations, it is the nature of the mind to put things together. Therefore, disjunction suggests a user who displays constructional and conceptual creativity consistent with our purpose. This also negates the common architectural concept of designing a

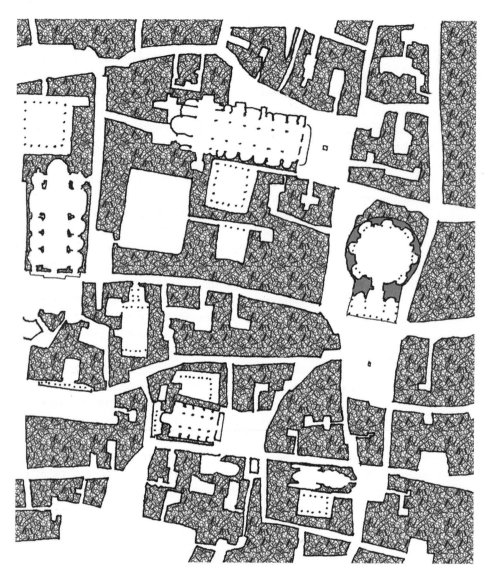

Figure 3.1
ROME 1748, taken from
the Nolli Plan, conceptual
organization.

school as an object in space. The effort (in the latter years of the last century) to raise the meaningfulness of schools through better looking buildings has not only been a futile exercise, it has been counterproductive. The shift is from objects in space to place making space.

The example

The thrust of school design in the recent decades has been the maximization of the archaic educational philosophy of 'Sage on the Stage' and the exclusive use of the architectural mentality that 'Form follows Function'. This thrust is well intended, and these ideas worked in the past.

However, the relevance of education has shifted and therefore so should the design of learning environments.

Rather than doing more of the same, this example exhibits how we might expand the possibilities of learning and learning environments. The example stems from a collaboration in Scotland to redefine learning environments for secondary school students. The groundwork came out of a Design Down workshop in Edinburgh in May 2003. The objective was to define an exemplary learning environment in order to inform other projects.

Because this design was not site specific, only a site strategy was applied. Consistent with the

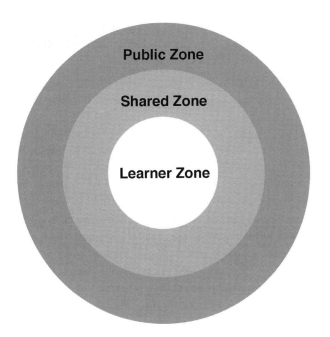

Figure 3.2
Public (community) and private (student) zones.

Design Down directions, the siting approach considered the school as public space. This is similar to the way churches were perceived in Rome around the eighteenth century. Public space included streets, parks, plazas, courtyards, and churches, as depicted in Figure 3.1. This is a portion of a 1748 map of Rome by Gianbattista Nolli. The shaded area shows all private buildings and the white space is the public space including the inside of churches. This is an exemplary case of place making. The round building to the right is the Pantheon, built nearly 2000 years ago. It has had several functions and still serves the community well as public space. We should be able to say the same thing about the schools we build.

The objective therefore is to make major portions of the school accessible to the public. This is consistent with today's desire for the school to be the centre of community. Other portions of the building would be the exclusive realms of the learners. Because both students and public share the use of some places, a third, shared zone in between the other two is envisioned. This is shown in Figure 3.2. The diagram is circular to depict the possibility of multiple entrances from various directions.

The programme is straightforward. Fifty per cent of the space is to be 'useful space' and the other fifty per cent is to be 'useless space'. With the exception of a lecture room and a theatre, each with sloped floors, all other occupied spaces are functionally undefined. See Figure 3.3.

The white boxes represent learning labs (useful space). They are accessible by the public, the students, or by both, depending on their location. The other white space is support space. The light shaded area is useless public space and the dark shaded area is useless learner space. The textured space represents courtyards.

The useful spaces are supported with an intense infrastructure underneath (hot and cold water, waste systems, compressed air, exhaust, gas, multiple power levels, hardwire and wireless networking, etc.). Furnishings are movable and designed for interactive use. This allows the particular use of the space to be established by the users and the equipment they bring to the box. The possibilities include small or large group discussions, various forms of research, multiple means of production, experimentation, performance, indoor sports, etc.

The useless spaces have only minimal support infrastructure (power and networking). Furnishings are available for various forms of social interaction. This allows for the natural formation of communities of practice.

The useful spaces gain meaning through the establishment of activities developed in collaboration with the learning programmes. The useless spaces gain meaning through the creative interactions of the learners and the environment.

Figure 3.4 begins to suggest the architectural character of the design. The experience of inhabiting this space is to experience a montage of gaps. It is an experience that demands the creative participation of the learner. The environment is incomplete without the learner's involvement. The architect and the learner share authorship for creating the situation. The architect primarily takes the setting apart and the learner puts the setting back together. Flexibility is meaningless because functionality is not fixed; therefore there is no need

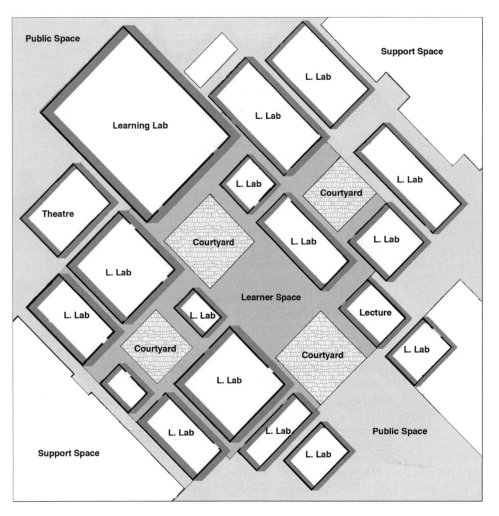

Figure 3.3
Plan – conceptual layout for a new model school.

Within the plan (Figure 3.3): Public Space, Support Space, L. Lab, Learning Lab, Theatre, Courtyard, Learner Space, Lecture, L. Lab, Public Space, Support Space.

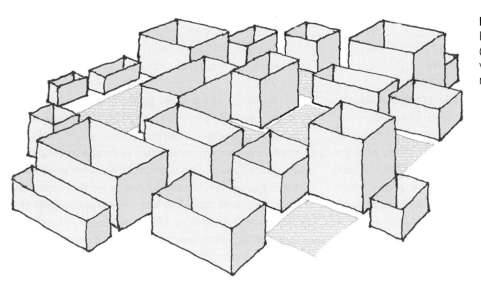

Figure 3.4
Image of learning labs (exterior walls, roof, windows and doors are not shown).

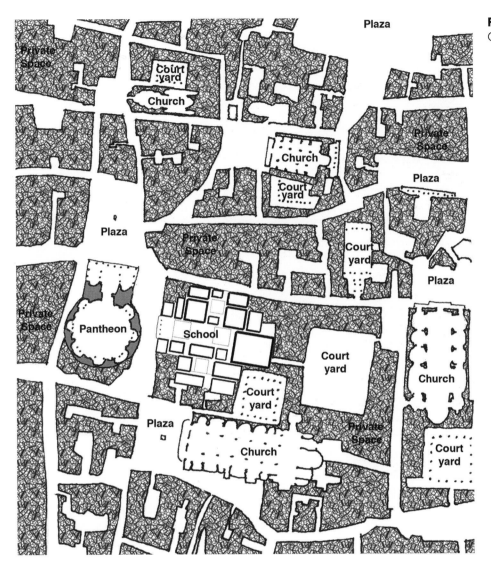

Figure 3.5
Conjectural siting, Rome.

for movable walls. An environment for 'Critical Pedagogy of Place' is an environment where standardized 'placeless' curriculum cannot survive.

This concept would fit into an urban setting (in this case historic Rome). The exterior enclosure would take on an appearance in keeping with its surrounding historical context. Daylight would come through a glass roof vaulting over the complex. Like the Pantheon and other churches, the school becomes public space.

However, the design is also adaptable to suburban or rural locations. In a rural setting the enclosure could be a geodesic dome and thereby enhance the place-based pedagogy and become its own ecological system. In a suburban location the enclosure would become a closer articulation of the plan's masses and voids, with materials, colours, textures, and a scale consistent with the existing context. The objective of the design is to support creative pedagogy and powerful place making. The exterior enclosure can be anything. It should reflect the context of the site and not be an end in itself (designed as an object in space). This adaptability illustrates another dimension on how the design fits the concept of contingency. Its location is indeterminate.

Figure 3.6
South view of scale model.

Evolution of a design for change: a case study

Ingunnarskoli in Reykjavik is a new school design model for Iceland. This learning environment design integrates educational planning, programming and design during the decision making. The school is a new basic school at Grafarholti, a new neighbourhood on the edge of the capital. It is designed for 400 students in grades one to ten, the standard basic school configuration in Iceland. The school aspires to be a place for learning that is based on the needs of children, their families and their communities. The project is under construction.

The process for making decisions about this new school is called 'Design Down'. It starts with the biggest issues, such as the overall context, and moves toward more detailed aspects. Its goal is to make all the parts (expectations, process, partnerships, technology, etc.) complement each other. Through this process, the physical space will support all elements of how the school is organized (students, time, curriculum, staff, etc.) and thus fit with the learning process. The Design Down

Committee, a multi-stakeholder group of parents, teachers, administrators, students, employers, neighbours and other concerned citizens, makes the decisions.

Signature

Early in the design process the learning signature is developed. The learning signature focuses on what is special and unique; it becomes the identity of the school. While most school-planning processes include consideration of mission, vision, values and logo, these components are rarely linked together in a compelling and highly meaningful concept for the school. Giving a school a special focus provides coherence, consistency and spirit to the school and thereby adds to the quality of the learning experience and accomplishments. At Grafarholti, the Design Down Committee defined four themes as their highest priorities: community, nature, spirit and flow.

The signature for Ingunnarskoli integrates these themes into a graph image (see Figure 3.7). A circle represents community, nature is indicated by a green colour, a wave symbol is incorporated which is symbolic of flow, and the image of a child

Figure 3.7

imbedded in the graphic implies the spirit. The signature becomes a major driver of the physical design itself.

Learning process

The learning process consists of the design for curriculum, instruction and assessment. As learning is viewed as a continuous process, learning inside the school and in the community are valued and closely coordinated. The learning process for the school at Grafarholti includes the following:

- Integrate the subjects.
- Use individual, small group and large group learning.
- Include learning in multiple settings: outdoors, elderly care centre, homes and Internet.
- Integrate learners of different ages.
- Involve students in managing their learning, teaching them to take responsibility to plan, organize and maintain their environment.
- Involve teachers working together and being trained in new teaching methods.
- Address the real needs of the community, producing useful products and services.

The signature and the learning process set the spatial concept: light as the spiritual essence of the design; the forum as the major organizing space; the interior being visually connected to the exterior; vertical level changes being limited to 'split levels'; and the roofing includes grass.

Design concept

The design concept is a synthesis of the Design Down parameters, the site, the landscape and the historic precedents. Three 'use variations' are embraced by the design concept in order for the school to start with what its users are familiar with and then 'grow' into the more innovative learning systems. The three variations are on a continuum from the 'traditional classroom' to the more personalized 'students at their own workstations in small groups' to a future-focused 'learner- and teacher-determined' environment. Corresponding space-defining elements include non-permanent walls (traditional variation), landscaped partitions (team-based variation) or what the learners develop (learner-determined variation).

To accommodate these variations only an armature for learning is built. This is organized into two components: the fixed, service zones (shaded in Figure 3.8) and the flexible, served space.

- The service zones include all the structure, pipes, ducts, and conduit. The zone's space supports utilitarian needs.
- The served space is flexible for numerous use configurations. Flexible walls can be placed as desired.

The service space elements are located in defined zones that are mostly enclosed. All serviced spaces have ready access to all utilities. How the space is used is up to the users (Figure 3.9).

Variation one

A traditional classroom layout can be achieved by filling in the wall zones. In our arrangement, four classroom areas for 20 students each can be readily

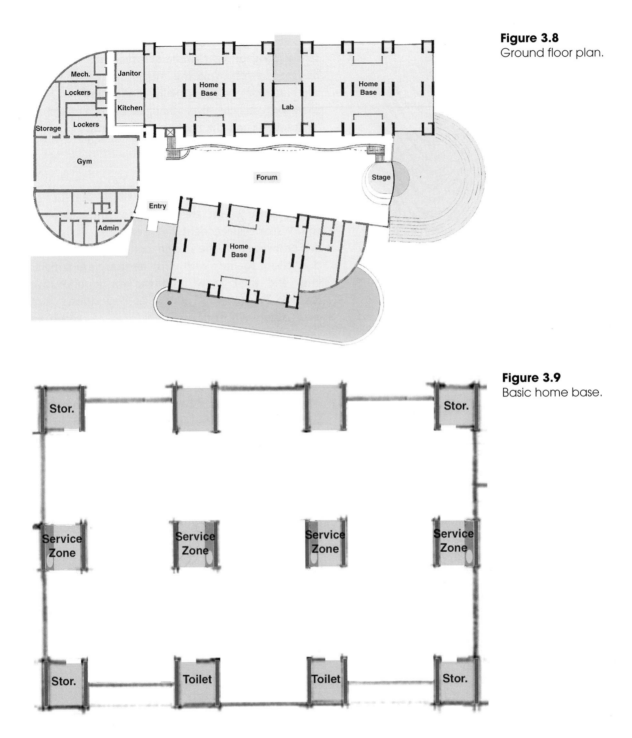

Figure 3.8
Ground floor plan.

Figure 3.9
Basic home base.

provided. There is also a common activity space, a small group room, and a teachers' planning room. Although partitions between the classrooms and the activity centre are not shown (owner's choice), they can be added to the base plan illustrated (Figure 3.10).

Variation two

A cooperative, individual workstation layout. In Figure 3.11, four team areas for 20 students each are shown. Each student has their own workstation. The common space functions for large group instruction. The work zone is for

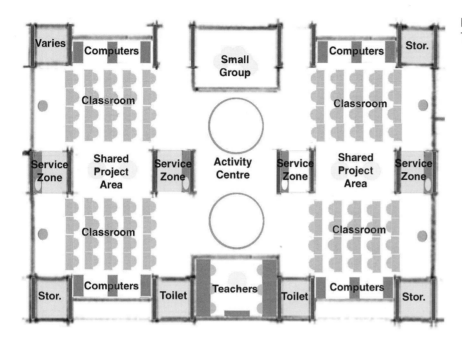

Figure 3.10
Traditional layout.

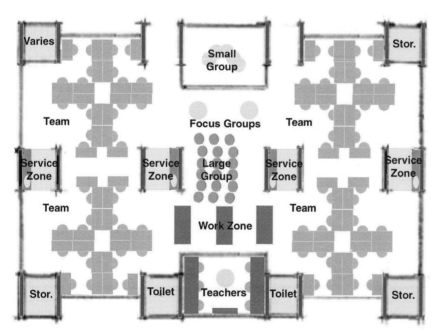

Figure 3.11
Cooperative layout.

project work. As in the traditional layout there is a small group room and a teachers' planning room. Although partitions between the team areas and the activity centre are not shown (owner's choice), they can be added (Figure 3.11).

Variation three

A creative, user-determined layout. This is based on the belief that what is best for the learner is best determined by the students and their teachers. This layout emphasizes that the freedom and

41

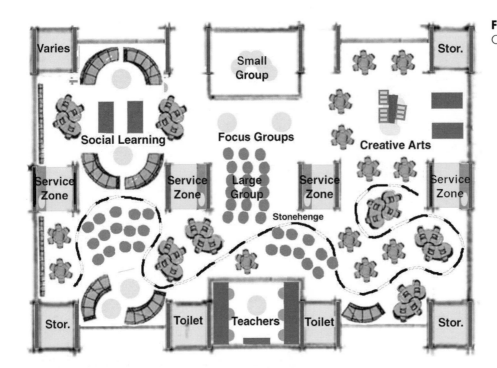

Figure 3.12
Creative layout.

Figure 3.13
Roof view showing the 'forum' at the heart of the plan.

creativity of the users is enhanced (not restricted) by the built environment. Multiple student groups around multiple learning tasks are possible at a moment's notice. Although partitions between areas are not shown (owner's choice), they can be added. The curved, broken black line indicates a flexible, movable space divider as an option to fixed partitions (Figure 3.12).

Freedom and creativity

The key element in this physical environment design is the ability of the children and teachers to create their own learning environments rather than having everything predetermined for them, as is the case when schools are over-designed. Predetermining nearly every aspect of children's interaction with their environment limits the range of possible learning experiences, minimizing the development of creativity. The approach to the design of Ingunnarskoli has intentional ambiguities to provide a space that enriches creativity by allowing children the freedom to create their own environments.

Summary

For education to be meaningful it needs to be relevant. The primary issues today revolve around cultures and ecologies. Approaches to learning, like a 'Critical Pedagogy of Place', draw upon components such as politics, society, environment, economy, etc. These disciplines and their relationships are analysed and then synthesized. It is a process of taking apart and putting back together. This requires creativity. Learning itself is not a passive mode of behaviour; rather it is an active, creative action.

Learning environments should mirror the learning they are to support. The dominant approach to twentieth-century learning followed the era's focus on mass production; school facilities were even called the 'school plant'. Today's issues require creative engagement. This can be reflected in building learning environments that invite learner participation and belong to the community. This happens when the environment is not a 'solution', but a setting that needs the learner to establish the full situation.

The ideas presented here are not intended to totally replace the existing system. Rather, like the electromagnetic spectrum, the idea is to reach out into those realms that have not been visible. Based on today's knowledge about learning, the intent is to expand the possibilities.

Notes

This chapter is an assimilation of numerous books, articles, and works of others. The following are the key references that include additional references to be pursued.

Gruenewald, D. A., The Best of Both Worlds: A Critical Pedagogy of Place. *Educational Researcher*, Volume 32, Number 4, May 2003.
Further references: Bowers, Freire, Orr and Soja.
Hill, J. (2003). *Actions of Architecture*. Routledge: London.
Further references: Barthes, Benjamin, Forty, Foucault, Tschumi.
Jilk, B. and Copa, G. (1997). The Design Down Process. Council of Educational Facility Planners International Issue, Trak Number Six: Phoenix.
Sarkis, H. (2001). *Le Corbusier's Venice Hospital*. Harvard Design School/Prestel: Munich, London, New York.
Further references: Hughes, Sennett, Smithson, van Eyck.

Bruce Jilk has been working on the design of learning environments since his first school project in 1961. Currently, he consults internationally on the design of learning settings for all ages. In the last decade he participated in three US Department of Education funded research projects centred on secondary and tertiary learners. This research has been implemented through projects in over thirty countries. In 2002 Bruce chaired the American Institute of Architects' Committee on Architecture for Education. He is currently the US delegate to the Union of International Architects. He has written for numerous publications and has made hundreds of presentations focused on innovation in learning environments.

4

The school building as third teacher

Eleanor Nicholson

Editor's introduction

'Wouldn't it give us pleasure to see a string of meaningful details in a children's world? Things that admittedly serve trivial purposes, that stand for themselves and their function and, besides, come together in the realm of fantasy, of poetry. They could be minor details: a star of light, patterns in a wall.... Little things, showing that we have made an effort to understand the world of children; that we have overcome what stands between us – age, drawing board, cost calculations ... ambition, architecture.'[1]

Since the late nineteenth century, children have gone to school. They have gone to all kinds of schools; small schools, big schools, friendly schools and forbidding schools. In the early stages of mass education school buildings were often little more than rudimentary conversions of former church or even industrial premises. During the twentieth century, throughout Europe and the USA, new purpose-built structures appeared, designed by architects with the needs of education and teachers in mind. Many of these structures are now coming to the end of their useful life and are being replaced. For example, in the City of Exeter, SW England, all five of its high schools are being rebuilt. The chronic underperformance of Exeter's state schools is the main reason for this (along with the evident need for radical solutions to old, badly maintained buildings). One local

headteacher stated that the city suffered from an anti-education culture, a commonly perceived view that would resonate around the state sector both in the UK and USA. This is due in no small part to the alienation children feel attending poorly maintained, outdated educational facilities. The message they send is one of failure and lack of respect for education and those intended to benefit from it.[2]

So, how should the new generation of schools be designed? Often the primary concern of school developers and the governments who allocate public finance is cost, which is determined by the use of time and the allocation of space. Consequently, pragmatic guidelines and standard schedules of accommodation tend to dominate the procurement agenda. With the recognition that schooling has a pivotal role to play in the general well-being of society, the importance of the place in which education takes place is now frequently discussed and debated. We are open to new ways of doing things, yet the reality of building seems to be that we are confined within systems which have been in place for decades, unchecked and unquestioned by school developers.

Eleanor Nicholson presents evidence that children and young people are extremely aware of the symbolic messages which these buildings transmit. The issue therefore is not simply one of educational outcomes, to use the current jargon; of equal importance is making schools attractive for the future generations of young people who will use them. Issues which are often deemed to be of secondary importance, such as the design of children's toilets, the quality of social and waiting spaces outside the classrooms, locker areas and the meaning or the ways in which architecture is represented, are often overlooked.

Nicholson presents a historical perspective, quoting the key educational visionaries such as Piaget, Montessori and Dewey, and illustrates a number of contemporary examples where good school design and enlightened educational strategies go hand in hand to create a humane learning system appropriate for the twenty-first century. She makes a plea that all of those within a community should have a stake in the design of the new school buildings and the form that the education should take. She sees the building as 'the third teacher' a tripartite alliance between teachers, parents and the environment within which it takes place. Perhaps there is an even more profound message here – the very fabric of the school building can teach children about many things which will be important ideals which they can grasp and hold onto throughout their lives. This is a plea for a better understanding of place, to enhance environmental literacy as part of the evolution of education towards a more humane individual framework which reflects the profound social changes which have taken place over the past 25 years.

Introduction

In an ideal world, there are supportive, experienced teachers; there is an engaging and experiential curriculum; and there is a school climate that supports a sense of mutual respect, warmth, fairness, aesthetic pleasure and the US traditions of democracy and opportunity for all. Do we need especially designed buildings to promote these values? Not necessarily. Fine child-centred programmes can exist in less than wonderful buildings. Conversely, rigid, unjust, cold and insensitive programmes can take place in state-of-the art buildings.

However, after a lifetime spent inspecting and supporting school communities in California, there

is no doubt in my mind that the school building is, and should be a player. A building can reflect and perpetuate ideas about how children learn, what they learn, how they are taught, and to what end they are taught. Beyond purely educational objectives, a building can also communicate to children a great many subtle messages about what is important and what is deserving of respect. This is crucial in an age where education is viewed with a certain degree of contempt by many young people in society, whilst paradoxically, education is conceived by those who govern us as a crucial component in making a fairer, more civilized society, now and in the future.

It is my view that school buildings really make a difference, not just in the education, but also in life experiences of the children who use them. In this chapter I intend to make a direct connection between children's learning and the buildings they inhabit, by way of a number of built examples. But what kind of learning do I mean here?

In 1990 James H. Banning addressed a gathering of architects and school people at a conference in Winnetka, Illinois, the proceedings of which are printed in a small booklet entitled *Children, Learning and School Design*. Rejecting a causal link between the built environment and student behaviour and student learning, Banning posits a possible or probable link. This, he says, '*not only appears more realistic; it also captures our intuitive notion that school buildings can make a difference in the lives of children.*'[3]

Every aspect of an educational environment represents a choice about what is to be provided and what is not to be provided. Implicit in those choices is someone's judgement about what's important for children. However, most of the battles on school turf are about three things – use of time, use of space, and use of money. There are but so many hours in the school day and the school week and the school year; there are only so many square – or even cubic – feet permitted in the school building. There is only so much money available from the Board, or in the case of private schools, from the Archdiocese or the Board of Trustees or the parents. For every choice made during the development of any school design, something is put into the school and something is left out. Those choices reflect priorities, which in turn manifest basic values. As such, even the most trivial as well as the most fundamental decisions about school design carry symbolic messages.

There is, for example, a difference between an assembly room designed to host the entire school for regular community gatherings and a hall that is designed primarily for sport. These two spaces are furnished differently, used differently, and viewed differently by the students and teachers. As such they represent different priorities. The message of the first is that building a sense of community has top priority; the message of the second is that the value of community is equal or secondary to physical education. It is a subtle but important distinction. Children read meanings about themselves and the wider world into the environment of their school. It is so important because it is designed specifically for them.

In his contribution to the 1970 Yearbook of the National Society for the Study of Education, Robert H. Anderson wrote:

> ... *Historically, the school building has influenced not only what might be learned but also what might not be learned. The primitive resources and limited size of schoolhouses placed definite restrictions on other than sedentary activities, and hampered the development of curriculum offerings in the creative and expressive arts, in physical education, in vocation education, and in other areas having specialized space needs. In recent times, despite a growing clamor for kindergarten and other preprimary services, many states have moved slowly in providing such services because of the high cost of providing the space such programs require. Thus both quantitatively and qualitatively, the physical environment has over time exercised a peculiar power, often repressive, in the educator's world.*[4]

The phrase 'the high cost of providing the space such programs require', demonstrates the priorities at work here. This statement not only implies an economic decision but one which, as Banning points out, promotes certain symbolic meanings,

advocating the primacy of financial decisions over and above the child centred agenda. It is the intent of this chapter to explore those symbolic meanings both in terms of architecture and of iconographic interpretations, and posit an alternative more inclusive approach to designing the next generation of school buildings. I would ask those who are reading this from the perspective of a professional training in architecture and space planning to bear with me and excuse some of the architectural references I make, which I appreciate may at times appear a little naïve and sentimental. As an educationalist rather than a building professional, I am aware that I am writing about the architectural side of this from the perspective of an informed amateur.

Messages of a good society

In his book, *The School and Society*, John Dewey, one of the key educational pioneers of education during the twentieth century, states:

> *What the best and wisest parent wants for his own child, that must the community want for all its children. Any other ideal for our schools is narrow and unlovely; acted upon, it destroys our democracy.*[5]

What values from our homes, our communities, and our democracy do we wish to communicate to children through architecture, both overtly and symbolically? What is the reality of the child's experience?

We are all familiar with the traditional public school where, in the words of Robert Sommer:

> '*Movement in and out of the classrooms and the school building is rigidly controlled. Everywhere one looks there are "lines" – generally straight lines that bend around corners before entering the auditorium, the cafeteria, or the workshop (or, I might add, the bathroom). The straight rows (of the classroom) tell the student to look ahead and ignore everything except the teacher; the students are so tightly jammed together that psychological escape, much less physical separation, is impossible. The teacher has 50 times more free*

space than do the students with the mobility to move around...teacher and children may share the same classroom but they see it differently.

From a student's eye level, the world is cluttered, disorganized, full of people's shoulders, heads and body movements. His world at ground level is colder than the teacher's world.[6]

This cannot be what the wisest and best parents want for their children or what the democratic society wants for its children. By comparison the model home is warm, loving, and beautiful; the complete community is fair, cooperative, collaborative, and respectful; democracy requires inclusion, commitment, and justice.

Figure 4.1
Elm Street School, Camden, Maine, 1869. (Photo: Eleanor Nicholson.)

Figure 4.2
Racht School, Harbert, Michigan, 1928. The two images on this page illustrate the intermediate development of the American school from the earliest nineteenth century school houses (see Plate 4) to the large-scale developments from the 1940s onwards. Note the iconographic architectural references to the home and the church seen here in these two examples (Photo: Eleanor Nicholson.)

Figure 4.3
Frederick John School, Chicago, IL, Arch. Dwight Perkins. The evolution of the American school from the small-scale school-houses of the late nineteenth century to the 'egg crate' blocks of the 1940s. (Photo: Eleanor Nicholson.)

There have always been schools that abide by these values. Even in fifteenth-century Mantua, Vittorino da Feltre, at the behest of the Gonzaga family, created a school that represented the best in humanist thinking and could take its place today as a humane yet challenging school environment for children. When the Gonzagas asked Vittorino, one of the foremost scholars in Italy, to establish a school for their children and the children of other prestigious Mantua families, it was a little like asking one of the Nobel laureates from the University of Chicago to go over and teach in a Laboratory School. The Gonzagas offered Vittorino a beautiful palazzo for his school, La Joiosa, or what might be translated as 'the Pleasure House'. Vittorino changed the name to La Giocosa, stripped the place of its opulent furnishings, decorated the walls with frescoes of children at play, and let the light and air in through the tall windows and spacious halls. It was open to all children, not just the aristocratic friends of the Gonzagas, but children of scholars and of the poor, whose tuition was paid for by Vittorino. They all wore the same simple clothing, regardless of rank. The children played in the meadows in front of the palazzo. Vittorino took them on field trips, tutored them individually as well as collectively, and watched over their health like a protective parent.

Vittorino's model, alas, saw little replication in the centuries that followed. To pick up the threads of this humanistic approach we can turn to some exemplary early nineteenth-century thinking. Horace Mann, father of the Common School in the United States, was outspoken in his feelings about the school architecture of the time. In 1840 he wrote the following:

The voice of Nature, therefore, forbids the infliction of annoyance, discomfort, pain, upon a child, while engaged in study. If he actually suffers from position, or heat, or cold, or fear, not only is a portion of the energy of his mind withdrawn from his lesson, – all of which should be concentrated upon it; – but, at that indiscriminating age, the pain blends itself with the study, makes part of the remembrance of it; and thus curiosity and the love of learning are deadened, or turned away towards vicious objects.[7]

The essay continued:

The first practical application of these truths, in relation to our Common Schools, is to schoolhouse architecture, – a subject so little regarded, yet so vitally important. The construction of schoolhouses involves, not the love of study and proficiency only, but health and length of life ... It is an indisputable fact that, for years past, far more attention has been paid, in this respect, to the construction of jails and prisons, than to that of schoolhouses. Yet, why should we treat our felons better than our children?[7]

Deeply concerned about poor ventilation in the schools of the day and dripping with irony, Mann continued his essay:

I have observed in all our cities and populous towns, that, wherever stables have been recently built, provision has been made for their ventilation. This is encouraging, for I hope the children's turn will come, when gentlemen shall have taken care of their horses.[7]

And finally,

I cannot here stop to give even an index of the advantages of an agreeable site for a schoolhouse: of attractive, external appearance; of internal finish, neatness, and adaptation.[7]

This particular lecture by Horace Mann covers a great many other topics in addition to school architecture, among them the multiplicity of school books, which he ascribes in part to the profits book companies wished to make out of the constant replacement of old, nevertheless usable books with new ones. He called for 'apparatus' which would 'employ the eye, more than the ear, in the acquisition of knowledge'. Such manipulatives, as he would call them, would include a globe, a planetarium, microscopes, telescopes, and prisms. Clearly he wished children to experience much more practical instruction over and above the purely academic lessons with children sitting passively, hearing and listening.

He discussed libraries, curriculum reform, corporal punishment, and teacher training. Throughout the lecture there emerges a passionate interest in the needs of children, how they should learn, and how they should be taught. Unlike the

stern Puritans who came before him and like the child-centred educators who came after him, Mann believed that the child was innately curious, eager to learn and capable of assuming responsibility for things of beauty and value. 'Nature has implanted a feeling of curiosity in the breast of every child, as if to make herself certain of his activity and progress'. He believed that children enjoyed finding things out in their own way and in their own time. Before the argument is raised, 'that mischievous children will destroy or mutilate whatever is obtained for this purpose [apparatus]', he countered,

But children will not destroy or injure what gives them pleasure. Indeed, the love of malicious mischief, the proneness to deface whatever is beautiful, – this vile ingredient in the old Saxon blood, wherever it flows, originated and it is aggravated, by the almost total want, amongst us, of objects of beauty, taste, and elegance, for our children to grow up with, to admire, and to protect.[8]

Mann would surely have hoped that the messages of the school building itself, as well as what is inside it, would proclaim to children the importance of beauty, taste and elegance.

With the diffusion of the various forms of childcentred active education into the mix, new ideas of beauty, respect for the child and attention to his or her developmental needs – emotional, physical as well as intellectual – entered the architectural consciousness during the second half of the twentieth century. Building on Froebel's Kindergarten ideals, succeeding waves of schools – progressive schools, Montessori and Waldorf schools – have all reflected and shaped new ideas about education. Almost unique in the present educational climate are the pre-schools in Emilia Romagna, Italy. There, an early years system has evolved which illustrates a clear philosophical commitment to architecture and its role in learning – the so called 'third teacher'. The words of Lella Gandini demonstrate explicitly that schools have messages:

The visitor to any institution for young children tends to size up the messages that the space

Lea Cromwell

gives *about the quality and care and about educational choices that form the basis of the program. We all tend to notice the environment and 'read' its messages or meanings on the basis of our own ideas. We can, though, improve our ability to analyze deeper layers of meaning if we observe the extent to which everyone involved is at ease and how everyone uses the space itself. We then can learn more about the relationships among children and adults who spend time there.*[9]

The underlying assumption of the Reggio approach is that space matters enormously. It reflects the vision of those who inhabit it and it shapes those visions. The system recognizes that children are born with a natural sense of exploration and that they interpret the realities of the world through their senses of touch, sight, smell and hearing. Neurobiological research has demonstrated how important this dimension is to children in their development of knowledge and the important social concept of a group memory. It follows that unstimulating environments tend to dull or deafen the child's perceptions. Schools must be capable of supporting and stimulating sensory perceptions in order to develop and refine them. This is an essential aspect of education, part of the hidden curriculum if you like.

The messages of the Reggio approach are transparent and powerful, both spatially and philosophically. Communication is the core of their research-orientated approach to pedagogy. Encouraging communication between three subjects – children, teachers and parents, makes these 'community-orientated' projects in a real sense. Whereas many childcare centres and most schools exclude parents 'at the front door', at Reggio childcare centres, there is always a large community space at or around the entrance where parents can linger and even participate in some of their child's activities. However, the listening or so-called 'pedagogy of relations' does not stop at the doors of the childcare building. Rather, the listening and collaboration take place on a city-wide basis and even spread to other cities and cultures. Given that fundamental premise of communication by the building, it might be explained as a second skin that covers the school, a sort of child-orientated architecture overlying the basic architecture. Therefore, a number of spatial characteristics follow, such as walls where displays of all kinds are presented in a coherent and aesthetically pleasing way, and different and varying levels of transparency between spaces inside (windows between different functional spaces which permit views which may be altered

Figure 4.4
Scuola del' Infanzia, Diane, Reggio Emilia, an image of an integrated approach to architecture and education. The courtyard just within the entrance, a communal area full of light and activity. (Photo by permission of Diana Municipal Preschool Reggio Emilia.)

with curtains or blinds, for example). This ensures that the environment reflects and communicates the life of the school and the activities carried out with and by the children. What Reggio describe as filter zones are also needed, situated outside but close to the classrooms. This enables an easy and unhurried exchange of information in the daily communication with the families and the children. It is also important that each space within the childcare centre is organized efficiently so that the work and projects carried out with the children can be documented. Each child (with its parents) develops a scrapbook to maintain a ready record of his or her progress. This then forms part of a growing archive to aid knowledge and understanding for future generations.

Philosophy, programme and architecture go hand in hand in the Reggio approach, thanks to a combination of superb care and education which is matched by excellent local state funding. At Reggio, you cannot talk about the architecture without understanding the education or pedagogy. They are mutually dependent.

In spite of the possibilities that exist for the development of schools that respect and facilitate the holistic development of the child, generally we are stuck with the facilities of yesteryear. Many of

the public schools in the great urban centres of the United States were built in the very latter years of the nineteenth century and the first two or three decades of the twentieth century. At that time, immigrants from central Europe and from the American South were coming to the USA on a daily basis and in their thousands. The Northern cities required new schools and they were needed in a hurry. Furthermore, the kind of research that has been done in recent decades into issues of child development, meaningful curriculum, and optimum teacher education was not available at that time.

Then, children were expected to be docile, obedient, and industrious; they were likely to be punished physically if they were not. The thought that children might enjoy school and actually might want to learn seemed to be an alien concept. For teachers, often young and with little training themselves, control was the overriding issue. The curriculum focused on the three 'Rs'. That was believed to be all that was required in a society in which most students could anticipate a life spent in low skilled factory work. It is easy to see why, given these considerations, the urban public schools built during this period are large, cold, even in some cases, forbidding. Classrooms are planned to cater for as many as forty or forty-five children. The

Figure 4.5
Original plaques on the William B Ogden School, Chicago, Illinois. (Photo: Eleanor Nicholson.)

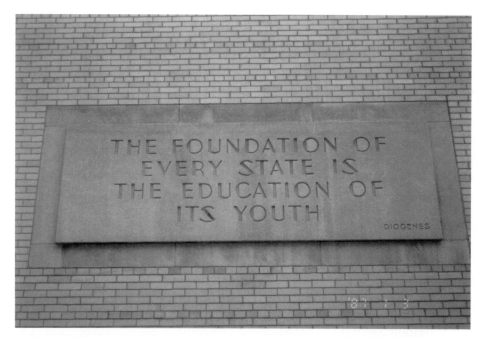

Figure 4.6
Original plaques on the
William B Ogden School,
Chicago, Illinois. (Photo:
Eleanor Nicholson.)

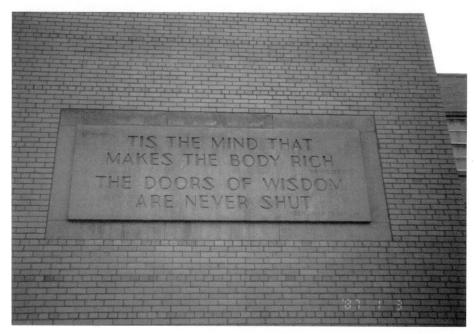

Figure 4.7
Original plaques on the
William B Ogden School,
Chicago, Illinois. (Photo:
Eleanor Nicholson.)

teacher is in a central position of surveillance. This is the overriding design principle; it is a message which is not lost on the children.

These massive structures are forbidding yet some of them were softened and humanized by the inclusion of important details. For example the plaques on the exterior walls of William B Ogden Public School in Chicago explain to children the

value of academic excellence, and the life of the mind. In their pure simplicity they communicate the importance of the American dream as propounded by Horace Mann. The message of a love of country was considered to be important for a relatively young nation, its cities filling up with immigrants. The individual ethnic identity of the immigrant families was not questioned, rather it

Figure 4.8
Original plaques on the
William B Ogden School,
Chicago, Illinois. (Photo:
Eleanor Nicholson.)

was complemented by the celebration of the new place in which they found themselves and all that had to offer. Ogden School, even in a busy urban area, strives to create a beautiful surrounding for its huge institutional form. As part of an urban community, Ogden welcomes neighbours to its asphalt-covered playgrounds by inviting them through an ornately inscribed iron gate which literally asks them to respect their environment, and trusts that they will do so. Ogden's gracious invitation for all comers to use the grounds is a contrast to the more typical dictate of the average Chicago public school. These are clear iconographic messages, legible, and articulate, if a little doctrinaire. The building speaks.

Another and older example of architecture that communicates consistent humanistic messages to American children is Crow Island School in Winnetka, Illinois. Now over sixty years old, Crow Island is a designated national historic landmark. The school is what it sets out to be; in the words of Francis Presler, Director of Activities at Crow Island (whilst briefing the architects Eero Saarinen and Dwight Perkins in 1938) the school was to be *'a place that permits the joy in small things of life and in democratic living'*, *'a place for use, good hard use, for it is to be successively the home, the abiding place for*

the procession of thousands of children through the years'.[10] He continued,

'The school must be honest and obvious to childish eyes as to its structure, its purpose, its use, its possibilities. Strength shall be evident. Genuineness shall be visible. Materials shall say "things are as they seem."... It must be inspiring, with a beauty that suggests action, not passiveness on children's part.... It must be democratic. That above all is necessary. School must not create an illusion, otherwise children will fail in more mature life. The classrooms shall express inner tranquility that can be sustained. The atmosphere of these rooms, which particularly are the school homes, should give feeling of security. These are especially the places of living together and should give feeling of inviting home-likeness.'

Note the emphasis on home spun values: home, democracy, security, beauty, action, tranquillity and continuity. Crow Island consciously, and to a unique degree, offered an education tailor-made to the emotional and cognitive needs of the younger child, and the building itself played a fundamental role in their education. The task of this age is to achieve competence at useful skills and tasks, and develop a positive self-concept, pride in accomplishment, and the ability to participate cooperatively with age mates. The honest forthright way in which Presler speaks mirrors the dawning sense of moral responsibility inherent in Erikson's tasks, while the tactility of the building's materials reflect the concrete nature of the thinking of this stage of child development, as outlined by Piaget, that children learn through all the senses. Crow Island classrooms fully meet standards for the physical setting as outlined by Sue Bredekamp and Charles Copple in *Developmentally Appropriate Practice in Early Childhood Programs*:

> *Space is divided into richly equipped activity centers – for reading, writing, playing math and language games, exploring science, working on construction projects, using computers and engaging in other academic pursuits. Spaces are used flexibly for individual and small-group activities and whole-class gatherings.*[11]

For the fiftieth anniversary of the school in 1990, 400 Crow Island alumni completed a questionnaire that probed specifically the effect of building design on their early learning. Here are some of the statements from the alumni:

'At Crow Island I felt at home.'; 'Crow Island just always felt cozy'; 'The building was very friendly and comfortable for us little ones, even then we knew it.'

Children's physical needs were considered and respected. Every classroom has its own bathroom accessible directly. A general comment made time and time again was the fact that as children they did not have to ask to go to the bathroom or to go down the hall to get to it as is generally the case. Perhaps you have seen children in public schools lined up at an appointed time so all can go to the bathroom one by one while the others remain in straight lines waiting. What adult would suffer the humiliation of being told that she or he may go to the toilet only at a given time?

Seats in the assembly are graduated in size, with those for the youngest in the front of the room. Light switches and door handles are at child level. Window openings are safe, yet accessible to children's hands so they can provide ventilation under adult supervision. Children felt safe there. Different ages played in different age-related playgrounds. Doors were colour-coded so a child could always find his or her own room.

Figure 4.9
Mature trees grow close to the building. Crow Island School, Winnekta, Illinois. (Photo: Eleanor Nicholson.)

Children's work was respected. 'We could build things in the workroom and leave them up 'til we finished them.' Children's work was displayed elegantly in the classrooms and in the halls.

Children were affirmed in their growing stature, skills and power. It was 'a wonderful moment when I moved to a new wing of the school (and) became a BIG kid'. Classrooms were orientated in different directions so that 'In each grade you looked out onto a whole new world as you changed wings'. Thus, the change from one grade to the next gave the child new perspectives on the environment around them.

The outside play areas were accessible directly from the classrooms. Large full height windows give views into the woods surrounding the site to provide a stimulating alternative to class lessons. The close proximity of each classroom to the outside areas extends a sense of space and light. As one former pupil remarked ... 'the windows to the courtyards and the wings gave the feeling of endless space'.[12]

Attention to natural as well as man-made beauty is manifest everywhere. Natural materials – wood and brick – are used inside and out. Sculptures enhance the environment, acting as fixed features, complementing the evolving displays of children's art. In my view, all spaces in the school have distinct

messages for the children. There is an assembly hall rather than an auditorium, because auditoriums are only for listening. Presler's stated goals for the assembly were clear.

The assembly has a unique place in the school. It is the one part of the building in which all come together simultaneously, obviously, and consciously to form the school body as a whole .... The room must have dignity for large group consciousness' sake. It must be buoyant for emotion's sake. But it must not be adult, sophisticated or over-stimulating. It may awe slightly – for children must be lifted to levels they did not know were inside.[13]

There was to be an art room where, according to Presler, '... beauty should be a background setting kind, and one not too finished, lest children feel it beyond them to make contribution'. The library was a place for 'lingering with energy' while the shop and science room should say to children, 'This is your place of finding out, of trying out, of doing and making'. This charge to the architects is consonant with the standards of developmentally appropriate practice:

The curriculum is implemented through activities responsive to children's interests, ideas, and

Figure 4.10
The courtyard with full height windows and doors opening off the class-room. Crow Island School, Winnekta, Illinois. (Photo: Eleanor Nicholson.)

everyday lives, including their cultural backgrounds[iii].

It is interesting to reflect upon what alumni remember from their childhood at Crow Island. Were they aware of the kind of messages being communicated to them when they were children? Harlan Stanley, who attended Crow Island in the 1950s, recently shared some of his memories with me. He recalled the auditorium with its seats in graduated sizes to fit differently aged children, the sense of privacy in the classroom courtyards, the fact that the door handles were at child level, and the ease of movement around a single storey building with broad well-lit circulation areas. 'We took these things for granted at the time. Only in going back later did we understand what it was all about'.[14]

What is surprising about the alumini survey is that the memories are mostly positive and remain vivid to this day; particularly in relation to the architecture itself. Children felt special attending the building, particularly in its early years; there was something communicated through the building fabric that could be later understood. Interestingly, Harlan's memories were more affecting than most of his more recent adult experiences. This, he assumes, is because children are so open to their experiences during these formative years. They have not yet learned the adult ways of sifting out unwanted sensory information which they do not perceive to have instant value. This view is supported by the words of John Holt:

> We all respond to space, but most adults so seldom see a space that they want to and can respond to that we lose much of this sense. Our surroundings are often so ugly that to protect ourselves we shut them out. Children, on the whole, have not learned to do this.[15]

Does the building enhance learning? There is no hard evidence to support a connection between the built environment and academic attainment. But the kind of learning supported at Crow Island is appropriate, non-verbal, intangible, symbolic and long lasting. Children must be challenged educationally, however the wisdom emanating from the building itself is explicit: children deserve and flourish in an atmosphere of love, community, mutual respect, beauty and a connectivity to nature. These are truths that we probably knew all along, however it is important to hear the comments of some of its alumni affirming these views.

The Reggio schools are for very young children, infants, toddlers, and preschoolers; Crow Island is an elementary school. They are separated in time by World War II and in distance by thousands of miles. But both systems communicate through their very buildings, important messages about the developmental needs of the children who attend them and they succeed uniquely in the positive support of young developing minds. What kinds of school buildings come to mind when we turn to members of that prickly, volatile group – the adolescent middle schooler? What is, in fact, a middle school?

In *School and Society*, John Dewey outlined his historical analysis of the development of the American school system. Decrying waste in education, Dewey said, 'I desire to call your attention to the isolation of the various parts of the school system, to the lack of unity in the aims of education, to the lack of coherence in its studies and methods.[16]

Dewey outlined the differing origins of the eight key blocks of the educational system. According to him, the aim of the kindergarten should be to support the moral development of children rather than to instruct them in a disciplinary way. The primary school developed during the sixteenth century when, along with the invention of printing and the growth of commerce, it became a business necessity to know how to read, write, and count. The aim was a practical one; getting command of that knowledge was not for the sake of learning, but because it gave access to careers in life otherwise closed. This is a principle adhered to by most contemporary elementary school systems.

Dewey's historical analysis proceeded to the grammar school or intermediate school and the high school or academy. Originally their aim had been to counter the elitist character of the university by enabling ordinary people to access learning so that men could broaden their horizons. That larger horizon originated in the Renaissance when Latin and Greek connected people with the cultures of antiquity. The aim of the grammar school and secondary school education was therefore to promote culture, not discipline. Dewey continued:

> It is interesting to follow out the interrelation between primary, grammar, and high schools. The elementary school has crowded up and taken many subjects previously studied in the old New England grammar school. The high school has pushed its subjects down. Latin and algebra have been put in the upper grades, so that the seventh and eighth grades are, after all, about all that is left of the old grammar school. They are a sort of amorphous composite, being partly a place where children go on learning what they already have learned (to read, write, and figure), and partly a place of preparation for the high school. The name in some parts of New England for these upper grades was 'Intermediate School'. The term was a happy one; the work was simply intermediate between something that had been and something that was going to be, having no special meaning on its own account.[17]

Believing that the different parts of the system were separated historically and had differing ideals ranging from moral development and general cultural awareness to self-discipline and professional training, Dewey concluded that the challenge in education is to establish the unity of the whole system, in place of a sequence of more or less unrelated and overlapping parts. Dewey recognized the need to reduce conflict and repetition within the disparate systems.

The need for a proper bridge between lower and upper schools became more and more evident as the decades passed. The methods used in the middle school made it a high school in all but name. In the traditional junior high, students changed classes at the end of each subject period, classes were of a given length and were taught at a given time. Teachers taught one subject four or five times a day to different groups in succession.

In 1968, British educator Charity James laid out a series of *desiderata* for the improved intermediate school. She agreed with Dewey's view that there is no justification in the profound social differences between the elementary and the junior high school. This is a time during young people's lives when they are embracing puberty and the profound personal transformation that entails:

> … can we really be content with the way our young people's days are spent? Would we allow them, if we had a choice, to spend this time in squads (groups is too rich a word) being addressed or grilled by adults, one adult after another, in totally incoherent order? … Would we not like them to work cooperatively rather than in a moral climate so competitive that sharing is denigrated as 'cheating' and actually punished?[18]

James is concerned with the arbitrary structure of the school day, divided as it was into 45-minute lesson periods, punctuated by the violent clanging of bells. And between each lesson, class groups moved around the building, creating log-jams in corridors and at classroom entrance areas. This planned incoherence does not treat people as individuals and thus negates the rhythms of learning that different individuals have at this time. She emphasizes the critical nature of these adolescent years and asks for new possibilities for individual learning to replace the group mentality. She questions the necessity for middle (high) school children to move around their school buildings all day, whereas elementary school children, by and large, stay put. For James, these are not merely organizational issues. The continuation of these practices is inimical to adolescent growth, if not even dangerous.

This urgency is echoed by Erik Erikson, for whom adolescence was a life stage of particular characteristics, tasks, and challenges. In his essay *Youth: Fidelity and Diversity*, Erikson states, 'In no other stage of the life cycle, then, are the promise of finding oneself and the threat of losing oneself so closely allied'. The fact that the emergent adolescent can, as Erikson interprets Piaget, 'now operate on hypothetical proposition, can think of possible variables and potential relations, and think of them in thought alone, independent of certain concrete checks previously necessary', can mean an investigation of happenings in reality and a consideration of other possibilities, often with an idealistic or ideological thrust. Adolescents are deeply concerned about issues of fairness and justice, both as applied to themselves personally and to society and societies as a whole.

At the same time, their emotional and physical development has taken an entirely different turn. The individuals in this age group are often characterized by mood swings, uncertainty, self-absorption, an evolving discovery of the self and its identity, a focus on the peer group, a need for supportive caring adults (while seeming to reject them), and a need for active learning. Their bodies are developing with dazzling and confusing rapidity; their energy levels are high and outlets for that energy are essential. Their ability to think abstractly has soared, while their ability to handle life calmly and acceptingly, as is characteristic of the successful younger child, has been for the most part set aside.

Adolescents are developmentally unique. They are different from the elementary children they so recently were, different from the high school students they will become, different from each other, and different from week to week, day to day, and hour to hour.

Maria Montessori, whose schools for preschool and elementary children are familiar to us, also planned a less well-known programme for adolescents while also rejecting the contemporary secondary school programme. Describing the child from 12 to 18, she wrote:

> *The secondary school as it is at present is an obstacle to the physical development of adolescents. The period of life during which the body attains maturity is, in fact, a delicate one: the organism is transformed; its development is rapid. It is at that time so delicate that medical doctors compare this period to that of birth and of the rapid growth of the first years.... This period is equally critical from the psychological point of view. It is the age of doubts and hesitations, of violent emotions, of*

> *discouragements. There occurs at this time a diminution of the intellectual capacity. It is not due to a lack of will that there is difficulty in concentration; it is due to the psychological characteristics of this age. The power of assimilation and memory, which endowed the younger ones with such an interest for details and for material things, seems to change.*[19]

Montessori compares the relative stability of the elementary school to that of the secondary school. There, the student changes teacher almost every hour. Montessori believes that it is impossible for the adolescent to adapt to a new teacher and a new subject every hour. Change brings mental agitation. A large number of subjects are touched upon, but all in the same superficial way.

Charity James called for middle schools that were to be totally different from the 'bossocracies' of the day where 'the value they represent is power, not growth. They mirror a social condition outside the school which is destructive to human dignity and ultimately endangers the species'. What she calls for are schools for adolescents that are non-bureaucratic, characterized by small groups, community involvement, an open evolving interdisciplinary curriculum, and teacher collaboration, all aimed at establishing loving, truthful, and hopeful human relationships. Human diversity should be respected and celebrated.[20]

Montessori recognized similar educational problems and envisioned the same kind of problematic atmosphere for the adolescent as a consequence. Reflecting on her background developing schools in the urban slums of Rome during the 1930s, her model school was to be in the country. There, the child would be outside his or her habitual surroundings in what she viewed as a peaceful place, in the bosom of nature. Perhaps most contentious was her view that the adolescent child should develop better outside the family, a painful by-product of her model school.

Her programme, called 'Erdkinder', or 'Children of the Soil', would provide experience in agricultural work, running a shop and maintaining a hotel annex for parents or guests who might visit. The work with the soil would offer an educational curriculum with a limitless study of scientific and historical subjects. Living outdoors in the open air, with a diet rich in vitamins and wholesome food furnished by the nearby fields would improve health. The harvest that followed the agricultural labour provided by the children would be sold and the funds from the sales would constitute an initiation to the fundamental social mechanism of production and exchange, the economic base on which society rests.

Thus, her visionary programme was to be self-contained, self-governing, and self-supporting. The environment was to be respectful of children and adults, and essentially collaborative rather than dictatorial. However there would need to be strict rules to maintain order and assure progress.

Montessori first published her insights into the nature of the adolescent in 1939. She herself summarized her vision as one where children would no longer take examinations in order to move into higher education. Rather, the secondary school would be a place where individuals passed from a state of dependence to a condition of independence through their own efforts, working within a living community. Although she never realized her agricultural society school, the message was a good one in its proposition that a school based on a collaborative social model connected to practical rather than theoretical activities would be more effective for the majority of adolescent children.

In 1973, the National Middle School Association was founded in the United States to improve the education of young adolescents. In 1985, the National Association of Secondary School Principals was responsible for the publication of *An Agenda for Excellence at the Middle Level;* this was followed in 1989 by the landmark report of the Carnegie Council for Adolescent Development, *Turning Points: Preparing American Youth for the 21st Century.* Echoing both Maria Montessori and Charity James, the task force found 'a volatile mismatch ... between the organization and curriculum of middle grade schools, and the intellectual, emotional, and interpersonal needs of young adolescents'. The report set forth recommendations for transforming the education of young adolescents. These have been examined,

modified, expanded, and made more meaningful both by a revision of the 1989 report entitled *Turning Points 2000: Educating Adolescents in the 21st Century* and various reports of the National Middle School Association, culminating in their publication, *This We Believe ... and Now We Must Act.*

In its work on best middle school practices, the National Middle School Association promotes a view of the middle school student characterized as one who wants to be seen as competent, accountable and responsible, as individuals who wish to be respected by peers and adults, as good people of high moral standing, concerned about justice and fairness.[21]

Such qualities will emerge and be supported in an environment that offers an integrated interdisciplinary curriculum, experiential learning, ample opportunities for socializing and interacting with a variety of others, both within the school community and with the wider community. The strategy requires close meaningful relationships with adults who understand the whole child and are themselves bonded together in a team relationship that is a community of learners. The community should plan a variety of individual, small group and whole group learning experiences within a flexible schedule.

What kind of school building addresses the unique social, intellectual, physical and emotional needs of this age group? The older stacked egg crate format of the traditional school makes the operation of a best practices programme difficult, just as the same format can repress the spontaneous exploratory learning and need for community of the younger child. It is simply too inflexible, the very walls seemingly dictating a nineteenth-century form of education.

This is what the criteria developed by the National Middle School Association look like when translated into architectural features. The list ranges from the broad and general to the detailed and specific:

1   Educators committed to young adolescents
     Needed architecturally: the building must be fun and an exciting place to be, filled with colour and light. There should be provision for

places to hang out and with overlooks, places to see and be seen.

2   A shared vision
    Needed architecturally: a planning process informed by the commitment and the vision of all the stakeholders.... The board, superintendent, principal as leader and informed faculty/staff, all participating, and 'on board'.

3   An adult advocate for every student
    Needed architecturally: space for files, activity space for advisory groups to meet, involving all faculty and staff.

4   Family and community partnerships
    Needed architecturally: parents' room, office, lounge, as well as community access to facilities such as the gym, the auditorium and the media centre.

5   Varied teaching/learning approaches, cultivating multiple intelligences, providing hands-on experiences, interdisciplinary, actively involving students in learning; a curriculum that is challenging, integrative and exploratory
    Needed architecturally: facilities to enhance the intelligences – music, art, drama, dance, film and video, out-of-doors, social spaces. Also required are classrooms of varying sizes and classrooms that permit varied activities; project rooms that are not necessarily science rooms; places to work and to be alone; places to accommodate a wide range of equipment.

6   Assessment and evaluation processes that promote learning
    Needed architecturally: authentic assessment involves spaces to create, perform and present student work for evaluation.

7   Flexible organizational structures
    Needed architecturally: provision for individual and team planning; team offices that are not departmentalized; team areas for kids, flexible spaces for flexible grouping; planning time and spaces to work that are not in the lunch room; teachers seen to be professionals.

8   Programmes that foster health, well-being and safety: comprehensive guidance services

Needed architecturally: alternatives to corridor locker areas, instead student areas which communicate a sense of trust and safety; a clinic with a nurse; counsellors whose offices are located where the reason for going is not clearly evident, to encourage a relaxed view on the discussion of personal problems; nutritional planning in the cafeteria.[22]

A number of these design and development criteria can be discerned in the floor plan of Central Middle School in Tinley Park, Illinois. Extensive consultation with all the users informed the process from the very initial planning concept right up to the construction of the building itself. Rejecting usual design strategies such as the 'egg crate' plan and the customary closed suite of departmental offices, Central Middle School accommodates the needs of students, teachers, administrators, staff, parents, and the community in an entirely different way.

Each of the three grade levels has a commons, around which wrap the classrooms. These accommodate 120 students in each grade. Immediately adjacent to the commons are the teacher workshops, conference rooms, project rooms, computer rooms, and bathrooms. Each grade level has its own science/project rooms. These are not so committed to advanced science that their furnishings exclude other kinds of projects. They are very flexible in use, a move carefully thought through by the faculty and the principal.

Each of the commons is large enough for all the children at that grade level to gather, sit on the carpets – each being a different colour according to the grade – and to discuss and plan together. Each commons leads not only to the other commons, but also to Main Street or central hall. This latter hall passes by the offices and special area rooms so when classes need to move to the art and music rooms, industrial arts shop, media centre, gym and auditorium/cafeteria, they can do so without disturbing a single other classroom.

The media centre, the auditorium/lunchroom, and gyms have outside entrances, making them accessible to the community during non-school

Figure 4.11
The Cafetorium, a multi-functional space distinct from the main hall. Thompson Middle School, Newport, RI, designed by HMFH Architects, Cambridge MA.

Figure 4.12
Locker rooms overseen by the head of department's office. (Photo: Jonathan Hillyer.)

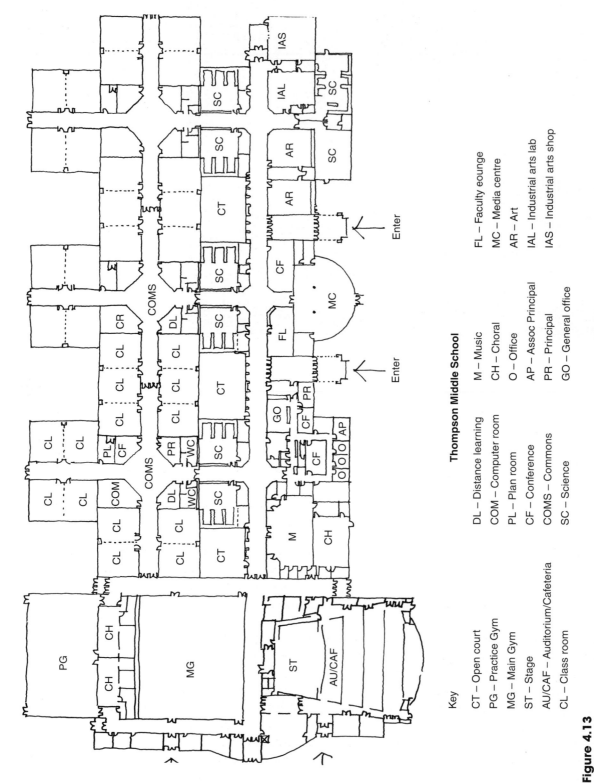

Key

CT – Open court	DL – Distance learning	M – Music	FL – Faculty eounge
PG – Practice Gym	COM – Computer room	CH – Choral	MC – Media centre
MG – Main Gym	PL – Plan room	O – Office	AR – Art
ST – Stage	CF – Conference	AP – Assoc Principal	IAL – Industrial arts lab
AU/CAF – Auditorium/Cafeteria	COMS – Commons	PR – Principal	IAS – Industrial arts shop
CL – Class room	SC – Science	GO – General office	

Thompson Middle School

Figure 4.13
Thompson Middle School, Newport, RI, designed by HMFH Architects, Cambridge MA.

Figure 4.14
Science labs express their function in the use of pure neutral colours and semi translucent walls, providing even, natural light set out in the form of a graph paper grid at the Little Village Academy, Chicago, Illinois. (© Steve Hall, Hedrich Blessing.)

hours. Some classrooms between the commons are designated as 'flex' rooms to accommodate differing numbers of children in the grade levels; a room could be a seventh grade classroom one year if enrolment there were higher or an eighth grade classroom the next as that group moved on.

Conclusion

Tinley Park is not a wealthy suburb. What was in place as the building was being planned was a knowledgeable, experienced, and determined principal, supported by an equally knowledgeable superintendent, both of whom matched the criteria listed in *This We Believe ... And Now Must Act*.[21] They shared a vision for a middle school programme that met the needs of their constituency and they built a building that both reflects and facilitates that programme. This was in no small way down to the sensitivity of the architectural team responsible for the building.

Charity James puts it this way:

... when I speak of the need for schooling to be living, my language is deliberately value-laden. I believe that the living behaviours are to explore, to make, and to enter into dialogue, and that these are the ways members of a school should engage themselves.[23]

Other exemplary middle school buildings exist and, fortunately, are becoming more visible in those communities who have listened to principals, teachers, parents, members of school boards, and the adolescents themselves, all spokespersons for a way of teaching and learning that is truly developmentally appropriate.

The messages of these buildings, to and about the adolescent, are that he or she is understood and his or her many and even competing, even occasionally conflicting, needs are respected and accommodated.

However, children are not usually the ones who are planning the buildings they live in. They are, in fact, the invisible clients. Perhaps three, six or even nine years of their lives will be spent in the building in question, yet they have no input into the design, iconography, uses, patterns or aesthetics of the building. It is therefore up to the adults in charge to develop what Thomas David calls 'environmental literacy'.

> *The development of environmental literacy involves the transformation of awareness into a critical, probing, problem-seeking attitude towards one's surrounds. It entails the active definition of choices and a willingness to experiment with a variety of spatial alternatives and to challenge the environmental status quo. Old roles, which were characterized by submission, or apathy or dependency on the 'experts' to determine one's environment, must be unlearned.*[24]

If, as Robert Sommer says, 'A design problem is a value problem' and the question is 'Whose interests are to be served?', how do we better serve the interests of children?[25] What do we *really* want to say to them? Their buildings and what goes on in them communicate, whether that is our intention or not, where they stand in the wider world. Do we want to communicate to them that they are not worth safe, well-maintained and child- and adolescent-friendly buildings, rich in beauty, interest and opportunities for engagement? Or do we want to communicate to them, overtly and symbolically through the built environment, that they are to be inspired, trusted, respected, loved, protected, and understood in all the developmental aspects of their being? If so, we will help them live in model homes, complete communities, and embryonic democracies. If we don't, we have made choices that are, in the words of John Dewey, 'narrow and unlovely' and we put our very democracy at risk.

Notes

1 Behnisch & Partner, Architekten Behnisch und Partner Arbeiten aus den Jahren 1952–1987, exhibition catalogue, Stuttgart, Munchen PT, p. 60.

2 'Gleaming Spires', *Education Guardian*, 13 April 2004, by Peter Kingston.

3 Banning, J. H. 'The Connection Between Learning and the Learning Environment" in *Children, Learning & School Design: A First National Invitation Conference for Architects and Educators*. E. Heber and A. Meek (eds) Winnetka, IL: Winnetka Public Schools, 1990, p. 21.

4 Anderson, R. H. (1970). 'The School as an Organic Teaching Aid'. Robert M. McClure (ed). *The Curriculum Retrospect and Prospect; The Seventieth Yearbook of the National Society of Education*, Part 1, Chicago, IL: The University of Chicago Press, p. 277.

5 Dewey, J. (1990). 'The School and Society'. Intro Philip W Jackson, Chicago, IL. The University of Chicago Press, p. 7.

6 Sommer, R. (1969). *Personal Space*. Englewood Cliffs, New Jersey: Prentice Hall, Inc. p. 99.

7 Mann, H. (1840). Lecture on education. Boston: Marsh, Capen, Lyon and Webb, pp. 20–24.

8 Mann, p. 32. (Details as note 7 above.)

9 The term 'third teacher' was derived from the Reggio Emilia approach, a powerful and arts-based pre-school curriculum first developed in Reggio Emilia, Italy and published in C. Edwards, L. Gandini, G. Forman (eds). *The Hundred Languages of Children; The Reggio Emilia Approach to Childhood Education*, Norwood, New Jersey: Ablex Publishing Company, 1966, p. 136.

10 Presler, F. (1990). 'Letter to the Architects' the Afterword in E. Heber and A. Meek (eds). *Children, Learning and School Design*, Winnetka, IL: the Winnetka Public Schools, pp. 59–60.

11 Bredekamp, S. and Copple, C. (eds). (1997). *Developmentally Appropriate Practices in Early Childhood Programs* (rev ed.), Washington, DC: National Association for the Education of Young Children.

12 Comments excerpted from the questionnaires are to be found in Herbert, E. (1990). 'Crow Island: A Place Built for Children' in *Children, Learning and School Design*, Winnekta, IL: Winnekta Public Schools, ch. 4.

13 Presler, p. 28. (Details as note 10 above.)

14 Personal phone call with Harlan Stanley, March 17, 2002.
15 Holt, J. (1975). *Learning Environments*. Chicago, IL: The University of Chicago Press, p. 141.
16 Dewey, p. 64. (Details as note 5 above.)
17 Dewey, J. Included in the chapter Waste in Education in School and Society, pp. 65–71. (Details as note 5 above.)
18 James, C. (1973). *Young Lives at Stake*. New York, NY: Schocken Press, pp. 14–16.
19 Montessori, M. (1973). *From Childhood to Adolescence*. New York, NY: Schocken Books, p. 100.
20 James, p. 15. (Details as note 18 above.)
21 Stevenson, C. 'Curriculum that is Challenging, Integrative and Exploratory' in *This We Believe and Now We Must Act*. Westerville: Ohio National School Association, 2001, pp. 65–67.
22 A summary of a talk given to the National Middle School Association in Washington DC in November 2001 by Julia Nugent and the author with the collaboration of Eliza Davey.
23 James. p. 96. (Details as note 18 above.)
24 David, T. (1975). *Learning Environments*. Chicago, IL: The University of Chicago Press, p. 167.
25 Sommer, p. 171. (Details as note 6 above.)

Eleanor Nicholson is currently adjunct faculty at Erikson Institute in Chicago, Illinois. Erikson is dedicated to the graduate level education of future teachers, administrators, policy makers and researchers in the field of early childhood education. Prior to joining the Erikson Faculty, she spent twenty-three years in school administration in four different Chicago independent schools. She currently lives in Evanston, Illinois and will spend the 2004–2005 school year in India as an interim head of an international boarding school.

5

The classroom is a microcosm of the world

John Edwards

Editor's introduction

'… everything we make must be a catalyst to stimulate the individual to play the roles through which his identity will be enriched … form makes itself, and that is less of a question of intervention than of listening well to what a person and a thing want to be.'[1]

The author has recently completed an exhaustive study of the classroom environment, talking to teachers and observing within a range of existing primary schools in the north of England. Here he explains the research process, describing in some detail how a combination of quantitative and qualitative methods have informed his thinking about design. He emphasizes that despite the wish to provide new school buildings wherever possible, by far the majority of primary education throughout the UK will continue to take place in adapted existing accommodation. Understanding the activities of the users within a range of representative classroom environments illustrates the need for an imaginative approach to instigate new ICT learning strategies, a recognition of special educational needs and an understanding of the notion of active learning, an essential principle enshrined in enlightened curriculum strategies which have developed over the past forty years.

In this chapter, the issues which affect an efficient classroom will be explained. Typical classroom layouts from the past will be illustrated by way of previous research; the principles of the educational curriculum in Key Stage 2 classrooms will be presented and, finally, Edward's key research findings from observation in classrooms and discussion with educationalists over a two-year period will be presented. This research clearly recognizes that the activities the classroom needs to support are critical and should largely dictate the form. The chapter is a useful briefing tool for architects embarking on the design of new or refurbished classrooms who are interested in gaining a deeper insight into the education which takes place there.

His studies represent a significant contribution to our understanding of how children, staff and other members of the education community relate to their existing physical settings. In its incorporation of a broad range of research techniques and educational data, Edwards has worked towards an integration of both architectural and educational concerns, to provide a bridge between the two disciplines by asking teachers to explain the various aspects of classroom design which are important to them. In search of a common language his work sets out to translate the misunderstandings, which often occur when architects try to talk about education and when educationalists try to discuss architecture and space.

Introduction

Children's experiences of school are framed by time as well as space. Most of a child's life in a primary school is spent in the classroom; there might only be two breaks from study during the day, once in the morning and once for lunch, with children essentially confined within a single room from 9 am to 3.15 pm for the majority of the day. There is a range of research from the past twenty years by educationalists which describes the ways in which time is spent within the primary school classroom. For example, *Life in Classrooms* is a closely observed and engaging account of the complexities of classroom life:

> *'Aside from sleeping, and perhaps playing, there is no other activity which occupies as much of a child's time as that involved in attending school. Apart from the bedroom where he has his eyes closed (most of the time) there is no single enclosure in which he spends a longer time than when he does in the classroom.'*[2]

With great periods of time spent there, the range and breadth of curriculum and pastoral activity which this single space must support is daunting. The classroom becomes a container of the child's life expectancies and ideally it should represent a sort of microcosm of the world. However, within the framework of existing research, there is very little which deals with architectural issues relating to actual space and its physical disposition. Previous research which has been undertaken limits itself to the environment on offer and those aspects which are controllable by teachers themselves, such as the organization of furniture and the grouping of children. The actual architecture of the classroom is usually deemed to be beyond the scope of classroom teachers and not particularly relevant to the ongoing education debate.[3]

Designing any classroom is about understanding the activities which take place there, and the way

in which the class lessons are structured to facilitate teaching and learning in line with the demands of the National Curriculum. Different aspects of organization are discussed here to provide an overview of how current practice has developed, whilst, in turn, revealing the relationships between classroom organization and teaching, which are framed by space and time. Finally, some key research findings will be summarized as a series of design process recommendations.[4] The chapter is presented in six sections: forms of classroom organization; the use of the classroom environment and resources; child-centred learning – developments over the past 30 years; a survey of classrooms in use; the UK National Curriculum; and key research findings.

The use of the classroom environment

Bennett and Kell's 1989 study described poor classroom organization and its effects, which showed in a lack of pupil involvement in the lessons (with some pupils wandering about inanely), interruptions which disrupted the whole class, and a general lack of interest or motivation on the part of the pupils.[5] Children played about without the teacher apparently being aware of it. There was little or no teacher control.

The key way in which teacher control can be improved is through the organization of the classroom; this is viewed by many educationalists as the Holy Grail. Currently, educationalists recognize four main types of classroom organization which takes place in primary schools: whole class, individual, paired and group working.

Whole class teaching is where all the pupils undertake the same activity, at the same time, whilst usually being addressed by the teacher positioned at the front of the room. This is successful for starting and ending the day, for giving out administrative instructions, general teaching, extending and reviewing work, and controlling the pupils during unruly periods of the day. The whole class can be organized so that everyone is being taught the same thing at the same time. This type of organization is particularly useful where a lot of discussion is required. Group or individual work often follows this, with children coming together again to discuss and review what they have been doing during individual or smaller group work.

Individual work will often follow a whole class briefing. This process is thought to be particularly useful for developing children's ability to work independently at their own pace through a structured work scheme. Children may work on individual tasks which may be of their own creation or an interpretation of a group theme suggested by the teacher. Paired as opposed to individual working allows children to collaborate on a task with one other pupil. This not only helps by making different aspects of a problem more explicit through collaboration in a limited and controlled form, but it also helps to develop each child's language ability.

There are many situations when a class of children needs to be divided in order to undertake particular activities. A powerful argument for grouping is that it encourages collaboration and supports the interactions and discussions through which much learning and socialization develops. It also helps with competency in social and language skills and as a means by which pupils can support, challenge and extend their learning together, through problem solving or working on a joint creative task. Different types of grouping are needed for different activities and children should have the opportunity to be part of a variety of groupings; ideally groupings should be flexible and varied. There are seven types of grouping arrangements: grouping by age, ability grouping, developmental grouping, grouping by learning need, interest groups, social learning groups and friendship groups.[6]

Learning activities can be thought of as falling into five categories. The activities differ in many respects including variable factors such as the number of pupils involved, the interactions they involve and the nature of the attention they require. However, the key groupings can be summarized as follows:

1　Pupils taught directly by their teachers;
2　As individuals;
3　In small groups;
4　As a whole class;
5　Or, when not with their teacher, alone or in collaboration.

It is also clear from the literature reviewed that the use of these types of activity differs, with individual work and whole class teaching tending to feature most prominently. While group seating makes sense for two of the five types of learning activity, it is not suited for individual work.[7] A balance needs to be struck regarding the time spent on individual work, whole classwork and smaller group work. This must be organized with regard to both pedagogical and practical considerations relating to the space in which it takes place.

Barker (1978) and Bronfenbrenner (1979) have discussed the importance of the quality of the environment and the fact that it can influence behaviour, a view which is commonly stated by teachers.[8] Space in classrooms is often limited and must be utilized with great skill to enable the activities, which form essential components of the primary school curriculum, to take place effectively. The organization of space may have a profound effect on learning because pupils tend to feel connected to a school that recognizes their needs through the provision of good architecture and good resources:

When children experience a school obviously designed with their needs in mind, they notice it and demonstrate a more natural disposition towards respectful behaviour and a willingness to contribute to the classroom community.[9]

It is axiomatic that a beautifully designed school, like any public building, is good for its users. However, there is much anecdotal evidence supporting the view that new 'landmark school architecture' does not always satisfy its users functionally. Architects do not get the classroom design right, often as a result of too little consultation. In the primary school classroom the teachers' task is to ensure that children experience the curriculum, develop and learn and are seen to be making progress. Therefore the presentation of children's work is most important and should be constantly updated. The primary school classroom should be aesthetically pleasing; stimulate children's interests; set high standards in display and presentation of children's work; and be designed in such a way that the room can be easily cleaned and maintained.[10]

Educational attainment has been shown to correlate with spending levels in each locality, so that in theory the higher the resource provision, the higher the attainment and the greater the educational life chances in that area. Investment in UK schools comes about via a complex combination of school-based decisions, numbers of pupils on the roll and the priority given to education by national and local government at the time. Presently within the UK, the quality of education and the buildings that support it have been widely condemned and with such obviously badly maintained old buildings, pupils and their parents can readily see how little investment there has been in education over the years. This has a great political significance, hence a lot of new capital investment is now beginning to happen within the UK.

In educational terms 'resources' are materials and equipment used in the classroom (as opposed to the buildings) and the quality of learning experiences will be directly affected by their provision. Materials include things such as paper and pencils and can be considered as consumables. Equipment is also very significant in primary education because it is usually through the use of appropriate equipment that the pupils get enhanced learning experiences. Both in quality and quantity these resources have an impact on what it is possible to do in classrooms. A good supply of appropriate resources is essential.[11] However, these older research studies referred to here do not consider ICT (information communications technology) in any great depth, a recent and profoundly important dimension which now also needs to be considered as part of the resource structure.

There are three criteria that must be considered when organizing resources:[12]

1   Appropriateness. What resources are needed to support the learning processes which are expected to take place?

2   Availability. What resources are available? What is in the classroom, the school, the community, businesses, libraries, museums, local resource centres? Are there cost, time or transport factors to be considered?

3   Storage. How are classroom resources stored? Which should be under teacher control? Which should be openly available to the children? Are resources clearly labelled and safely stored.

Clearly, an effective classroom needs to be designed ergonomically so that storage is designed into the architecture in an appropriate, safe and accessible form. Close discussion with teachers will enable this to happen.

As previously stated, the way in which time is used in the classroom is very important. Pupil progress is undoubtedly related to the time that is made available for effective 'curriculum activity'. However, many educationalists believe that the amount of pupil time spent in 'active learning' is more important. This is a qualitative criteria not a quantitative one, in that it implies a more positive engaged learning mode for the pupil. In order to maintain active engaged learning, an appropriate variety of activities offered within the classroom is necessary. This has clear spatial implications, for example, the availability of discreet work bays off the main teaching space or separate study areas to support pupils with special needs.

Findings from Pollard's 1994 study showed considerable variations between the proportion of pupil time spent in different modes and various levels of pupil engagement in passive as opposed to active learning in various classroom situations.[13] Mortimore et al. (1988) noted that between 66 and 75 per cent of teachers used a fairly precise timetable to order the activities during each session and noted that the older the children the more organization and lesson planning was required.[14] The study found that managerial aspects of a teacher's job took approximately 10 per cent of the time available within each teaching period.

The establishment of the UK National Curriculum in 1988, the need for public accountability and the subsequent numeracy and literacy strategies developed successfully since then have brought about an even more rigid allocation of time within the classroom environment. A study by Campbell and Neill (1994) illustrated the important concept of 'time available for teaching'. They show that almost 10 per cent of teaching time is lost as 'evaporated time' in the management of classroom activities, which is necessary to create teaching and learning opportunities within the framework of the increasingly proscriptive educational curriculum.[15] However, it was not estimated how much time was lost to teaching as a result of poor environmental conditions.

Child-centred learning – developments over the past 30 years

In mainland Europe forms of classroom organization vary, although over the past 30 years there has been a gradual move away from the organization of pupils in formal rows focusing on a single teacher at the front of the space. Now, smaller more informal groupings organized around tables of 6 to 8 pupils is the norm. Elsewhere, in Russia and India for example, pupils are still generally organized in rows as they were in UK primary classrooms until the mid-1960s, when practice changed dramatically as a result of the findings of Plowden.

The report published by the Central Advisory Council for Education entitled *Children and their Primary Schools*, but better known as 'The Plowden Report', was published in 1967.[16] It brought about a radical transformation in primary education. Before Plowden 'traditional' primary education was predominant, with children taught in whole class groups and typically sitting in rows focusing on the teacher's desk, which was often raised up on a plinth. The 'progressive' era was characterized by profound changes to the curriculum and, in particular, to teaching methods. These were described as 'pupil-centred'; the principle was that education should engage with children as individuals. This was a philosophy that placed the child at the heart of educational methods and extolled the virtues of individualization within the framework of collaborative learning. Rather than sitting at the front, the teacher now moved around the classroom, facilitating in turn individual or smaller groups of children often carrying out different tasks in the same lesson period. As a result, whole class teaching would be minimized.

A glance at some of the photographs taken from the report illustrates a variety of classroom arrangements proposed by Plowden with children in smaller, less formal groupings. The comparison between figures 3/A and 3/B is stark, with the 1937 arrangement showing children sitting in well-ordered ranks enclosed by four walls, whilst the 1966 image is a space which is higgledy-piggledy and open plan. In reality, most schools favoured the ordered discipline and predictability of the 1937 arrangement until Plowden enforced new informal layouts from 1967.

The Plowden Report endorsed a reduction in the proportion of time that teachers were spending teaching the whole class and a drastic increase in the proportion of time that children should be taught as individuals or as members of small groups. However, there was a problem. This proposition did not provide additional teachers or more space in order to make the new teaching strategies workable, as one might have expected. In addition, ever more complicated forms of classroom organization were introduced, such as the 'integrated day', to provide individual children with appropriate direct learning experiences relating to their own individual needs. Here, the implication was that children themselves would begin to take more responsibility for their own activities, so that learning would be based on their natural desires and motivations, as their interest in learning was stimulated. In hindsight this appears to be a somewhat idealistic aspiration. The reality of the integrated day for many teachers was an environment where art took place at one table with maths at another adjacent table simultaneously; this necessitated even more control by the teacher. For many teachers the atmosphere in the classroom became increasingly fraught as the day progressed. The ideals of

Figure 5.1
(a) Children at work, 1937; (b) Children at work, 1966; (c) Children at work, 1966; (d) Children at work, 1966.
(Source: DES (1967).[16])

Plowden, to create a generation of adults more socially adept as well as being better educated, was turned on its head. Discipline and restraint had to be increased in order to maintain some semblance of order. Resourcing of the new approach was simply inadequate.

Nevertheless, this radical educational approach was enforced and it is generally acknowledged that the Plowden Report was substantially responsible for the development and nature of primary practice over subsequent decades up to the introduction of the UK National Curriculum. During this period the only systematic surveys of junior school classroom organization were those carried out by Moran (1971) and Bealing (1971), which concluded generally that teacher control remained tight within the framework of the 'integrated day'.[17] However, much anecdotal evidence suggests that this was not the case. By 1970 the transition to 'informal' classroom structures had been widely adopted, however there was little evidence to support the idea that primary school children would or could take more responsibility for their own learning, and more evidence built up over intervening years that education was poorer and children less disciplined:

> *Despite the relatively informal classroom layouts adopted by the vast majority of teachers there was so much evidence of tight teacher control over such matters as where children sit and move that it seems highly doubtful that there is much opportunity for children to organize their own activities in most classrooms.*[18]

Following the implementation of Plowden, the first large-scale observational study of primary classrooms in use was undertaken; ORACLE (Observational Research and Classroom Learning Evaluation) took place between 1975 and 1980. The main focus of the ORACLE study was the curriculum; the way teachers taught it and how the pupils responded. Looking back it is surprising that spatial or architectural issues were largely ignored. The study followed pupils during their last two years of primary school and through the first year of their secondary school. The study used systematic observation techniques in a wide range of classrooms to gather data on the nature of classroom events. Much of the research focused on a somewhat reductive question – which worked better, combined individual teaching and small group teaching in informal groups, or traditional whole class teaching?

This obsession with the effects of individual pupil activity, as opposed to whole class pupil activity, disguised a hidden agenda which was perhaps somewhat ideological; the progressives favoured the notion of free self directed learning, as opposed to the traditional virtues of 'instruction', a single message given to the whole class simultaneously. Galton *et al.* (1980) showed that although the majority of primary class children sat in small groups around 4–8 person tables, they rarely interacted. Instead, children worked either alone or collectively as a whole class. An accurate portrayal of classroom organization at a time when the pre-war image of the primary classroom, as a place where children sat in serried rows of desks, had virtually disappeared, with children only sitting in rows in four of the fifty-eight classrooms surveyed. Further observations from the study reveal that the teacher no longer stood in front of the blackboard, or instructed the pupils from behind a centrally positioned desk, but instead moved around the room interacting with pupils continuously. However, teachers tended to spend time with the most engaging pupils whilst others missed out on individual instruction.

Figure 5.2 compares children's activities between the 1976 ORACLE study and a subsequent 1996 ORACLE study which revisited the same schools. Information about the use of collaborative learning comes from the records of activities that pupils

	ORACLE 1976	ORACLE 1996
Individual	55.8[a] (71.2)[b]	43.1 (48.4)
Group	7.5 (9.8)	14.6 (16.4)
Class	15.1 (19.0)	31.3 (35.2)
Total	78.4 (100.0)	89.0 (100.0)

a: Figures in first column represent the percentage of all interaction

b: Figures in brackets represent the percentage of teacher–pupil interaction.

Figure 5.2
Changes in the form of classroom organization 1976–1996. (Source: Galton *et al.* (1999).[30])

were set. Comparing the data, it can be seen that there is a decline in individual interactions and a corresponding increase of teacher–pupil interaction with both group and class activities. Individual interactions have increased from 43.1 to 48.4 per cent, group interactions have changed from 14.6 to 16.4 per cent and class interactions from 31.3 to 35.2 per cent.

Like Plowden, *Curriculum Organisation and Classroom Practice in Primary Schools* conceptualized primary teaching in terms of individual, group and whole class teaching activities.[19] The main task of their research was to make recommendations about curriculum organization in the classroom. Groups were considered in terms of children collaborating in their learning and of the teacher's role as manager of a class comprising of groups working on different tasks. The report also made recommendations about effective methods of teaching and classroom organization:

> *The organizational strategies of whole class teaching, group work and individual teaching need to be used more selectively and flexibly. The criterion for choice must be fitness for purpose. In many schools the benefits of whole class teaching have been insufficiently exploited.*[20]

The report also went on to make recommendations about the deployment of teachers beyond the traditional 'one teacher one class' model, stating that:

primary teaching roles in the past have been too rigidly conceived and much greater flexibility of staff development is needed.[21]

What the report failed to recognize was the importance of the environment in this regard. Because of the need for constant supervision, the limitations of 'one teacher one class' can only be overcome if the staff pupil ratio is increased or team teaching is enabled by physically combining two or more classrooms. This requires the arrangement of classrooms in suites with flexible partitions which can be removed at certain times. Coming full circle from the original aims of Plowden, the Alexander report affirmed that primary teachers had been devoting too much time to individual instruction and making insufficient use of whole class teaching methods, concluding: '*In many schools the benefits of whole class teaching have been insufficiently exploited.*'[20]

Another more recent study, *The Nature and Use of Classroom Groups in Primary Schools* (Blatchford et al., 1999) found that teachers taught a large range of group sizes including pairs, small groups, and groups with 7–10 pupils, in addition to working with individuals or with the whole class.[22] The study revealed that large groups of 7–10 pupils were in greater use in Key Stage 2 classrooms than smaller groupings. It also indicated that there was little correlation between grouping characteristics, such as size and composition, learning task type and interaction between group members.

To summarize, the grouping of children for instruction is widespread in British classrooms today, a practice encouraged in the Plowden Report, conceived as the best compromise in achieving individualization of learning and teaching within the teacher time available. Among the benefits the report envisaged for group work, were that children learn to get along together, to help one another and realize their own strengths and weaknesses by comparing their work with the work of their peers. Much of the research illustrates that most of a child's contact with a teacher happens when the teacher is working with the whole class, consequently in classes where teachers do more whole class activities, children get more teaching contact. This view is supported by McPake et al. (1999), whose study of 12 Scottish primary school classrooms found that overall, children were in direct contact with their teacher for 41 per cent of their classroom time. This was only achieved because for 32 per cent of the time their teacher was interacting with the whole class.[23]

Plowden was a radical experiment which was imposed upon an education system ill prepared and under resourced. Teachers found it challenging as control was the price paid for pupil freedom within the classroom, yet this freedom to discover (and it seems to also disrupt the learning of others) was the philosophy which lay at its heart. Furthermore, the available buildings were inappropriate for the new system, lacking flexibility and enough space for the system to work properly. Many classrooms were acoustically disastrous when fifteen or so 9-year-olds were attempting to express themselves simultaneously. Nevertheless, Plowden was pushed through and took some of the blame for poor educational standards in state schools over subsequent years. Politicians blamed new fangled trendy ideas and by the beginning of the 1980s set out to re-create a more traditional approach to education. The result was the new UK National Curriculum.

The National Curriculum was in part a reactionary return to older values. However, after 15 or so years of tinkering since it was first introduced, there is now a recognition of the need to make education at Key Stage 2 much more tailored to the child's individual needs, reflecting the culture in which most children now grow up. 'Individual learning plans' are perhaps the latest exemplification of this, yet there still appears to be little discussion regarding how best to design buildings which will support this strategy. A 'one size fits all' approach to education is a neat exigency for politicians wishing to understand their brief, but widely understood to be inappropriate in modern Britain. It is unfair to deal with a group of middle class children in a leafy middle class suburb of Surrey in the same way you would with a refugee community on a sink estate in post-industrial Sheffield. When a primary school has 45 per cent of its pupils requiring special needs support, the key requirement is for more specially trained teachers, and a whole range of smaller self-contained rooms in which small group and individual work may take place outside of so-called mainstream teaching; the notion that five identical classrooms can support such a diverse learning community is rather like suggesting that every family should live in an identical house.

The UK National Curriculum

The 1988 Education Reform Act heralded the introduction of the National Curriculum for all children of compulsory school age.[24] The National Curriculum sets out learning objectives and attempts to provide coherence in the teaching of pupils, whilst also clarifying the role of teachers within the classroom. The following four criteria summarize the government's key ideological aims:

— to establish entitlement to a number of areas of learning for all children irrespective of their social or ethnic background. In particular it seeks to promote the development of people as active and responsible citizens.
— the National Curriculum makes expectations for learning and attainment explicit and establishes national standards for the performance of all pupils.
— it promotes continuity and a coherent national framework that ensures a good foundation for life long learning.
— it promotes public understanding providing a common basis for discussion of educational issues among lay and professional groups.

In reality, its introduction was a rather desperate response to the perceived failure of education during the 1970s and early 1980s. Students were emerging from the system with very poor social and literacy/numeracy skills. Politicians felt they had no control over what was happening and sought to disguise the general underfunding of the system in the cloak of new educational strategies. The need for new and refurbished schools was largely ignored at that time. Significant government funding has only come on stream since 2001, and this is largely directed towards secondary schools rather than primaries. However, it is fair to say that most primaries are receiving more resources, improvements to the maintenance and repair, and additional classrooms to support community links (ICT training suites which can be used outside school hours), early years facilities (nursery units) and after school clubs. Although the National Curriculum does not refer to the environment specifically it is possible to interpret the spatial implications of its content.

The related framework of the National Literacy and Numeracy Strategies contains detailed guidance about planning and teaching from which spatial issues can be ascertained. It is important to understand the key ideas of the curriculum and how these are put into effect in the classroom, which in turn will help to identify the architectural requirements of the classroom's design, now and in the future.

There have been some significant developments in primary education in recent years, due to legislative changes to make the National Curriculum more effective. The early stages of its implementation were problematic; most teachers found it difficult to cope with the large subject content they were expected to cover. A period of review led to a reduction in the amount to be taught in most subjects and the introduction of a proscriptive element of time to be spent on certain subjects over and above others. Recent modifications to the National Curriculum, including the introduction of the National Literacy and Numeracy Strategies and the evolving of ICT (information communications technology) into a separate dedicated subject within the curriculum, have had a positive effect on education and its delivery, requiring a new approach to the design of schools. The numeracy and literacy strategies for primary schools give guidance ranging from how each individual minute of classroom time should be used to the arrangement of classroom furniture.

The government has taken control over not only the objectives, but also the teaching methods.

The National Curriculum Handbook for Primary Teachers in England (1999) identifies three core subjects: English, Mathematics and Science. In addition to these, there are seven non-core foundation subjects: Design and Technology; Information Communication Technology; History; Geography; Art and Design; Music; and Physical Education.[25] For each subject and each key stage, programmes of study set out what pupils should be taught, and attainment targets establish expected standards of pupil performance. National frameworks for literacy and mathematics are published by the Department for Education, and exemplar schemes of work are jointly published by the DfEE and QCA; they illustrate how the programmes of study and attainment targets can be translated into practical, manageable teaching plans.

The National Curriculum identifies six skills areas, which are described as 'key skills' because, according to government dictum, they help people of all ages to improve their learning and performance in education, work and life (DfEE and QCA, 1999:20). These skills are: communication, application of numbers, information technology, working with others, improving learning performance and problem solving. In addition to these key skills the National Curriculum identifies five thinking skills which complement the key skills. These are: information-processing skills, reasoning skills, enquiry skills, creative thinking skills and evaluation skills. This provides a theoretical justification for the core subject areas, as they are thought to encompass knowledge, skills and understanding without which it is not possible for other learning to take place effectively.[13] The National Curriculum Programmes of Study set out what pupils should be taught in each subject and provide a basis for planning schemes of works. The programme of study sets out two areas of benefit:

- *Knowledge, skills and understanding – what is to be taught in the subject during the key stage.*
- *Breadth of study – the contexts, activities areas of study and range of experiences through*

which the knowledge, skills and understanding should be taught.[26]

For example, the skills of speaking (from a text) and writing are viewed as fundamental aspects of English as a core subject taught at both Key Stage 1 and 2. The Programme of Study for English states that:

In English, during key stage 2, pupils learn to change the way that they speak and write to suit different situations, purposes and audiences. They read a range of texts and respond to different layers of meaning in them. They explore the use of language in literacy and non-literacy texts and learn how language works. Speaking and listening: during key stage 2 pupils learn how to speak in a range of different contexts, adapting what they say and how they say it to the purpose and the audience. Taking varied roles in groups gives them opportunities to contribute to situations with different demands. They also learn to respond appropriately to others, thinking about what has been said and the language used.[27]

The National Literacy Framework for teaching sets out teaching objectives for Reception to Year 6 to enable pupils to become fully literate. Literacy unites the important skills of reading and writing. It also involves speaking and listening, which although not separately identified within the framework, are an essential part of it. The National Literacy Strategy contains detailed guidance on the implementation of literacy hour, in which the relevant teaching will take place. The Literacy Hour is designed to provide a practical structure of time and class management which reflects the overall teaching objectives (a step by step guide is included in Appendix A). The National Literacy Strategy defines the structure of the literacy hour quite precisely. It should include the following:

a. *Key Stage 1 and Key Stage 2: Shared text work, a balancing of reading and writing. (Whole class, approximately 15 minutes)*
b. *Key Stage 1: Focused word work. Key Stage 2: A balance over the term of focused word work*

or sentence work. (Whole class, approximately 15 minutes)

c. *Key Stage 1: Independent reading, writing or word work, while the teacher works with at least two ability groups each day on guided text work, reading or writing. Key Stage 2: Independent reading, writing or word and sentence work, while the teacher works with at least one ability group each day on guided text work, reading and writing. (Group and independent work, approximately 20 minutes)*

d. *Key Stage and Key Stage 2: Reviewing, consolidating teaching points, and presenting work covered in the lesson. (Whole class, approximately 10 minutes).*[28]

The literacy hour offers a structure of classroom management, designed to maximize the time teachers spend directly teaching their class. It is intended to shift the balance of teaching from individualized work, especially in the teaching of reading, towards more whole class and group teaching.

The essential elements of the literacy hour are: shared reading as a class activity using a common text, e.g. a big book, poetry poster or text extract. At Key Stage 1 teachers should use shared reading to read with the class, focusing on comprehension and on specific features, e.g. word-building and spelling patterns, punctuation, the layout and purpose, the structure and organization of sentences. Shared reading provides a context for applying and teaching word level skills and for teaching how to use other reading cues to check for meaning, and identify and self-correct errors. Shared reading, with shared writing, also provide the context for developing pupils' grammatical awareness, and their understanding of sentence construction and punctuation. At Key Stage 2 shared reading is used to extend reading skills in line with the objectives in the text level column of the framework. Teachers should also use this work as a context for teaching and reinforcing grammar, punctuation and vocabulary work.

At both Key Stages, because the teacher is supporting the reading, pupils can work from texts that are beyond their independent reading levels. This is particularly valuable for less able readers who gain access to texts of greater richness and complexity than they would otherwise be able to read. This builds confidence and teaches more advanced skills which feed into other independent reading activities.

We have quoted at some length from the National Curriculum (in one core subject only), in order to give the reader a flavour of the tasks and functions which need to be considered when designing a classroom. The way in which the classroom is organized affects the extent of each child's contact with the teacher and the opportunities for effective learning. A functional, well-organized classroom will have teaching materials, tools and equipment arranged efficiently so that they are easy to find, use and keep in order. The planned layout of an activity area should match the intentions of the activity, with resources in close proximity. As will be seen in later sections, the space standards recommended by the Department for Education are, in my view, inadequate for many classes, particularly where pupils have a high level of special educational needs. That is why all aspects, such as storage, become critical. There should be a definite place for everything and storage should be labelled appropriately, making it easily accessible. Children's personal storage should be allocated a particular place which is secure, yet positioned so that it does not obstruct learning and spatial efficiency. This will enable children to be given responsibility for taking out and putting away their own materials and equipment. Materials should also be stored at appropriate levels, so that access to certain equipment can be controlled by keeping it out of reach of pupils.

There is very often surplus equipment and resources lying unused in classrooms. The development of Information Technology resources in schools is essential for every pupil, to contribute towards the development of other curriculum themes, skills and personal qualities. Grouping such resources and sharing them between selected classrooms would usually be more efficient and economies could be made in the provision of

Figure 5.3
Equipment store, Millennium School, Greenwich. A long corridor storage area which doubles as an occasionable circulation route out to the playground. (Photo: Mark Dudek)

specialized equipment and resources, such as a shared information technology suite. The pairing, or grouping, of classrooms enables flexibility in areas such as the sharing of practical areas, allowing teachers to work together or separately as and when required, with a variety of different teaching group sizes this flexibility enables.

Primary classrooms should not simply provide a neutral space for teaching and learning, but should also communicate to children something about the ethos of their education, what is being offered and what is expected from them as pupils within the school community. An ordered spacious environment gives them a natural sense of well-being, however, other features, such as the use of colour, the controllability of their environment, and good acoustics will all help to communicate essential messages. The Government wishes to see schools designed to a standard 'comparable to that found in other quality public buildings, to inspire pupils, staff and parents'.[29] This means that a far more sophisticated array of design skills needs to be brought to the table for discussion with future users, especially teachers. Space in classrooms is always limited; yet the space that is available must be utilized in such a way that a wide range of

activities, which form essential elements of the National Curriculum, can occur simultaneously. This is some challenge.

A survey of classrooms in use

In his study entitled *Inside the Primary Classroom*, which was published in 1999, Galton found that the majority of classroom spaces in use were simple enclosed rectangular rooms which were difficult to adapt.[30] Of the various twenty-eight classrooms observed, twenty-two were of the type generally referred to as 'box like', the key characteristics of which were self-contained rooms enclosed by walls and a door which closed them off from the rest of the school as opposed to more open plan arrangements (which can be seen in many working environments today such as contemporary offices, and many institutions of higher education).

The example of a classroom arrangement in an early Victorian building was nicknamed the 'shoebox'. It illustrates even more limitations of space with severe restrictions on the scope for flexibility. This shows how staff delivering the curriculum had to adapt to problems inherent in the building. Teachers used the classroom environment efficiently and ingeniously so that, although the size of the classroom meant that it was impossible to create work bays for different activities, the teacher managed to teach (with some difficulty), all curriculum activities in the space available. A high level of organization and a number of space saving techniques helped to achieve this. These included children being assigned a specific group for each activity organized around a single 6–8 person table. The size of the room meant that the whole class could not sit together within a dedicated 'carpet space' for whole class activities such as story time. Nevertheless, by using rigorous organizational methods the teacher had been able to introduce, in a severely restricted space, a level of flexibility which allowed for individual, group and whole classwork, and which could be tailored to a variety of curriculum activities, without any rearrangement of furniture. However, the effectiveness of these activities is not commented upon. It is likely that the proximity of desks would make it difficult for children to concentrate because of noise and visual disturbances within the confined classroom environment. There was little scope for additional activities such as teacher demonstrations and dedicated ICT zones.

Another example of a classroom type illustrated by Galton is the L-shaped classroom. In this example the smaller part of the 'L' was deemed to be unsuitable for teaching and was therefore used only as storage area. So the remaining teaching area was rectangular and of reduced size, and the presence of fixed storage cupboards down the longer side of the room further reduced the available space for teaching. This resulted in an awkwardly shaped teaching area to accommodate twenty-eight Year 6 pupils. A similar L-shaped configuration was discussed by James Dyck in more positive terms. Describing it as the 'Fat L' he illustrates a much wider variety of layouts than the traditional rectangular form allows, however, it also implies that the overall area requires significantly more space in order for it to work effectively.[31]

Rearranging furniture within the framework of an existing rectangular room to create an inner rectangular row of desks has a number of social benefits. The so-called 'horseshoe' arrangement was used for many activities including class discussions and for most written work, and it also facilitated paired working arrangements. However, it should be noted that the teacher used other furniture layouts according to the demands of the curriculum, particularly when the task required was designed around small groupwork, when the tables needed to be rearranged in blocks. Clearly an important criteria here is the ease with which furniture can be moved around and reconfigured by teachers.

This U-shaped furniture arrangement is claimed to be the most effective for allowing the three main working styles – individual, group and whole class, with a minimum of modification.[32] The other six classrooms in the survey were part of open-plan teaching spaces referred to as 'home units'. The reviewed evidence suggests that the U-shaped or 'horseshoe' arrangement can be an extremely effective way of making the most of any rigid enclosed classroom environment.

As Galton *et al.* (1999) state:

'the "horseshoe" and "shoebox" layouts demonstrates the need for a high degree of flexibility in terms of his or her teaching techniques on the part of the teachers in question. They represent a considered and deliberate response to a difficult situation, overcoming the constraints on an environmentally inadequate or overly confined classroom environment'.

An earlier study assessed the use made of available spaces by both teachers and pupils in open-plan classrooms.[33] A scale plan drawing of each grouping of rooms was made; on this, different functional zones were identified by the teachers in the unit. Observations of the number of pupils and teachers in each space and the activities in which they were engaged were made every 20 minutes throughout the day for a total of three days. Interestingly, the descriptions by Bennett *et al.* (1980) of the use of available space include dedicated 'quiet rooms' which are defined as:

rooms varying in size but not larger than 32 m², having four walls and a door located within the

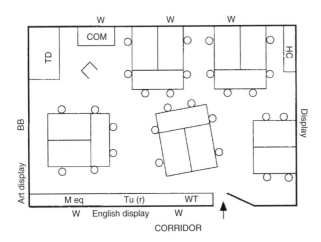

Figure 5.4
Shoebox layout. (Source: Galton *et al.* (1999).[30])

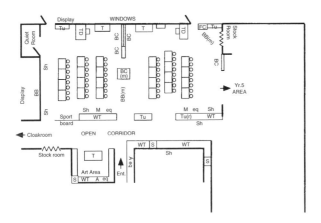

Figure 5.5
L-shaped layout. (Source: Galton *et al.* (1990).[30])

teaching unit. Originally they were conceived to be a self contained room of less than classroom size for the purpose of small class teaching or for noisy activities such as music or TV which could be carried on without distracting children in the rest of the unit.[33]

It was noted that patterns of use were very diverse with the average use of such rooms, in both infant and junior units, ranging from between 4 and 5 per cent for both pupils and teachers; with major factors of under use including, the space being too small for use by the whole class or large groups,

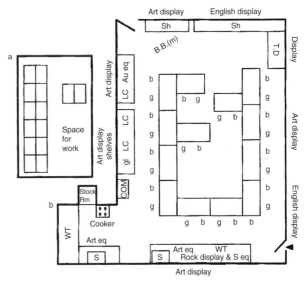

Figure 5.6
Group activity within an L-shaped classroom.
(Photo: Brian Vermeulen.)

Figure 5.7
Horseshoe layout. (Source: Galton *et al.* (1999).[30])

or their location away from other working areas making supervision of the children difficult. The units that teachers felt worked well had two quiet rooms (each 20 m²) either side of a central link area that was used constantly by teachers accessing other areas. The research summarized that:

Quiet rooms that are square and large enough to take the whole class sitting on the floor and

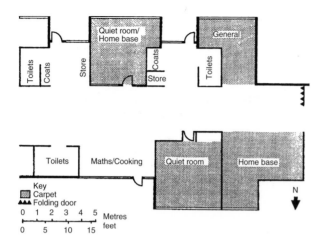

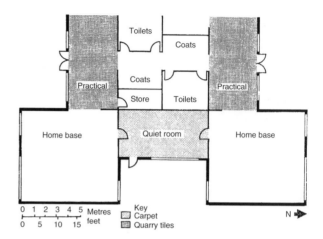

Figure 5.8
Typical open-plan classroom showing quiet rooms. (Source: Bennett *et al.* (1980).[33])

Figure 5.9
Typical open-plan classroom showing location of practical areas. (Source: Bennett *et al.* (1980).[33])

placed centrally for easy supervision would seem to be the most satisfactory from the teacher's point of view.[34]

The next types of space described are 'practical areas' defined as:

those areas which have sinks and floor finishes that are suitable for wet activities such as quarry tiles and vinyl tiles, and are situated within the teaching unit.[34]

It was found that these areas were used slightly more than the 'quiet rooms' with 8.4 per cent of pupils and 13.2 per cent of teachers in infant units, but less, at just over 6 per cent of pupils and teachers in junior units. The study goes on to reveal how the location of a practical wet area can affect its use, with the majority being positioned so that circulation, and therefore organizational problems resulted. Examples of good and bad practice are illustrated in this study. These include, placing the area around a central courtyard which was effective and worked well when access areas were sufficiently wide to allow easy circulation, adequate work space and storage for materials. But if the area was used for dining, or contained toilets, or was used to access other parts of the school it became a source of continual disturbance

and distraction. Placing the activity area centrally generally worked well, however, poor access and visibility were often the by-product.

The 'use of space' observations by Bennett *et al.* (1980)[33] concluded that the way in which teachers and children used space was different in every instance even when the design of the unit was identical. It was also noted by Galton *et al.* that:

Whilst the dimensions and design of a classroom are fixed, and therefore largely beyond the control of the teacher, the challenge is, and always has been, to make the optimum use of what space is available.[35]

Galton *et al.*[30] examine three features of the primary classroom – the teacher's desk, the 'carpet area' and the computer zone, and their effects on the organization of the primary classroom. They recognize that in earlier times the teacher's desk dominated the class. By the 1970s the hierarchical arrangement had changed, with the desk often being found in the corner of the room. The second feature, the carpet areas, are described as 'spaces which have traditionally been marked off as places of shared activities which often involve the whole class with the teacher'.

In both the 1976 and 1996 ORACLE studies the 'carpet area' was an important space, used by

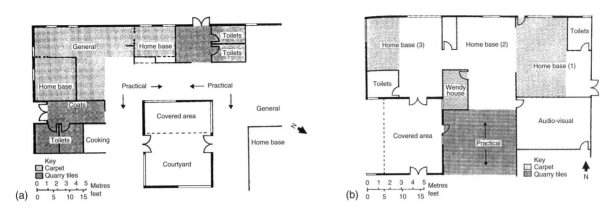

Figure 5.10

(a) Typical open-plan classroom showing location of practical areas (left), and (b) Typical open-plan classroom showing location of practical areas (right). (Source: Bennett *et al.* (1980).[33])

teachers who wanted to talk to the whole class at the same time and independently by children who required additional work space, or as a place for silent reading. Galton *et al.* (1999) noted that:

> these carpet areas continued to be an important part of classroom life, and even in the case of some modern classrooms that were carpeted throughout, a space was often marked out in some way.[36]

It was also noted that this area in many classrooms was used more frequently in the 1996 ORACLE classrooms, with children being moved away from their desks to sit on the carpet midway through the lesson for whole class instruction or discussion, or to bring some variety to the lesson format. In the 1976 ORACLE study on the other hand, the carpeted area was mainly used first thing in the morning to take the register or to outline the day's activities, or at the end of the day to sit and listen to a story. Another development found in the 1996 study was the increased importance of information technology (IT), or as it is now referred to in National Curriculum documentation, information communication technology (ICT). This confirmed the general findings of the Mckinsey survey, *The Future of Information Technology in UK Schools*, which showed a national average of one computer to every seventeen pupils, and that in 40 per cent of primary schools the ratio was 1:20:

> although there was often a dedicated space for a computer, occasionally accompanied by a printer, much of the equipment was relatively old, of varying make, of low specification, and rarely used, so that out of almost a 1,000 records of curriculum activity, just twelve recorded the use of IT.[37]

Eight years on, it is likely that this observation is widely out of date as most UK schools now have reasonably effective ICT, either in the classroom or within dedicated ICT suites.

Past research has tended to identify where classroom arrangements are ineffective rather than informing how the spaces may be adapted to the teacher's advantage. From this it seems clear that teachers and pupils will find it difficult to teach and learn in classrooms organized in a manner that does not match and support the learning activities precisely enough. Children are grouped together in class sizes of around 30 pupils, however in today's classroom they are rarely taught as a single group. Therefore, whole group teaching is not on its own a good enough reason to have group seating arrangements as the overriding design criteria for new primary classrooms. The way teaching is conducted would seem to have implications on how a classroom should be organized; although Alexander *et al.*[19] make reference to the fact that group seating may not be suitable for all learning tasks, none of the literature reviewed makes any recommendations on the physical organization of classrooms. Organizing primary classrooms so that children sit in smaller groups is substantiated by a number of observational studies, however it does not take us very far in understanding the classroom of the future.

Dipping into this educationally derived research, the conclusion must be that the physical context of the classroom should support the teaching and learning methods, and each organizational arrangement should support the particular teaching and learning strategy being implemented at any one time much better than it presently appears to do. As architects working in this field, there is a need to gain further understanding of the best organizational principles for the primary classroom environments and to identify physical organizational needs more precisely. However, it is apparent how little 'architectural' concerns have informed the research which is helping to dictate classroom design. The functional layout is surely not the only factor which affects the success of the education. It perhaps signifies how low architecture has been rated by educationalists responsible for these research studies.

Both the size and layout of the classroom environment in which learning takes place and its overall design have implications on the way in which teachers operate. The range of classrooms in the present school building stock provide some spacious classrooms, which allow for adaptation and movement; by far the majority are small, confined and awkwardly shaped which places constraints on the degree of flexibility possible. How then, should teachers in current classroom environments respond to the demands placed on them, and what is the impact of the National Curriculum on the architecture of the classroom environment of the future?

Key research findings

Whilst investigating aspects of the learning environment, we found relationships between behaviour and human experience on the one hand and the design of the physical setting on the other.[38] It is a complex relationship and evaluation naturally incorporates a degree of personal interpretation. The most common method used in qualitative

research is participant observation, which entails the sustained immersion of the researcher among those whom he or she seeks to study, with a view to generating a rounded, in-depth account of the group. Behavioural mapping has been the key tool in this study, together with key research questions which have been addressed to those teachers involved.

Behavioural mapping is a form of direct observation, tracking the movements of subjects through existing physical settings, whilst observing the kinds of behaviour that occur in relation to these settings. It is empirical, describing observed behaviour both quantitatively and qualitatively. There are three components to this: the description of the environmental setting; the description of the subject; characteristics and the description of the behaviour.

Behavioural mapping is a naturalistic time-sample technique for describing patterns of activity and the use of the physical space. A scaled drawing or a floor plan of a physical space provide the basis of the observational studies, with each area labelled according to the kinds of behaviour expected to occur there. The research refers to classrooms built within the existing building stock. The main body of the research refers to Key Stage 2 classrooms, which accommodate children aged between 7 and 11 (in year groups 3 to 6), exploring the relationship between the classroom environment and the implementation of the National Curriculum.

The study's initial research questions provided the structure for the research methods applied. The prime research question is:

How does the physical environment of the primary classroom influence the effective delivery of the National Curriculum?

From this, five sub-questions can be extracted to determine the parameters of the research. These questions are associated with the classroom environment, teaching and learning, physical organization, and the final question concerning the implications of the study.

1   *What are teachers' perceptions of their classroom environments?* This question utilizes teachers'

experiences in classrooms as a method of gauging how classroom environments currently work.

2 *What is the structure of teaching and learning activities associated with the National Curriculum and the differing uses of the National Curriculum?*

3 *How is the classroom environment being used during the teaching and learning activities associated with the National Curriculum?*

4 *How does the organization of resources in the classroom environment support the teaching and learning activities associated with National Curriculum?* These three questions examine the physical environment in relation to the spatial implications of the National Curriculum through a series of observational studies.

5 *Is it possible to support and improve the design of primary classroom environments to enable a better delivery of the National Curriculum?* This question challenges existing approaches to the design of classrooms.

Of the 44 lessons observed in this study, 12 adhered to the *standard lesson structure*, which ranged in duration from 30 to 70 minutes. *Dual activities* were observed taking place in 20 lessons, with durations ranging from 30 to 100 minutes, and finally 12 lessons were categorized as *multiple activity* lessons, that ranged in their duration from 70 to 100 minutes.

In addition to the order in which activities took place, the amount of time noted in each category was recorded by percentage for each lesson, informing the amount of time spent in each category. It was observed that the percentage of time relating to administration varied from 5.0 to 16.7 per cent of the duration of lessons, and periods of introduction ranged from 2.0 to 16.7 per cent. The periods of the lesson devoted to teaching activities took up the most time and ranged from 50.0 to 85.7 per cent of the lessons observed. Periods of transition between teaching activity in dual and multiple activity lessons ranged from 2.4 to 12.0 per cent. Plenary took between 5.5 and 23.0 per cent of the duration of lessons and concluding stages ranged from 2.8 to 16.7 per cent of the total duration of lessons.

In the lesson structure outlined previously the pupils were all involved in similar teaching activities simultaneously. However, field notes revealed that individual pupils moved on to other activities whilst other members of the class concluded their teaching activity. This often took place in the same location but children were sometimes observed moving to other areas of the classroom as illustrated by Figure 5.11, where children finish an activity and go on to collect books from shelves in the corner (Lesson: 03, Classroom: 01, Time: 34 minutes).

The five main types of pupil activity were recorded using the following categories:

1 Engaged on task
2 Task related
3 Distracted
4 Waiting
5 Other.

The data indicates a considerable degree of consistency across most of the lessons observed. Pupils spent on average 85.2 per cent of their time engaged in tasks, with differences in task engagement ranging from 60.0 to 92.1 per cent. This included periods of administration, introduction to activities and the plenary.

The whole class being distracted was never recorded. However, individual pupils were recorded in the field notes as being distracted by something going on in the classroom, as illustrated by Figure 5.12 (Lesson: 31, Classroom: 11, Time: 16 minutes). The classroom was a converted dining hall, which also served as a corridor between two other classrooms and the rest of the school. Here, another class and teacher are observed moving through the classroom to gain access to another part of the school.

Distractions were also caused by something taking place outside the classroom, such as another class walking past the classroom entrance. Other teachers experienced no interruptions during lessons. This was a chance finding but it was clear that it had a marked effect upon the lesson structure and some pupils' concentration.

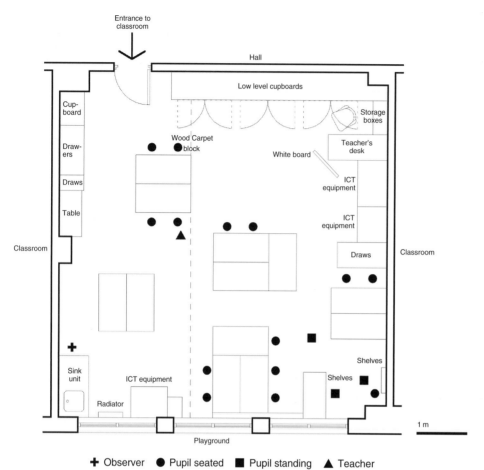

Figure 5.11
Pupil movement between activities (Lesson: 03, Classroom: 01, Time: 34 minutes). (© John Edwards.)

Three main types of teacher activity were recorded using the following categories:

1　Teaching
2　Managing
3　Unrelated.

The data shows that teachers spent on average 81.3 per cent of their time teaching, which in the 44 lessons observed ranged from 66.6 to 93.8 per cent. Time spent managing was very varied ranging from 7.2 to 53.0 per cent, with on average almost one fifth (17.5 per cent) of their time spent managing. A little less (14.8 per cent) was spent on unrelated issues, such as dealing with school administration.

There appeared to be a complex relationship between teaching and managing. The reasons for this included factors such as the teacher wishing to use his or her time differently with different groups, with some activities requiring the minimum of the teachers' or learning support staffs' input. Other reasons included a shortage of equipment required for that particular activity so that only small groups of children could use it at any one time. An important concept here is differentiation. Pupils do not learn at the same rate or in the same way. They need different sorts of instruction, different access to subject matter and varying amounts of practice and reinforcement. Sometimes whole class teaching may provide this, but at other times only differentiating the learning situation in a more radical way can provide this. If an activity requires a substantial teacher input, the teacher must manage his or her time carefully to respond to these needs.

Within the classroom environment learning support staff were observed supporting teaching

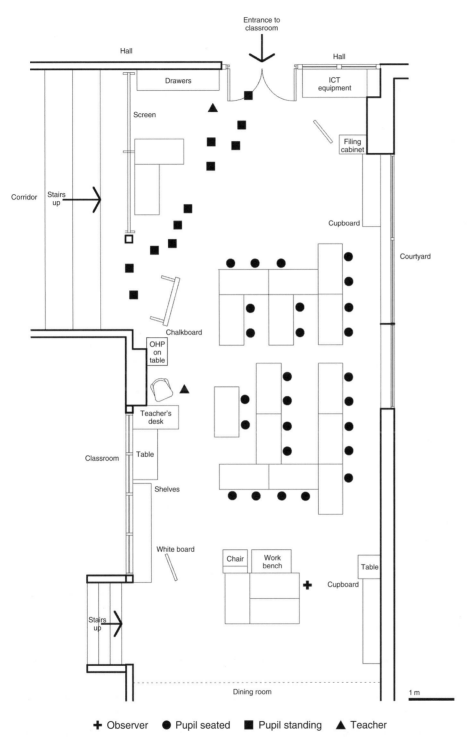

Figure 5.12
Internal distraction (Lesson: 31, Classroom: 11, Time: 16 minutes). (© John Edwards.)

Hall

Entrance to classroom

Drawers

Hall

ICT equipment

Screen

Filing cabinet

Corridor

Stairs up

Cupboard

Courtyard

Chalkboard

OHP on table

Teacher's desk

Classroom

Table

Shelves

White board

Stairs up

Chair

Work bench

Table

Cupboard

Dining room

1 m

+ Observer   ● Pupil seated   ■ Pupil standing   ▲ Teacher

activities, which included consolidating learning, and keeping children engaged in tasks, as well as reading with small groups and individuals. They were also observed supervising practical activities and resolving minor difficulties, often circulating from one group of pupils to another, as well as working with pupils from the class in another location, such as the school library. Their presence

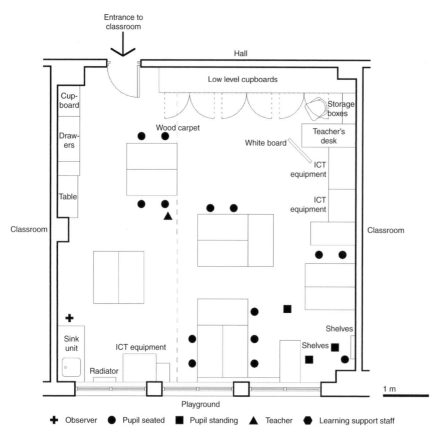

Entrance to classroom

Hall

Low level cupboards

Cup-board

Draw-ers

Wood carpet

Storage boxes

White board

Teacher's desk

ICT equipment

ICT equipment

Table

Classroom

Classroom

Sink unit

ICT equipment

Radiator

Shelves

Shelves

1 m

Playground

✚ Observer   ⬤ Pupil seated   ■ Pupil standing   ▲ Teacher   ⬢ Learning support staff

Figure 5.13
Whole class teaching activity seated at desks (Lesson: 08, Classroom: 03, Time: 10 minutes). (© John Edwards.)

freed the teacher to give more attention to teaching other individuals or groups.

The most common form of class organization recorded was whole class and individual arrangements. Whole class organization was encountered at some point in all 44 lessons ranging from 10 to 100 per cent of the lesson duration. Groups were encountered in only 4 lessons, ranging from 47.0 to 70.9 per cent of the lesson duration, and paired organization in 3 lessons, ranging from 32.3 to 90.0 per cent. Individual organization was noted in 34 of the lessons and varied from 17.0 to 90.0 per cent. The classes were observed leaving the classroom twice. This was for school assembly, however, it was noted by class teachers that the whole class sometimes left the classroom with the teacher to work in another part of the school, such as a computer suite or quiet room.

When the children were observed as a whole class they were undertaking the same activity at the same time, often seated focusing on the teacher at one end of the classroom, which meant some pupils had to turn their chairs in order to see the teacher, as in Figure 5.13 (Lesson: 10, Classroom: 04, Time: 30 minutes), or they were gathered together in one part of the room, such as a carpeted area of the room, as in Figure 5.14 (Lesson: 42, Classroom: 15, Time: 8 minutes). Pupils often worked in groups with another child or individually after a whole class session, during which the teacher had explained the task or activity to follow.

During the course of lessons pupils were observed working with the teacher or a member of support staff in a particular part of the room, as demonstrated in Figure 5.15 (Lesson: 02, Classroom: 01, Time: 03 minutes). Sometimes they were organized in ability groups for specific lessons, which was most common during literacy and numeracy lessons.

However, although there was a high level of variation observed in class organization, the layout

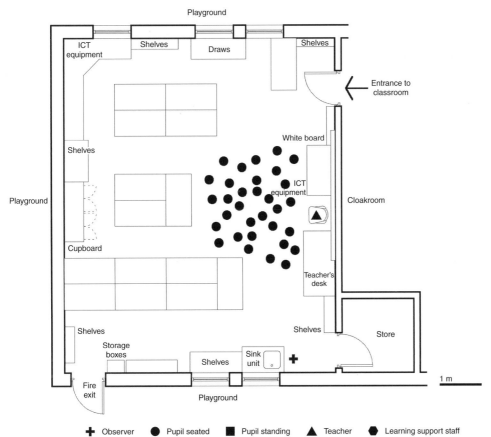

Figure 5.14
Whole class teaching activity seated on floor (Lesson: 42, Classroom: 15, Time: 8 minutes). (© John Edwards.)

➕ Observer ⬤ Pupil seated ⬛ Pupil standing ▲ Teacher ⬡ Learning support staff

of the classrooms did not change significantly and therefore did not reflect the mode of working. Studies of primary classrooms consistently report that primary school pupils spend most of their time working alone. They also show that they get most of their limited direct teaching contact as whole class members, not as individual learners and though teachers spend more of their time with their class as a whole, individual work remains the most common type of activity for children when they are not working with the teacher, amounting to between 17.0 and 90 per cent of a pupil's classroom time.

Although the data collected did not include the type or duration of interactions the teacher had with the pupils, the field notes taken during the observations revealed that the teacher interacted with the whole class, with groups of pupils and individually with pupils. Working individually with the teacher or learning support staff member was a

relatively rare occurrence. This usually depended on the individual needs of each pupil as well as the type of class organization adopted during teaching activities.

By far the greatest amount of time spent interacting with the teacher was as part of whole class teaching activities. The teacher would interact with the whole class, either by addressing pupils where they sat as Figure 5.13 (Lesson: 10, Classroom: 04, Time: 30 minutes) or by arranging the pupils to sit around the teacher on the floor as illustrated in Figure 5.14 (Lesson: 42, Classroom: 15, Time: 8 minutes).

In all the lessons observed there were variations in the time pupils worked in whole class, and in mixed ability groups with the teacher or member of learning support staff. However, these variations took place within the framework of established routines. It appeared that in most classrooms, each pupil had a regular place, but they often moved

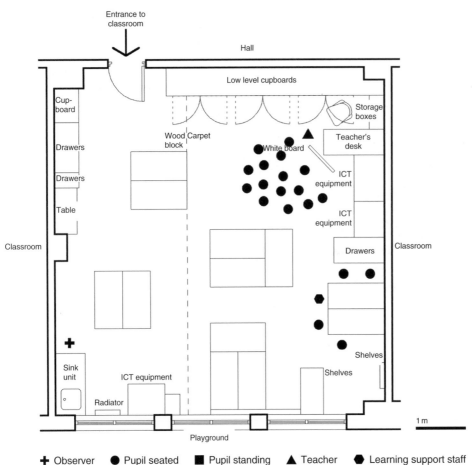

Entrance to classroom

Hall

Low level cupboards

Cupboard

Drawers

Drawers

Table

Wood block

Carpet

White board

Storage boxes

Teacher's desk

ICT equipment

ICT equipment

Classroom

Drawers

Classroom

Sink unit

ICT equipment

Radiator

Shelves

Shelves

1 m

Playground

✚ Observer   ● Pupil seated   ■ Pupil standing   ▲ Teacher   ⬡ Learning support staff

around the room to be seated in ability groups or to work with learning support staff that were present. Pupils were also observed interacting socially with other pupils during the main teaching activity.

Teachers have a tendency to spend extended periods of time in specific locations within the classroom and certain areas were identified as being used more than others. When teachers were interacting with the whole class, they were observed to be less mobile. When teachers were interacting with individual pupils or small groups their movement around the classroom increased.

When analysing the *Classroom Data Sheets* it was found that the teacher's movement around the classroom was very repetitive. However, there was always a preferred route taken by the teacher and usually it was a repeated and predictable route. From this main route the teacher branched out to other locations in the room. No pattern was

found in relation to its location in the classroom layout, but this main route was always present. In summary, the location and movement of the teacher within the classroom does not relate to the layout of the room but to the teaching activity and organization of the class.

Observational studies summary

The lesson observations took place in a varied age range of classroom environments and the research instrument used provided a detailed and descriptive analysis about the structure of lessons and the varying uses of the primary classroom environments. The following is a summary of the research findings:

- Classroom layouts were arranged in either rows, group seating arrangements or a combination of both.

Figure 5.16
A classroom session, briefing and numeracy, whole class. Little space to organize the pupils on the floor, some pupils appear to be sitting partly beneath the tables. Woodlea Primary School, Bordon, Hampshire, UK. (Photo: Tony Weller, the Builder Group Library.)

- Neither classroom age nor size dictates the layout of the classroom, although it was thought to limit the possible arrangement of furniture and resources and was observed to cause circulation problems for both pupils and teachers when too small.

- Lesson structures were found to be a combination of standard, dual activity or multiple activity types. The periods of the lesson devoted to teaching activities took up the most time in lessons and ranged from 50.0 to 85.7 per cent of the lesson. Periods of transition between teaching activity in dual and multiple activity lessons ranged from 2.4 to 12.0 per cent. Plenary took between 5.5 and 23.0 per cent of the duration of lessons and concluding stages ranged from 2.8 to 16.7 per cent of the total duration of lessons.

- The data shows that teachers spent on average 81.3 per cent of their time teaching, which in the 44 lessons observed ranged from 66.6 to 93.8 per cent. Time spent managing was very varied ranging from 7.2 to 53.0 per cent, with on average almost one fifth (17.5 per cent) of their time spent managing; this shows a complex relationship between teaching and managing, and pupils actually learning.

- The most common form of class organization recorded was whole class and individual teaching. Whole class organization was encountered at some point in all 44 lessons ranging from 10 to 100 per cent of the lesson duration. Time spent exclusively in group teaching was seen in only 4 lessons, ranging from 47.0 to 70.9 per cent of the lesson duration, and in paired organization in 3 lessons, ranging from 32.3 to 90.0 per cent. Individual organization was noted in 34 of the lessons and varied from 17.0 to 90.0 per cent.

- By far the greatest amount of time spent interacting with the teacher was as part of whole class teaching activities. The teacher would interact with the whole class, either by addressing pupils where they sat or by arranging the pupils to sit around the teacher on the floor.

- The location and movement of the teacher and learning support staff in the classroom did not relate to the layout of the room but to the teaching activity and organization of the class.

Teacher questionnaires

With regard to questionnaires within the study, three questions were asked of the teachers. The questions were as follows:

Q1   Does the way you teach or the subject matter you teach require any special physical needs within the classroom?

Q2   What do you think about the classroom environment? Do you think the layout and organization of the classroom interferes with the way you teach and if so, how?

Q3   What would you change about your classroom to achieve a more effective teaching/ learning environment?

In the following section a number of the most interesting answers have been chosen to illustrate the range of responses. The restrictive size of classrooms was a recurrent issue commented on by 11 of the teachers questioned. A shortage of teaching space was a concern as well as the lack of storage space and provision of specific resource areas such as ICT. The following response illustrates this:

TIS: C13. *The classroom is not big enough to accommodate all the different [teaching] areas needed, and storage is very limited. The shared area is not utilized to its maximum capacity to avoid disturbing the other class. Carpet area is too small for the whole class, and the display boards are badly placed. A larger carpet area and computers that work would be better. Bookshelves, pupil drawers, and teacher storage are required. We would like a more open environment to enable easier movement.*

There was a strong response in the sample relating to the ability to alter the layout of the classroom environment. In most cases this concern was due to the size of the classrooms, as indicated by the following response:

TIS: C05. *Lots of things are needed but the classroom is too small to fit them in. It would be better if we did not have tables on the carpet area, but at present we take groups of children to the library. The limited space means having to pack away some curriculum activities*

to accommodate others. There is a lack of space and the classroom is too cold in winter, too warm in summer. Blinds on the windows are inadequate. The adjoining walls to the next classroom are thin and therefore acoustics are very bad. An area for two or three computers, and space for children to sit around them comfortably would be ideal. We could also create better learning areas within the classroom, i.e. specific areas for art, however the restrictive size of the classroom makes this impractical.

The acoustic quality of most classrooms was rated as poor, for reasons including noise from other spaces such as halls, other classrooms and dining rooms, and external noise sources such as roads, as indicated by the following responses:

TIS: C01. The floor space near my desk is used a lot by the whole class and the sink and art area in the opposite corner of the room is another important resource for art and science activities, but this may have to reduce in size if the class gets bigger. The classroom is large enough, but there are only 19 children in the class. More children will make it more crowded. In the winter there is inadequate heating and there is insufficient ventilation in summer; the blinds are inadequate on sunny days. *Sometimes noise from the hall and the playground can be disruptive to the pupils, especially when they are setting up dinner tables and clearing away afterwards.* I would like to develop learning areas within the classroom, like the art area and reading and literacy corner, where children could work independently, and an area for plants.

Classroom lighting was only mentioned in 4 responses, all negatively. Responses related mainly to the inability to control natural illumination and the quality of natural illumination, either there being too much or too little. The responses highlighted that a common problem in classrooms was the inability to control or adjust lighting levels as exhibited by the following response:

TIS: C02. The shared workspace is used a lot by the classroom assistants who are working there with numeracy and literacy booster groups all the time. *The classroom has many physical constraints, in* particular the poor lighting (*you have to have the lights on all year round due to the limited number of windows*); not enough plug sockets, and too little space to rearrange the furniture. There is a lack of space and not enough power points to integrate technology properly within the classroom. More storage is required and I would like a cupboard to put teacher's resources securely away from children.

Issues relating to temperature and ventilation were only mentioned in 3 responses (TIS: C04, C05 and C08), which were all negative as the following example illustrates:

TIS: C04. Yes an area or floor area so that the children could be seated as a class. But the classroom is too small to accommodate this and our quiet room is too small. Resourcing all the classrooms would be difficult and some resources may be better grouped in other locations in the school. A balance needs to be met between specialist spaces and classroom activities. It is important to have a variety of spaces within a school that complement the classrooms. I think we definitely need a separate ICT area. *This classroom also has very poor ventilation, the new double glazed windows cannot be opened fully and it can get very hot in summer.*

When analysing the information gathered from questions 06, 07 and 08, many of the teachers identified specific features within the classroom, including floor space, carpet areas and quiet rooms, as well as art and messy areas and book corners or literacy areas, as illustrated by the following responses.

A number of teachers gave detailed responses about what they could change or develop to create a more effective teaching/learning environment. This not only related to specifics within the classroom, but also issues relating to the wider school environment as illustrated by the following responses:

TIS: C14. The classroom is one of the biggest I have ever worked in and generally I am satisfied with it as a teaching environment. *But I would like to develop various areas of the classroom with displays*

and resources that the children can interact with. There is one problem with noise and it is not from the children but from the rain on the roof, this is very noisy.

TIS: C15. I have too many resources and not enough storage space (or teaching space). This is difficult for hands-on activities and science experiments. *I think that some activities cannot be supported properly in the classroom and it would be better to have other [dedicated] spaces for drama, ICT and arts and crafts. We need as many practical areas as possible, without losing any classroom space. We need more shelves/cupboards, art storage areas.*

When comparing the responses of the *Classroom Survey Questionnaire* and the *Teacher Interview Sheet* responses, the most common concerns related to the restrictive size of the classrooms and the ability to alter the organization and layout of the classroom, which were perceived to hinder the delivery of National Curriculum activities. Acoustics, lighting and temperature and ventilation problems were also referred to on both.

Summary of the study

With reference to the question: *Does the primary classroom environment enhance the effective delivery of the National Curriculum?* The study clearly indicates that there is a strong relationship between the classroom environment and the teaching and learning strategies associated with the National Curriculum. The explanation of this answer lies in the collection of the research findings relating to four sub-questions, which are associated with the classroom environment, teaching and learning, and physical organization, and the final question concerning the implications of the study.

What are teachers' perceptions of their classroom environments? The data gathered suggests that teachers both question and recognize problems within their own classrooms and could be considered as experts. Teachers were able to identify problems occurring in the classrooms in which they taught. They have a real need for classrooms that support the teaching and learning strategies of the National Curriculum much more precisely than in previous times. The teachers surveyed were poorly served by the classroom environments in which they work.

The data collected revealed a strong negative response regarding the teacher's ability to alter the layout of the classrooms; clearly they would like to effect change more readily. Similarly, teacher access to resource/storage areas was relatively poor. Pupil access to resource/storage areas was seen as slightly more satisfactory but was still predominantly rated as poor. This is an important aspect of any successful learning space. It felt that there was a lot of pressure on pupils and teachers and the classroom needed to be a more efficient 'machine' for learning in.

Responses to the question of access to the outside of the classrooms varied, but it was seen as being generally satisfactory or not an issue. However, this is more likely down to the lack of any features within the classrooms surveyed that enabled direct access to the outside areas from the classrooms. This suggests that they do not make enough use of the inside—outside dimension in their teaching and pastoral care.

The integration of IT was rated in a range from very poor to very good. However, the majority of responses indicated poor or very poor integration which suggests that some schools are way behind others in this respect.

The most frequent concern by far was the restrictive size of classrooms and the inadequate amount of space available for storage and resources. Issues relating to other criteria used for the coding of responses, i.e. acoustics, lighting, temperature and ventilation, although mentioned in the responses, failed to reveal much evidence about the issues. However, this may have much to do with the low aspirations many teachers have got used to over the past thirty years. Evidence suggests that teachers believed that there was a relationship between teaching activities and the flexibility and adaptability of the classroom layout, indicating that teachers recognize the important role the classroom has in supporting a variety of activities. The need for specialist areas was a frequent response, but not enough space within the existing classroom was available.

The following four questions examine the physical environment in relation to the spatial implications of the National Curriculum.

What is the structure of teaching and learning activities associated with the National Curriculum and the differing uses of the National Curriculum? Lesson structures were found to be a combination of *standard*, *dual activity* or *multiple activities*. The periods of the lesson devoted to teaching activities took up the most time in lessons and ranged from 50.0 to 85.7 per cent of the lesson. Periods of transition between teaching activity in *dual* and *multiple activity* lessons ranged from 2.4 to 12.0 per cent. Plenary took between 5.5 and 23.0 per cent of the duration of lessons and concluding stages ranged from 2.8 to 16.7 per cent of the total duration of lessons.

How is the classroom environment being used during the teaching and learning activities associated with the National Curriculum? The data shows that teachers spent on average 81.3 per cent of their time teaching, which in the lessons observed ranged from 66.6 to 93.8 per cent. Time spent managing was very varied ranging from 7.2 to 53.0 per cent, with on average almost one fifth (17.5 per cent) of their time spent managing. This illustrates a complex relationship between teaching and managing, and affects the amount that pupils actually learn.

The two most common forms of classroom organization recorded were whole class and individual. Whole class organization was encountered at some point in lessons, ranging from 10 to 100 per cent of the lesson duration; as groups in only 4 lessons, ranging from 47.0 to 70.9 per cent of the lesson duration; and as paired organization in 3 lessons, ranging from 32.3 to 90.0 per cent. Individual organization was noted in 34 of the lessons and varied from 17.0 to 90.0 per cent. By far the greatest amount of time spent interacting with the teacher was as part of whole class teaching activities. In this, the teacher would interact with the whole class, either by addressing pupils where they sat or by arranging the pupils to sit around the teacher on the floor.

How does the organization of resources in the classroom environment support the teaching and learning activities associated with the National Curriculum? Classroom layouts were arranged either in rows, group seating arrangements or a combination of both. Neither classroom age nor size dictated the layout of the classroom, although its size was a limitation to the possible arrangement of furniture and resources, and was observed to cause circulation problems for both pupils and teachers. The location and movement of the teacher and learning support staff in the classroom did not relate to the layout of the room but to the teaching activity and organization of the class. Pupil movement within the classroom during teaching activities took place for a number of reasons, for example, to collect materials and equipment.

The final question challenges the existing approaches to classroom design. *Is it possible to support and improve the design of primary classroom environments to enable a better delivery of the National Curriculum?* The study has revealed that the environment is an important resource for teaching and learning. Furthermore, teaching strategies could be better planned and organized to implement the delivery of the National Curriculum. The study provides evidence that is particularly supportive to teachers and architects, and it is hoped that the following sections regarding professional implications and classroom design guidelines can be utilized in a process of collaboration to promote the development and design of better primary classrooms over the next decade.

Conclusion

Initially, this chapter outlined some of the physical implications of the National Curriculum, pointing out that it does not refer specifically to classroom environments and specific ways in which this relates to teaching. However, the research has demonstrated that there is a strong relationship between the physical environment of the classroom and the teaching and learning strategies associated with the National Curriculum. In order to advance this concept through the complex processes of procurement, design and implementation, both

architects and teachers need to be aware of this critical relationship.

Traditionally, classrooms have been designed on the basis of a generalized prediction of activities, functions and teaching styles, with users having to accept what they were given with very little scope to change or adapt the space after it has been handed over. This is especially common in primary schools where teachers 'inherit' a classroom designed for an earlier generation of teachers. They may attempt to make the best of things but they are rarely able to create conditions which optimize contemporary teaching strategies. Therefore, due to the hierarchical nature of the process by which primary classrooms are designed, with little end user consultation, there is a tendency for teachers to be passive and accept the obvious shortcomings of the spaces that they are given.

Teachers are clearly able to identify problems occurring in the classroom environment. This awareness is important, but this alone is not enough to bring about change and there is far too little respect given to teachers' views within the design process. The primary classroom can support or restrict the primary teacher's organizational decisions, decisions about the location of resources and much else. The quality of the classroom environment in general is a significant component of educational efficiency. Teachers who recognize the role of the environment and are dissatisfied with their present classroom environments will be an important catalyst for change, however the teaching profession must be more articulate and knowing in their arguments for better architecture.

Recommendations regarding the physical environment of the classroom have mainly been limited to the enforcement of minimum space standards across the board. Design professionals who can offer creative design solutions often do so with an inadequate understanding of the educational process. All classrooms should meet minimal standards pertaining to the Premises Standards Regulations, however, this alone does not ensure an effective teaching and learning environment. Architects need to go much

Figure 5.17
The architectural pleasure of any school goes beyond the mechanistic functioning of the classroom. Burr elementary School by Architects SOM. Curvaceous internal courtyards are cut out of the traditional block plan, so that the natural semi wooded setting appears to bubble up into the centre of the building. Thus a conceptual rather than a formal process is what makes it architecture according to designer Roger Duffy. (Photo: SOM.)

further. Unfortunately there is a void between meaningful architectural discourse and educational discourses when it comes to conceiving classroom space. This approach often ends with classrooms that provide only a narrow repertoire of dedicated teaching and learning zones. With a few exceptions, even the latest schools designed from department of education guidelines appear to be little different from their twentieth-century counterparts.

The difference between statutory regulations and what are non-statutory guidelines is often confusing. For example, in theory there is no statutory minimum for classroom floor areas, but a precise framework which is accepted as the standard. In practice this forms a straitjacket within which budgetary and procurement systems dictate the end product. It is very difficult for school user clients to tailor their classrooms to the particular context and community within which they are working. It also makes it difficult to innovate and step beyond the constraints of the $54\,m^2$ standard classroom as defined by the guidelines.

One of the key lessons of this study is that there is no standard approach to the design of classrooms. A classroom is not 'a machine for learning in' (although it needs to be efficient); it is more an organic, dynamic entity which should grow to fit a number of variable criteria which are interpreted in a unique way each and everytime.

So there is a need for solutions to meet the existing standards, but also a need to interpret guidelines creatively and to develop design criteria in collaboration with the teachers, which are specific to the context within which the school is located. This will require variations in capital budgets between schools.

To initiate this, two things need to be done. Firstly, staff in particular and pupils should be more articulate about their natural understanding of the environment in which they work. Developing environmental awareness involves understanding the effects that the classroom has on implementing the National Curriculum, through continually reflecting on its different physical characteristics and in turn how these affect the processes of learning and teaching. It is necessary to find ways to give teachers greater authority in both the design and redesigning of the space in which they teach. Things change and the shape of the classroom must be allowed to evolve as teaching strategies move on. Secondly, being environmentally capable of responding to knowledge requires architects to look beyond the statutory and recommended guidelines, which are so often the minimum that government can get away with financially. In areas of high social deprivation, for example, different classroom forms are almost certainly necessary. Architects must have enhanced knowledge about education in order to transform the school environment more efficiently. This requires ongoing research and consultation between teachers and architects about the evolving needs of education. The analogy might be drawn between civil aircraft design, which constantly adapts to the changing needs of its customers and advances its technology due to its manufacturers' deep and intimate relationship with its users, and the economies which dictate competition between Boeing and Airbus.

A clear brief makes it easier to ensure that the classroom environments and supporting spaces within a primary school meet the expectations of the users. However, the brief should be much more than a finite schedule of accommodation. It should also incorporate a process which engages the users through graphic demonstrations of the available options following extensive consultation at early design stages. The brief describes the users, their activities, their needs, preferences and expectations and this is something which should be open to interpretation. Architects rely on this conceptual model of the users during the design process. However, if these models are inadequate the environment will fail to meet the users' needs. If the designs of primary classrooms are to be effectively developed by architects, then it is important that this is done in close collaboration and discussion with teachers. Good clients create good buildings.

The classroom brief should not be seen as a static document and should be developed, allowing time to advance and refine its objectives, particularly as teaching methods and classroom resources are continuously developing. Not only do architects need to know what kind of teaching and learning they are supporting in primary school environments, it is also necessary to appreciate that the needs of users is a constantly evolving process.

In relation to this there are numerous matters to consider, including individual learning styles, pedagogical strategies and learning objectives. Teachers must be critical and active participants in the classroom design process, with the process being as broad and as inclusive as possible. If

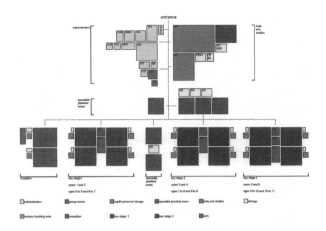

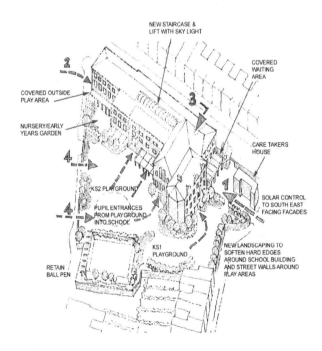

Figure 5.18
The author prepared this summary of key site issues which emerged as a result of an extensive process of consultation with the existing school users. The design development process was intended to heighten awareness of design issues amongst the school users prior to actual design proposals by the architect. Mark Dudek Associates, working for Lewisham Schools PFI as design adviser, May 2003. The schedule of accommodation is laid out as a colour-coded block diagram. This shows the relative scale of all rooms, so that staff can compare the staffroom with a year three classroom. The lower image shows the existing school as a sketch aerial view.

95

the impact of primary school investment is to be optimized, the way forward is through designing, renovating and remodelling primary school environments so they provide not only sufficient space and adequate conditions, but also inspirational places for learning. Physical changes could include simple modifications such as choosing more appropriate age-related furniture types, arranging furniture according to activity needs, or acquiring and integrating learning technologies that work into everyday curriculum activities. Detail design is important, but so too are large-scale changes that may include redesigning the entire school building in order to cluster certain activities, such as information communication technology, or offer an additional range of spaces to complement existing classroom environments which may be difficult to adapt. It is something of a conundrum, how do you design for change in the future, yet also for quite specific functional requirements in the present? Like airplanes, it may be necessary to build classrooms which are disposable after a certain time, to accommodate the evolving needs of education and society. Governments need to think seriously about the undoubted financial implications; in other words, how committed they are to educating their people? Education is failing too many. We need more funding, more flexibility, more freedom for teachers to customize the curriculum to individual children, more mentoring, better classrooms, and more imagination. That is how important changing attitudes are and making the classroom fit for the twenty-first century.

What follows is a checklist to consider, which it is hoped will help architects, clients and users. These recommendations can also be considered in both the refurbishment and the extension of existing facilities.

The classroom is a shared space and a balance needs to be struck between the needs of the teaching staff, the needs of children and the resources available. The architecture, furniture and technology must be integrated to provide quick, easily reconfigurable rooms. To accommodate these changes the classroom needs to be larger, more flexible, and technology enhanced, promoting relaxed interactions and encouraging a sense of community:

- Consider the need for secure storage for teachers' personal possessions
- Provide storage which is only accessible to teachers but storage which is accessible to children as appropriate
- Particularly at key stage 2, the classroom needs enough space for pupils to be organized in different groupings
- Circulation routes around the classroom need to be clear and unencumbered; the primary route should remain the same even when furniture layouts change
- The National Curriculum dictates specific activities; zones for these activities within the classroom should be identified and provided for in addition to the general teaching area, space permitting
- The position of the teacher's desk needs to be considered, particularly as the teacher moves around the space constantly; it may need to be centrally located
- Whole class teaching will require a single focus for teacher demonstrations to all 30 children; consider the shape of the space to provide minimal distraction when children adopt a single focus
- Instructional resources such as white boards require space for teacher demonstrations and pupil interaction
- Furniture should be robust but also attractive to encourage and help motivate children
- The classroom will support a range of activities simultaneously, a single rectangular form may not be appropriate, rather subsidiary spaces off the main space to provide special interactive learning zones
- Adaptable lighting, which supports a variation in the location, and focus of activities should be considered
- Acoustics are important when different activities are taking place within the same space
- The integration of computers and digital technology needs to be anticipated

- A well-organized classroom will be functional with materials, tools and equipment arranged ergonomically so they are easy to find, use and store away
- Curriculum resources needed to support learning activities should be identified and should dictate the layout of the room
- The display of children's work should be integrated into the classroom and should not be too distracting or overpowering.

The planned layout of an activity area should match the intentions of the activity, with resources in close proximity, making sure that frequently used classroom materials are accessible to pupils. This will minimize the amount of time preparing for activities, concluding stages and periods of transition from one activity to the next. In addition, the rapid advances in information technology are and will continue to have a major impact on classroom design and it is likely that new classroom spaces will be needed for new educational purposes as these are developed and introduced to primary practice.

The influence of the classroom environment is continuous and how well the environment works over time will relate directly to the teaching and learning strategies imposed. If done correctly the resulting classroom will be perceived as flexible and/or adaptable. Teachers may override the system, so they always have other options. Such approaches aim to maximize the amount of time that teachers can spend teaching.

As has been shown in this chapter, teaching and learning methods associated with the National Curriculum are very varied, ranging from whole class instruction to individual, self-directed learning. There is a tendency for primary classrooms to be perceived as inflexible. Given the opportunity and appropriate tools, alternatives and modifications to existing classrooms could be explored, and these explorations would suggest interesting alternatives to present classroom environments. Making active changes through experimenting with a variety of spatial organizations and layouts would challenge the accepted norm and develop more innovative classrooms. It does feel as if we

are still using a nineteenth-century model – the very term 'classroom' emphasizes this antiquated form.

Appendix A

Literacy hour lesson structures are as follows:

1. Approximately 15 minutes shared reading and writing – whole class

   Shared writing provides many opportunities for pupils to learn, apply and reinforce skills in the context of a larger group with careful guidance from the teacher. Teachers should use texts to provide ideas and structures for the writing and, in collaboration with the class, compose texts, teaching how they are planned and how ideas are sequenced and clarified and structured. Shared writing is also used to teach grammar and spelling skills, to demonstrate features of layout and presentation and to focus on editing and refining work. It should also be used as a starting point for subsequent independent writing. Wherever possible, shared reading and writing should be interlinked. For example, over a five-day period a teacher may plan to (a) introduce a text, (b) work on it through shared reading and then (c) use the text as a 'frame' for writing or as a stimulus to extend, alter or comment on it.
   (DfEE, 1998: 11)

2. Approximately 15 minutes word level work – whole class

   There must be a systematic, regular and frequent teaching of phonological awareness, phonics and spelling throughout Key Stage 1. Teachers should follow the progression set out in the word level objectives carefully. It sets out both an order of teaching and the expectations of what pupils should achieve by the end of each term. The work must be given a specific teaching focus in the Literacy Hour.

Although it is essential that these decoding skills are practised and applied in shared reading, they also need to be taught through carefully structured activities, which help pupils to hear and discriminate regularities in speech and to see how these are related to letters and letter combinations in spelling and reading. The majority of pupils can learn these basic phonic skills rapidly and easily. Word recognition, graphic knowledge, and vocabulary work should also have a teaching focus during this period of 15 minutes. At Key Stage 2, this time should be used to cover spelling and vocabulary work and the teaching of grammar and punctuation from the sentence level objectives. For Key Stage 1 pupils, these sentence-level objectives should be covered in the context of shared reading and writing and this remains an important context for teaching skills at Key Stage 2. Nevertheless, teachers will need to plan a balance of word and sentence level work for this second part of the Hour, across each half-term, to ensure that all these objectives are covered. (DfEE, 1998: 11)

3   Approximately 20 minutes guided group and independent work

> *This section of the Literacy Hour has two complementary purposes:*
>
> - *to enable the teacher to teach at least one group per day, differentiated by ability, for a sustained period through guided reading or writing;*
> - *to enable other pupils to work independently and individually, in pairs or in groups and without recourse to the teacher.*
>
> *Guided reading is the counterpart to shared reading. The essential difference is that, in guided reading and writing, the teacher focuses on independent reading and writing, rather than modelling the processes for pupils. Guided reading should be a fundamental part of each school's literacy programme. In effect, it takes the place of an individualised reading*

programme and, as a carefully structured group activity, it significantly increases time for sustained teaching. In ability groups of four to six, pupils should have individual copies of the same text. The texts need to be carefully selected to match the reading level of the group. In the early stages pupils should meet texts of graded difficulty as they progress. These texts will often be selected from reading schemes or programmes and can usually be built up from existing book stocks with some careful supplementation. At Key Stage 1, teachers should introduce the text to the group, to familiarise them with the overall context of the story and point out any key words they need to know. Pupils then read it independently, while the teacher assesses and supports each pupil in the group. The same principles apply at Key Stage 2. However, as pupils progress, the teaching should focus increasingly on guided silent reading with questions to direct or check up on the reading, points to note, problems to solve etc., to meet the text level objectives in the Framework.

Guided writing – as with guided reading, these writing sessions should be to teach pupils to write independently. The work will normally be linked to reading, and will often flow from work in the whole class-shared writing session. These sessions should also be used to meet specific objectives and focus on specific aspects of the writing process, rather than on the completion of a single piece of work. Often, these teaching inputs can be followed through during independent work in subsequent sessions. For example, pupils might focus on:

- *planning a piece of writing to be continued independently later;*
- *composing a letter;*
- *expanding or contracting a text to elaborate, summarise, etc.;*
- *constructing complex sentences;*
- *connecting points together in an argument;*
- *editing work into paragraphs, headings, etc. for clarity and presentation.*

Independent work – often this happens at the same time as the guided group work. The class needs to be carefully managed and the pupils well trained so that they are clear about what they should be doing and do not interrupt the teacher. There are many forms of organisation ranging from a carousel of ability groups, with a rotation of activities for each group, to completely individual work, e.g. a whole class writing activity derived from an earlier shared writing session. Independent tasks should cover a wide range of objectives including:

- *independent reading and writing;*
- *phonic and spelling investigations and practice;*
- *comprehension work;*
- *note-making;*
- *reviewing and evaluating;*
- *proof-reading and editing;*
- *vocabulary extension and dictionary work;*
- *handwriting practice;*
- *practice and investigations in grammar, punctuation and sentence construction;*
- *preparing presentations for the class.*

Pupils should be trained not to interrupt the teacher and there should be sufficient resources and alternative strategies for them to fall back on if they get stuck. They should also understand the importance of independence for literacy, and how to use their own resources to solve problems and bring tasks to successful conclusions. (DfEE, 1998: 12)

4   Final 10 minutes – plenary session with the whole class:

The final plenary is at least as important as the other parts of the lesson. It is not a time for clearing up and should be clearly signalled as a separate session when the whole class is brought together. It should be used to:

- *enable the teacher to spread ideas, re-emphasise teaching points, clarify misconceptions and develop new teaching points;*

- *enable pupils to reflect upon and explain what they have learned and to clarify their thinking;*
- *enable pupils to revise and practise new skills acquired in an earlier part of the lesson;*
- *develop an atmosphere of constructive criticism and provide feedback and encouragement to pupils;*
- *provide opportunities for the teacher to monitor and assess the work of some of the pupils;*
- *provide opportunities for pupils to present and discuss key issues in their work.* (DfEE, 1998: 13)

Notes

1 Article by Herman Hertzberger, *Harvard Educational Review*, 1969
2 Jackson, P. W. (1968). *Life in Classrooms*. New York: Holt Rinehart and Winston.
3 Architecture as opposed to building has been described and explained in many different ways; the following is from Laugier (1753): 'The sight of a building, perfect as a work of art, causes a delightful pleasure which is irresistible. It stirs in us noble and moving ideas and that sweet emotion and enchantment which works of art carrying the imprint of a superior mind arouse in us. A beautiful building speaks eloquently for its architect' from *Companion to Contemporary Architectural Thought*, Farmer, B., Louw, H., (eds). Routledge: London, Preface.
4 Bennett, N. and Kell, J. (1989). *A Good Start? Four Year Olds in Infant School.* Oxford: Blackwell.
5 Dean, J. (1992). *Organising learning in the primary school classroom* (2nd ed). London: Routledge.
6 Hastings, N. and Wood, K. C. (2002). *Reorganizing Primary Classroom Learning.* Buckingham: Open University Press.
7 Barker, R. G. (1978). *Habitats, Environments and Human Behaviour.* San Francisco: Jossey-Bass.
8 Herbert, E. (1998). How school environment affects children. *Educational Leadership*, **56**(1), 69–70.

9 Clegg, D. and Billington, S. (1994). *The Effective Primary Classroom: Management and Organisation of Teaching and Learning.* London: David Fulton.

10 Stewart, J. (1986). *The Making of the Primary School,* Milton Keynes: Open University Press. House of Commons, Select Committee on Education, Science and the Arts (1986). *Achievement in Primary Schools,* London: HMSO.

11 Byrne, D., Williamson, B. and Fletcher, B. (1974). *The Poverty of Education.* Oxford: Martin Robertson.

12 Pollard, A. (1997). *Reflective Teaching in the Primary School: A Handbook of the Classroom* (3rd ed.): London: Cassell Education.

13 Mortimore, P., Sammons, P., Stoll, L., Lewis, D. and Ecob, R. (1988). *School Matters: The Junior Years.* Wells: Open Books.

14 Campbell, R. J. and Neill, S. R. (1994). *Primary Teachers at Work.* London: Routledge.

15 DES (1967). *Children and their Primary Schools. A Report of the Central Advisory Council for Education (England). Vol. 1: The Report. (Plowden Report):* London: HMSO.

16 Bealing, D. (1972). The Organization of Junior School Classrooms, *Educational Research*, **14**, 231–235. Moran, P. R. (1971). 'The Integrated Day', *Educational Research*, **14**, 65–69.

17 Bealing, p. 235. (See note 17.)

18 Alexander, R., Rose, J. and Woodhead, C. (1992). *Curriculum Organisation and Classroom Practice in Primary Schools: A Discussion Paper.* London: DES.

19 Alexander, *et al.* p. 35. (See note 19.)

20 Alexander, *et al.* p. 43. (See note 19.)

21 Blatchford, P., Kutnick, P. and Baines, E. (1999). *The Nature and Use of Classroom Groups in Primary Schools.* Final report to ESRC.

22 McPake, J., Harlen, W., Powney, J. and Davidson, J. (2000). *Practices and Interactions in the Primary Classroom.* Scottish Council for Research in Education Interchange Number 60.

23 Great Britain (1988). Education Reform Act 1988. London: HMSO.

24 DfEE and QCA (1999). *The National Curriculum Handbook for Primary Teachers in England, Key Stages 1 and 2.* London: HMSO.

25 DfEE, p. 26.

26 DfEE, p. 50.

27 DfEE, p. 9.

28 Commission for Architecture and the Built Environment

29 Galton, M., Hargreaves, L., Comber, C., Wall, D. and Pell, A. (1999). *Inside the Primary Classroom: 20 Years On.* London: Routledge & Keegan Paul.

30 Illustrated in *Architecture of Schools*, Dudek, M. (2000). Architectural Press: London.

31 McNamara, D. and Waugh, D. (1993). 'Classroom Organisation: A Discussion of grouping Strategies in the light of the '3 Wise Men's Report', School Organisation*, **13**, 1, 44–50.

32 Bennett, N., Andreae, J., Hegarty, P. and Wade, B. (1980). *Open plan schools: teaching, curriculum, design.* Windsor: NFER Publishing for the Schools Council.

33 Bennett, *et al.* pp. 168–170. (See note 33.)

34 Hastings, N. and Schwieso, J. (1995). Tasks and Tables: the effects of seating arrangements on task engagement in primary classrooms. *Educational Research*, **37**, 279–291.

35 Galton, p. 43. (See note 30.)

36 Galton, p. 37.

37 Proshansky, H. M. (1976). Environmental Psychology: A Methodological Orientation, in H. Prohansky, W. H. Ittelson and L. G. Rivlin (eds) *Environmental Psychology – People and their Physical Settings* (2nd edn). New York: Holt, Rinehart and Winston, pp. 59–69.

John Edwards works with various architects and designers whose hands-on experience give an important insight about value and quality in the education sector.

6

The classroom as an evolving landscape

Prue Chiles

Editor's introduction

Twenty-seven of the recent UK Government's 'classrooms of the future' pilot projects are now complete. Prue Chiles reflects on this important Government initiative as one of four architects building classrooms in the Sheffield area. She explains how she responded to the challenge of designing a 'classroom of the future', combining extensive consultation with the users, particularly the children, with the usual restrictions of a tight budget and safety concerns. She was keen to hear what children had to say, and to act on their advice. Her views on this process are particularly interesting viewed in the context of the constant presence of teachers, who often tried to influence and interpret the opinions of the children.

There is a clear philosophical view on the difficult subject of 'the future' and all that implies. During the twentieth century, the future was viewed as being unequivocally about the liberating effects of science and technology on our lives. Today, we are less sure about this, as the exploitation of the planet is becoming much more apparent. The concept she grapples with here is balancing technology with issues of accountability to the wider environment. She brings in the concept of nature as a civilizing counter weight, and

uses the external areas around her new building to encourage more interaction.

The relationship built up with the school after a three-year relationship with its staff and pupils is one which enables the architects themselves to learn. Ballifield Primary School is used as a test bed to explore both the school childrens', teachers' and the architect's attitudes to what a classroom of the future should be and to describe how these aspirations were transformed in the final built project. What is most gratifying is to hear about the mistakes and problems which the architects confess to; this is no egotistical vanity building, it is a flawed piece of work, with compromises which mean some aspects of its technology work, and some do not. Her honest self-reflective approach is unusual, and lends weight to the need to view these projects as evolving processes, which must be able to adapt and change to the needs of the users. As architects, we can learn a lot from this process.

Introduction and background to the project

In 2000, the Government's Department for Education and Skills (DfES) piloted twenty-seven new school projects around the country in an initiative called 'classrooms of the future'. By starting with a polemical question 'what is "a classroom of the future"?', it encouraged both a design-led approach and an exploration of where the theory of the classroom design meets practice. David Miliband, the government minister involved, described the challenge as 'designing inspiring buildings that can adapt to educational and technological change'.[1]

Chris Bissell from the DfES, the initiator of 'the classrooms of the future' initiative sums up his expectations:

> *to deliver the best and most effective education exploiting all the possibilities of the information age, school buildings need to reflect advances in technology. They need to provide a pleasant and comfortable environment for learning and to use architectural and design features to stimulate children's imaginations. And they need to be open to wider use, binding schools to their local communities.*

The project encapsulates all the Government's latest education initiatives. The classrooms need to be technology-led, open to local community use, matched to the curriculum and to be comfortable, healthy and inclusive. ICT is being championed by the DfES and others as the key to flexible ways of teaching and communication. It was clear that using new technologies was the most important theme – the future embodied in technology generally and information technology in particular. There was also an interest in the 'classroom of the future' initiative to develop a new modular or universal solution to the existing challenge of replacing all the delapidated mobile classrooms currently littering our school sites up and down the country. The argument for universality and prototypes is powerful. It is consistent with contemporary forms of building procurement, and in a return to 1960s thinking, some of the classrooms of the future nationally are suggesting prototypes for modular buildings; repeatable units to be attached to any school. This gives ease of erection and much reduced design time and costs in the long run.

The argument for individual, special buildings with specific details is inevitably more difficult to justify and is arguably less cost-effective in the long run. Discussions between the architects and the four chosen schools in Sheffield had already established an understanding of what each particular school required, the schools' teaching and learning agenda and their individual characteristics. All the schools had very different priorities.

Ballifield Community Primary School, one of the schools chosen, is a successful and popular school in the local community. It was built in the early 1970s. It is a single storey brick building with an interesting open-plan layout. However, the school has particular problems. Ballifield's priority was to replace two rundown, temporary classrooms with technology-filled new classrooms. The school is also completely inaccessible with level changes throughout its interior landscape. Ballifield has never had a disabled child or parent in the school because they can not be catered for – there are too many steps everywhere.

The school is right on the edge of Sheffield, a former industrial city which now suffers from considerable deprivation due to the loss of its industrial base over the past thirty years. However, it is surrounded by generous green sloping grounds and looks over fields separated from the school by a recently restored ancient hedge.

The final brief for the 'classroom of the future' project at Ballifield incorporates two new classrooms with a new main entrance, cloakroom, toilets and offices. We decided that the new classrooms were to be placed at the front entrance to the school instead of being hidden away as stand alone classrooms on the edge of the playground, like the rundown mobile classrooms they were replacing. The project aimed to solve the inadequate entrance and access problems, discussed by staff and parents, and create a new image for the school for both the children and the community. The new entrance became nearly as important as the classrooms, changing the character of the whole school and raising aspirations as an important by-product of its novelty.

Although new technology was a crucial element in the scheme at Ballifield, the project developed as a part of an exploration of themes in children's lives today. We, the architects, took the opportunity to design classroom environments specifically tailored to the needs of the school and the children.

In this chapter the key themes are explored and then put in context of the consultation we carried out with the teachers and the children, and the resulting building that took shape. As with all of our work, we place the users at the centre of our design process. With a school this has significant additional implications, as we need to consult with the children as well as the teachers. The process was helped in this respect by our relationship with the School of Architecture at the University of Sheffield. Students helped to develop and sustain a deep process of participatory design.

The relationship between children, technology and nature

Technology changes our whole outlook on life; it has acquired the power to determine ideas, beliefs and myths to such an extent that all our thinking, as well as our activities, is now situated within that technological context. The word 'nature', which in the past described the natural world, has been displaced by 'environment' – which has a more technological resonance. More than that 'Technology has been used to change so much of our surroundings that it is rarely correct to talk of the natural environment – this is observable and quantifiable'.[2]

One of the key themes to be explored in the classroom is the relationship between nature and technology. Nature is still key in fashioning our lives; take the natural weather conditions for example. For the past thousand years we have been influenced by the Benedictine idea of the world of Mankind within the world of nature. This notion stressed the creative transformation of nature and the idea of the careful stewardship of resources. Now, with the technological 'know how', we can help solve the problem of dwindling resources with man-made systems that are superior to natural systems.

Technology versus nature is one of the most poignant relationships in our world today. Many

of us have a desire to return to a more natural way of life but we also need and use technology, devouring the latest gadgetry and innovations it provides us with. This relationship is played out in the classroom. Blue-tooth technology and laptops can allow the children to wander around with their technology, even outside. They can explore natural phenomena with the help of high technology, either by using the internet, using video technology, or by recording and analysing what they can observe on the computer.

However, in the design of classrooms it also becomes a dilemma. There is, in our view, a direct conflict between the amount of technology used and the strain that has on the natural environment. The more ICT equipment in the classrooms, the more heat extraction is needed. The more white boards are used the less natural light, and particularly sunlight, are welcome in the room. Using more natural materials, that are often quite hard, and having light airy spaces can make it more difficult to maintain the required noise levels. Just as one primary school is exposing the original Victorian high ceiling and opening up the classroom to light, air and space, other primary schools are installing suspended ceiling tiles to improve acoustic and thermal performance. Being aware of these conflicts is crucial in overcoming them successfully and creatively.[3]

Ballifield School received funding awards to provide ICT equipment in the new classrooms. This included 30 laptops and an interactive white board provision. Undoubtedly, technological advances allow a flexibility in the classroom in terms of wider communication and global reach. However, technology should also be in the service of the natural world, not only helping us to understand the world around us but also to achieve a healthy, breathing, responsive classroom environment. This is part of the lesson to be learnt through our new classrooms.

The healthy classroom

Closely associated with a natural environment is a healthy environment. It is now widely known that a healthier environment, with more natural light and ventilation, aids concentration and therefore learning, but we are still designing school classrooms that are not as healthy as they could be, with too little ventilation and too much unnecessary artificial lighting and heating. They are filled with unhealthy cheap materials, for example, carpets that give off chemicals known for their carcinogens and the copious use of medium density fibreboard (mdf). We are still solving the practical problems of the last forty years in classroom design; this fundamental building ecology still needs to be solved and should form the basis for any classroom of the future.

The dilemma here is that it is as much about how the classrooms are used as how they are built. The teachers and the children need to feel comfortable, and a combination of never having been shown how to use the technologies properly and the need for immediate comfort, sometimes negates the positive effect of the natural technologies. Children

have a higher resistance to cold than adults and our experience during this project is that most classrooms are too hot.

The design of Ballifield classrooms prioritized the less visible sustainable technologies associated with a healthy environment. Specifying healthy materials is still a price lottery and we are working within the framework of very tight budgets. Good quality 'new' materials and interesting shapes are undoubtedly more expensive than the 'bog standard' approach to specification. There were a number of difficult choices to be made between different forms of technology in this respect. We lost the battle with rainwater recycling but kept the healthy breathing wall and recycled insulation. We achieved the healthy natural carpet on the balcony but lost on the type of natural paints we wished to use. We lost the wind power operated laptops but managed to encourage recycling, by making it explicit in the fabric of the classroom.

Figure 6.1
Detail of flap down table showing Warmcell recycled newspaper insulation.

Schoolchildren are knowledgeable about their environment and vocal, as the consultation process showed, but they need to be convinced that the adult world takes sustainable issues seriously. What better place to do this than in the classroom, with the classroom as the raw material for this rhetoric. At Ballifield the sustainable issues and the construction itself became a teaching device – apparent and visible. If the children can see how their recycled newspapers and plastic bottles from home can be used, recycling seems more worthwhile and understandable.

As part of an early evaluation we are writing a classroom manual with the children on the materials used and the structure and construction. Important information and instructions are being inscribed on the walls.

The paradox we are left with is that Government spending limits per school prohibit most sustainable technologies being employed, and the de-skilled and conservative construction

industry still finds it difficult to implement these new technologies. Until sustainable materials are common currency and therefore inexpensive, we will have to carry on proving their worth.

A classroom appropriate for the curriculum and new ways of learning

In recent years, there have in our view been enormous steps forward in the curriculum and the way our children are taught, but very little has changed in the classrooms we are providing for that new learning. The 'classroom of the future' initiative made the assumption that classrooms are still appropriate environments to initiate new ways of learning.[4] So this project is limited in its scope in terms of the relationship of the classroom to the whole school environment and how that might be challenged. In mainstream primary classrooms the curriculum needs are more diverse than in specialist facilities for senior schools or specialist schools. In primary schools, the curriculum has

Figure 6.2
Recycled worktop.

different emphases. It relies almost entirely on the different ways teachers team teach together in paired classes; their teaching methods change over the academic year, and will again over the coming decade. Therefore the need for flexibility is paramount. We were, then, looking for solutions that were transferable. We saw the future as a place where the curriculum and method of teaching will change but in which the environment, both technological and natural, plays a crucial part in the development of a child's knowledge and understanding of the world. We used the model of paired classrooms which are interchangeable and flexible as a fundamental design principle.

After the consultation phase, which is explained in more detail later, we were quite confident at Ballifield that we understood how a particular pair of teachers taught in two class bases together and we thought we understood what we could include in one room and not the other. One room became about technology and the other more about

nature. They would look visibly different and they would share or swap facilities in the afternoons. By and large the rooms work well and everyone seems to be enjoying the spaces, but we learned some important lessons about being too prescriptive. We also learned that usually specific facilities are adaptable and are the ones that are most enjoyed and cherished.

Placing facilities, such as a sink, for example, in only one of the classrooms was not ideal; it reduces flexibility in the future. The head teacher is now planning to put a sink in the technology classroom where jointly we decided not to put one. The experiment at Ballifield in swapping the class bases over works for some lessons, but the number of children and the demands of the curriculum mean the same facilities are sometimes needed in both classrooms.

The most important element between the classrooms is the sliding screen. This allows the classroom to be opened up and closed down at

Figure 6.3
Two classrooms working together with folding screen in open position.

will. We tried to make this look as if it is just another wall, that you can move at will, covered in the same birch veneered plywood. This element has not been without its problems. It worked well for a while in use, but the way it was being opened, and the way it was built, meant it became heavier and soon too heavy to open. These are difficult elements to get right. This has proved an annoyance to both class bases as it prevents the free flow, mobility and flexible use – one of the most important factors in the whole design.

In consultation, pupils asked for their own private space. They also wanted something that would be a little different. We suggested a balcony or mezzanine, responding to the need for creating a space to withdraw to, one that could be fun and different. The DfES are recognizing that with a policy of inclusivity there is a greater need to be able to take children away, but not completely away, from the classroom. Also, the initiative of Quality Circle Time, an established social skills/citizenship aspect of the curriculum requires a space where all children sit in a circle and each child talks about a given subject equally and democratically. This needs to be a special place away from the tables and chairs, the stuff of everyday.

The balcony was designed with a ship metaphor in mind, a popular theme in the children's ideas which came out of the consultation, with a crow's nest or maybe a top cabin with portholes for long views. At Ballifield, out of one window on a clear day, you can see as far as Sherwood Forest, twelve miles away. It has a sloping balustrade to lean against and a soft natural carpet to lie on. It should have brightly coloured cushions to sit on, as requested by some children in the early post-evaluation, but these have not materialized yet.

It was enormously difficult to make this balcony work. Initially we were told it would need a lift. We resisted saying the staircase with portholes and low level lights was part of the experience and so a chair lift was more appropriate. The door to the balcony is quite a secret, looking like the other storage cupboard doors. The whole experience encourages the children to remove themselves from their day to day classroom environment and to dream ... Perhaps this has been too successful, as

the teacher says he forgets it is there and finds it difficult to use it for the whole class, although it is big enough. It also has some unexpected uses. Eye tests, for example, and counselling sessions in small groups. There were some reservations that it was a little dangerous, as the children could swing from the roof structure or throw themselves over, but this worry has abated. Unfortunately, I noticed it was also being used for storage too. New and unusual spaces have to be worked at, tried out and experimented with and the design team need to help in this and persuade teachers to take time out of a curriculum-packed day.

The inside and the outside

The very nature of Sheffield as a city of hills and valleys means many schools in Sheffield enjoy great long views. Ballifield is no exception. The exterior space around the classrooms has the potential to provide different experiences on different levels. We reflected this in the design of the external spaces. Working with a landscape architect,[5] we tried to reflect the inside spaces outside and to wrap different types of the planting around places that the whole class or smaller groups might congregate. The outside classroom became as important as the inside. It seemed to be the key for exploration – more liberating and free than the inside in good weather. There is a pond, a wetland area, fruit and nut trees, paths, steps, slippery grass slopes, rope balustrades and hedges. One enormous (or it will be in 15 years) hedge in the shape of a whale will swim alongside the building. A long-term plan such as this is totally dependent on the will of the school and the head teacher. Of course maintenance is a huge issue. There are two planted walls, with an evergreen honeysuckle that will need to be maintained. Hopefully it will be so much part of the building it will be maintained as a matter of course; particularly the hedge that forms around the main entrance, which will give the whole school its 'image'.

It was less easy to pin down teachers on how the new pond (larger and more accessible than the previous one) will be used. They need time to develop lessons around it. This goes for the whole outside environment. It is so much more ambitious and varied than before that it needs time to develop ways of using it as the planting grows and matures. It is hoped that parents and the community will use the building and the outside landscapes, and indeed help to develop the different zones of planting. The classrooms can dislocate themselves functionally from the rest of the school, like a pavilion surrounded by gardens.

The relationship between the outside and the inside of the classrooms and how that related to the curriculum became a key theme at Ballifield. It was expressed as a fluid teaching relationship between the outside classroom and the inside classroom. For example, the box bay with windows opening fully inwards flat against the reveal, allows the children to sit half inside and half outside. Many of the children commented that they felt like they were hiding when they were right inside the bays

Figure 6.4
Box bay open makes a connection between the inside and outside spaces.

with the table flapped down. Two sets of double doors open on to the external classroom, one is a balcony to look down on to the pond and another opens straight on to a terrace. Outside the classroom, entrance area is designed to feel like it is almost outside, with a polished concrete floor and ramp, roof lights and a totally glazed end. It is as if the classrooms are totally surrounded by the outside environment.

The process of consultation

Before the design stages of the project began a programme of consultation was devised. This was carried out by diploma architecture students at Sheffield[6] with us, the architects. The intention was to make this consultation a key part of the briefing process for the classrooms and to involve the children in designing the process of building and to make them more aware of architecture generally.

The head teacher, the teachers and the pupils were supportive and generous with their time during the consultation process. The children aged between 8 and 10 were genuinely delighted at the prospect of being invited to participate in the design process and to add to the architectural debate, but it was difficult to know where to begin the consultation process with young people on a subject area they have not been formally taught. The workshops varied depending on the teams and the schools. An introductory session used cartoon strips to introduce the job of the architect and flash cards showing some interesting images. The students looked in detail at the built environment with the children showing slides and more specifically looking at inspirational school buildings. In four sessions they modelled an ideal classroom, surveyed favourite places and places to avoid, walked through an ideal school and answered a hundred questions. The aim in all these exercises was to allow the children to be expressive. Drawing was encouraged at every stage. The children kept notebooks and carried out further exercises at home for the following sessions.

The teachers provided a strong influence on the children and it was sometimes difficult to stop the teachers enforcing their ideas; through design we were trying to break down both the children's and the teachers' preconceptions. When a child was asked what they should do, the teacher often told them, rather than the children thinking about new possibilities. Research on how design is taught and learned in schools cites the attitude of the schools and the teachers towards design, as the greatest reason design is marginalized: 'it tends to be treated as an artsy frill rather than something that has real impact on our lives'.[7]

It was in the children's words that many of the most interesting ideas came forward. This again conforms to recent research indicating that drawing is not habitually demonstrated as a useful tool for organizing and representing ideas. More usually drawing is seen as a 'servicing agent for the real work of writing stories'.[8]

In most of the workshops asking the children to imagine and draw a new classroom, the children associated the future with 'high-tech' gadgetry and technology in general. However, during an exercise investigating children's favourite places and least favourite places, the nature of their ideas became softer, smaller and a lot more natural. This inclination proved true when a pilot evaluation on Ballifield, after the children had moved into their new classrooms, showed that 57 out of 60 children drew the red box bays for sitting in as their favourite part of the classroom.

The consultation process was undoubtedly creative and educational for both the schoolchildren and the architects and most importantly it raised children's awareness of design issues in the building of classrooms. However, it was clear from some of the more general comments we received from the children that we weren't specific enough in our questions in the early sessions. The children were knowledgeable and useful about more practical issues, such as having views and light and water in the classrooms, and it was clear they were interested in a less institutional environment. The consultation process is a way of drawing out the tacit expertise in children as opposed to the explicit expertise of the professional. In the later consultation after the classrooms were finished we could be very specific and we got very precise answers.

Findings that came out of the early consultations and workshops were totally consistent with the results of a poll of school children in the *Guardian*[9] asking them what they would like to see in their classrooms. The most popular were a 'home from home' and a safe environment, quiet study rooms, drinking water easily available, better toilets, and storage lockers. Also, the desire for exciting new ways of learning and a magical atmosphere were articulated in various ways. It was more problematic asking the children to actually imagine spatially and formally how this could be achieved. The children's response, understandably was to make the classrooms look like something else – an anthropomorphic response – for example a space ship or an animal. Later, when more specific tasks were asked for, for example at Ballifield the children were asked to imagine the entrance space as a forest, they engaged with the ideas immediately and came up with imaginative ideas and designs incorporating rainforest canopies and all kinds of hanging wildlife.

Finally, and perhaps most importantly, the consultation served to instil a sense of excitement, expectation and anticipation. Knowing that it was really going to happen and the classrooms were actually going to be built, and the fact they had been asked their views, had an enormously positive effect on the whole school.

However, whether we as the architects actually engaged and used the consultation work as effectively as we might have done brings up a critical point. The findings of a lot of creative participatory work are not filtered effectively into the briefing process – a more traditional 'top down' approach takes over exclusively. We had a genuine desire to use the material generated in the consultations, but the different agendas of the students doing the workshops with the children, and the architect's role in the consultation process limited the study. A carefully thought out method of communication between all parties is imperative to the effective passage of information from user to professional. A report written by the students involved in the consultation was exhaustive, but difficult to extract specific information from – a common problem of too much information not being prioritized or being too abstract to be incorporated into the building directly.

Using the consultation and designing the building

It was often the informal issues and incidental remarks that had the most lasting influence in the design of the classrooms. More than anything it was the realization that the classrooms were places children had to be inspired by to have fun in; places of wonder and surprise, somewhere for children to explore, both formally and informally. Formally, the classrooms became teaching tools and every time we specified a material or a particular technology we thought whether it would be interesting for the children. Being able to put some of the children's imaginings, and indeed our own desires from childhood into what a school could be, was both a privilege and fun. We encouraged the children to

continue to think of the classrooms as an animal, the whale, and the entrance as a jungle, an unknown world the other side of a hedge. Children and visitors will enter the building through a door in a hedge, when it has grown, reminding them of the ancient hedge running along the boundary of the school. In the end we did not build the jungle canopy – the entrance did not seem to need it, but the light from above makes that space feel special even on a dull day.

Outside, the two classrooms, each with their own expressed form, are clad in timber or ply. The nature classroom wall is planted with climbers – a living wall. These will be evergreen honeysuckle that will be scented as well as quite profuse. The oiled larch boarding will weather in time. A copper datum strip reflects the copper roof and indicates the colour change that will happen there too. The building will look very different when the copper has patinated. The nature classroom has the green, living wall externally and the technology classroom

Figure 6.5
The new entrance gives children a sense of pride in their environment, particularly as they helped to design it.

has painted panels. Although they do not look particularly unusual, the painted panels are a papered and sealed ply, a new product from Finland. We will see how well that new technology stands up to the English climate!

The building is designed to be light-hearted and fun, both inside and outside; to be non-institutional, playful and to have places to hide. The balcony, as discussed before, is a result of mainly the teachers'

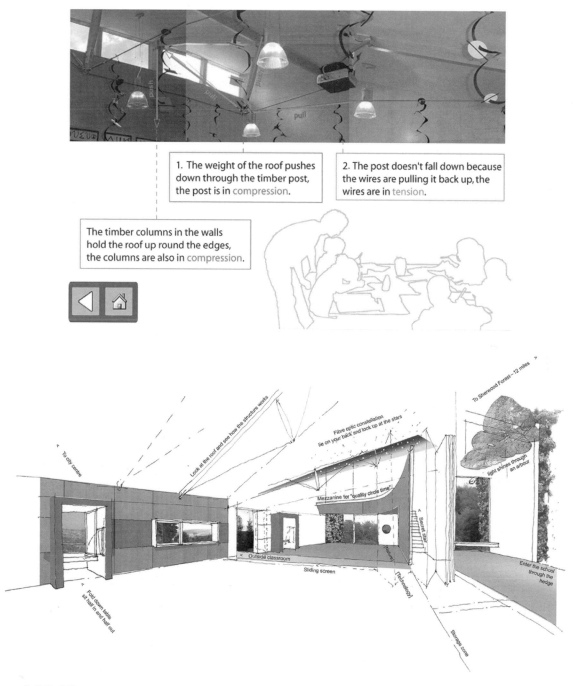

Figures 6.6 & 6.7
Extracts from architecture students' user manual.

input but the children talked about spaces to look down from and to hide away in.

Toilets and cloakrooms featured as particularly unpleasant parts of the existing school and were commented on often by the children. We thought it was important to make ours luxurious and colourful. Both toilets are big enough for changing rooms and both are suitable for disabled children; but they are everyone's toilets.

After the children had moved into their new classrooms I asked a boy whether he liked the new toilets and he said he did, but he had been in it rather a long time trying to get out – the door handle had come off in his hand. He said he had had a long time to look at the coloured panels and liked them a lot.

Also, try as we might to achieve a tidy cloakroom by giving the pegs more room, there is still the odd coat on the floor and bag hanging out of the lockers. The teachers have reassured us that even if every child had a metre of space and a hand grapping their coats, there would still be some thrown in the direction of a peg and left where they landed, on the floor.

Technology is very present in the classrooms; the white boards are designed to be a focal point. All the cabling for the services and computer cabling is hidden behind the ply panels and in the roof soffit. These removable panels allow for changes in the requirements for cabling. We also wanted to indicate how invisible new technology is.

Where architects also need to improve the communication is in the feedback to the users. What is often forgotten in the process is feeding back and explaining the building once it is built – the other end of the consultation process. We need to work with the teachers to help them to make better use of their space. Anything new and different needs explaining, from how to use the under-floor heating to how to exploit the new construction in teaching, i.e. the recycled materials. To learn from the ideas emerging from the project and to monitor their success once the pupils started using the classroom, we carried out an initial post-occupancy evaluation and this now forms an important part of the continuing life of the project.

This also gave the teachers an opportunity to discuss their problems and dislikes, as well as what they loved about the building, directly and without compromise.

One of the most frustrating things about the early period after practical completion and handing the classroom over was the number of small things that could have been avoided if it had not been such a rush at the end. All the ironmongery was not tightly secured, and the teachers were not handed over keys or talked through the use of the services, such as the heating. As a result of this we asked some diploma architecture students to prepare a 'Users Manual' for the classrooms. The manual, both digital for projection on the white boards and hard copy for hanging in the classroom, has become an important document to help both the teachers and the children understand the technologies and how to use them. This includes everything from how to open the sliding screens to how to change bulbs in particular types of light fittings. This can be a teaching aid too, discovering about the different types of artificial lighting and qualities of light, about the structure and the forces working in the roof, and the nature of the materials. The standard issue Health and Safety Manual certainly does not satisfy these everyday requirements. Knowing how the building works is empowering and liberating.

The evolving classroom landscape

A classroom is not finished when it is finished, far from it; its life is just beginning. We would like to carry on charting the progress of Ballifield over the next few years to see how the landscapes inside and outside change. New agendas and ideas will inevitably mean changes to the plans as they are now; including the use and ideas for the external classroom and playground. Notions of health and safety might change too; now it is considered too dangerous to have an open pond. In other European countries the attitudes in playgrounds appear to be changing to place more emphasis on the children and parents taking responsibility for their behaviour and use of the public domain. However, most importantly children need to continue discovering ways of using their environment, changing it, understanding it and even re-imagining it.

Notes

1   David Miliband, the ministerial design champion writes in the foreword to a promotional book '*Classrooms of the future – innovative designs for schools*', written by the DfES and published by The Stationery Office in London, 2002.
2   Simmons, I.G. (1993). *Interpreting Nature: Cultural constructions of the environment.* London: Routledge.
3   Anecdotal evidence from two neighbouring Sheffield primary schools taking diametrically opposed approaches to solve their conflicting problems.
4   *Daily Telegraph*, 28 June, 2003
    Sarah discusses this issue in relation to the exemplar school initiative (the design of a whole school) that followed the classroom initiative.
5   Cathy Dee.
6   This was one of the 6-week 'live projects' carried out by all diploma students every year.
7   Anning, A. and Hill, A. (1998). '*Designing in elementary/primary classrooms*'. IDATOR Loughborough University of Technology.
8   Anning, A. (1993). '*Technological capability in primary classrooms*'. IDATOR Loughborough University of Technology.
9   The *Guardian*, 5 June 2001.

Schools Building and Design Unit – DfES 2002 '*Schools for the Future – designs for learning communities*' Building Bulletin 95 The Stationery Office, London.

Prue Chiles combines practice with teaching and research. Prue Chiles Architects, established in 1999, carries out private commissions including the DfES funded 'classroom of the future'. At the University of Sheffield, School of Architecture, Prue runs a diploma unit and directs the Bureau of Design Research set up in 2002 to work with both local communities and national groups on research-based design consultancy projects.

7

The schools we'd like: young people's participation in architecture

Ben Koralek and Maurice Mitchell

Editor's introduction

The view that children's perceptions of space are different to those of adults is the central premise of Chapter 7. What follows is the proposition that children and young people have a democratic right to be heard about the make up of their education, and most importantly the form of their school buildings, many of which were designed for the nineteenth century. The authors illustrate a range of initiatives which have been implemented within the UK over the past ten years which have transformed the perceptions of those who have participated. For example, the work of the Building Experiences Trust and then School Works has challenged the conventional professional view that children have nothing to offer to the design process.

The second part of this chapter describes in some detail a number of participatory projects which have bridged the gap between architecture and education. The creativity of the end result illustrates how good school design could be if the views of its users were heard. This illustrates how important it is to get children's views about their lives and the kinds of spaces they would like to have for themselves. However, it is not a straightforward discursive process. Detailed case studies where school students have actually worked with designers illustrates what is possible if appropriate inclusive methods are used to talk and listen to schoolchildren properly.

Although full of childlike fantasy, there are some remarkably grounded ideas to transform existing and new school environments and to make them more appropriate for the present and future generations who will be expected to use them. The authors argue that as huge amounts of investment flow into the state education system, the need to 'get it right' has never been more critical. The commitment of professional designers would help to transform the urban fabric and make school attractive to young people.

Those architects and designers who are truly interested in the possibilities of a participatory approach will find this chapter particularly enlightening. How do you make meaningful consultation with school students within the PFI (Private Finance Initiative) process for example? When is the right moment to gauge the views of school students and what is the best process to use in order to get the best and most exciting design ideas? Here, the process is as important as the end result. In an era where the democratic process appears to be peripheral for many people, is this an approach which should be adopted more widely, to enable the future citizens of this country to engage with their world in a positive way?

Introduction

Like other mammals, our children are born inextricably linked to the environment around them. In this respect, childhood is an ecosystem whose success and well-being depends equally on complex biological, social and cultural systems. As well as these non-material relationships, children are also dependent on tangible, physical environments in which to grow. Buildings, the spaces between buildings, streets, green fields, playgrounds and parks all play a significant part in shaping children's experience of the world and their place in it.[1] For the large majority of children today, one part of the built environment in particular shapes their experience of the world, that is the school.

In retrospect, we tend to associate our own childhood with pleasant domestic experiences such as slides and swings in the park, quiet rooms at home for drawing or reading, hidden spaces under an old table (ideal for listening to the radio), the local swimming pool and secret camps at the end of the garden; for many of us, our daily experience of school plays a less dominant role in our memories of childhood.

The role of memory in the design of school buildings should not be underestimated. Where our memories of specific rooms, places and buildings are concerned, adults and children have very different perceptions of architectural space.[2] With our own sense of scale and proportion, adults experience places of childhood, including our former schools, as much smaller in size than our memories tell us.

Perhaps because of this difference of perception between the adult and the child, the school building provides a unique subject for collaborative working in the conception and production of space.[3] As we hope to show in this chapter, a dialogue on the design of school buildings can provide a bridge between adult and child perceptions of architectural space because it is a space they both share during the most formative years of child development.

Until very recently, UK school buildings in all their many shapes, styles and sizes, represented children's space as conceived by adults, and adults alone. This chapter focuses specifically on recent projects and participatory design processes in which young people have collaborated with professional and student architects in the remodelling and the making of new learning environments.

In exploring the production of children's spaces, and school buildings especially, it is worth acknowledging that virtually all of the spaces used and inhabited by children today are still designed, made and managed by adults. This is just as true at the beginning of the twenty-first century as it was for the great European interpreters of childhood of the past: Rousseau (in the eighteenth), Froebbel (in the nineteenth) and Montessori (in the early twentieth century).

In her seminal research on children's cognitive development, Montessori acknowledged both the need to develop new ways for adults to work with children in educational settings, and the importance of the environment on children's learning.[4] In these ways, Montessori's work holds a special relevance to this chapter's analysis of the production of children's spaces. Just as children require time for their cognitive development, their socialization and their individual journeys along the play–learning continuum, children and young people also require a range of spatial settings: play areas, learning environments and buildings in which to experience their world and develop their identity.

As has been well documented (by Montessori's natural 'successors') in the municipality of Reggio Emilia in northern Italy, children growing up in the urban environment play a key role in shaping a city's identity and civic culture.[5] As Loris Malaguzzi, the principal founder and key protagonist in establishing the approach to early years education in Reggio Emilia reminds us:

children ask us to be their allies in resisting hostile pressures and defending spaces for creative freedom which, in the end, are also spaces for joy, trust and solidarity.[6]

Indeed, as those working in and supporting the Pre-Schools of Reggio Emilia demonstrate, the life and healthy evolution of a city depends on the well-being and creativity of its young people.

In Reggio Emilia, for example, children are actively engaged in an ongoing discourse with the urban and learning environments in which they work and play. Supported by studio-based 'learning supervisor-researchers' – the atelierista, children at these state-funded pre-schools investigate and manipulate their studio spaces and explore their home city as a matter of course. They draw, make models and create stories about the things they touch, see, hear and experience. Their journeys across the urban environment become familiar and highly personalized elements within their cognitive development; many of which have been further celebrated, recorded and animated on return to the pre-schools and their creative studio spaces which provide an adaptable container for the children's expressive work, or as Malaguzzi says, 'a kind of aquarium which reflects the ideas, ethics, attitudes and culture of the people who live in it.'

The interior architectural environments of the Reggio Emilia pre-schools must, by definition, allow for flexible remodelling prompted by the activities and ideas of the children. For this reason, and the fact that their 'pedagogical coordinators, teachers, and parents met to plan with the architects' in the design of their learning environments, the pre-schools of Reggio Emilia provide a very useful precedent to our analysis of young people's participation in the architectural process; and a point of reference to which we will return later in this chapter.[7] However, whilst the influence of the pre-schools of Reggio Emilia continues to spread across continental Europe and in north America, the state education system in the UK has been slow to absorb the important pedagogical

insights and professional practice pioneered in what is now referred to as the 'Reggio approach'. Likewise, British architects are only now rediscovering the creative challenge in designing learning environments which take into account contemporary educational practice for the benefit of UK schoolchildren.

To this day, school communities in the UK are still – typically – housed in Victorian or post-1945 buildings designed by adults to contain and condition young people into being responsible citizens capable of taking their place in a productive society.[8] Children's learning and early social experiences are still shaped in much older rooms, playgrounds, laboratories, corridors and halls designed by distant generations of architects in response to very different pedagogical, social and cultural criteria. For some, like child psychologist David Elkind, schools, and by default the buildings in which they operate, 'represent our past rather than our future'.[9] Authoritative antique Victorian school building stock still commands a powerful physical position in the British landscape of childhood.

As we explore in Part Three of this chapter, as an expression of governmental control of children's time and space, the school 'boards' of the Victorian era (established as part of the 1870 Education Act) set a new standard. Not only did the school boards have the power to make their own by-laws, decide whether or not to charge fees for schooling, determine what subjects 'Masters' were to teach their pupils in the classroom, they also exercised the authority to build and maintain school buildings using public finances ('rates'), for the first time in British history.

The motives behind the establishment of the school boards may have been mixed. Whether philanthropic in essence, or as an agent of social control (or both), the school boards' attempt to hold young people in custodial care also defined a relationship between central government and children's education which has become the foundation for the industrialized world's contemporary school system (Friere, 1971; Illich, 1971; Gatto, 1992 *et al.*). At the same time, the school boards defined a very specific form of architectural children's space; many of which are still in use today.

In a world where young people were to be 'seen and not heard', Victorian children had absolutely no chance to voice their opinion as to how these new spaces would be arranged or their school days organized, let alone what the new school buildings would look like. British children would have to wait a hundred years for such a privilege.

In Part Three of this chapter, through an examination of some recent case studies, we will explore ways in which children's design ideas can be developed with architecture students to reinterpret and adapt formal board school spaces from the inside out. As we will show in Parts Two and Four, the idea that children might work alongside architects as they have done at Lightwoods Community primary school in the West Midlands and with School Works at Kingsdale secondary school in London is only now becoming a viable reality.[10] However, the roots of this kind of participatory collaboration go back approximately thirty years.

Our title for this chapter takes its name from the *Observer* newspaper's 1967 competition – 'The School That I'd Like', which invited British secondary school students to reinvent their schooling at a time when their experience of education was still that of containment 'in the prison of a most dreadful conformity'.[11]

At the height of 1960s radical student activism, and in the same year that the benefits of a more 'child-centred' primary education became more formally acknowledged (in the 1967 Plowden Report), 'The School That I'd Like', gave young people the chance to collectively, and very publically, voice their opinion, and vent their spleen, on both the organization of learning and the quality of school buildings.[12] Of the subsequent contributions, children's author and the competition's 'patron' Edward Blishen reflected that 'most, however, were either out of patience with school buildings as they are, or were profusely able to think of improvements. Most were tired of squareness: where an actual shape was suggested, nine times out of ten it was a round one. Domes were yearned for'.[13]

In 1967, the *Observer* received almost 1000 ideas for new schools: 'some half a million words, innumerable charts, collages, architectural or pseudo-architectural drawings'.[14] Thirty years later, in the midst of New Labour's successful 1997 General Election campaign, the *Guardian* newspaper repeated 'The School I'd Like' competition. Second time around, 15 000 primary and secondary pupils sent their ideas on video, in 3-d model form, in drawings, photographic collages and in text (epic poems, plays, dictated comments and in Braille); and in response to newly-elected Prime Minister Blair's now infamous declaration of a Labour government's top three priorities to be: 'Education, education, education' (on April 15th 1997), just seven weeks later, and as a product of the second 'The School I'd Like' competition, the *Guardian* also published *The Children's Manifesto* calling for beautiful, comfortable, safe schools.

With the reappearance of 'The School I'd Like' competition format in 1997, and the active involvement of the (then) New Labour think-tank DEMOS and London's Architecture Foundation, the quality of school building design was placed back on the political agenda.[15] Second time around, a generation of more politically-enfranchised school children would have an even louder voice thanks in part to the formal framework established by the UK Children's Act (1989) and Article 12 of the United Nations Convention on the Rights of the Child (1990) in which children and young people 'had the right to express an opinion on all matters which concern them.'[16]

With New Labour's commitment to a greater degree of public participation in the delivery of public services, it appeared (to many) that young people now had a direct invitation to take part in the political process. For the first time, perhaps, it seemed that children's requests for a respectful school with flexible timetables and a more relevant curriculum would also be heard. For the first time, young people would be able to express their perception of the quality of school buildings, and the adults around them would have to listen.

With projects like School Works and The Sorrell Foundation's 'joinedupdesignforschools' initiative established in 2000 to 'join up UK designers with schools across the country to demonstrate how design and creativity can improve the quality of life and learning in schools', calling for a new kind of working partnership between professional adult designers and young people, and given the enormous sums of public and private finance going into new schools production in the UK, the stakes were (and remain) high. Could young people express their design ideas clearly enough for them to be incorporated into new schools' architecture? Would architects be able to listen and work with a young public looking to participate in the planning and design processes? Whilst managing expensive building programmes, would local education authorities be prepared to allow additional time to engage with young people? These kinds of questions continue to vex design and education professionals seeking to develop and improve new learning environments.

Through the examination of some important recent participatory collaborations between designers and young people, we hope to sketch out some answers, and in doing so, to show the simplicity of our argument.

With the hundreds of expensive new schools currently scheduled for design and construction in the UK, and despite the engagement of advice and support of advocates of good design, few students, teachers or parents will be allowed the time to actively engage with the design process before the building starts.[17]

Whatever kinds of old, new or remodelled spaces a school community has to work in, young people and their teachers should be allowed and encouraged to take the time to engage in their own *ongoing* process of site-specific investigation, analysis and creative design. Their collective expertise of what works best in their environment is overlooked to their (and our) cost. As our survey of projects in Part Four, and our experience from the case studies in Part Three suggests, this kind of knowledge emerges within the framework of working relationships developed over time and from direct experience of a pragmatic and participatory collaboration with designers.

To avoid, or repair the costly errors of judgement or almost inevitable misunderstandings and compromise in large-scale, 'fast-track',

multiple-school new-build projects, a modest, (comparatively) inexpensive, continuing, and – above all – child-centred design process might ensure the best possible learning environments for young people.[18]

However, in rethinking our approach to the design of learning environments and school buildings, we should remember that despite the growing number of school building design projects, and the subsequent opportunity for dialogue between adult designers and school children, the knowledge gap between architects and young people is still too wide. 'As a society, we are shamefully ignorant of the positive impact that architecture and the design of cities can have on our lives. We need to make far-reaching changes in our approach to the built environment, and should be prepared to legislate for them. Education is one important component in remedying the situation, and a new system of participatory planning is essential.'[19] Despite some significant progress in these areas (as we shall see), Richard Rogers' 1997 general criticism is, largely, still accurate.

A brief history of built environment education in the UK

At the time of the original 'The School I'd Like' competition in 1967, young people in Britain had virtually no contact with architects. However, in the early 1970s, somewhat lagging behind built environment education in Denmark and the USA, the Royal Institute of British Architects' traditional Christmas children's lectures (in London) were reinvented to give a more hands-on introduction to architecture and experiences of the built environment. Like the Chicago Architecture Foundation, for example, the RIBA organized a team of volunteer architects to deliver a mixture of 'walk around the block' events and space-making activities for children and parents. Following the success of these experiential learning projects, and in order to extend the invitation to learn about architecture to more children and young people, during the mid-1970s 'architecture workshops' were established in Cambridge, Hull, Plymouth, Stevenage, Halifax, London, Leeds, Bradford, Glasgow, Newcastle and Manchester. By 1980, some architecture workshops had established ground-breaking educational projects; and other schemes, like teacher-designer Nigel Frost's Cambridge Architects & Teachers (CAT), had formalized links between architects and school teachers.

Building on this pioneering work in 1985, and signalling an historic commitment to general education, the RIBA appointed Frost as its first Architects-In-Schools Coordinator, where he developed his work on CAT to pilot an 'architects-in-residence' scheme for schools in England and Wales. Thanks to this successful programme, some children will have had an opportunity to explore aspects of building design and construction from a visiting professional, at their school.

Paradoxically, alongside this important cross-fertilization between education and architecture during the 1970s and 1980s, children and young people grew up in a negative climate in which, more often than not, architecture was seen as part of the problem, rather than part of the solution. Indeed, architects are still seen – by some – as professionally distant, arrogant and fixated on stylistic dogma. Until recently, public opinion has been highly critical of contemporary British architecture.

> 'As a nation...we are very partisan in the way we make decisions about what we think is good – it tends to be about heritage. For this to change...it's important for children to be made as aware of the built environment as they are of the natural environment.'

Architect Ros Diamond's view, supported by extensive research for her 1996 Arts Council report. *The Built Environment & the National Curriculum*, is one that has echoed through the architecture cognoscenti for decades and is as true today as it was in the 1990s.[20]

Indeed, frustrated by repetitive, high-profile assaults on the work of twentieth-century British architects, by the mid-1980s, the country's architectural community united in a mission to raise public awareness of architecture generally, and more specifically to increase understanding of contemporary design in the built environment.[21] In rallying to the cause, from necessity, architects cast themselves in the role of educator.

Architects as educators

At the forefront of this educational 'crusade' was architect Richard Rogers. As architectural advisor to both New Labour and (later) Mayor of London, Ken Livingstone, Rogers is now as famous for being the public voice – and face – of British architecture as he is for his practice's iconic, high-tech buildings. Passionately committed to the civic experience and urban life, Rogers also played a pivotal role in establishing two organizations which would change the relationship between British architecture and its public forever.

Indeed, arguing that 'the most useful act that any socially-minded architect could do would be to spend a few hours each year at his/her school trying to explain the effects of the environment on people, the development of the senses, art and technology and the responsibility of the individual to the global village', Rogers found a natural ally in Nigel Frost.[22]

By 1989, Frost had contacted Rogers to discuss the establishment of an educational charity which would be dedicated to continuing and extending the successful built environment education work he had pioneered with the RIBA and other architecture workshops across the UK. Frost proposed a programme of educational workshops for primary and secondary schools to be delivered by a team of specially-trained animateurs under the auspices of 'The Building Experiences Trust' (BET).

Seeking to further built environment education in the UK, and by then already involved with the establishment of London's first 'architecture centre' – The Architecture Foundation, Rogers agreed to support Frost by acting as Chairman for the Building Experiences Trust. Both organizations focused their energy on creating dialogue between architects and the public; and between them, both ventures would create an accessible context for learning about the built environment for adults and children respectively.

Of the two organizations, Rogers and Frost's Building Experiences Trust (1989–2003) focused specifically on designing and delivering an education programme for the (then) 32 700 primary and secondary schools across the country.[23] With its mission to 'advance the education of young people about architecture and its related disciplines', the BET introduced young people to a creative design process through the construction of large 3-d (frame) models of famous buildings and architectural structures. At its heart – as the name suggests – the Building Experiences Trust aimed to raise young people's awareness of their own experiential responses to architectural spaces and the buildings around them.

Frost's workshop format was highly successful in its ability to equip participants with a very personal – albeit universal – range of experiences of constructed forms and enclosures to the extent that some participants would be inspired to discover and use a new language with which to articulate their (emotional) experience of being enclosed, or feeling safe, or excited and energized by the spaces they had created.[24] *The architecture workshop 'movement': defining a new architectural and educational language.*

In educational terms, with its emphasis on empowering children with a kineasthetic 'language' derived from the manipulation of simple, tactile materials, Nigel Frost's system can take a legitimate place in a pedagogical lineage of hands-on experiential learning stretching as far back as Froebbel and Montessori. Indeed, it could also be argued that the system developed by Frost had its roots in an even older tradition of educational construction 'toys'.

In discussing education as a training for later life, Plato in the fourth century BC, for example, instructs that 'the future builder must play at building … and those who have the care of their education should provide them when young with mimic tools.'[25] During the modern era, in nineteenth-century Germany, the work of former architecture student and educational philosopher

Friedrich Froebel, translated Plato's concept quite literally. Froebel's 'Gifts' and 'Occupations' for young children included sets of mathematically derived wooden blocks specifically designed for building (Gifts 3–6 were, for example, a set of blocks cut from an eight-inch wooden cube).[26] Nearly a century later, in Italy, doctor of medicine and educator Maria Montessori, also included building blocks with which children could construct a tower and a stair in her 'prepared environment' for children's learning (1912). Now commonplace in children's spaces at home and school, largely thanks to the pioneering work of Froebel and Montessori, wooden blocks continue to provide the most accessible introduction to architecture to countless children around the world. For those growing up in the pre-Lego era, like writer and structuralist philosopher Roland Barthes, 'a few sets of blocks, which appeal to the spirit of do-it-yourself are the only ones which offer dynamic forms.'[27] In keeping with Barthes' spirit of 'do-it'-yourself', the sense of creative freedom could also be expressed whilst using Frost's construction system.

Inspired too by the geometrical and structural insights of twentieth-century designer-engineers Richard Buckminster Fuller and Santiago Calatrava (with whom – in 1991 – he collaborated on children's workshops within an exhibition on bridge design), Frost's elegant modelling system placed the humble tetrahedron (and other Platonic solids) centre stage. With tetrahedra and the equilateral triangle as universal building blocks, Frost devised an engaging, effective and highly theatrical way to explore 3-d structure through hands-on participatory learning.

During the 1990s, and alongside his work in museums, learning centres and galleries in the UK, Europe and the USA, Frost was careful to tailor the content and structure of the workshops to respond to, and enhance, the newly-imposed National Curriculum for schools in England and Wales.

Typically, during one of Frost's workshops, participants are introduced simultaneously to a kit of simple materials (lengths of dowel and rubber bands), a logical construction system and, where

Figure 7.1

Figure 7.2

Figure 7.3

relevant, to certain key moments in the history of architecture. Leading the workshop (with up to seventy participants at one time), a workshop animateur demonstrates and explains with clarity and precision how to fix the materials together – in stages – to make specific architectural/engineering forms such as triangular trusses or portal frame arches. In the now famous Pyramids workshop, participants start with just six sticks and four rubber bands, to make one small tetrahedron each. These are then assembled – usually in a school hall or gym – sequentially in groups of four until one, very large pyramid remains, towering over its young builders.

Participating children love the immediacy of the workshop process, taking inspiration from, and great delight in, the success of the 'massive' structures they have just made by hand. Young children especially thrive on the chance to make a 3-d structure big enough to get inside or underneath. From this new vantage point, they have the opportunity to test out the structural integrity of what they've made – to see how it works and to understand why it doesn't fall down!

For many workshop participants, the experience of building these giant pyramids is simply unforgettable. In establishing a highly visible, educationally valid and genuinely participatory learning process, Frost has successfully crystallized a vital means of communication for British architecture and its young public. Perhaps unwittingly though, he had also devised a construction kit and system that could rival Lego for its accessibility and Meccanno for the structures' engineering authenticity.

Free of the demands of covering surfaces of any kind, the tetrahedral and triangulated structures reveal their skeletal structure for all to see. This is – one might say – architecture stripped bare. Free of the need to wall, roof or clad the models, the construction system speaks for itself. Like the 'exoskeletal' hi-tech structures being crafted in the built environment around them, the structures made by children as young as six years old clearly express their own engineering.[28] The structures 'speak' to young people in an architectural language of their own.

To this day, through the continuing work of the Cambridge-based Architecture Workshops Association, children and young people across the UK find themselves central protagonists in live architectural modelling/story-telling dialogues.

Plate 1
The new castle – anchor and all. (Photos: Kompan.)

Plate 2
An old bent crooked tree ... a wonderful tree, in Guell Park, Barcelona. (Photo: M Laris.)

Plate 3
Colour variation promotes invention.
(Photo: Kompan.)

Plate 4
Spring Creek School, Three Oaks, Michigan, 1886. (Photo: Eleanor Nicholson.)

Plate 5
Warm burnished brickwork is embellished with decorative iconography. Crow Island School, Winnetka, Illinois.

Plate 6
View into the main hall showing the door case from the original school building, fully integrated into the new building. Thompson Middle School, Newport, RI, designed by HMFH Architects, Cambridge, MA. (Photo: Jonathan Hillyer.)

CHAPTER 5: THE CLASSROOM IS A MICROCOSM OF THE WORLD

Plate 7
King Alfred School,
Hampstead, London.
Interior of classroom:
an ordered, calm
environment. Van
Heyningen and Howard
Architects. (Photo: Dennis
Gilbert.)

CHAPTER 6: THE CLASSROOM AS AN EVOLVING LANDSCAPE

Plate 8
Ballifield Community
Primary School, Sheffield:
new entrance and
classroom. (Architect:
Prue Chiles.)

Plate 9
Ballifield Community Primary School,
Sheffield: exterior of classroom. (Architect:
Prue Chiles.)

Plate 10
Children's toilets are designed to the
same standard as the classrooms,
which encourages a healthy attitude.

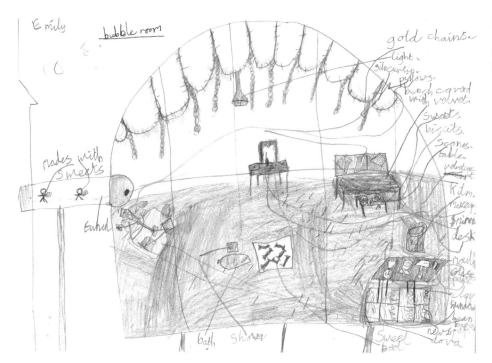

Plate 11
'Bubble' room concept for a new children-only space.

Plate 12
A small personal pod equipped with sofa, beanbag and cushions; supplied with a dream cassette machine and a rack of computer games.

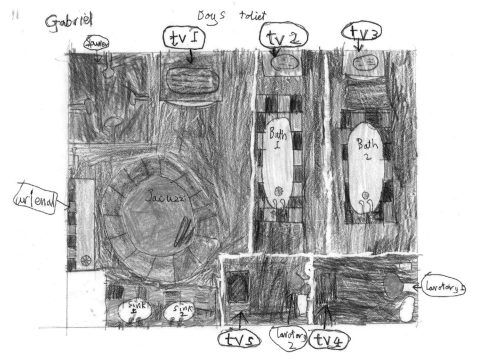

Plate 13
A 'bubble' room with stained glass windows displaying the planets in glorious technicolor.

Plate 14
Exploring the issue of personal space at Kingsdale School.

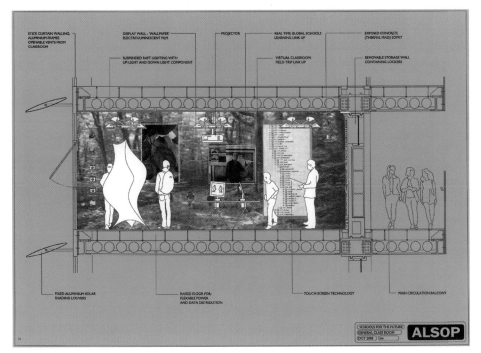

STICK CURTAIN WALLING,
ALUMINIUM FRAMES
OPENABLE VENTS FROM
CLASSROOM

DISPLAY WALL - 'WALLPAPER'
ELECTROLUMINESCENT FILM

PROJECTOR

REAL TIME GLOBAL SCHOOLS
LEARNING LINK UP

EXPOSED CONCRETE
(THERMAL MASS) SOFFIT

SUSPENDED RAFT LIGHTING WITH
UP-LIGHT AND DOWN LIGHT COMPONENT

VIRTUAL CLASSROOM
FIELD TRIP LINK UP

REMOVABLE STORAGE WALL
CONTAINING LOCKERS

FIXED ALUMINIUM SOLAR
SHADING LOUVERS

RAISED FLOOR FOR:
FLEXABLE POWER
AND DATA DISTRIBUTION

TOUCH SCREEN TECHNOLOGY

MAIN CIRCULATION BALCONY

SCHOOLS FOR THE FUTURE
GENERAL CLASS ROOM
OCT 2003

ALSOP

Plate 15
Conceptual section
through the classroom of
the future with Real Time
Global Schools Learning
Link Up and Virtual
Classroom Field Trip Link
Up. ALSOP Architects.

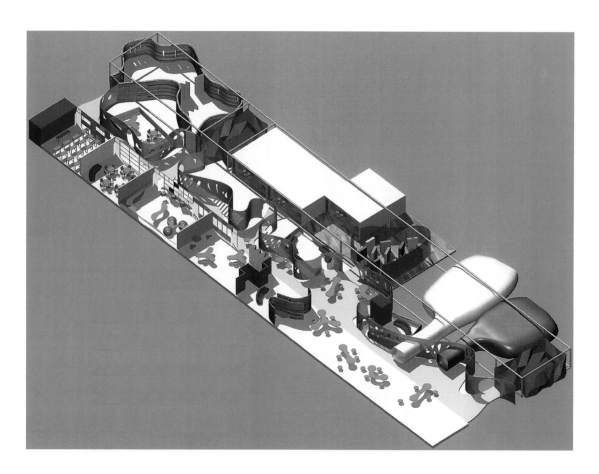

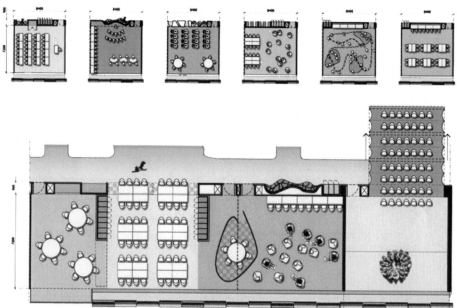

Plate 16a,b
We can predict that in the future, teaching will take place in a variety of group sizes ranging from 90 students to the traditional 30 pupils per class. ALSOP Architects.

LA JETEE

Plate 17
First prize site plan.

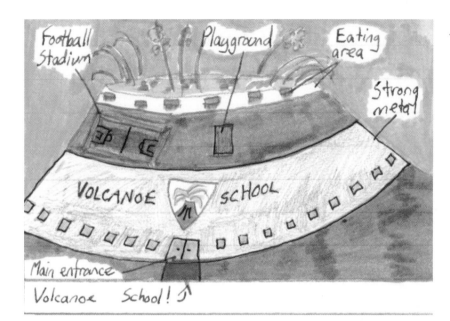

Plate 18
Volcano school.

Plate 19
The ideal school canteen.
(Nicholas, age 6, Barnsley.)

Plate 20
Washington School yard,
Berkeley, California,
May, 2002. (Photo: Cathy
Burke.)

Plate 21
The edible schoolyard, Martin Luther King Junior Middle School, Berkeley, California. (Photo: Cathy Burke.)

Plate 22
The Grandview
Uuqinak'uuh community
garden. (Photo: Cathy
Burke.)

Figure 7.4

Whether building pyramid forms, models of the Globe Theatre or Richard Rogers Partnership's Millennium Dome, these are important, perhaps seminal experiences for UK schoolchildren (see Figure 7.4). As one Year 5/10-year-old pupil says following her participation in a 1998 Architecture Workshops Association (AWA) Tudor workshop:

> *Thankyou very much for doing the [Design & Technology] Workshop. I had great fun learning words like octohedron and tetrahedrons. It reminded me of the Tudor houses at St Fagons. I like making the pyramid and the roof for the Globe Theatre. I would like to be a architect when I grow up. I enjoyed doing it ... I wish I could do it again.*[29]

In more holistic educational terms, working with geometry and 3-d forms, workshop participants are prompted to problem-solve and to think laterally. In turn, their existing, theoretical classroom understanding of shape and space is developed through practical, investigative work whilst constructing elements of the large models. Through this process, participants are given a 'real-world' opportunity to test and expand their own

mathematical vocabulary – 'vertical', 'horizontal', 'space', 'volume', 'surface', 'vertices', 'angle', 'depth', 'weight', etc., with renewed purpose. Children participating in a workshop of this kind also become confident in using another vocabulary made up of architectural and technological terminology, i.e. 'structure', 'truss', 'tensile', 'compression' 'torsion', 'oscillation', etc.

At the same time, working with a combination of rigid and flexible materials, participants can test their own scientific understanding of compression, tension and torsion, whilst bringing to life highly imaginative, often beautiful sculptural forms – as if by magic revealed to the eye via a shift in perception. As if describing an AWA workshop, pioneer of visual education Kurt Rowland observed (in 1976) that: 'the design of structures which make use of the material in the most efficient manner, without any waste or left-overs, is not only economical and elegant but magical.'[30]

Within this learning experience (which complements the existing UK National Curriculum pedagogy so well), participants also have to adjust their own thinking to address the three-dimensional qualities of the structures, and the fact that there are no flat surfaces to assist one's preconceived idea of how a building fits together.

The experience of arranging frame elements (each with their own spatial volume) and fixing them together to make a larger structure provides a range of experience which empowers young people to understand some of the core principles of architectural design and construction. This challenging process, dependent on manual dexterity and some first-hand knowledge of materials, also helps formulate a new 'grammar' of space and structure; in short a new, child-centred experiential 'language'.

Learnt 'by hand', the language embodied in the Frost/AWA workshop format also has its roots in that known by master builders and craftsmen for centuries. This is the language of building craft tradition; the same kinaesthetic language which comes from 'that unique repository of intimate knowledge and understanding of natural materials and processes, which provided the technological base on which recent generations of innovation and technical discovery stand'.[31]

Most importantly for our purposes here, the kind of experiential process embodied in Frost's workshop format also gives young people a *common* language with which to communicate with architects.[32]

Architecture and education: a national context

Running in parallel to these ground-breaking developments was the establishment of a national network of architecture centres, in London (The Architecture Foundation, RIBA Gallery and The Building Exploratory, Hackney), and in Kent (Chatham), Glasgow, Bristol, Plymouth, Liverpool, Manchester, Birmingham, Newcastle, Leeds, Hull the East Midlands and Cambridge.[33] Whilst each of these centres is unique and specific to its host city, local region and community, they all have one thing in common. As The Architecture Foundation puts it: architecture centres exist to 'promote the importance of high quality contemporary architecture and urban design to as wide an audience as possible ... to encourage public participation and debate on the design, planning

and sustainability of our cities ...' and to actively bridge the gap 'between decision-makers, design professionals and the public.'[34]

To complement the growing network of architecture centres, and to add to this new public interface with design in the built environment, two annual events were established to celebrate both existing and new British architecture. National Architecture Week was established in 1997 to run each year in June; and London Open House over a September weekend was first launched in 1992. Both provide a wide range of opportunities for young people to interact with architects and their work.

Architecture Week's 'Open Practice' initiative in particular is 'a great chance to ask architects face to face about their buildings and see how they work'.[35] As if calling out to a younger audience, Tom Dyckhoff declares: 'There's no doubt about it, architecture's suddenly become hot. The big debate these days isn't about classical v modern but whether it's the new sex or new rock'n'roll'.[36] At last, a group of secondary students visiting an architect's practice would be an annual event and not a once-in-a-lifetime fluke.

Perhaps, after ten years of gradual and incremental education work by the likes of the Building Experiences Trust, the Architecture Workshops Association, Kent Architecture Centre, Manchester's CUBE (Centre for Understanding the Built Environment) and The Building Exploratory in Hackney, East London, for example, a new generation of young people had grown up with the idea that architecture was 'cool'. This same generation had – perhaps – also developed their own understanding of architecture and the impact of design on their lives. From a few solitary architects venturing into their local schools to help with a one-off curriculum project, we now have young people turning up on the doorsteps of architecture practices all over the country.

These first building blocks have laid the foundation for a new kind of dialogue between schoolchildren and architects. Alive with a new awareness of design in the built environment, empowered with a shared architectural language and in an era in which public participation is becoming common place, young people and the architect-educators of the architecture workshop movement have co-created a context for meaningful collaboration on the design of new school buildings.

Young people's collaboration in the architectural process

In the UK, the idea that schoolchildren could contribute to an architectural design process in a meaningful way has at last been tested through practice. As we will see below, a few young people of both primary and secondary school ages have been given the opportunity to investigate the architecture of their school, analyse the school's current and future needs and – in collaboration with architects – to offer practical solutions on renovation, remodelling and refurbishment projects.

As a result of the wide range of innovative built environment education work of the 1990s, young people at the beginning of the twenty-first century are now more confident in approaching architects and are excited at the prospect of applying themselves to a creative process in which real change takes place in real buildings. With their enthusiasm to see concrete alterations in their own school buildings, young people are ready now to participate in a culture of rights to, and responsibilities for a 'healthier' built environment. Against the backdrop of 'Citizenship' in the National Curriculum (for secondary students in England and Wales since September 2002), the School Council movement and even the practice of Circle Time in Primary schools, young people – increasingly – know that they have the right to voice an opinion, and that their views should be considered.[37]

In a global context too, as we have seen, children's participation in decision making is on the political agenda. Since the ratification of Article 12 of the United Nations Convention on the Rights of the Child (1990), public services in the UK, including health and education, have been required to glean and incorporate children's views.[38]

The implications of this new approach have particular significance for the traditional masters of decision making over children's learning and school buildings – the Local Education Authorities (LEAs).

The political context: from Welfare State to Private Finance Initiative

Following the 1902 and 1903 Balfour Acts, and the later Butler (Education) Act of 1944, local borough and county councils took responsibility for the statutory provision of formal education and the subsequent organization, funding and construction of the great majority of the state's school buildings.

As the public agency responsible for the maintenance of essential social infrastructure (including schools), and working with the construction industry to build thousands of new schools across England and Wales, these new Local Education Authorities acted on behalf of Head Teachers as architectural clients for new capital works. Paradoxically, the vast majority of new school buildings (opened between 1950 and 1970) were also designed by the local authority's own architect's.

This duality has given way to the current dichotomy growing within local education authorities wrestling with the financial, legal, contractual and ethical conditions of central governments' Private Finance Initiative (PFI). With New Labour's proposed spending and release of public funds via the PFI totalling £8 billion during 2003–2006, the question of whether it is possible for an organization designed to deliver a public service to reorientate itself into a more product-focused commercial operation in order to provide public facilities, is currently being explored in some contemporary PFI schools projects like that at Castle Green School, Sunderland.[39] At the very least, it is fair to say that the corporate culture of the protection of commercial interests within the PFI is at odds with the current culture of participation in the delivery of public services.

Contrary to the PFI's tendency to work with a minimal allowance of time for design and a more standardized design template; and the inherent

125

contractual pressures to 'design and build' fast, young people's participation in schools design projects also challenges LEAs to redefine the client in terms of a collective. On new participatory, collaborative design projects (discussed in more detail below), the 'client group' has been redefined to represent the whole school community: children, parents, head teachers, support staff, local community groups and teaching staff alike.

The Department for Education and Skills' (DfES) own School Buildings & Design Unit's 2002 guidelines sets the tone for this new relationship between the LEA and school communities: 'It is very important that right from the beginning of a school building project there is proper consultation with the staff and pupils of the school and the wider community.... This approach will help to encourage greater use of the building, develop trust between all parties and add to the feeling of community and ownership'.[40]

Further to this, the DfES's own 'Departmental Investment Strategy, 2003–06' published in December 2002 points out – in reference to the commissioned Pricewaterhouse Coopers' report 'Building Performance' (2001) – that 'external evaluation is revealing the quantitative linkages between investment in school buildings and increasing pupil performance'.[41]

Whether or not it is possible to prove in quantative terms that a better-designed school helps pupils 'perform' better in academic tests, some schoolteachers have been quick to recognize the cross-curricular potential in design projects relating to proposed on-site building works. Education professionals and designers alike appreciate the value in encouraging children and young people to develop their own design ideas, as a way of incorporating into the architects' main design brief their insights into, and understanding of, the school organization. Initiatives like School Works (see Part Four below), have been especially effective in this aspect of participatory school building renovation projects. In the last few years, as School Works demonstrates, significant strides have been made in finding new ways to link children's perceptions of architectural space to new school design projects.

Young designers working with professionals

At the same time the DfES launched their own 'Classroom of the Future' initiative in July 2000, some Local Education Authorities allowed schools to facilitate a greater collaboration between their pupils and their project architects.[42] Pupils at Cottrell & Vermeulen's prize-winning Westborough Primary School in Essex worked, for example, on a 3-d modelling project looking at alternative structural forms during the design process for their new school. Taking this approach a few stages further, St Jude's Primary School in Glasgow undertook a 'Designing for Real' process to investigate possible improvements to the design of their school buildings.[43] The three-year 'Making Fish' project involved children of all ages in a process that would enable them to re-examine the strengths and weaknesses of their existing primary school environment. To make this possible, St Jude's had to 'provide the pupils with sufficient skills and understanding of their environment, of the needs of their school in the future, and in drawing and modelling, in order to propose designs that could then be translated, by the professionals involved into a possible reality'.[44] Without the pressures of a looming building programme, this kind of collaborative 'Designing for Real' project benefits young people and their school community through a greater provision of time to conceptualize and explore design ideas.

As an extension of the hands-on approach taken at St Jude's Primary School, a team of architects working on a 'Classroom of the Future' scheme at Ballifield Primary School, Sheffield have tried to devise small-scale projects in which schoolchildren themselves can physically alter and reinterpret both the interior and exterior (playground) environments of their school. With Ballifield pupils working as 'designers, makers and implementers', architects from the Research Design Unit at the University of Sheffield School of Architecture devised ways for their young colleagues to redecorate walls and ceilings with personalized ceramic tiles and to construct large playground benches from rammed earth, concrete or cob (refer to Chapter 3).[45] To the extent that school-children

A large timber bench with solid base has many functions, spanning various activities. It acts as a plinth for improvized play and forms a basic building block for the children to use in various ways. The complexity of the unit can be designed to suit budget and needs.

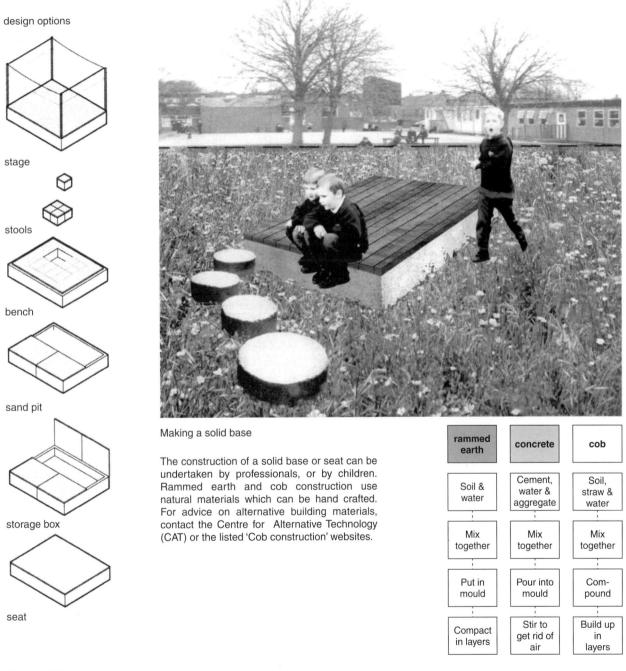

design options

stage

stools

bench

sand pit

storage box

seat

Making a solid base

The construction of a solid base or seat can be undertaken by professionals, or by children. Rammed earth and cob construction use natural materials which can be hand crafted. For advice on alternative building materials, contact the Centre for Alternative Technology (CAT) or the listed 'Cob construction' websites.

rammed earth	concrete	cob
Soil & water	Cement, water & aggregate	Soil, straw & water
Mix together	Mix together	Mix together
Put in mould	Pour into mould	Com-pound
Compact in layers	Stir to get rid of air	Build up in layers

Figure 7.5

might actually construct some parts of an architect's scheme, projects of this kind take young people's participation to a new level. Hot on the heels of this innovative work at Ballifield Primary School, in 2003 the UK's Construction Industry Training Board (CITB) launched 'Creative Spaces' – a national competition scheme offering 11- to 14-year-olds the chance to experience the excitement of working in construction while developing ideas for improvements to their schools. Winning students get to see their design proposal actually built, with up to £50 000 worth of construction costs being met by the CITB.

Again in Glasgow, and this time via The Sorrell Foundation's independent 'joinedupdesignforschools' scheme, seven 11- to 12-year-olds at Quarry Brae Primary School worked as a 'client team' with architect Ross Hunter and graphic designer Janice Kirkpatrick to 'create a new type of learning space within a classroom setting.' In response to the cramped conditions of the 1903 Edwardian school building, and as an investigation into 'the thinking behind the space above us', the Quarry Brae team's highly successful project to design a treehouse above an existing classroom evolved as the result of a creative participatory process to find more working area in a school where 'space is at a premium'.[46] As Kirkpatrick says of the process: 'I thought this was a great idea – asking children to imagine a different kind of life in which they are in control. For me that's the most important aspect – asking them to behave in a way that's contrary to the traditional curriculum … They had pretty strong ideas of what they wanted. Some were really great – especially the treehouse idea. We might never have come up with that solution without them.'[47]

Giving young people control lies at the heart of the new collaboration in schools design. The positive aspects of allowing young people to take control in participatory design and planning processes has been well documented (see Bibliography at end of chapter: Hart, 1992, Trafford, 1997 and Adams & Ingham, 1998). For example, the opportunity for young people to work with professional designers stimulates pupils' own learning processes whilst challenging them to think critically about the organization of architectural space around them. With collaborations of this kind, the rigid boundaries between 'school life' and the world/s beyond the school gates become a little more blurred. As one young Quarry Brae client team member says, relishing his new sense of ownership: 'I enjoyed it because we had to think of our own ideas. I really enjoyed working with the designers. It was a lot of hard work – just working as a group. People were thinking of different things and it was so hard to get agreement sometimes. It made me feel good because it was all our own ideas. I will be proud to see it happen – my parents are proud. It makes me like the school more.'[48]

The importance of ownership should not be underestimated. In her comprehensive and indispensable survey of current UK practice in the design of new learning environments, Helen Clark reminds us 'that "aspiration of space" is intrinsic to the well-being of those inhabiting it.' As well as enhancing their own mental health and well-being, 'reducing the likelihood of vandalism, neglect and costly replacements in the future,' as a result of this process, the unforgettable educational value of a project like Quarry Brae's treehouse learning space, rests in the fact that the adult designers' collaboration with children as young as eleven years old produced the most effective design solution.[49] With flair, and a sometimes more liberated imagination, young people can – and do – formulate effective design solutions to specific architectural problems. As architect Keith Priest attests to his (2001) experience working with 16- to 17-year-olds on a 'makeover' for the English Department at Monk Seaton Community High School, Newcastle: 'There's no doubt that school students should be involved in a wide range of decisions about their school – they certainly can contribute.'[50] As Blishen (1969, see Bibliography) too has shown us: 'our children are immensely anxious to be reasonable, to take account of practical difficulties.'

With Blishen's observation's in mind, it is worth reflecting here on the pedagogical implications of collaborative projects of this kind.

Working over time, within school settings, architects and designers can take on a catalytic role. Invited to contribute to the life of a school community and its environment, creative professionals bring an 'ingredient x' into the usual teacher–pupil exchange. At its most creative, collaborative partnerships between professional designers and architects and young people can also redefine traditional teacher roles to the extent that the more formal, institutional teacher–pupil relationships can be transcended to the benefit of both parties.[51] Mirroring the capacity of design projects like that at Quarry Brae to redefine boundaries between school learning and 'real-life' learning, collaborations of this quality can reinterpret teacher–learner relationships in ways which open up new possibilities for young people to reflect on their own propensities and preferred modes of learning (Gardner, 1983).

'Live' design projects of this kind, where there is a shared responsibility for the outcome, prompt in young people an alternative kind of learning experience in which another range of abilities comes into play. Young people fortunate enough to have participated in these recent design experiments have also benefited from a renewed sense of self-esteem, confidence and empowerment. Regrettably, this kind of educational process and the experience of the children at the schools mentioned above is the exception, not the rule. In spite of all the pioneering work described above, there is still too great a perceptual and professional distance between architects and young people. There is certainly no shortage of opportunity for collaboration between architects and school children. With the enormous quantity of school building projects scheduled for remodelling or new construction across the UK, we have before us an historic moment of great potential in rethinking the ways in which school buildings and learning environments are designed. To capitalize on this, we need to invent, develop and refine new working relationships between architects and young people.

To bridge the gap between contemporary designers and school children, Clark[49] proposes that architects 'become trained in understanding pedagogical and curricular requirements'. Like Clark, we would also propose that a more participatory design process requires that learning between young people and architects becomes a two-way exchange. Schoolchildren can learn a spatial language from professional designers, but architects too must learn an environmental language from their young collaborators. We would further argue that a good place to develop this capacity is within the architect's own education and training.

Board school bubbles: action research and the new collaboration between architects and primary children

While some architecture departments at universities like Sheffield and North London have started to work more closely with schools, academic studio design work rarely addresses the needs and ambitions of the occupiers of their hypothetical schemes directly, as there are no real clients to interrogate and learn from.

This is despite a growing realization that the psychological reaction of individuals to their spatial surroundings has a primary influence on their perception and understanding of modern urban space. Whether a 'situationist' or a phenomenological approach is taken to increase contextual understanding and generate a design strategy, the problem is still one of assessing the reaction of an individual (whether designer or occupier) to their surroundings.[52] In primary schools, pupils bring their own fantastical imaginings with them from elsewhere and overlay these on what exists. What has gone before and what is proposed then moves into a newly active realm where the interlopers attempt to impose their preconceptions.

The relative permanence of a school's fabric is occupied by rapidly changing cohorts of pupils. Each pupil will have their own perception of the school environment and will attempt to engage with these relatively timeless edifices as a backdrop to their own fleeting fantasies.

There is an enormous gap here in the knowledge available to architects. It is clear that techniques are required allowing the political, psycho-geographical and phenomenological responses of occupiers to penetrate the studio teaching cycle and the architects' design process. But in order to contribute to better school design, some way should also be found to understand the potential of spatial design to facilitate the exploration and creative expression of the pupils' own imagination. As we have seen already, the work of the architecture workshop movement has provided some important first steps in enabling young people to express their own design ideas.

However, such an understanding implies a structured dialogue between architect and building user which is seldom found in practice. There are, however, a few precedents. Pioneering architect Walter Segal thought that as a profession, the architect's role could no longer be 'one of taste maker' and that it would be desirable 'for those for whom architects are building … to bring their own talents to bear'.[53] In his own work this dialogue involved the manipulation by individual self builder/house owners of a basic kit of parts designed by the architect. Cedric Price thought that this dialogue with the user was the 'delight' in architecture (Price, 1984, see Bibliography). The uncertainty over time of the interaction between the elements of his Fun Palace projects and their users distorted 'time and place, along with convenience and delight [which] opens up a dialogue that reminds people how much freedom they have.'[54]

The kind of intellectual freedom identified by Segal and Price is represented exactly in the kind of creativity which has been illicited and utilized in schools design and refurbishment projects like those at Ballifield (sic.) and Kingsdale (see below). As we will show, this interactive approach has also been explored by architecture students investigating the implications for design in changing public buildings within the framework of a 'Designing for Real' (D4R) collaborative design process, in the context of Victorian school buildings.[55]

London Board schools as a fertile ground for studio design work

Undergraduate studio 6 at the School of Architecture and Interior Design at the University of North London had been concerned for many years with the decline of public space and the way that this space was being used in a climate of diminishing resources. The studio had observed the shifting relationship between urban landscape, both natural and artificial, and its occupation, both ephemeral and enduring. This relationship appeared obscure and unpredictable.

In order to explore further, the studio began looking for a typical family of existing buildings each set within its own topology, with established social uses, and occupiers who were accessible to questioning and might even be persuaded to take part in the design process. If there was a pressing programme for change that could be enlivened by animated interaction with the users then the imagination and creativity unleashed by such a process might be profound.

In the teaching year 1999–2000 the studio focused on the problems and opportunities of London Board schools. The design briefs of the architecture students were to be derived from both their own empirical responses to the fabric of the school and their dialogue with pupils and staff.

London Board schools

As we have seen, London board schools were built as a direct response to the government's decision to provide primary education for all in the late-nineteenth century. They are usually four- or five-storey redbrick structures designed in the 'Queen Anne' style by E. R. Robson and his successor at the London Board, T. J. Bailey, and are far more elegant than the dreary, hermetic Gothic structures, which represented the church-sponsored education on offer previously (Girouard, 1984, see Bibliography). The new buildings provided extensive cross ventilation and daylight within an open secular environment, a truly modern universal experiment of its time. They were built high in dense urban environments because land was scarce and they needed to be located within walking distance of the pupils' homes.

Soundly constructed, many are now 'listed' as having architectural merit. Most have continued for over a 100 years to house state primary schools. Over this period the buildings have undergone a number of physical changes. Originally separated, infants and junior schools have been combined. Sanitation has been improved. Gender separation between boys and girls has been abolished.

However, in some respects their physical fabric has resisted change, remaining intact well after their generating educational concepts have disappeared from the agenda. Board schools were meant to provide a 'healthy' educational environment. It was thought that physically and mentally weak children would benefit from large amounts of sun and fresh air in a climate of close supervision. This has left a heritage of cold, over-ventilated, monolithic cellular classrooms that are expensive to heat and difficult to adapt to the flexible and more open teaching spaces favoured now.

On tight sites the ground floor was sometimes left open at first, to act as a playground and then enclosed when sufficient surrounding land was acquired. Many board school roofs continue as 'playgrounds with a view'. Corridors were kept to a minimum to save space. Each floor was centred on a hall. Classrooms started as alcoves off the hall, being curtained off according to the number of teaching staff available. Eventually the standard board school plan emerged, with classrooms leading off both these halls and secondary corridors that in turn served a series of staircases (Kelsall, 1983 and Dark, 1994, see Bibliography). Each hall is not usually large enough to allow the whole school to gather for assembly or to eat school dinners at a single sitting. Currently, halls are vestigial spaces requiring careful management of the timetable by the head teacher to put them to good use.

Originally, parents rarely passed through the school gates; these previously hallowed portals are now thrown wide open at the start and end of the school day and parents are welcomed into the classroom. With falling rolls, schools now need to

attract new pupils by displaying an attractive public face. In many of these more forward thinking schools, foyer spaces, located next to entrances, often house changing displays of school work. With such permeability comes the danger of unwanted intrusion highlighted by the 1996 Dunblane tragedy.[56] CCTV cameras have been installed to monitor school entrances that have become shop windows with a security filter.

In the UK, even in inner city locations, there are few examples of multi-storey primary schools built after the First World War.[57] This is in contrast to the situation in the Netherlands. Jan Duiker's Open Air School (1928–29) in Amsterdam and the work of Herman Hertzberger today are just some examples of Dutch multi-storey schools.

Even more so today there is a question mark over the suitability of London board school buildings for continued use as state primary schools. Their fabric is the antithesis of that of post Second World War primary schools that are long and low, well-insulated, lightweight, single-storey structures, painted in bright colours with warm wood finishes, broad areas of glazing and bright internal lighting. Board schools remain multi-storey structures with tall ceilings, multiple staircases and no lifts. They are thermally massive buildings with little or no insulation, and large areas of single glazing absorbing a disproportionate share of the school budget to heat in the winter.

In some areas where school age populations have diminished and board schools have been sold to developers, their striking and often listed façades have been successfully renovated and their interiors divided into lofted residential accommodation. Because of their centrally located city sites, these properties have proved irresistible to city workers, providing a vision of cleaned up heritage with superb views and a central location within a secure compound.

'Designing for Real' case studies

Carlton School, Kentish Town, London

Carlton school was built in 1883 to accommodate 1800 pupils who were previously being taught in cellars and under railway arches. Originally there was an infants school, together with separate entrances to a junior school for girls and boys. By 1986, all had been combined into one primary school teaching 420 pupils.

The building consists of three tall halls stacked on top of one another facing south west. Classrooms make up the remainder of this and the whole of the opposing north east façades. Projecting slightly into the playground, this tower of three halls is flanked on either side by six half-height floors of stairs, toilets, offices and store rooms.

Access to the school was seen as confused by both staff and pupils. Set back from the road the school had minimal presence on the street. Reception and administration needed relocation adjacent to a new entrance and foyer space. The pupils lamented a lack of green areas within the playground and longed for a more colourful and natural play environment.

Pupils' proposals for change

Pupils were asked to draw and paint snapshots of their school, chosen by looking through a framing device or viewfinder. They were also asked to trace their routes through the school using coloured string, later marking these routes on a plan. Using collage and modelling they then made proposals for changing the playground and entrance spaces.

On the street frontage a new colourful entrance wall was proposed leading to a garden full of trees, ponds, race tracks, slides, swings, 'movement tubes' and a swimming pool. The ponds would be home to a family of frogs, fully supplied with lily pads and toys to jump off, together with fountains from which the pupils could drink and in which they could refresh themselves. Trees would both support dens out of the reach of teachers and troublesome peers, and frame the new building entrance with luxuriant foliage. Snacks and hot food were available from a garden kiosk and coin-operated vending machines. A large neon sign of the figure 2000 was featured in several drawings either in the garden or fixed to the façade of the school, perhaps to emphasize a new start or to suggest that the school was not so old after all.

The framed snapshot approach highlighted the ambiguous message presented to the visitor by the existing façade. For example, there were several entrances but these were marked confusingly: 'fire exit' and 'office'. Their true function was actually indicated by the presence of bicycles chained to railings. Using the framing device, pupils picked out two pairs of doors set symmetrically at the foot of the lower hall which they all agreed should be the location of the new school entrance, but confusion remained over which pair of doors this should be.

Just inside the new entrance pupils sensibly located the administration and head teacher's offices and toilets. Here, most importance was given to a 'place to be' with 'a little quiet' where pupils and visitors might wait and anticipate what was in store. These drawings were amongst the most severe and subdued, suggesting control (remotely-operated sliding doors, CCTV, touch screen information booth) with just a chink of openness (glass block wall, helper's room).

The weaving of thread from each individual entrance to the various classrooms provoked a study of the multitude of doors which had to be negotiated on the way, their direction of swing, their scale (compared to the child) and the part these doors played in providing thresholds between each domain of the school.[58] All this was circumvented by proposals for passenger lifts. Lifts would not only shuttle pupils rapidly from entrance to classroom but also provide an alternative map of the school. A separate button in the lift car would identify each class and teacher. Pupils only had to press the appropriate button to be transported rapidly and unambiguously to their destination. The lobby outside each lift stop would be a friendly and optimistic space with a colourful mat on the floor, a tea-making device and lots more buttons to press to other destinations.

The most expressive proposal for vertical movement was for a bulbous, tubular shoot fixed to the outside of the building taking rubbish for recycling from each classroom and hall of the building, rapidly and noisily, to an enormous cylindrical dustbin marked with the school's new logo: a tree.

Daubeney School, Hackney, London

In 1884, at the time of Daubeney's construction, some education experts preferred schools to be of a village-school scale, trying to resist the pressure of expensive land driving such buildings as tall as Rhyl, Carlton or New End. As a result, the buildings here are lower and more spread out, but no less important than these others. The façades of Daubeney School were listed some time ago as they are a prime example of this smaller-scale type (Saint, 1991, see Bibliography).

Over the years the curtilage of the school has been extended to include elements located within a distinct rectangular urban plot, shared with houses, offices and warehouses and surrounded on all four sides by roads. The original single-storey infants block and the two-storey (plus two roof space classrooms) junior school are located on adjacent sides of the playground. Elsewhere are a new nursery, a vacant corner plot and a 'hop garden' which leads off the playground and has been partially landscaped with a pond and wildlife garden.

The current pupil role is 480 and is falling slightly as local tower blocks have been demolished. Maintaining the external fabric of the buildings is expensive due to the relatively large surface to volume ratio and has largely been neglected. Temporary 'prefab' buildings erected within the playground 25 years ago, and used for both storage and dining, consume most of the annual maintenance budget. The listing of the premises had inhibited minor improvements, such as building covered walkways, incorporating external toilets within the building and providing direct access for the pupils to the playground.

Proposals by both pupils and students

The tasks that the students introduced to the pupils were unlike those undertaken at the other schools studied. Exercises were mostly carried out together as a group, often in the hall on a large scale. The work produced was a collective expression of the pupils' ideas rather than a series of individual pieces.

For the first session the students presented a scale model of the school and asked the pupils what

Figure 7.6

they would like to change. Later, both pupils and students overlaid sketches of their proposals on plans or photographs of the school for general discussion. Pupils were also asked to write down their proposals for improvement.

The following week pupils jointly produced a large map collaged from coloured paper and drew on it their route to school, method of transportation, the entrance used, and their favourite place within the school. Pupils were also asked to associate words of their choice such as 'smelly', 'noisy' or 'fun' to enlarged photographs of spaces which were of particular interest to the students. In subsequent sessions pupils built large-scale mock-ups of their ideas using cardboard boxes (to make walls, entrances, corridors), or – as a variant of Frost's modelling system (sic.) – with bamboo sticks and elastic bands (to erect a framed enclosure) in real space.

Whilst some of the later exercises were designed to explore the pupils' own spatial experience, most were intended to elicit their response to the architecture students' proposals. Unlike work in the other three schools there were no drawn proposals from the pupils themselves.

The exercises confirmed that entry to and movement around the school was problematic; halls were too small and hall-based activities, such as dining or physical education, interfered with classroom activities. Whilst pupils had difficulty separating the qualities of spaces themselves from the activities carried out within them, the favourite place in the school was undoubtedly the playground. Enjoyment of this space would be enhanced even further if food and improved play equipment were provided.

In the last session the students organized a discussion with the pupils of some simple proposals based on the ideas which had emerged from the previous sessions. The students used the original cardboard model of the school, enlarged to include the whole urban block containing the grounds of the school, to illustrate proposals for a larger hall, a lift, shelter and a café.

All the children liked the idea of a bigger hall but were unsure about what to do with the old one. In response to the problem of moving large numbers of children around in lifts, pupils suggested that each class on the upper floor should have its own lift. They were concerned however that this would not be allowed because of the perceived mismatch of an array of modern lifts superimposed on a listed façade. A shelter should be provided at the main entrance which should be top lit, inward looking and contain lots of chairs, allowing parents to chat to each other whilst they attended to their children's arrival and departure from school. A number of locations were proposed for a café or tuck shop as it needed to be immediately accessible at all times except during classes.

The excitement and inventiveness of the children during this last exercise was particularly notable. They responded with easy and frank approval or derision to each other's ideas that ranged from the practical to the fanciful. Nevertheless, in the students' view they were all capable of providing the basis for a valid design proposal.

Rhyl School, Kentish Town, London

Rhyl Primary School, built by Bailey in 1898 and listed in 1999, is a large, turreted and pedimented, standard 'triple-decker' building in Kentish Town (Saint, 1991, see Bibliography). The main school entrance is off-axis on the north, classroom-dominated, street-facing façade. In contrast, the more broken, hall-dominated southern elevation overlooks a generous, warm, colourful, leafy playground filled with a set of new play equipment.

Arranged around the major route from front to back, the entrance area has been assembled by knocking holes in the thick brickwork separating corridor from classroom, leaving the resulting space extensive but contorted. Using an abundance of furniture, locations have been defined within the entrance area for meeting, waiting, crèche and adult literacy classes. These activities are provided with a coffee machine and surrounded by corners, niches and walls displaying items such as: the school uniform, a fish tank, the work of the Art Club, the Declaration of Human Rights, an RSPCA board, an exhibition of Chinese artefacts and a Hindu shrine.

The children's view of the school

Using drawings and collage, pupils were asked to represent spaces both inside and outside the school building and then to illustrate their preferred changes. Later they were given enlarged photocopies of photographs of spaces in the school and asked to draw over them changes they would like to see.

The pupils saw the northern approach frontage as grim, dirty and out of date. They indicated that parts might be painted in bright colours. Soft white pods were shown fixed to the façade to be entered through classroom windows. Ponderous horizontality and heavy enclosure characterized external brickwork whilst window areas were under-represented.

A sense of the building as a dense high container was contrasted with the open, colourful, natural

Figure 7.7

and playful spaces outside. Children had a formal sense of their school building as a rectangular block with which they had a physical relationship in terms of shape and scale. Classrooms were shown as cluttered, busy, homely and inward looking, whilst outside, football, trees and play equipment predominated. Attempts to improve horizontal circulation included proposals for a rocket-powered lift carrying at least 30 pupils and a helter-skelter or roller coaster attached to the southern façade. Powered three-wheeler beach-buggies, water slides and Ferris wheels are located in the playground; sweet shops, ice cream kiosks and 'MacDonald's' hamburger stalls service these activities.

Surprisingly, the need for pupils to withdraw and set themselves apart from the rest of the school was expressed in a variety of drawings. One pupil even went so far as to show herself reclining in an oasis surrounded by palm trees. One sketch shows the entrance to a 'Year 6 Club' at the top of a set of tiny stairs, whilst another displays a notice advising when pupils can attend. Perched atop a stepladder on the ground floor is an individual platform provided with a large pair of bright red spectacles for the retreatant to look down on her peers. In another version the class is cocooned in a red translucent bag with the artist climbing a ladder to a different world suspended from the ceiling. Quiet rooms and music practice rooms are raised above their classmates and, in contrast to depictions of the busy, colourful and textured classrooms, are sparsely furnished, coolly decorated and clearly articulated spaces.

New End School, Hampstead, London

Built in 1905 on a tight, steeply sloping site described as an 'inadequate wedge of left-over land', in what was then the poorer part of Hampstead, New End now epitomizes the more well-endowed board school. Pupil numbers have surged to 430 in the last 10 years and the accommodation is somewhat cramped. Consequently, classrooms have recently been added to the lower floor and on the roof. The school was listed in 1988 for its 'one-off tall symmetrical design' and its 'strong contextual value' (Saint, 1991, see Bibliography). The southern façade is an impressive assembly of redbrick and glass towering over the urban landscape of narrow alleys and small walkways from behind a high brick perimeter wall that seals off the whole site.

The students developed a strong working relationship with two of the teachers and their

135

pupils and this enhanced communication and creativity. Pupils were asked to draw and model spaces within the school building and suggest improvements to their use and fit out. Each session was concluded with a discussion on the ideas generated. In a later exercise pupils were asked to comment on the students' own designs which had incorporated ideas generated during the three sessions.

The pupil's proposals

Pupils' proposals centred on the need for escape, relaxation and fun; perhaps indicating perceived stress in the school programme. A 'loft of wonders' on the roof of the school consisted of seven zones containing toys and games surrounding a quiet area. Four pupils proposed 'bubble' rooms.

'A bubble room is a sort of extension to the school (Plate 12). It has a door then a tunnel to a classroom or hall. In the bubble room there is a comfy area. This has lots of cushions and beanbags. There is also a sweaty (sic) pool, this means if you have a bath or a shower you can dive in and eat all the sweets. There is also a mucky place, a nice tea and coffee place but I will leave you to imagine them'.

One contained a whole wall of bright lights shining on a disco ball and mirrored walls. Music was provided to allow dancing on a cleared central area edged with beanbags on which to languish between dances. The second more detailed schematic involved bathing as a method of relaxation served by maids bearing sweets and biscuits who entered the bubble from a side tunnel. Central place was given to a dressing table with a mirror and a central light. Furnishing was sumptuous and womb-like with gold chains and silk curtains hanging from the ceiling. The third drawing shows a small personal pod equipped with sofa, beanbag and cushions; supplied with a dream cassette machine and a rack of computer games (Plate 12). The fourth and last 'bubble' room is notable for its stained glass windows displaying the planets in glorious technicolor (Plate 13).

Rather than an emblem of disgust, school toilets have become the place where pupils can escape and relax. Here, washing (using baths, basins and showers) has become distinct from relaxing (in jacussi and sauna). Gabriel explains his ideas (see Plate 13):

I chose the toilet. I don't know why I chose this room. I just had some good ideas. I am going to

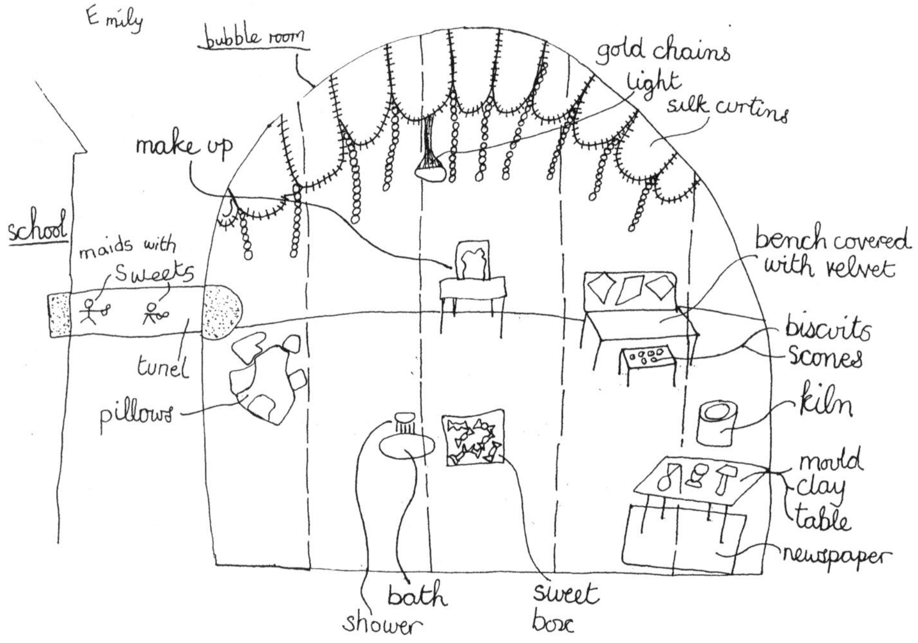

Figure 7.8
Theatrical concept for a 'bubble room' (see also Plate 11).

use a playstation box and two breakfast boxes (for the model). I put two baths, a Jacuzzi, some TVs, a shower, a urinal, some sinks and some lavatories. I chose the Jacuzzi because if you wanted to relax you could hop into the Jacuzzi and relax. I chose the baths and the shower because if you got dirty in school time you could hop in the bath and go in the shower. This space is supposed to be very enjoyable and fun.

Instead of ventilated lobbies, boys toilets (but not girls toilets) are to be fitted with electronic smell traps. Girls toilets are provided with mats and carpets together with soft chairs so that pupils can sit, wait for and talk to friends whilst they ablute.

The student response to the fantasy agenda

The studio programme had been set up so students had a range of different opportunities to develop their own individual design programme. They were asked to generate a strategic brief from the general literature on board schools, talks with school staff, a measured survey of their particular school and their own personal response to their individual site. They were also challenged to adopt some of the fragmentary and often fantastical pupil-generated ideas, using the design process as a line of enquiry into their project.

Most of the students found it easier to respond to the explicit agenda coming from teachers and school governors rather than creatively interpreting the fantasies generated by the pupils. The discussion below is restricted to those ideas that emerged from dialogue with the pupils and used by students in developing their proposals. These included ways of moving rapidly around, and particularly up and down the school, and the provision of small 'retreat' spaces or pods.

Rapid vertical movement

Pupils' imagination was stirred by the possibility of some type of automated mass transit system to move pupils (and rubbish) vertically up and down the school façades. This was to be a fast, visible and indeed thrilling experience akin to a roller-coaster ride.

Matthieu Tisserand proposed a dramatic full height glass screen stretching across, and several metres in front of the already impressive southern façade of New End school. Most of the old wall was removed to reveal and unite a layer of spaces sandwiched between the northern row of classrooms and the new glazed wall. These were the new spaces – light, open and brightly coloured. They were punctured by stair towers and toilet blocks but combined by their shared southern aspect.

Lifts and escalators begin to meet the pupils' desire for rapid, expressive and 'fun' transit facilities: a traveller's progress being visible from the south through the façade. Previously, time was represented by the lazy, subtle, seasonal play of sunlight on red brick. Now the contrast was between conditions of bright daylight when interiors receded and the dark winter afternoons when artificial lighting would display the school like a doll's house.

Once available, this ability to display itself needed to be managed. So the southern screen was engineered to project messages, timetables and images to inform itself and the local community of current programmes.

Pods

Amongst the pupils there was a clear awareness of the potential for relaxation provided by reformulating the idea of school toilets into bath and chat rooms. This was just one type of retreat (bubble, pod, soft) space which emerged from the 'Designing for Real' (D4R) (sic. footnote 30) exercises which variously provided for especially focused study, protection, observation, relaxation and an opportunity for intimate control over a pupil's immediate environment.

Steven Van Der Heijden found teachers and pupils at New End particularly enthusiastic about developing an idea for a space that would be an adjunct to the classroom called the 'softspace'. Class 5J's teacher at New End explained that rather than tables and chairs there would be 'soft cushions for circle time, group games or class discussions. I have often had classroom assistants coming in, assisting in teaching small groups of

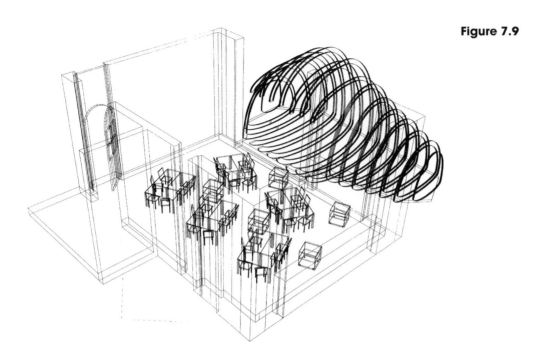

Figure 7.9

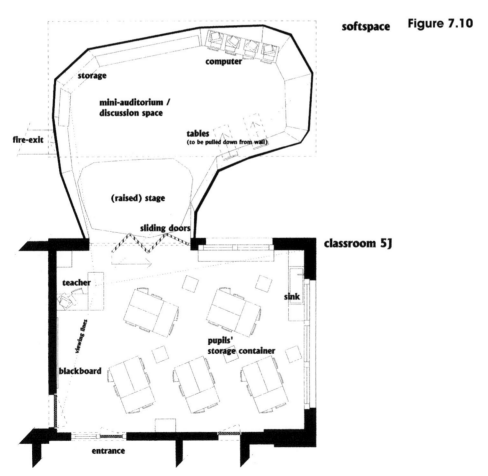

softspace   **Figure 7.10**

computer

storage

mini-auditorium /
discussion space

fire-exit

tables
(to be pulled down from wall)

(raised) stage

sliding doors

classroom 5J

teacher

sink

viewing lines

pupils'
storage container

blackboard

entrance

the class, and I have to arrange some tables for them in the corridor. At the moment it is impossible for me to monitor these and other activities outside the classroom. The additional "softspace" could maintain a mini-library, resources and reading station with headphones, computer and display wall'.

Van Der Heijden chose to hang extra space on to the outside of the existing building. His 'softspace blobs' projected from the north facing wall of classrooms and were supported on a steel framework, filling the space between the building and the northern boundary of the site. This framework also accommodated a new entrance on the ground floor. Penetrating both the old school and new steel frame was a new enlarged whale-like hall.

A series of drawings tested the proposed 'softspace' and its relationship with the classroom. Comments from 5J's class teacher on the detailed proposals led to further changes. Pupils responded well, imagining the 'softspace' as a refuge or a secret panopticon and incorporating these ideas into their own drawings. Emily, aged 10, said that a bubble room was a sort of extension to the school and it had 'a door, then a tunnel to a classroom or hall. In the bubble room there is a comfy area. There is also a nice tea and coffee place, a wonderful art area and a bath or shower.'

Gabriel, aged nine, said that: 'you could have a big pole which goes out of the school with a bubble at the top. So that instead of going round Hampstead, we could just go up some stairs to the bubble at the top to see.'

With a strong design idea and extensive involvement with the D4R exercises, Van Der Heijden was able to unlock the creative contribution of pupils and teachers and enrich and articulate the design of an important fragment of his scheme.

Lessons learned

Pupils saw their tall brick board schools as ponderous monolithic structures; as out of date as their designers had perceived their Gothic predecessors. Nevertheless, through the D4R exercises, the pupils managed to overlay upon this

perception, snapshots of their dreams, aspirations and obsessions. These took the form of colourful interventions providing for relaxation and fun – perhaps an escape from the stress of the well-used, homely but work-focused classroom. The collective methods employed at Daubeney were in marked contrast to those employed at other schools where exercises were designed to provoke individual vision and creativity.

Daubeney group exercises elicited a general preference for outside (associated with fast food, movement and freedom) over inside (associated with conflicting activities, deteriorating fabric and restrictions on building improvement). From this, students developed schemes that dispersed activities around the site rather than rehabilitating existing buildings. Students were also able to get a positive critical response to their proposals from pupils.

So whilst the methods employed at Daubeney were perhaps most useful at informing a strategic response to the problems of the school, they were less useful in unlocking images of children's most vivid and imaginative ideas. The work which most nearly achieves this is the 'soft space' proposal at New End where images derived from the drawings of pupils were developed to link in with and enhance the existing classroom routine.

But there is much further to go. Schemes which derive their agenda and design idea from a fragmentary moment captured during interaction with the pupils rather than (or as well as) being informed by a strategic response to the school's overall ambitions, promise a richness lacking from standardized output. The evocative drawing which shows a girl in conversation with her friend in the toilets at New End, the faith in technology mixed with homely comfort of the lift lobby drawing at Carlton and the whole plethora of bubbled retreat spaces emphasized in so many pupil drawings, are the potentially rich sources of invention and imagination usually missed during the design process.

Whilst perception based on the five senses might be regarded as changeless, the relationship between what we occupy and how it is perceived psychologically, changes not only with the age of the occupier but also with the age of the different layers of landscape being occupied. Board schools provided a fertile illustration of this phenomenon. Pupils' imaginary representations, partly derived from film, television and advertising, were juxtaposed with the 'listing' imperative and historical interpretations of board schools as 'beacons of light' and 'open air' environments superseding their Gothic predecessors.

Many architects will argue that they have the capacity to not only interpret, but also invent spatial and material qualities and processes that transcend the dreams and fantasies of the users – making them at the same time real and better. This may well have been true of board schools in the time of Bailey and Robson, who provided an inspirational backdrop to the efforts of Victorian schoolchildren. But this inspirational relationship between architecture and pupil presupposes a timelessness to the built product which is less evident in those London Board school buildings which continue to be used as primary schools today.

We all overlay our experience of the physical environment with our current fantasies. Children are perhaps able to express this more easily than most adults because of the immediacy of their artwork. Most importantly, the D4R research showed that the landscape of the board schools was less an active generator of a pupil's spatial perception and more a passive backdrop on which their imaginations were actively projected.

If architects are to provide landscapes for dreams, rather than nightmares, they should avoid allowing their own cultural obsessions to dominate school designs, which are more appropriately intended as neutral serviced containers for the more tentative and changing imaginings of their occupiers. Cedric Price referred to this when he insisted that his Potteries Thinkbelt project should be 'capable of being … supplanted, with the minimum amount of physical (that is, built) fuss in order to avoid … being branded for all time as the ideal spot for scientific education' (Price, 1984, see Bibliography).

In the private realm of housing, the work of Walter Segal and the self-build movement have demonstrated that successful inhabitation should involve some significant level of capacity for spatial manipulation by the occupiers (Segal, 1981/2, see Bibliography). In schools, this might at least imply a looser fit between major building works and anticipated occupation. The potential of the building and its grounds for make-believe might be reassessed with each facelift and redecoration. In the classroom, the artwork associated with discovering psychological perceptions can overlap and be extended to encompass actual changes, allowing a pupil's imagination to reverberate and echo for a little longer.

In the D4R exercises the student working process might be seen as a line of enquiry seeking to project, through a form of dialogue, the individual creativity of the pupils within the public space of the school. Whilst Segal and Price focused on interactive technologies of making and use respectively, the D4R students concentrated on proactive dialogue in the briefing process to incorporate users creativity. Further understanding needs to be developed in all three areas of architectural performance.

Architecture can provide both the conduit and the structure for such a dialogue. It can set boundaries, particularly in the public realm and offer the challenge of new representational technologies and bodies of thought. But architects can only help interpret and orchestrate this process of dialogue if they have the tools to understand the changing relationship between physical fabric and fantasy amongst users of all ages.

Young people's creativity and artistic talent has also been harnessed at perhaps the UK's most high-profile (and well-documented) participatory school design project: 'School Works'.[59] Collaborating with the school community at Kingsdale Secondary School in Southwark, South London, School Works took 'student's interest in the arts as a starting point to explore issues of morale, self-esteem and identity … [and] the links between transforming the school structure and the spirit of the school.'[60]

At the time of School Works' intervention in early 2000, the Kingsdale School community was struggling in a dilapidated late-1950s triple-decker,

Modernist building which, as well as hindering effective teaching and learning, had sustained a number of significant social and behavioural problems. Significantly, for example, essential ICT (Information Communications Technology) learning resources were kept out of reach of students for fear of theft and/or vandalism; lacking sufficient personal storage space, students failed to arrive at lessons prepared with the right resources; and perhaps most alarmingly, the students' toilet and washroom facilities were so appalling that many preferred to go home instead, effectively creating a significant truancy problem for the school. Under these conditions, Kingsdale's young people voted with their feet.

The offer of help with reinventing the culture of the school through redesigning its architecture was especially welcome to Kingsdale's newly-appointed Head Teacher: 'When he was approached by School Works, he jumped at the chance to give Kingsdale a fresh start.'[61]

School Works: new user-group participation in secondary school design

Established between 1999–2000, and originally an Architecture Foundation project, School Works was devised as a way of bringing a new awareness to the relationship between the architecture of secondary school buildings and effective learning. On the one hand, the project seeks to address the gulf between education professionals who don't appreciate design concepts and find it hard to prioritize or envisage the level of environmental change needed in school buildings. On the other hand, School Works seeks to inform designers and architects who know little about developments in pedagogy, curricula or educational technology and their impact on schools design in buildings which need to work now and into the future.

As the DfES-sponsored initiative declared from its outset: 'We cherish our homes; we aspire to beautiful places of work. Why should our schools be different?' (School Works, 2000, see Bibliography).

Indeed, at a key moment in the development of New Labour's education policy, School Works' opening rhetorical question set a new and dramatically simple benchmark in the school design debate of the new millennium. Fresh on the heels of Blair's now infamous sound-bite commitment to education (sic.) and in anticipation of significant capital expenditure on new school buildings at the beginning of the twenty-first century, the School Works project sought to ignite a new level of interest in the architecture of schools and the relationship between building design and pupil achievement.

In response to the growing body of mostly American research evidence (Edwards, 1991; Earthman *et al.*, 1995; Hines, 1996 and Maxwell, 1999) showing that there is some relationship between (a) architectural design, (b) shifts in perception, organizational self-esteem and aspiration within a school community and (c) higher student achievement, School Works set out to show a UK government that high quality design in the architecture of schools can make a qualitative and quantitative difference in the academic and social lives of secondary school students.[62] To further this aim, with support from the New Economics Foundation and with reference to the DfES' own quantitative and qualitative indicators, School Works established a set of measures to assess the impact of streamlined architectural design on pupil achievement.[63]

Ideologically and historically, School Works has its roots in the simple idea of giving your school a 'make-over'. Adopting this young person's term – fresh from the Valley area of southern California, and an ever-popular topic of conversation amongst the female protagonists of US TV series 'Beverly Hills 90210' (aired weekly on British TV during the mid 1990s) – 'Makeover At School' was devised by SENJIT (the Special Education Needs Joint Initiative for Training at the University of London Institute of Education). Like School Works, Makeover At School (M@S) set out to find new ways for architects to explore design solutions in the remodelling of school buildings.[64] Extending SENJIT's M@S's work, a small Architecture Foundation team (including social anthropologist

Hilary Cottam and architect Dominic Cullinan) tested the beginnings of a new, creative process in six London schools in which 'teachers, pupils, classroom assistants, educational psychologists, Special Educational Needs coordinators, caretakers, heads of departments, parents and residents' would all be included in giving 'direct input into the design process, and indeed, be responsible for developing the design brief, supported by independent consultants with technical expertise.'[65] With the launch of School Works as an independent initiative, English secondary students would – for the first time – have a voice in the design process for the refurbishment and renovation of their old school buildings. Largely thanks to School Works' Director Hilary Cottam's recognition of their meaningful position in the overall equation, young people could now also take their rightful place within the client team.

Working with the RIBA Competitions Office, School Works also devised a new competition format recommending that architects be appointed on the strength of both their design portfolio *and* the practice's 'proposals to engage with the potential users of the new building'.[66] Specifically, School Works' competition criteria placed a much greater emphasis on the architect's ability to communicate with and respond to the needs and vision of the whole school community. Competition winners de Rijke Marsh Morgan's proposal and presentation for School Works included architect Alex de Rijke taking on the role of TV news reporter in a series of 'live' investigative interviews taken with staff and students around the school. The choice to engage with a large (1100-strong) school audience via the most accessible mass-communication medium proved to be a smart one. In early 2001, de Rijke Marsh Morgan were appointed as project architects for School Works' £8.5 million pilot experiment at Kingsdale School, south London.

With political support from the think-tank DEMOS and financial seed-funding from the London Borough of Southwark's education authority, School Works assembled a multi-disciplinary team to work with dRMM and the whole school community.[67] Acting as a facilitatory agent and catalyst, Cottam called on her team of professionals to devise a series of investigative workshops and activities for students, staff and Kingsdale's neighbouring residential community.

The workshops themselves (many of which have been well documented in School Works' own 'Tool Kit' publication) ranged from discussion groups, to qualitative ranking exercises, to performance art projects (see Figure 7.11). All members of the school's community were invited to engage with the participatory exercises to help elicit how the school was functioning and to scrutinize the relationship between the architectural design of the school's buildings and the educational, cultural and managerial organization of the school. Central to the project's mission was a belief in the ability of the whole school community to reveal possible solutions to improve both the performance of the school's buildings and Kingsdale's students (see Figure 7.12).

Cottam's School Works team were able to animate Kingsdale's community to such an extent that a wide range of spatial, social and administrative issues were investigated and analysed within a three-month period.

For example, one group of Year 7 (12–13-year-old) students managed to show that the school's actual provision of ICT (Information Communications Technology) hardware was much greater than the school's operational provision. The self-named 'Maverick Explorers' revealed that perception of security and vandalism within Kingsdale was such that a significant amount of computer technology had been stored out of reach of the student community behind locked doors. In parallel to this, the issue of personal space and storage was investigated from the perspective of the students themselves. By asking some seemingly straightforward questions like 'What is a locker?', School Works were able to explore the more subtle importance and meaning for Kingsdale's student community, of personal space within a large institutional building (see Plate 14). The locker workshop raised the fundamental, and in the case of Kingsdale, neglected issues of both individual and corporate identity within the school.

Figure 7.11
Investigative workshop
as part of 'School Works'
consultation at Kingsdale
School.

Figure 7.12
Solutions to funding the
school's problems is
part of a collaborative
process.

In concert with these activities, sensory audits, social mapping exercises and workshops investigating stress levels within the school all combined to provide a thorough and perceptive overview of what life inside Kingsdale was like for students and staff alike. Most importantly, the three-month process of collaboration and dialogue also opened up a forum for a kind of 'plurilogue' on a new vision for the school, with greater aspiration and a more focused direction.[68]

By the end of the 2002 school year, Kingsdale students' experience of the School Works project had already fulfilled elements of the very new secondary 'citizenship' curriculum launched in September of that year. In 'developing skills of enquiry and communication, and participation and responsible action', dRMM's young collaborators had also shown the value of architectural process within a more formal curriculum context.[69] Rather than learn about the social functon of architecture in the form of a lesson in a classroom, Kingsdale students had their own first-hand, 'lived' experience of design and decision-making processes. At the same time, rather than learn about what it means to be a 'good citizen' from traditional textbook exercises, young people had participated in round-table discussion groups, 'community listening' workshops, new forms of 'active audits and surveys' and had tested their own set of tailor-made indicators to measure and analyse their findings (Seymour, J. *et al.*, 2001, see Bibliography). Through these aspects of the Kingsdale project, School Works has shown a new way of integrating elements of the architectural process within the secondary school curriculum.

Whilst the full achievement and implications of School Works' Kingsdale project might be revealed following the 'post-occupancy evaluation' advocated by School Works, the participatory work undertaken at the school has shown that intelligent and well-synthesized collaboration between architects and young people is both possible and highly rewarding, for students, the designers and the whole school community.[70] As an experiment in a new, more inclusive design process, School Works has set a new standard in the production of children's spaces.

As well as this, despite the lack of formal assessment of the Kingsdale project's success (according to School Works' own, DfES' and/or PwC's as yet unpublished criteria), the project might, justifiably, already claim some part in a significant change in pupil and school motivation which has already swept through the culture of the school like a breath of fresh air. Indeed, if Ofsted's measurement system of the performance of London's Southwark schools is anything to go by, Kingsdale has seen the highest increase in 'improvement in 15-year-olds achieving 5 grades

A*–G' during the 1999–2002 period.[71] The project has also set a precedent for client groups to take on a more proactive role in defining design briefs for school building projects.

As well as challenging the imaginations of children and adults alike, School Works also confronts the educational infrastructure with a recommendation that 'the users of the building... [are] viewed as the client during the entire process.'[72] Whilst questioning the traditional role of local education authorities to act as client and primary decision maker, this bold assertion raises an expectation of school communities to take on the role of client (in addition to their other existing duties). Where schools have the facility and are confident to take on a participatory process as recommended by School Works, secondary school communities are much more likely to realize effective, successful new building designs.

However, on the other hand, the assumption that secondary schools have the organizational capacity, sufficient time, political flexibility and business sense to manage and sustain their role as client (dealing with consultants and stakeholder groups, for example) whilst simultaneously running a complex and large-scale learning organization, is problematic. In addition to this, Clark has found that teachers are not always confident or proficient as 'placemakers'.[49] School Works' aspiration also assumes that there is sufficient activity, outreach and support within our wider education authority, design and developer communities with which to foster an ongoing culture of learning about what it means to be a good client in the first place.

Perhaps the greatest challenge to those architects, designers and facilitators seeking to engage school communities in a participatory collaboration lies in the paucity of our spatial and design awareness. Whilst as a nation Britain can pride itself on her great world-renown literary culture, we are – by and large – spatially illiterate.

Against this and the wider context of the UK National Curriculum, the achievement of School Works' Kingsdale project is perhaps doubly significant. Despite the advent of Design and Technology in both the primary and secondary school timetable, most school children in England

and Wales have very little chance to investigate or learn about the buildings they work in. At the secondary level too, very few young people are given the opportunity to systematically explore the social and civic function of architecture in the urban environment.

For young people and adults alike, the lack of a more than surface understanding of the architectural process sustains a culture of low expectation as to what is possible, by design, in the built environment. The appreciation of what architectural imagination can do for a community or a city is still a mystery to most people. To a certain extent, with their lively imaginations, children especially are able to meet designers halfway. Thanks to projects like School Works and joinedupdesignforschools, the education outreach of the UK's architecture and built environment centres and organizations like the Architecture Workshops Association, young people (as we have seen) are now empowered with an architectural language and an understanding of building design that their parents and teachers never were. In the production of children's spaces, these participatory collaborations provide us with a living example of what is possible in the design of new learning environments, and a golden opportunity to create a new generation of user-friendly, efficient and inspirational school buildings.

Conclusion

It is no exaggeration to say that man who up till now has built on a world for the adult must set to work to build up a world for the child.[73]

Maria Montessori

In Britain, we have moved from a period in the history of schools' architecture – the 1930s – in which no time at all has been allowed for architect–pupil collaboration, a time when, according to Saint (1987, see Bibliography), even 'progressive educators thought "architecture" as such was to be avoided for schoolchildren', to a moment, seventy years later, when School Works' four-year Kingsdale project was born out of a twelve-week 'intensive consultation exercise with pupils, staff, parents and the wider community to identify existing problems, encourage debate and develop ideas as to what a beautiful and functional school would look like ... [culminating] in the production of an agreed building plan addressing the immediate architectural needs of the school environment.'[74] This trajectory represents a significant movement towards more intelligent thinking about the design of school buildings in the UK.

In renovating and remodelling existing, older buildings, a very small number of young people have had the chance to interact with architects and designers for a few days, or a few weeks, on realized design schemes or D4R exercises of the kind described above. Beyond the ongoing 'Architects in Residence' schemes at schools like Hills Road Sixth Form College, Cambridge, for example, contact between architects and young people has typically been based on a single day visit by an architect – as part of an RIBA scheme, either a consultative service provided to LEAs by organizations like SENJIT or as a curriculum project delivered through national Architecture Week, or the Architecture Workshops Association, for example. Whilst these opportunities for exchange play a crucial role in maintaining contact between the worlds of school and contemporary architecture, they give little opportunity for informative dialogue between these two professional communities on the (seemingly) continuous process of 'change' within the UK educational system.

Increasingly politicized, often irregular, sometimes circuitous and sporadic, the organizational framework for children's learning is subject to a significant level of uncertainty of direction over the long term (Lucas & Greany, 2000; Sterling, 2001, see Bibliography) in which repeated structural reform is a common denominator.

In response to, and as an expression of this degree of change within educational thinking, central government has, in recent times fuelled a new flourishing of 'diversity' and 'flexibility' in (Secondary) school types. The days of 'one size fits all' are over (Rotherham, 2001; Clark 2002, see Bibliography). City Academies, Technology

Colleges, Specialist, Beacon and Launch Pad schools (for example) have all been developed and built since New Labour's 1997 general election victory. Whilst it is too early to tell whether local authorities now understand the need to move away from a culture of 'homogenized schools. Schools as McDonald's, plonked down with no feel for the local context', there is a growing appreciation in central government of the importance of individual design in contemporary schools architecture.'[75] Not only does this approach allow School Governors and Head Teachers to tailor the school building to fit its curriculum, its delivery and the particular strengths and aptitudes of the school's teachers and learners, but it also makes it more likely that the school provides a meaningful (and ideally profitable) service for the wider surrounding neighbourhood.

With more community-specific school designs – so the rationale goes – public funds will be spent more wisely, the needs of the user will be met, and each school community is freer to express its own unique qualities. With a more responsive architecture, schools can reorientate themselves towards new roles within their neighbourhoods. With community-specific design at the forefront of a new collaborative process, schools will be better equipped (both figuratively and metaphorically) to realize a new culture of learning as an ongoing 'life-long' process.

However, there is more to this happy equation than at first meets the eye.

Unlike the buildings which house it, thinking on education and learning never stands still. Academic theory and political management play their part in stimulating an ongoing process of debate, interpretation and revision. Ideas about the use of space lie implicit within this complex dynamic.

The opening of a new, or reopening of a refurbished school creates an illusion in time. A building's 'newness' suggests to the outside world that the complexities of teaching and learning have been resolved. Just as a building is literally fixed together, in space, rooted to its foundations so that it will not move, a new school building lulls us into a false sense of permanence. Once a school building has been finished and the school community moves

in to its new home, the process of change starts up again. The building might be fixed in space and time (quite literally 'cast in stone'), but – once opened – the intellectual, philosophical, professional and political discourse which accompanies any formal schooling mechanism shifts a gear again. The history of schooling clearly shows that ideas about teaching and learning change from generation to generation. Alongside this, efforts to adapt to new governmental initiatives, schemes and proposals and new findings in educational theory also bring with them added pressures on a school's already complex organization.

In this quite common situation, Head Teachers can find themselves in a position where their building's design no longer matches its function. After an initial 'honeymoon' period between the school community and its building, it soon becomes clear that their working environment (whether Primary or Secondary) can no longer cope with the range and diversity of activities and functions being performed within it. With layers of change being worked into the fabric of a school's organization and culture, year by year, large school buildings – old and new alike – almost creak with the strain being placed upon them.

> *Some commentators have argued that designing schools without recognising the shifting boundaries of ways in which we learn, and the subsequent need for flexible and adaptable spaces for multi-purpose building use, means new school buildings could be in danger of being 'obsolete' before they even open.*[49] *This is perhaps especially true of school buildings procured and operated under the PFI.*

How then are schools to cope with this mismatch between their architectural environment and their learning culture?

Making children's spaces and the schools they'd like

Set against the backdrop of the secondary citizenship curriculum, increased children's participation in decision making, and more opportunity for contact between young people and architects, the stage is now set for new ways of working between school teachers, architects and young people. As we have shown, a younger generation of architects like van der Heijden and de Rijke Marsh Morgan are able to collaborate with young people on the basis of interpreting their imaginative representation of the spaces they use in school buildings.

Hopefully, school children will continue to be given the opportunity to collaborate with architects and to have access to design projects of the kind seen at Kingsdale (with School Works), at New End and Quarry Brae Primary schools (joinedupdesignforschools/Sorrell Foundation). As well as complementing existing National Curriculum work and having significant impact on pupils' confidence and self-esteem (Adams & Ingham, 1998; Seymour *et al.*, 2001; Bentley, Fairley & Wright, 2001, see Bibliography), projects of this kind open up whole new ways of understanding the evolving nature of both education (pedagogy and practice) and of school buildings as an architectural form. With this twin approach, we move closer to a new conception of how young people and children explore and define their space at school.

Prompted by the prospect of working with architects appointed to make actual, structural change to the fabric of school buildings, the collaborations between architects and young people which we have looked at in this chapter succeed on the basis that the school children and teachers involved have been given enough time to develop their own understanding of architectural space and the built environment around them.

Indeed, we would argue that investment in time embedded within projects like School Works and Making Fish (at St Jude's Primary, Glasgow) lies at the heart of their success. These initiatives in particular have benefited from the built-in ingredient of elongated collaborative periods in each project timetable. Young people and architects alike need this kind of creative gestation period during which there is enough space to allow design ideas to develop and for them to be explored in both conceptual and detailed terms. Given enough time, the inherent creativity of educators and

architects can transform perceptions of what is possible and of what works. For collaborative school design projects of this kind to succeed, we also need to allow for working relationships between architect and student which can be sustained over time.

By definition then, the projects discussed above place a particularly strong emphasis on process, rather than on product alone. If we are to realize the political vision of bespoke, community-specific designs for individual schools, each with their own specialized identity and learning resources nurtured at the heart of the community, we will need to engage pupils, teachers and parents alike in a creative and responsive process based on mutual understanding and a collective vision.

To better support schools managing change, we need to develop an ongoing discourse within the school community, using the kind of architectural language discussed above, in which ways are found for young people to articulate their own insight into the workings of the architectural space around them. Educationally, we need to develop an ongoing relationship in space and time between the pupil and the school environment. We need to find ways of linking National Curriculum schemes of work to a sustained, ongoing analysis of the school's architectural form and the building's users, not simply in response to an architect's proposed scheme in school, not for a day alone, but every year, perhaps even every term, as needs dictate.

Like the adults around them, schoolchildren too adapt to the difficulties inherent in school buildings. Whether in terms of air quality, temperature control (and poor ventilation), unforgiving acoustics in circulation spaces and large open halls, for example, or cramped 'one-size fits-all' accommodation and furniture – to name just a few – young people develop their own highly detailed knowledge and highly personal experience of the spaces within school buildings. There is a wide range of architectural and design problems in the current UK school building stock; and as the new buildings are user-tested and lived in, new problems will emerge. Leaving recent reports of PFI 'disaster schools' aside, there will be a need to build capacity within school communities to analyse and resolve design faults as new buildings 'learn' how to service their occupants (Brand, 1997, see Bibliography).

In order to better resolve issues around lighting, for example, a school might take upon itself to embark on a learning project on 'Light', to explore aspects of lighting in its building/s. Children's insight into aspects of the quality of natural daylighting, glare, heat loss, the combination of tall ceilings and high south-facing windows, for example, in specific rooms and spaces, might open up whole new areas of design possibilities. It is the intimate and detailed nature of children's knowledge of specific spaces in school buildings which might best illicit design ideas which, over time, emerge from a creative exchange centred around attitudes to the quality and qualities of space.

Not only does work of this kind create opportunities for applied curriculum work and this kind of ongoing dialogue help bring about a more articulate, focused client group with which to engage architects, but sustained, ongoing dialogue of this kind might also help bring about a new relationship between young people and the built environment around them: both inside school and outside it.

On the basis that, as Worple (2000, see Bibliography) suggests, 'it is the people who *use* space who "create" it just as much as do those who design it; indeed arguably more so'; and in order to build capacity in schools, we might shift our traditional expectation of architects (as consultants able to resolve all the problems of a school's infrastructure in one go), towards a new collaborative process in which the ongoing development of children's design ideas becomes part of the school's learning programme and culture.

This in turn calls for a more generous, 'loose-fit' type of school architecture which is more responsive to the changing needs of the school community. As has been tried and tested in the pre-schools of Reggio Emilia, educational space might be reinterpreted as a '"container" that favours social interaction, exploration, and learning' and not as an institution built on the shifting sands of received wisdom.[76] Rather than a fossilization of received policy at a given date, such an architecture would be more of a supportive, infrastructural backdrop onto which pupils and teachers could project, test and remodel their own ideas about the physical environment in which they work.

As adults, we might at the same time foster a whole generation of young people who understand and care more about the architecture of their own school buildings and who are more able to take on greater responsibility for children's spaces in the built environment around them. Schoolchildren in turn might just get the school's they'd like.

Notes

1 See in particular Chapter 1 in Worple, K. (2000). *Here Comes The Sun: Architecture and public space in twentieth-century European culture*. London: Reaktion Books.

2 Bachelard, G. (1958). See in particular Chapter 1: The House. From Cellar to Garret. The Significance of the Hut. In *The Poetics of Space*. Boston: Beacon Press.

3 Henri Lefevre's *The Production of Space* (1970) remains one of the most persuasive analyses of the social, political and cultural mechanisms at work in the organization of the built environment.

4 Montessori, M. (1936). *The Secret of Childhood*. London: Longmans, Green & Co.

5 Edwards, C., Gandini, L. and Forman, G. (eds) (2000). See in particular Chapter 9 in *The Hundred Languages of Children: The Reggio Emilia Approach, Advanced Reflections*. Greenwich, CT and London: Ablex Publishing Corp.

6 Malaguzzi, L. (1996). cited in The Municipal Infant–Toddler Centers and PreSchools of Reggio Emilia. Reggio Emilia: Reggio Children Srl, p. 29.

7 Gandini, L. (2000). Educational and Caring Spaces in *The Hundred Languages of Children: The Reggio Emilia Approach, Advanced Reflections* pp. 161–177, Greenwich, CT and London: Ablex Publishing Corp.

8   Saint, A. (1991). *Towards a Social Architecture, The role of school building in post-war England.* New Haven and London: Yale University Press.

9   Elkind, D. (1981). *The Hurried Child.* Reading, Mass.: Addison–Wesley, p. 47.

10 Discussed in detail in Part Four, School Works is a DfES-sponsored secondary school 'design initiative' looking at new ways to link schools design to pupil achievement. Primary children at Lightwoods school worked with architect Will Alsop on the design of a new school art space, as reported in *The Guardian*, May 27, 2003.

11 Blishen, E. (1969). *The School That I'd Like.* London: Penguin, p. 9.

12 See also: Burke, C. and Grosvenor, I. (2003). *The School I'd Like: Children and Young People's Reflections on an Education for the 21st Century.* London: RoutledgeFalmer.
    Whilst essentially a comprehensive review of the whole state education system, Lady Plowden also observed that 'more architects need to spend more time in schools getting to understand their needs', Plowden Report, (1967) London: HMSO, p. 397.

13 Blishen, E. (1969). *The School that I'd like.* London: Penguin, p. 12.

14 ibid p. 9.

15 With research and lobbying relationships to New Labour, DEMOS and The Architecture Foundation both played key roles in arguing for and establishing the School Works project between 1999 and 2001. See http://www.demos. org.uk and http://www.architecturefoundation. org.uk

16 UN Convention on the Rights of the Child. (1989).

17 In October 2002, *The Times Educational Supplement* reported 'a nationwide PFI construction and maintenance programme worth £45 billion' with the front page headline: 'Private building deal for every secondary school in England'. (October 4, 2002.) By July 2003, the Government's own advocate for design quality, the Commission for Architecture & the Built Environment (CABE) was deploying 'enablers' on 190 PFI schools projects with 26 local education authorities around the UK. See http://www.cabe.org.uk

18 As an indication of the sheer scale, volume and market-driven pace of construction demanded by the UK Government's Private Finance Initiative (PFI), it is worth noting Phillipa White's 2002 report in the TES that Stoke-on-Trent LEA has 'handed over' its 122 schools to private construction company Balfour Beattie, for example, and that construction company Jarvis has a contract with Scotland's Dumfries & Galloway LEA for 130 schools, another with Norfolk County LEA to rebuild 15 schools and a third to build and remodel 89 schools for Liverpool City Council to the tune of £300 m. *TES*, October 4th, 2002.

19 Rogers, R. (1997). *Cities for a small planet.* London: Faber & Faber, p. 107.

20 Cargill Thompson, J. (1999). Early Learning, *RIBA Journal*, September 1999, p. 15.

21 Amongst the most infamous of criticisms was that made by HRH Prince Charles of Sir Denys Lasdun's National Theatre building, opened in 1976 on London's South Bank. The Prince suggested that Lasdun's design was 'a clever way of building a nuclear power station in the middle of London without anyone objecting.'

22 Cited in the Introduction to: Frost, N. (1987). *Architects-In-Schools.* London: RIBA.

23 In the spring of 2003, the Building Experiences Trust was reconstituted as The Built Environment Education Trust, based in Cambridge and operating as a member of the Architecture Centre Network under the name 'shape Cambridge' See http://www.shape-cambridge. org.uk

24 At the Bauhaus, Laszlo Moholy-Nagy 'spoke of the emotional content of mathematical forms, which … seem to express universal laws which can be *felt*.' Cited by Rowland, K. (1976). *Visual Education and Beyond.* London: Ginn & Co., p. 114.

25 Read, J. (1992). Cited in Plato's *Laws*, 1953 trans. Para 643, p. 24, in Exploring Learning: young children and blockplay. London: Paul Chapman Publishing.

26 As well as deciding that her son would be an architect, Frank Lloyd Wright's mother bought a set of Froebel Gifts for her young son. In his autobiography, the great American architect recalls: 'the smooth shapely maple blocks with which to build, the sense of which never afterwards leaves the fingers: so *form* became *feeling*…Here was something for invention to seize and use to create.' Lloyd Wright, F. (1932). *My Autobigraphy*, p. 11. original emphasis, cited in Read, J. (1992). ibid.

27 Barthes, R. (1957). *Mythologies*. Vintage, p. 53.

28 Kostof, S. (1985). *A History of Architecture*. Oxford: OUP, p. 748.

29 More information about the Architecture Workshops Association can be found at http://www.awa.ndo.co.uk (Child's own spelling.)

30 Rowland, K. (1976). *Visual Education & Beyond*. London: Ginn, p. 114.

31 Coleman, R. (1988). *The Art of Work*. London: Pluto Press, p. 6.

32 Largely thanks to the BET and Frost's small team of architects delivering architecture workshops around the UK to thousands of primary children and secondary students by the mid-1990s, it could be said that young people were engaged in a deeper understanding of what architects do and how an architectural process evolves.

33 See http://www.architecturecentre.net

34 Architecture Foundation. (2001). *10th Anniversary booklet*. London: Architecture Foundation.

35 Architecture Week. (2002). *Promotional booklet*. London: Arts Council.

36 Dyckhoff, T. (2000). Hot Property in *London Open House, A celebration of London's architecture*. London: London Open House/The *Guardian* p. 2.

37 'Circle Time' takes its name from the 'quality circles' which have been used as a mechanism for mediation in industry. Circle Time as practised in UK Primary Schools centres around small groups sitting in a circle together in order to discuss difficult aspects of the school day and/or to collectively facilitate conflict resolution. See http://www.antibullying.net/circletimeinfo.htm

38 Adams & Ingham, Participation Chapter 1.

39 In October 2002, the DfES announced proposals to refurbish *all* British secondary schools under the PFI worth up to £45 billion. (The *Guardian*, 4/10/02).

40 DfES. (2002). *Schools For The Future*. London: HMSO, p. 63.

41 See also Delivering Results, a strategy to 2006 (PwC, 2001). See http://www.dfes.gov.uk/delivering-results

42 The DfES' own 'Classroom of the Future' initiative shared £10 million between 12 LEAs for 'the creation of learning environments that are imaginative and stimulating, with the aim of inspiring children to achieve more'. By April 2003, 32 new school building pilot projects had been developed, some to completion. See http://www.teachernet.gov.uk

43 Coined by University of North London Architecture department's Undergraduate studio 6 (1999–2000), the phrase 'Designing for Real' (D4R) is derived from the Neighbourhood Renewal Unit's 'Planning for Real' process designed for local people to engage in local planning issues and procedures resulting in actual change to their neighbourhoods and communities.

44 Clark, H. (2002). *Building Education. The role of the physical environment in enhancing teaching and research*. London: University of London Institute of Education, p. 17.

45 Chiles, P. (2001). *Primary Ideas, Architectural projects for ages seven and over*. Sheffield: Research Design Unit, University of Sheffield. Contact p.chiles@sheffield.ac.uk

46 Bentley, T., Fairley, C. and Wright, S. (2001). *Design For Learning*. London: Demos, p. 32.

47 ibid. p. 33.

48 ibid. p. 32.

49 Clark, H. (2002). *Building Education: The role of the physical environment in enhancing teaching and research*. London: University of London Institute of Education.

50 Bentley, T., Fairley, C. and Wright, S. (2001). *Design for Learning*. London: Demos, p. 29.

51 Adams. E. (2002). *Breaking Boundaries*. Kent: Kent Architecture Centre, p. 42.

52 Both Situationism and Phenomenology offer ways for students to study the existing sensual, spatial and temporal context within which they are intending to design. Situationism's most famous proponent was Guy Debord. The movement was active in 1950s Paris and was a response to the belief that modern cities had reduced their occupants to being mere specators of life without taking part in or involving themselves in the events that were taking place around them. Phenomenology, as developed by Heidegger and Gadamer, is the study of the appearance of phenomena. It seeks a deep understanding of truth by interpreting a heightened sensory perception of a situation.

53 Segal, W. (1981/2).
Walter Segal was an architect who made a huge contribution to the self-build movement in the UK. He proposed a system of timber housing which made it easier for semi-skilled families to design and build their own dwellings.

54 Price, C. and Obrist, H. (2001). Unpublished transcript of conversation between Cedric Price and Hans Ulrich Obrist.

55 Undergraduate studio 6 (1999–2000) was run by Robert Barnes and Maurice Mitchell. Students involved in the D4R research were Matthew Barton, Miriam Bradford, Kim Chong, Carlos Efstathiou, Asua-Shirley Ellimah, Steven van der Heijden, Lesley Heron, Sonia John, Sam Jones, Ajesope Jumo, Christabelle Lim, Shereen Mahmoud, Rupali Mehendiratta, Alison Ng, Vanda Oliveira, Tea Puric, Martin Steele, Armelle Tardiveau, Matthieu Tisserand, Clifford Too, Dimitrios Vasmatzis and Ignazio Vok.

56 The Dunblane Massacre saw 16 children and their teacher killed and 12 other children and 2 teachers injured by a lone gunman in the grounds of Dunblane Primary School, Scotland (March 1996).

57 Taking some inspiration from the work of Duiker and Hertzberger, one notable exception is the rebuilt Hampden Gurney CE Primary School in London whose sheltered, but open-air play decks and 'six levels of teaching, sport, worship and play' rise up from the Westminster school's cramped central London site 'like a glass mirage, a brightly lit spaceship' (*TES*, 31/1/03). BDP architects' new design was nominated for the 2002 Stirling Prize.

58 This technique was invented by the UNL students as a gestural device to explore the lines of movement of pupils through space in the school.

59 See School Works Tool Kit and http://www.school-works.org.uk

60 Seymour, J., Cottam, H., Comely, G., Annesley, B. and Lingayah, S. (2001). School Works Tool Kit. London: School Works, p. 88.

61 Hartley-Brewer, J. (2002). Model school for the 21st Century. The *Sunday Express*, 22 January.

62 See Clark's more in-depth interpretation of the US research in her (see note 49) *Building Education*. The role of the physical environment in enhancing teaching and research, pp. 7–8.

63 Independent consultants Pricewaterhouse Coopers (PwC) were commissioned by the DfEE in 1999 to investigate the relationship between capital expenditure on school buildings and pupils attainment. Although to date still unpublished, as 'the first major attempt in the UK to examine empirically the relationship between capital investment in schools and pupil performance' the study, using PwC's own set of indicators, found 'some evidence of a positive and statistically significant relationship between capital investment and pupil performance' (PwC 2001, cited in Clark, 2002, see note 49).

64 Largely thanks to SENJIT's 1999 international literature review into research on school building design, enough material was gathered to give credence and impetus to the idea that student's achievement could be linked to the quality of schools' architecture.

65 Annesley, B., Horne, M. and Cottam, C. (2002). *Learning Buildings*. London: School Works, p. 45.

66 Seymour, J. *et al.* (2001), (see note 60).

67 School Works' multi-disciplinary team included the architects, an educational psychologist, an educational policy researcher, an engineer, a construction manager and a performance artist.

68 OECD Programme on Educational Building. (1976). Teachers and School Buildings. Cited in Clark, H. (2002), p. 16, (see note 49).

69 DFES/QCA. (1999). *Citizenship curriculum.* London: DfES, p. 14.

70 School Works are currently developing their participatory process with the DfES, LEAs and Pringle Brandon Consulting.

71 In the 2003 secondary school national 'League Tables' published in January 2003, Ofsted recorded a 26-point improvement in 15-year-olds achieving 5 grades A*–C at Kingsdale: 27 points higher than one of Southwark's wealthiest international fee-paying schools during the same period.

72 Annesley, Horne & Cottam. (2002), pp. 45–46, (see note 65).

73 Montessori, M. (1936). *The Secret of Childhood.* London: Longmans, Green and Co., p. 249.

74 School Works (2000). *School Works: a secondary school's design initiative.* London: The Architecture Foundation, p. 6.

75 Rouse, J., CABE Chief Exec. quoted by N. Pyke (2002) in Cardboard in a class of its own. The *Independent*, 29 August, p. 2.

76 Gandini, L. (2000). *The Hundred Languages of Children: The Reggio Emilia Approach, Advanced Reflections.* Greenwich, CT and London: Ablex Publishing Corp., pp. 166.

Bibliography

Adams, E. and Ingham, S. (1998). *Changing Places, Children's Participation in Environmental Planning.* London: The Children's Society.

Annesley, B., Horne, M. & Cottam, H. (2002). *Learning Buildings.* London: School Works.

Bachelard, G. (1958). *The Poetics of Space.* Boston: Beacon Press.

Bentley, T., Fairley, C. and Wright, S. (2001). *Design For Learning.* London: Demos.

Blishen, E. (1969). *The School that I'd Like.* London: Penguin.

Brand, S. (1997). *How Buildings Learn.* London: Weidenfeld and Nicholson.

Clark, H. (2002). *Building Education: The role of the physical environment in enhancing teaching and research.* London: University of London Institute of Education.

Ceppi, G. and Zini, M. (1998). *Children's Spaces, relations. Metaproject for an environment for young children.* Rome: Reggio Children and Domus Academy Research Centre.

Dark, R. A. (1994). *Save Our Schools. The history and conservation of London Board and London County Council Schools 1870–1914.* (Graduate Conservation Course, Second Year Thesis). London: Architectural Association.

DfEE and Department of Health. (1996). Children's Services Planning. London: HMSO.

DfEE/QCA. (1999). *Citizenship. The National Curriculum for England, Key Stages 3–4.* London: DfEE & QCA.

DfES/SBDU. (2002). *Schools For The Future: Designs for Learning Communities.* (Building Bulletin 95). London: The Stationery Office.

Dudek, M. (2000). *Architecture of Schools: The new learning environments.* Oxford: Architectural Press.

Edwards, C., Gandini, L. and Forman, G. (1998). *The Hundred Languages of Children.* Greenwich, CT and London: Ablex Publishing Corp.

Gardner, H. (1984). *Frames of Mind: The Theory of Multiple Intelligences.* London: W. Heinemann Ltd.

Girouard, M. (1984). *Sweetness and Light: The 'Queen Anne' Movement 1860–1900.* New Haven & London: Yale University Press, pp. 64–70.

Gura, P. (ed.) (1992). *Exploring Learning: Young children and Blockplay.* London: Paul Chapman Publishing Ltd.

Hart, R. (1992). *Children's Participation, from Tokenism to Citizenship.* UNICEF.

Kelsall, F. (1983). The Board Schools, School Building 1870–1914. In *The Urban School: Buildings for Education in London* 1870–1980 (R. Ringshall, ed.), London: Greater London Council/Architectural Press.

Lefebvre, H. (1991). *The Production of Space*. Oxford: Blackwell Publishers Ltd.

Lucas, B. and Greany, T. (eds) (2000). *Schools in the Learning Age*. London: Campaign for Learning.

Municipality of Reggio Emilia. (2000). *Reggio Tutta. A guide to the city by the children*. Reggio Emilia: Reggio Children Srl.

Price, C. (1984). *Works II*. London: Architectural Association.

Record, I. and Frost, N. (1991). *Design Technology and the Built Environment*. London: Building Experiences Trust.

Rotherham, A. (2001). Choice Among Schools. In *21st Century Schools*, London: Policy Network.

Rowland, K. (1976). *Visual Education and Beyond*. London: Ginn & Co.

Saint, A. (1987). *Towards a Social Architecture: The role of school-building in post-war England*. New Haven & London: Yale University Press.

Saint, A. (1991). Report on *Listing of London Board Schools*. (Unpublished report for English Heritage, London).

School Works. (2000). *School Works: a secondary school design initiative*. London: Architecture Foundation.

Segal, W. (1981/2). *View from a Lifetime*. RIBA Transactions (Vol.1, No.1).

Seymour, J., Cottam, H., Comely, G., Annesley, B. and Lingayah, S. (2001). *School Works Tool Kit*. London: School Works.

Sterling, S. (2001). *Sustainable Education: Re-visioning Learning and Change*. Devon: Green Books.

Trafford, B. (1997). *Participation, power-sharing and school improvement*. Nottingham: Educational Heretics Press.

Vitra Design Museum. (1997). *The material world of childhood*. Milan: Skira editore.

Worple, K. (2000). *Here Comes The Sun: Architecture and public space in twentieth-century European culture*. London: Reaktion Books.

Ben Koralek is founding Director of shape; the built environment and architecture centre in the East of England region. Since 1996, he has been designing and delivering built environment education programmes and workshops for children and young people in schools, colleges, museums and architecture centres in London, Cambridge and throughout the UK.

Before establishing shape, Ben was Head of Projects at 'School Works', the award-winning DfES-sponsored initiative focused on improving the architectural design and educational performance of secondary schools buildings through a participatory design process.

Maurice Mitchell was trained at the Architectural Association London. He has been a partner in Dwyer Mitchell Architects since 1988 and now runs a Diploma Studio at the Department of Architecture and Spatial Design, London Metroplitan University. He also teaches at Oxford Brookes University and the Centre for Alternative Technology. He is the author of *Rebuilding Community in Kosovo* (2003) and *The Lemonade Stand: Exploring the Unfamiliar by Building Large Scale Models* (1998).

8

Digital landscapes – the new media playground

Mark Dudek

Editor's introduction

Writing in 1992, architect Peter Eisenman states that since the Second World War, a profound change has taken place in the ways in which we interact with the world. He describes this process in somewhat jargonistic terminology as 'the electronic pradigm'.[1] This alludes to the shift from mechanical to electronic devices which, he stated, would increasingly dominate our lives; in this he included television, fax machines and photocopiers. What he did not predict was arguably the most profound social transformation since the industrial revolution – the advent of user-friendly personal computers, the Internet and the world wide web.

Over a relatively brief period of time, computers and related digital technology have become ubiquitous, dictating the ways in which people work and play. My personal experience of studying and working as an architect during the pre-computer era entailed long arduous hand-drawn renderings, with carefully graded shadows (sciography – the science of shadows was a subject taught in my first year at architecture school), and geometrically constructed perspectives (using, I seem to remember, long pieces of string to generate converging planes). These were the main antiquated tools we employed to communicate

architectural ideas. Even the photocopier, with its enlarging and reducing facility only came into widespread use towards the tail end of my studies.

Contemporary architects now have a sophisticated range of computer-aided design and presentational methods at their disposal. These can produce filmically accurate renderings of every form of building proposal, ranging from colour perspectives to fly through animations of incredible realism. The so-called information super highway, or world wide web, enables research and investigation to take place within the confines of the office or the home. A revolution has taken place which will have profound effects on the ways in which children spend their leisure time or their working time at school. In time it may even change the form the school takes completely.

This chapter is divided into two parts. The first is a comparative analysis of the way children play computer games as a result of the new culture. It includes a brief and selective history of computer games, and comments on the way these games may effect children's culture outside of school. The second section is a summary of recent initiatives in education which have computer technology at their heart. This tentative study should be read as the somewhat personal account of a digital sceptic who observes the activities of his own children and looks back at his own childhood with a certain degree of nostalgia for a time when children were more free to create their own (more physical) games.

Introduction

The advent of Information and Communications Technology (ICT) has transformed the world of work generally. In the USA it is estimated that 60 per cent of jobs now require ICT skills.[2] In the UK, governments have emphasized the importance of technology skills to combat social exclusion:

'Entrance to the new media playground is relatively cheap for the well to do, a small adjustment in existing spending patterns is easily accommodated. For the poor the price is a sharp calculation of opportunity cost, access to communication goods jostling uncomfortably with the mundane arithmetic of food, housing and clothing'.[3]

Whilst there is no doubting the brutal pressures placed on families by poverty, the reality would appear that no matter what their class, bright young students will develop ICT skills if facilities are provided for them in schools, libraries or commercially through high street outlets. Today it seems, the issue of education and ICT literacy is a generational problem, not just in terms of access, but also in terms of knowledge and understanding. Digital culture is central to the culture of childhood, outside and inside school.

The National Grid for Learning in the UK, which was launched in November 1998, was the initial political commitment. This investment was to help provide use of the Internet, to enable all 30 000 UK schools to be connected, allowing pupils internet access to libraries and museums and to allow parents to maintain remote communication with the school about their sons and daughters. Similarly in his 1995 State of the Union address, the then President Clinton declared that *'every classroom in America must be connected to the information superhighway with computers and good software and*

well trained teachers ...'.[4] Secretary of Education Richard Riley has stated that computers are *'the new basic of American education'*, with the Internet the *'blackboard of the future'*. Since those early days, the development of ICT as a learning tool has developed in most schools within the UK and USA.

Perhaps most profoundly, the world wide web enables children to participate in conversations instantly across geographical boundaries through its global networking capabilities. In the future, cyberspace is seen as a great social leveller, with its de-centralized structure bringing users of all media and speakers of all languages together in what Marshall McLuhan described as a *'unified public field of awareness ...'*[5] or 'the global village'.

The anonymity afforded by this digital technology has been used maliciciously: older men have posed as children themselves and lured young people into dangerous real (as opposed to virtual) encounters.[6] The unregulated nature of the Internet is what makes it so attractive for children, but at the same time represents the fear adults have about their children participating freely. Nevertheless ICT in schools and at home has become fundamental to almost every child's pattern of learning and social interaction, extending the field of communication for the new generation of computer literate learners. Here we will describe a number of educational initiatives which aim to fully exploit this, and speculate on their effect on staff and students, now and in the future as school pedagogy evolves.

Computer games also play an increasingly important role in the lives of children at home. Significant amounts of time are spent by many young people playing games with realistic animated landscapes, which can be explored. We will describe some of these games and assess their effect on the contemporary culture of childhood. To a certain extent this too is a generational issue. At least as adults we have, during the course of our lives, accumulated experience of the realities of life for ourselves (largely without the aid of computers) and hence have a perspective formed alongside the virtual realm. Increasingly however, our children's experiences of the world are effectively second hand, communicated through a voracious electronic landscape, detached from the real physical landscapes of earlier childhood experience.

In this chapter we will explore the wider influence information and communications technology has on the lives of modern children, by way of comparisons between earlier childhoods, and reflections on contemporary use patterns. We may bemoan the lack of physical activity our children experience as they sit for hours hunched over a computer keyboard or interactive console, yet the free time parents have in return is a positive benefit, especially as they are relaxed in the knowledge that their children are physically safe, yet occupied and stimulated. Many parents are fully aware of and concerned about the possible implications of so much time spent playing computer games or working on line at school. This is the electronic landscape, and it may be every bit as important as the landscapes of childhood discussed elsewhere in this book. Here childhood, and its status and meaning within the context of an architectural milieu, will be explored in relation to this most profound material change.

Many of the observations within this chapter are framed by my own personal view of the world. I grew up in an environment which was largely devoid of electronic devices (a telephone was only installed in our home when I was 14 years old). There is inevitably a certain amount of personal mistrust of this new electronic landscape and a good deal of misunderstanding regarding its effects on the lives of children. However I have tried to be reasonably positive and open about what it might hold in the future and in this regard, two publications have been particularly valuable in balancing my personal views. They are *Reading Digital Culture*, edited by David Trend, and the excellent *Cyber Reader – Critical Writings for the Digital Era*, edited by Neil Spiller. They are both cited as key references throughout the text.

Digital culture: the new frontier

Eisenman compares the fax machine (electronic) and the camera (mechanical) as examples of new and old paradigms stating that:

> '*with the fax, the subject [or the user] is no longer called upon to interpret, for reproduction takes place without control or adjustment ... The fax also challenges the concept of originality. While in a photograph the original reproduction still retains a privileged value, in facsimile transmission the original remains intact but with no differentiating value since it is no longer sent ... The entire nature of what we have come to know as the reality of our world has been called into question by the invasion of media into everyday life. For reality always demanded that our vision be interpretive*'.[1]

Even in the decade since Eisenman made his observations technological developments, in particular those relating to computers, have made transformations which are even more profound. This has altered the ways in which many children spend their lives, with computer-aided learning, the use of the world wide web and the Internet ubiquitous in most aspects of education, and computer games of an ever more sophisticated form directing children away from traditional pastimes. These games are especially interesting since there is much anecdotal evidence which supports the view that children, boys in particular, are experiencing an interactive three dimensional kind of play which demands an engagement with landscapes which are spatially challenging yet with no physical dimension for the participants. The health and safety agenda has overtaken the natural development patterns children were exposed to previously, restricting the healthy freedom children had to explore outdoors, free of parental supervision. The electronic landscape is filling this void, creating an environment where children hardly need to go outdoors at all. Today children spend hours immersed in their computer worlds at home, they are ferried to school in the family car and then may continue to work on the computer during their school hours.

Compare this to Joan Bakewell recounting her somewhat nostalgic wartime experience of a childhood in Stockport, England during the 1940s: '*Children were out of doors, playing on the streets. After* air-raids there was shrapnel to collect, bombed houses to loot, ruined buildings, their walls tipping dangerously, to be explored ...'. She goes on to describe a sense of freedom and excitement which came out of this uninhibited play: 'it made us self-reliant, responsible for our own actions. It was assumed we knew how to look after ourselves. We roamed the fields and streams, climbed trees, trespassed into grand houses, collected frog spawn in jam-jars, picked wild flowers and took them home to press .... Days when I wasn't at school were governed by nothing more than the need to get home in time for tea ...'.[7] Her childhood was distinguished by a closeness to the real landscapes around her home and an uninhibited freedom from adult supervision which has almost totally disappeared, except for the so-called feral children described in Chapter 9.

Photographer Ansel Adams was at the height of his creative powers forty or so years before the invention of the fax machine. His work captured the legendary qualities of the American landscape (see Figure 8.1). His images enhanced the natural beauty of its huge rivers, mountains and lakes.

Looking at these stunning images the viewer tends to load extra meanings onto each, over and above the intended surface meaning. These are more than just landscapes; in Eisenman's terms, these photographs are open to a variety of interpretations, just as the physical landscapes which were open to earlier generations of children could be interpreted in a variety of ways, through imaginative game playing and physical immersion in their real time spaces.

Whilst Ansel Adams was taking photos during the 1950s, John Wayne was appearing in feature films set in that mythical nineteenth-century landscape. That was a world where the horizon seemed to be never ending and the environment appeared to challenge man's everyday existence. The frontier exists beyond the edge of settled or owned land, and has a fatalistic charm for those looking in. These films encapsulated some of the most important electronic images of my childhood years. Narrative and metaphor could be interpreted by the childish imagination depicting man's actions as a moral choice between good and

Figure 8.1
Monument Valley by Ansel Adams (the Ansel Adams Publishing Rights Trust, Little Brown & Co., Boston).

bad, heroism and weakness. The ideas presented within this narrative were enhanced and amplified by the monumental landscapes within which the films were set.

The technology available to the film industry in the 1950s was limited; most of what we witnessed was real time. Within our suburban communities during the immediate post-war years, the release of big budget films into local cinemas was established as an important moment in the collective weekly experience. Joan Didion first saw Wayne on screen in 1943. She wrote that '*when John Wayne rode through my childhood, and perhaps through yours, he determined forever the shape of certain of our dreams … in a world we understood early to be characterized by venality and doubt and paralyzing ambiguities, he suggested another world, one which may or may not have existed no more: a place where a man could move free, could make his own code and live by it*'.[8] Yet there are a number of other levels at which this can be read.

When Wayne walks off into the desert at the end of *The Searchers*, the landscape is framed by the door of a settler's home (see Figure 8.2). The family have been rescued from the savage (as represented by the people who 'don't count' like native Americans), and the wilderness beyond is apparently tamed as Wayne returns to his footloose life of isolation and social deprivation (perhaps roaming the empty spaces between settlements). There is a sense of admiration for a man who requires no comforts; his comfort comes from the spiritual relationship he has with the natural world. His is a rejection of the modern western world of technological devices and ironically for an American icon, capitalism. There is, in addition, a physicality about the interaction between the actors and the landscape, a definition of all that is real, authentic, primordial. The Western narrative resonates to the American romance for a sort of individualistic masculinity.

Is this is a peculiarly male boyish take on the myth? Ask most women for their view of this drama and they might pose questions of rights, responsibilities and the need for people to take three steps back before they respond to a confrontational situation. Yet for many men there is something seductive about being immediate and spontaneous. The lawlessness of the relationships between men in the Western myth was what made it so attractive to young boys being drilled in the relentless lifeskills of discipline and self-control. Laura Miller describes it as '*a lawless society of men*' which gave men the scope to operate outside the rules of law and society within … '*a milieu in which physical strength, courage, and personal charisma supplant institutional authority and violent conflict is the accepted means of settling disputes …*'.

Monument Valley was the backdrop to many of John Ford's films, visually a highly charged

Figure 8.2
John Wayne, the final image from *The Searchers* (from the Art Archive Kobal Collection).

setting with its soaring monumental rock systems reminiscent of a Gothic cathedral. It is an environment which film critic Philip French has suggested, in his book on the Western, to be a moral universe, rugged and uncompromising. The landscape was never just a landscape, the films were about the earth itself. Wayne's myth is spiritual, a oneness with the natural world, yet seeking in some small way to control nature. The message had a moralistic tone, a human code in spiritual harmony with the wild environment to which all men remained subservient. Americans regard the loss of that wilderness with a sad regret, like the inevitable loss of innocence that goes with the transformation from being a child to being an adult.

However did this representation of a relationship between the early American settlers and the landscape ever really exist? Certainly Didion implies that it was a retrospective construction. It symbolized the loss of certain values which tied the refugees from the old world (mainly Europe) into the new world, where there was little of man-made cultural beauty. The landscape was the bond between the people and the state, the culture of the USA, expressed by wild and natural landscapes within which men could roam freely, prior to the development of an urban environment and the constraints of civilization. As Laura Miller points out in her essay 'Women and Children First' ... '*When civilization arrives on the frontier, it comes dressed in skirts and short pants*'. In other words, children and women need protecting, hence the imposition of law and order. Institutions like the prison are established and the first schools are built.[9] Civilization, it may be deduced, is primarily one which relates to mothers and their children.

We began this section discussing the romance of the frontier in nineteenth-century Western mythology. Many obervers of digital culture have drawn analogies between the Net and the frontier notion. The frontier is an apt description for all that limitless freedom young people can find there, which is largely uncontrolled or it may even be described as lawless. The romance of the Western relates to the instantaneous nature of conflict and conflict resolution played out in a theatre which

is a beautiful abstract representation of the great American landscape. The protagonists do not need lengthy discussion, negotiation and compromise, imposed by the rules of society, in order to resolve their differences. As previously stated, there is an instantaneous frisson of decisive action, a brief exchange of truths followed by assassination. There is usually only one winner, the person who is on the side of right and truth. It is that ultimate sense of power which was the basis of its appeal to so many young male children during the time I was growing up.

In a similar way, the many computer games give the participants that instantaneous hit of a connection with few rules or boundaries. They offer themselves for exploration like the frontier, yet are devoid of the physical dimension the Western landscape promoted. The Internet has evolved from an obscure system used by academics and scientists, into the global support system for millions of users worldwide. Like the Western frontier, the electronic frontier is largely unregulated and open to all sorts of misuse. Unlike the Western frontier, which was tamed as a result of its habitation by women and children, the Internet remains stubbornly free of effective controls (it was designed to be this way), and is to a large degree, a male domain.

For this reason, it feels slightly dangerous and risky, replicating the spontaneous collision of different anonymous people operating within a certain type of space, 'cyberspace', which arguably does not really exist. Francis Spufford explains the psychological pay-off for children using computer games ... '*in the small domain of a programme, he had what the big world rarely gives to 18 year olds: the chance to say yea or nay and have his instructions followed to the letter. It was a small but real power.*'[10]

Eisenman's view that reality was always interpreted in order to make it authentic and rich goes a long way towards defining the potential trouble for children operating within the new media playground. Whereas my childhood fantasies were for the most part played out in real landscapes, where everything was open to imaginative interpretation, and the 'real time' delays that entailed, the contemporary landscapes of computer games and the Internet are devoid of that potential for interpretation. Furthermore, they are immediate.

The instantaneous nature of the Internet and other electronic communications available to young people, such as the mobile phone, brings a sort of craving for progressively more extreme virtual worlds in which to live out their lives. This leaves very little which is open to their own imaginings. Modern digital culture is for the most part devoid of ambiguities. It is 'given' and to that extent it denies children their potential to stand back and develop thinking skills and the power of their own imagination. It limits the range of expressive mediums children are willing to explore with and restricts verbal dexterity. Take it away for a few

Figure 8.3
Matthew (aged 9) on a summer holiday deprived of his computer games is given a set of Froebel blocks.

weeks and watch how other forms of play will be exhumed, such as painting, drawing, block play (see Figure 8.3), and role play. Give it back to them and it will take over their lives again. Time will tell what effect this will have on coming generations brought up in the electronic landscapes of childhood.

Other dimensions of the transformation from the childhood experiences of the 1960s, and the way in which contemporary childhoods are now played out, should also be noted. The new computer games (a number of which will be described in the next section), present conflict situations devoid of any physical dimension and synthetic spaces with a dull abstracted terrain, across which the players float. This lack of a physical engagement with the landscapes of childhood, where the body becomes passive while the mind enters cyberspace, is very useful for adult carers and parents. We live in a world where the potential for violent physical dangers (at the hands of predatory strangers) is emphasized at the expense of the very real and widespread physical danger of too little physical exercise for our children. This goes largely ignored. The 'virtual reality pod' idea holds such attractions as an image of the future, yet it is pernicious for this very reason. Although Joan Bakewell's recollections of her childhood are imbued with a mischevious sentimentality for a golden past, nevertheless the unregulated, isolating and extremely male-orientated electronic landscape can only ever be half a place in which to grow up. We should ask ourselves very soon, do our children lack danger?

A brief history of the computer environment

Our escape (as children) from the ugliness of human relations as exemplified by the old city environments to the elegiac beauty of nature, was purely and simply escapism. Even today, most American city centres are largely ugly, anti-urban places, where the only safe way to negotiate the downtown areas is from the safety of a car. It is the places between the cities which become the living realm; these are the suburbs, a form of space which is low rise, green and defined by clear territorial family boundaries and peculiarly American in its myths and meanings. The picket fence and the veranda define ownership, a memory perhaps of the early settlers, who we are led to believe marked out their territory 150 years before when the land was still unoccupied. It is possible to imagine the settlers' homestead in *The Searchers* 150 years later, consumed and surrounded by numerous similar properties, a part of any American city suburb at the end of the twentieth century.

Of course there were many other reasons why the Western was such a powerful and resonant representation for children to mimic during the post-war years. The god fearing existence where homesteaders eaked out a living from the land, independent, solitary and noble in their physical and spiritual struggle, was one to which the immediate post-war generation of children could relate. It was an image seared into the memory because it was so evocative of a natural world (prior to the harnessing of electricity). Although this myth of the frontier and the early settler tied to the landscape helped to form part of the American dream itself, children growing up during the 1950s and early sixties were probably oblivious to it all. For me this was the childhood fantasy which was enhanced by cinema and (later) TV, which contained my childhood fantasies. It was the promise of a more beautiful physical existence, vast stretches of virgin territory, an escape from the restrictions of a society based on private property, which was restricted, out of bounds to small boys.

I grew up in the 1950s and early 1960s, the son of a Polish immigrant marooned in the suburban spaces of an English provincial town. My fantasies were perhaps understandably tuned into those American dreams since our suburbs felt claustrophobic and ugly. The first TV set in our household was only introduced in time for the 1964 Tokyo Olympics, when I was 9. The flickering black and white cabinet was like having a new friend in the house. Its effects were dramatic as it dictated a collective albeit passive lifestyle for the whole family as we gathered around the 'box' for our favourite programmes. Throughout the 1960s, the entire Apollo moon rocket sequence was televised

and became an essential component in our appreciation of a wider orbit. It was perhaps the first inkling of the new globalized culture which was to come.

Similarly for Stuart Piercy, an architect born twenty years later, his imagination was orientated towards the wonders of new technology as represented in science fiction films perhaps as a hangover from those televised Apollo space dramas which reflected the romance of technology with its potential for time manipulation. The inaugural commercial flight of Concorde in 1977 enabled the wealthy to arrive in New York before they left London. With the release of films such as *The Empire Strikes Back* (1981) and *Back to the Future* (1984) the Western myth was replaced by the time he was aware of film and TV narratives. More important for Stuart was the computer. The first home computer was introduced to his household when he was 9, in 1981. For a short time it had a galvanizing effect on male lifestyles in their household. However it was a more solitary form of viewing than the TV had been for me.

His father was an electrical engineer, and the first Sinclair ZX Spectrum was limited to conventional 2-d games; beyond its technical novelty, it did not dominate his life as computer games do today. In 1982 home computers were only a few years old. There was no such thing as a mouse or the 'desktop' with its little pictures of files where your information could be neatly stored. The hard disk was only available to well-endowed research scientists. Graphical user interfaces (GUIs) existed only as a promising experiment in an American research laboratory somewhere. It would be 1984 before Apple built a GUI into the Lisa and then into the Macintosh and created the mouse with icons to make computers user-friendly and available for everyone. Windows were even further away: Microsoft was just an obscure company in Seattle at that time. Yet there was definitely something in the air. The electronic landscape was beginning to stir.

It is worth describing the brief history of computer games in order to understand the amazing speed of development which has taken place over such a short period of time. The first computer game ever played on a monitor was called *Space War*. It was invented in 1962 by an MIT researcher called Steve Russell who developed the game on a large 'mini' computer called PDP-1. It was not designed for children, rather for scientists involved in computer development at that time. Small white dots dash around a flickering black screen. The aim is to avoid a white cross at the centre of the screen. The dots are controlled by a large 'sink plunger' joy stick. This is a game that is reminiscent of the first Disney animations. It is difficult to play, yet attractive to anyone interested in the early development of modern computer technology.

Ten years later the world's first video game machine was installed in a bar in America's Silicon Valley. It was a large machine with complicated controls and it appeared to be a somewhat quaint, almost anachronistic device. Nevertheless it suggested the great commercial potential of video games and convinced game developers worldwide to begin work on more compact and refined machines. The following year in 1973, the world's second commercial video game, Pong was released by Atari. This was a ball and bat game which was easy to control, with the ball represented by a square dot moving around the screen, and the bat as a white line which could be varied in length depending on the desired game difficulty. The ball bounced between one end of the screen and the other making an irritating pinging sound everytime the ball came into contact with the bat. Pong was installed in pubs and bars worldwide and it did not seem out of place; its appeal was its simplicity, similar to age-old pub games such as cribbage and dominoes.

On the basis of its success, other 'base line' games emerged without much note beyond the computer community until *Space Invaders* was introduced in 1976. Described by its makers Taito as an inter galactic battle ground, in reality it comprised of abstract pin prick blocks of light moving in formation across the screen towards the player's 'dot' or home planet. Its very name was reminiscent of space travel, and unambivalent conflict between good and evil appealed to the imagination; this and the novelty of its technology gave it instant appeal. By 1978 every coffee shop in

Japan had one. The Japanese economy was gearing up for unparalleled growth, whilst in the wake of the worldwide oil crisis, other nation-based economies were experiencing a significant period of recession. According to Masuyama, the game was so popular it created a scare over the shortage of 100 yen coins in Japan.[11] Amongst the game's major fans was a youthful Satoshi Tajiri, inventor of *Pokemon*.

Pokemon was one of the first worldwide hits which developed beyond the player's own personal computer to create a defining digital children's culture. Early on, the creator's background in games culture brought him to the view that if players could trade monsters or bugs it would give the participants an altogether more stimulating experience. Nintendo introduced the Game Boy in 1989 and its communications cable gave Tajiri the idea to develop his bug game to be interactive. The game took six years to develop and was introduced to an unsuspecting world in 1996. The network dimension to the game enabled numerous players to communicate and play together via their computers. The natural extension of *Pokemon*'s astonishing success was game cards, which were traded in school playgrounds worldwide. Magazines, books and films followed on. A further catalyst to its rapid success was the evolving use of the Internet, particularly in Japan during this time. *Pokemon*'s communication system was certainly unlike any other game system which had come before. Its success mirrored that of the Internet itself.

Meanwhile in the UK, the developers of a new space game were obsessed by the need to keep players interested for long periods of time. Space seemed to be the easiest and most interesting scenario for those first generation games: '*All you had to get right were twinkles against blackness and the environment was already persuasive.*'[12] It was an environment with no real architecture, therefore nothing in particular needed to be modelled. The very word 'space', came to mean everything and nothing beyond the imagination of the players. The 'space' was actually a void, to be filled in by those heads full of space travel myths and the desire to explore 'the final frontier' .... [13]

Space Invaders was all very well, however players became bored very quickly. Games culture had always applied the short attention span theory, that children can't spend elongated periods of time playing a single game. Short and simple had been the philosophy for any successful children's game up to that time with adult time frames dictating the length and depth of most games. Free play was potentially more open, however it only assumed a longevity when played outdoors. Indoors the space making activities of most children were usually curtailed by the adult need to clear things away at the end of each session.

To many children this may have appeared to be unfair, however it was usually a factor to do with the limitations of real space within the average family home or nursery. The virtual world was of course different since its space was not physical, rather it psychologized space through visual stimulation which became a real physical world for players negotiating their way through it. David Braben and Ian Bell, two university students, realized that the most exciting dimension of play was one where you became so engrossed in what you were doing that you could leave the game, go to school and come back home to pick it up where it had been left off the previous day. They wanted a game which would challenge the players and sustain their interest for days on end if possible. The new dimension they would bring to their game was time.

In 1982 they began to develop the software for what was to become the highly successful 'Elite'. In addition to building extended time frames through ever more complex scenarios, they also wanted their space game to have three dimensions with space craft which could carry out interesting manoeuvres. They had been taken by the space craft docking sequence in Kubrick's film *2001* and needed serious three-dimensional geography to provide a context within which players could negotiate the spaceship. They then applied ever-increasing levels of difficulty, enabling players to fly from solar system to solar system, fighting space pirates, and perhaps most interestingly, dealing in commodities ranging from vegetables to narcotics and then spending the profits on improvements to the player's space ship. The game's creator even set an almost impossibly difficult target which would

make only the rarest player 'Elite'. In order to qualify as an Elite player, you had to 'kill' 6400 enemies and in order to do this you had to spend countless hours in bedroom warfare. You could then send in a completed card to the makers to verify your commitment. Much to their astonishment, literally thousands of cards arrived at the makers' offices.

The worldwide success of *Elite* was one of the first examples of the new generation of games which were compulsive to the point of obsession. Players would dissapear from social contact and inhabit the world of the screen in their bedroom, complete with its cartoon 3-d images and complicated layered narratives. For the new generation of players, this was much better than a once weekly movie. With John Wayne you had to fill in the space with your own inventive play from one week to the next. The new games culture could, apart from a few other non-virtual commitments like school and family holidays, play computer games all the time if you so desired, and many do.

The Le Diberder Brothers in their 1989 study 'L'Universe des Jeux Video' defined three game types: firstly, thought games which have their origins in text adventure books such as *Dan Dare* and *Treasure Island*.[14] Secondly, there are action games such as reflex response games, the racing or fighting games where the player can compete with the computer or with one two or three other players. Finally, there is the category of computer games comprising simulation games played out within so called 'on-line worlds'. A popular example of one of these on-line worlds is called the SIMS. The player has a family of characters, he or she can build a house for them and effectively control their lives. As eight-year-old Matthew explains '*if you are getting bored with one of the people, you can get him run over in the street....*'

Eleven-year-old Tim's take on this is more representative of an academic adult perspective and one suspects his views are not entirely his own ... '*You get to mutate plants and animals into different species. You get to balance an ecosystem. You are part of something important*'.[15] Despite Matthew's rather anarchic view of the family, the idea of the SIMS is non-violent creative play, analogous to role play in the Wendy House or the home corner with its child-sized furniture. When Joan Bakewell describes her childhood experience of washing the dolly next to her mother, the importance of this mimicry becomes clear:

> *'I was given my own doll and encouraged to wash and dress her in parallel with my mother's own routine for the new baby. I copied exactly everything she did – the reaching for the soap, the washing of the hair, the flannel binder, which in those days was wrapped tightly round the child's navel as though it were a bandage healing a wound. All this I did to my doll, like a session of synchronized swimming, until my mother was driven mad...'.*[16]

Of course the SIMS does not permit physical mimicry, however for older boys aged 8+, it does allow a benign immersion in the life of the family, a psychologically valuable aspect of computer games, especially where family life is fragmented or difficult for children. It is also analogous to the most common architectural representation in its form as a set of interior room plans projected into three dimensions in isographic shape.

The complexities of a game such as 'Civilisation', which depicts history as a series of conflicts or contests over land and other resources, define rules and relationships which the players must respect, and in this sense there is a discipline which is more complex than a John Wayne film ever was, yet with the same 'black and white' morality. The landscape has a realism which is hardly ever monumental or beautiful yet it allows participants to move through it, developing mind maps of its features in a similar way one might explore a real landscape. However the 'top-down' maps encourage a disrespectful controlling perspective on the landscape. The screen represents the Middle East, its strategic location between Europe and Asia making it a highly volatile region, much as it remains today, and the landscape is a mixture of conventional maps and 3-d landscapes.

The modern equivalent of the backyard, fields and woodlands where previous generations played can be found in 'capture the flag' games such as *Castle Wolfenstein*, *Doom*, *Quake*, *Serious Sam* or *Unreal Tournament*. These are early examples of the more sophisticated second and third generation games played by so many children these days such as 'Halo' and 'James Bond'. Here the players are pitted against the enemy hiding in a landscape which comprises of more localized spaces such as streets, warehouses, rooms or corridors. Movement through these spaces is restricted to relatively plain environments and the physical features such as trees and shrubs are rendered in an unsophisticated abstract style. There is a sort of super realism or surrealism evident in these landscapes but, nevertheless, they are very architectural.

Exploration takes place through the gunsights or by the player seemingly hovering slightly above the friendly gunman (sic) as he moves through the landscape. There is a moment by moment immediacy about the struggles for spatial dominance. Single player games feature linear levels that are not meant to be explored, rather they must be cleared of hostile creatures, while multi player levels feature multiple overlapping paths with dangerous intersections. Exceptional players learn to read tactical possibilities from their knowledge of the spaces themselves. According to Jenkins and Squire, this draws on a concept from psychologist James Gibson that game designers construct spaces or objects for their games which offer players certain 'affordances' – spaces or objects embedded with potential for interaction and conflict.[17]

This notion of affordances is interestingly resonant with some early years developmental practice. In his study of children's play, Harry Heft states that environmental features should be described in terms of the physical activities they encourage.[18] He calls this concept 'affordance' in which, for example, a smooth flat surface affords or encourages walking and running, while a soft spongy surface affords lying down and relaxing. The affordance theory is one which relates to an integration between the body and the mind. It enables children to feel orientated, relating their self-image to a real space. Put in another way, there is a clarity about reality where children can touch and feel, orientating and learning through all of their senses. A pre-computer single reality. Today children deal with a dual reality, one which becomes distant as they grow up and seem to lose contact with the landscapes of previous earlier childhoods, moving as they grow older to a second altogether more disorientating reality, the realm of cyberspace.

The form of one particular cyberspace interaction has evolved out of the early 1970s role playing game, *Dungeons and Dragons*. For some reason, the term dungeon was adopted in the digital culture which was evolving at that time, to accommodate a number of individuals who wished to communicate together. Text messaging was the method of communicating, but the organization of the messages is within a conceptual representation of a physical space. So players may find themselves in a medieval church from which they can step out into a town square or a lakeside forest path. What was interesting about Multi-User Dungeons (or MUDs) was that prompted by the particular environment they stepped into, players could adopt and explore different identities, slipping into new and unexplored personae in response to the exchanges they had with other participants. The participants found this to be essentially far more creative and fluid than the average computer game.

According to Sherry Turkle, this was a new and exciting form of community, a virtual parlour game which encouraged the use of written text to create collaboratively written literature and would become the gateway to many other forms of joint creative activity: '…*MUD players are MUD authors, the creators as well as consumers of media content. In this, participating in a MUD has much in common with scriptwriting, performance art, street theatre, improvisational theater, or even commedia dell'arte …*'.[19]

The lavish claims made about the potential for this form of participatory approach may be treated with caution. However many people claim to utilize MUDs as a scaffold for their own personal problems, in that it allows them to play and therefore escape from the reality of a stressful life. And here there may be a hint of a less male-orientated digital form. Certainly the form seems less child-orientated, but to do with play

nevertheless, extending the limited possibility adults may have in ordinary life:

> *The psychoanalyst Erik Erikson called play a 'toy situation' that allows us to 'reveal and commit' ourselves 'in its unreality'. While MUDs are not the only 'places' on the Internet in which to play with identity, they provide an unparalleled opportunity for such play. On a MUD one actually gets to build character and environment and then to live within the toy situation. A MUD can become a context for discovering who one is and wishes to be. In this way, the games are laboratories for the construction of identity.*[19]

ICT learning in schools

There is little doubt that ICT is changing pedagogy radically and that existing schools will invest as and when technology advances. This goes hand in hand with the need for more flexible learning spaces, and a new approach to school design. The novelty and control this technology allows makes it particularly attractive to boys, who often have a more sensory approach to learning than girls. If it is used properly, ICT and the architecture of new schools have a fantastic potential to turn disaffected students onto education. This was not always the case.

Looking back to the first computers, the novelty value was significant. Architect Stuart Piercy remembers racing his father down the stairs each morning to get to the Sinclair first. For Stuart however, the computer only captured his imagination when the first 3-d games were introduced in 1983. That was by way of the Sinclair ZX Spectrum, which became a best seller because of its suitability for gaming. That first computer proved to be a much more revolutionary piece of kit than our black and white TV set had been twenty or so years previously. TV merely presented the dramas that were actually taking place (often far away) in a particular form (in that peculiarly restrained language of BBC science). Although initially exciting, as one grew older events such as the moonshots no longer fascinated because it was impossible to interact with what was happening, and TV became dull. It could never be interactive like computer games and the world wide web. In a similar way to the interaction children experience when using computer games, promoting a sense of control by each individual is a fundamental aspect of the new ICT enhanced learning strategies. Exploration is the key idea.

However it is fair to say that it has only been during the past three years that the full potential to use computer modelling as a creative tool has come into widespread use for architects and designers. During Stuart Piercy's architectural studies, the course work was limited to sketching and drawing traditionally, with few opportunities for 3-d modelling, since the university architecture department had little or no 3-d software. So although the computer was a constant in his life from the age of 9, it did not become an educational tool until relatively late. As a consequence he believes that his childhood was never dominated by the computer, rather he developed his childhood interests within the real landscape much more than the electronic landscape: '*I suspect that today it is much more addictive, the games are formulated by rules and relationships which are similar to the traditional goodies and baddies in my real time games.*'

Computer studies were part of the educational curriculum from the age of 13 at Stuart's school. A growing knowledge and understanding of its potential were part of his school's activities during these formative years, however teachers were to a certain extent intimidated by the use of computers in education. This issue delayed its effective use in the educational curriculum. Today, it is clear that the effectiveness of ICT is very much related to the teacher's ingenuity rather than to huge amounts of investment in expensive kit. The head of computer studies at the Docklands Community School in London explained that teachers have to learn to use computer teaching technology because the pupils expect it; often when a teacher who is new to the use of interactive white boards is presenting his or her first lesson, pupils themselves will demonstrate how it is done. They have to get used to it quickly, and pupils enable this to happen, acting as teaching mentors to the teachers themselves.

Today, the technology available in schools is evolving to a higher plain and at the same time becoming more affordable so that in theory everything from distance learning to video production (of lessons) in real time is possible. This will enable teaching and learning to be pre-prepared and tailored to the needs of a group, with the teacher's role one of supporting individual children. Today, cross-curricular links between PE, ICT and maths are widespread in more enlightened schools particularly at secondary school level. In the future, other cross-curricular links will develop so that learning becomes more integrated into the everyday lives of children. This means that students who have difficulty recognizing the academic value of school, can learn surreptitiously outside formal lessons. The architecture of the school and the architecture of its ICT systems (and to a certain extent the school–home interface) must be fully integrated so that each is mutually supportive.

In the future it is likely that the relationship between a charismatic teacher and his or her students will change as well. Larger teaching groups in lecture theatre format may prove to be a more economical approach to certain types of teaching at secondary school level. Digital technology enables this to happen now, however the architecture of most school buildings is generally neither flexible enough or suitably equipped with a variety and range of computer compatible spaces to enable this to happen. We can predict that in the not too distant future, teaching will take place in a variety of group sizes ranging from 90 students through to the traditional 30 pupils per class, to smaller group seminars and one on one special needs supported groups (Plate 16). ICT will help to provide education in a form which is again more tailored to the needs of individual pupils. A dialogue between ICT and architecture enables this to happen in appropriate settings, and the design of new school buildings, particularly at secondary school level should in future provide managed flexibility to accommodate change.

Of course it is possible to overestimate the significance of new technology and traditional teaching will always be important. However, the designers of Alsop's Exemplar School set out to

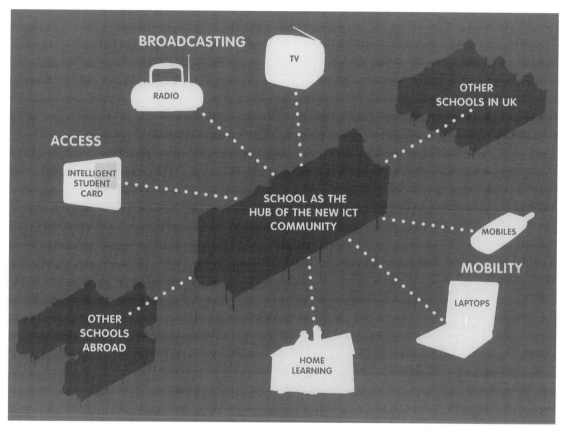

Figure 8.4
The future of learning in a digital culture: conceptual diagram.

create a building which optimizes the possibilities of ICT enhanced learning everywhere.[20] Classrooms are designed in such a way that they can be reconfigured to accommodate different forms of learning strategies. The school has breakout areas throughout, which can be used by pupils discreetly between lessons so that learning and personal development is a continuous process, enabled by the environment and through the student's own wireless laptop. Even the outside areas have safe enclosed 'pocket gardens' where students can sit and use their laptops. Each breakout area has discreet supervision by way of strategically positioned staff offices or properly policed video camera surveillance (see Plate 16a).

As stated previously, one of the main benefits of ICT is that it allows students to make cross-curricular links in almost every subject area. For example, in music lessons ICT enables students to advance quickly without compromising on the theory of music. Audiomulch, a sample-based studio environment in wide use within UK schools, can be introduced at GCSE (for pupils aged 16) and used on any computer with a reasonable sound card and headphones, and it doesn't need a musical keyboard. Although traditional musical performance spaces are still required, the technology means that musical creativity can in theory take place anywhere in the school.[20] This possibility was exploited within the Alsop exemplar scheme with acoustically treated breakout spaces where students can spend time between lessons sampling and exploring musical effects digitally.

Just got a Tutortext on my phone, reminding me where the Human Geography class is being streamed from today – Beijing, cool! It's great talking with kids in cities on the other side of the world, we did a course last term with a class in Sydney and we're still in touch, emailing and stuff.

*Oh no there's my mum, she'll have just dropped
off my baby sitter in the school crèche where they
train to be nursery nurses.*[21]

Fred Seddon of the Open University in Milton
Keynes sees collaboration between schools as a key
to understanding the global future for our children.
Pupils e-mail text and Midifile ideas for composition
back and forth and pieces are built up in dialogue.
He ran a project linking Lord Grey Secondary
School in Milton Keynes with one in Bergen,
Norway with great success. This helped to develop
further subject areas such as geography and
economics, with exchange visits a by-product of
the initial electronic dialogue relating to musical
composition. ICT enables international links to be
established and maintained – an important added
dimension to education within the global village.

ICT is an area, which if used properly can be
made to relate strongly to what is happening in
industry. Design Technology is a key curriculum
area in the use of advanced technology within the
UK educational curriculum. Jonathan Boyle, a D&T
teacher at Walsall Academy in the English Midlands,
uses the school's Intranet to place all of the
information he wants his students to know about.
He uses video clips to create a multi media file of
complex skills, such as modelling in poly-plastics
and vacuum forming. He also uses 'Camtasia', a
programme that records the teacher's voice and
everything on the teacher's screen as the lesson
progresses. Subsequently this is made available to
students who may need to follow the lesson at a
slower pace or were, for whatever reason, absent
from the lesson.

Rhys Errington Evans, ICT coordinator and head
of D&T at Ysgol Dinas Bran Llangollen in Wales has
tried the combination of Autodesk Inventor and
Rhino software. Inventor produces excellent 3-d
solid models, which students may develop
intuitively. Students can open and modify Inventor
files in Rhino and then export them back to
Inventor, giving a greatly enhanced workflow, thus
improving the student's productivity. This is an area
where ICT is making a significant input to build and
maintain enthusiasm in difficult subject areas. In the
long term this will help to create a more enhanced

skills base in areas such as UK manufacturing where
survival depends on its ability go upmarket. This is
viewed as a fundamental requirement, as most basic
manufacturing processes are priced out of western
economies to the lower wage economies of Asia
and China.[22]

A recently completed project at the Yewlands
Secondary School in Sheffield, UK develops and
extends its existing design technology department,
which is currently an antiquated workshop space.
This is an environment which was created for the
old steel bashing technologies of the previous
century. From the Industrial Revolution, Sheffield
was a world centre of steel production but has all
but lost its industrial base over the past 25 years,
largely because it failed to develop new technology
ahead of its cheaper international competitors. This
reality was at the forefront of the thinking behind
the Classroom of the Future. In 2002, the
school won funding to invest in a new building
which would transform the old 'dirty' workshop
environment into a clean state-of-the-art design
laboratory with ICT at its heart.

The designers explain the scheme in the
following way: unlike a traditional classroom where
knowledge is presented by a single teacher
to a group of 30 children under a continuous
supervisory presence, in Yewlands' Classroom of
the Future learning will be controlled virtually.
Pupils can work on projects at their own pace and
to a certain extent in their own way. The usual
classroom log-jam where 20 pupils want to use a
single piece of equipment at the same time will not
happen. An essential aspect of this learning
environment is to encourage students to develop
projects laterally; there is no single predetermined
sequence in design, rather it is up to students to
explore in their own way and at their own pace
using a lot of intuition and creativity along the way,
as opposed to predetermined rules and dogmatic
formulae. The student's awareness of a coherent
process is viewed as being as important as the end
product.

Head of D&T at Yewlands, John Innes, who
helped to develop a lot of the thinking for the new
building, ultimately wanted the Classroom of the
Future to provide individual pupils or small clusters

Figures 8.5 & 8.6
Yewlands Design and Technology Classroom of the Future. Learning largely takes place via computer teacher, enabling students to develop projects at their own pace in a spacious, post-industrial clean workshop setting (Figure 8.5). Presentation and discussion take place in small seminar groups. (Figure 8.6. Photos: Mark Dudek.)

the opportunity to pursue their tasks in different learning and activity zones spread around the department. He describes the concept in the following way:

> Learning is not sequential, rather it builds up as different activity areas become available. There will be no queuing; pupils wishing to use a piece of equipment already in use will know this from the virtual plan of the department on their monitors. They can go on to another task until the equipment they need is free. This process challenges them to think hard and be creative about their projects, there is no right and wrong way to design technology in the modern world ... the main priority is to encourage joined up thinking which is innovative. For example the new BMW group wide system called 'mechatronics' is an attempt to fuse mechanics, hydraulics and electronics in future cars.

Innes goes on to explain how a central space, or what he calls 'the stage', will be used to brief the entire class of 22 pupils at the beginning of each lesson. It will have a large electronic white board and be capable of fully closing itself off from other areas of the Design Technology Department for specific presentations. Here, the teacher will brief the whole class (for only twenty minutes) and only once during the two or so weeks of the project.

He or she will set out a range of menus from which individual pupils can draw down required information to carry out the task. Sources for this information will range from the Internet to pre-prepared teacher's notes and video clips. Pupils will sit at portable fold-out desks using their lightweight wireless laptops. When the initial briefing session is complete, the walls of the space will open up to provide a larger, more fluid forum for meeting and discussing ideas in a variety of group sizes. The use of wireless laptops and integrated interactive plasma screens is planned, to provide maximum flexibility. A full video-conferencing facility for communicating with other schools is the only closed off room in the scheme.

The new Classroom of the Future will then resume its role as a fluidly accessible zone within the rest of the department. Existing departmental zones will be complemented by quiet zones. These are best described as niche areas suitable for a maximum of three to four pupils at any one time, providing a more enclosed space for concentrated activities. The concept recognizes that different pupils learn and develop in different ways and at different speeds. The designers do not wish to hold back fast learners. However, the Classroom of the Future will support those who are perhaps slower, more sensory learners. New technology enables efficient monitoring of pupil activity and the dissemination of vital information. The room is an adult environment for learning where students will enact their roles in a space which is similar to a contemporary open plan office. The emphasis is on spatial flexibility and process flexibility to encourage the designers of the future to think and work in innovative ways.

Physical education is an activity which on the face of it may not fit with ICT. Yet digital cameras abound in effective PE teaching, where educators and pupils have quickly realized that by capturing physical performance and comparing and contrasting efforts with other pupils and top athletes, enthusiasm is generated and performance is enhanced. Gym equipment can be connected to computers to allow students to record their achievements and attempt to beat them. The bid for the 2012 Olympics in the UK, if successful, may also help to focus attention on future medal winners.

A recent initiative, which crosses the boundary between academic and social activity, is called 'Supaskills'. The tarmac playground of the Archbishop Ramsay School in Southwark, South London has been converted into an area where pupils can play football, netball and cricket and then use computer technology to test their scores scientifically against previous scores set by their peers and by professional footballers. The programme is based on a grid system with areas of the playground laid out for different sports, and relates to the maths/ICT areas of the curriculum. In the football part of the grid, for example, pupils can practise routines involving shooting, passing, dribbling and volleying in an ordered sequence, with numbers and scores determining the level of skill.

The football aspect of Supaskills has been devised by former Liverpool footballer Craig Johnston, who also provides regular after-school coaching. A huge mural of David Beckham plastered onto a grimy party wall overlooking the playground makes the environment even more attractive to those students who use it. This helps them to relate their environment to academic tasks, which would previously have been confined to the classroom. It helps to integrate the physical

Figure 8.7
'Supaskills' attempts to integrate sport into academic subjects to encourage and motivate pupil interest. (Photo: Michele Oberdieck.)

with the academic, assisting body and mind coordination; students can, if they wish, simply participate in a good old fashioned kick about.

Like the Supaskills playground, the Yewlands Classroom of the Future was designed to respond and interact with its users, just as they can interact with their computer. In some ways, the designers would like school students to be able to play with the building as they might play on their classroom computer. Thus, some of the façade glazing has electronically wired inserts which can be programmed to interface with computers. Interesting work pages can be projected onto certain parts of the façade, and at night visual messages will be beamed out into the surrounding

Figure 8.8
Architecture in the digital age. This proposal for a visitor centre in London's Crystal Palace Park looks like a spaceship; it isn't heavy and grounded like traditional architecture, rather it hovers with a temporal air above the ground, as if it may lift off at any moment and relocate to a distant planet. (© Wilkinson Eyre Architects.)

urban environment. The building becomes like an ever-changing advertising hoarding with education at its heart.

Hidden stairs are a source of bullying in many schools up and down the country; in our view it is not sufficient to simply place video cameras in the stairwells to reduce bad behaviour. Particularly in a vertically organized school building, stairs should be conceived as key areas of social contact, albeit fleeting. The internal architecture of each stair core should be designed around a strong sensory theme, to give the users a positive view of what are usually negative spaces. At Yewlands there is a soft stair (with quilt padding on its curved inner walls), a hard stair (with exposed concrete walls and faceted Core Ten steel cladding) and a natural stair (with birch timber cladding and water screen windows). Each of these spaces has a distinctive aroma to add to its particular sensory qualities.

The size of stair treads in each of the three cores varies slightly, thus broadly relating to a different age range. Although children of various ages may use any stair, there is a big stair, a medium-sized stair and a small-size stair to add to the other

Figure 8.9
One of the responses to new technology in schools is the need for incidental social spaces that allow for self- and project-based learning to occur. These spaces often take the form of smaller resource areas outside the classroom for use by different age groups, as here at the Millennium School in Greenwich, South East London. (Photo: Mark Dudek.)

sensory themes. This differentiation is explained graphically in the form of real time computer video screens located in atrium areas. They show children using the stairs, evaluating their movement around the building by way of a space syntax software programme.

At the Alsop Exemplar School, the school's heating and cooling systems are deliberately emphasized within the framework of the overall design with big cooling stacks at the centre of the atrium and simple control devices on the perimeter façades which enable staff and students to have a degree of control over heating and cooling. Having a sense of control of their environment develops spatial awarness and helps students to relate to their building. Even the plant room is centrally located with glazed walls so that students can see and begin to decipher the systems which support and control their environment. The building should be like a cryptic puzzle, constantly unfolding and sending out overt and subtle messages to students who have a natural interest in their environment.

The contemporary school building should become a lesson in its own right, communicating with its users, rich in texture and symbolism, a microcosm of the traditional city. One might add too, that the new school environment should complement the all-pervasive contemporary computer culture, which is rich in text and graphical-based messages, but poor on the level of textural-rich sensory stimulations.

Conclusion

In this chapter we have attempted to gather together the various elements which constitute the electronic landscapes of childhood today, including the application of ICT-enhanced learning in schools, the instantaneous globalized information flows of cyberspace, and the increasingly sophisticated interactive gaming culture which for many children commences in earnest around about the age of 7 and can become all-engrossing by the age of 10.[23] It seems that there is a whole series of spatial experiences that go with the new electronic landscapes of childhood, and worrying broader concerns which feel mostly negative to the older generation of parents. Those who accept cyberspace and gaming culture as a new form of architecture should also take note of the landscape qualities their children are immersed within.

Computer games create alternative landscapes of the eye and of the mind, which are impossible to re-create in the modern city. The sophistication and inventiveness of the new electronic playgrounds negate the need for children to invent their own fantasy within the real playground. We create a form of super realism or surrealism, which is an incredibly seductive narcotic for many children. However, the quality of a landscape is sterile and hygienic; it has no texture beyond the computer keyboard and denies children affordances which enhance their social and physical development. Compare this type of 'space' to the spaces children inhabited in previous generations.

In his biography of London Peter Ackroyd explains how in the past, contact with the physical textures of the city afforded children rich opportunities for play and development:

> Marbles were rolled in the gutters, and the paving stones were marked with chalk for a hopping game. Children made use of walls, against which 'fag-cards' were flicked in games such as 'Nearest the Wall Takes' or 'Nearest the Wall Spins Up'. It was remarked that these games make boys uncommonly nimble with their hands, and this must help them later on if they go in for certain trades such as watchmaking. Then there were the touch games, one entitled 'London'. The game 'Follow My Leader' was popular in the streets of London particularly in the suburbs: it included crossing the road at precarious moments, following the route of railway lines, or knocking upon street doors.

To emphasize the importance of danger and secrecy (from adult supervision), Ackroyd goes on to describe the interest children had in places such as churchyards:

> as one Cockney boy put it, 'You have to play in the dark because torches are no good in the daytime.' Street games can be played in the darkness of London because 'sport is sweetest when there be no spectators'. That is why old tunnels, disused railway lines, dilapidated parks and small cemeteries have become the site of games… From that secluded vantage, the boisterous may jeer or throw missiles at passing adults…An instinctive savagery and aggression often seem to be at work in the city air.[24]

Today, where conventional activities appear to sustain most children without resort to electronics, around about the age of 7, a transformation occurs. For many children, the power of straightforward electronic images usurps the power that more conventional mind and body activity previously had. Similarly, where 'conventional' fantasy figures such as *Bob the Builder* or *Postman Pat*, consumed as story-book narratives are achievable role models for younger children, the space-time fantasy fictions captured within games such as *Matrix* or *Halo* suddenly transform their worlds into malign manipulations of power and conflict. Whereas nineteenth-century London was open to children (and some were killed or injured as a result), today the city is a playground which is largely out of bounds to children independent of adult supervision.

Parents feel reassured that their kids are safely confined to their bedrooms, not roaming the city streets. In addition, the control afforded by computer games gives modern children something they used to get perhaps by taking real physical risks within the city streets or fields and by exploring intruiging features of the natural landscape they found in their travels. It is a strange characteristic of the new electronic landscape, that adults have created it, yet (this generation of parents) would appear to have very little comprehension or interest in its real effects on their children. As Paul Virilio observes, we should be taking note of its possible outcome… '*Why? Because never has any progress in a technique been achieved without addressing its specific negative aspects. The specific negative aspects of these information superhighways is precisely this loss of orientation regarding alterity (the other), this disturbance in the relationship with the other and with the world. It is obvious that this loss of orientation, this non situation is going to usher in a deep crisis which will affect society and hence, democracy.*'[25]

It seems that technology has overtaken the natural development patterns children were exposed to previously. As more and more sophisticated electronic images develop, an intensified form of urbanism is evolving which is completely out of the ordinary. Whilst the real textures of the city are out of bounds, subversion, which seems to be the natural provinence of healthy growing children, is somehow denied to them as health and safety paranoia restricts children's activities and their traditional patterns of play. A recently refurbished school we visited had even been equipped with video surveillance cameras in the classrooms; some hope for children to feel the thrill of secretive activity within that sort of an environment.

The computer with its element of edgy interactivity and privacy from adult supervision has filled the risk–secrecy void for many children. Whilst it gives a semblance of risk, it lacks the real risk of chance social interaction within a real urban environment. A space that fosters encounters, exchange and empathy is very much related to face to face interactions. Unfortunately, the streets of our cities are now viewed as dangerous places, particularly for teenage children. This can potentially have a detrimental effect on their lives, in replacing the freedom children previously had to explore their real environment, because there is little or no physical dimension, and therefore no touch–sensory stimulation to enable a sense of sharing, or community. The space of the historical city is imbued with this layered richness. From the material point of view, it is hard to think of any space more empty, more minimal than cyberspace.

Added to this, other synthetic lifestyles appear to make the child's view of the world one which is completely removed from 'real time'. For example, air travel can be a false truncated experience. Arguably, a family holiday to Florida will often confine rather than extend a child's experience of the natural world. Children may see exotic fish in the aquarium at Sea World, however their concept of distance is blurred and framed by the airport lounge, an air conditioned shopping centre sealed off from any natural sensory stimulations. Even during the flight, most of the time they will be engaged with on-board electronic games with only an occasional view out of the window. On arrival at their destination they will have had very little appreciation of the oceans and mountain ranges across which they have actually traversed.

There are many other examples of this falsified view of the world that children are now presented with, from food preparation to professional sport. How can children understand food production when all they see is the polystyrene packaging of a Mcburger appearing like magic down a shute, seemingly produced by robots. No wonder 20 per cent of Britain's children are obese when they are offered double cheeseburgers for 99p on sexy adverts costing millions to produce. The message is the product, the food is merely garbage.

Inevitably, the environment offered for any fast food interaction is a reflection of a number of these electronic obsessions. Firstly, it is sterile and hygiene obsessed, coinciding with a powerful health and safety agenda which, for example, restricts child play equipment to the overly safe and predictable. Secondly, the high street fast food outlet is predictable in design and standardized the world over (just like the food itself). Children recognize no distinctive sense of place in the restaurant architecture; this again challenges their sense of orientation and understanding of their distinctive place in the world. Finally, the space is like the food itself, lacking in texture and variety. With its flat even lighting, hard synthetic surfaces and inevitable piped muzac, there is no ambivalence about its architecture. It is in fact featureless, in cold comparison to Ackroyd's description of a texturally rich, albeit hazardous nineteenth century London. Therefore it is hardly open for playful interpretation. It is a form of architecture which offers few affordances for the young child; even the traditional zone for child play and activity, the floor, is out of bounds. No child would be able to spend more than a few moments scurrying around on its hard, cold ceramic tiled finishes. In this respect it is the most adult-orientated environment it is possible to find anywhere, except perhaps a high security prison.

Elsewhere children now hero worship professional footballers, who seemingly burst onto the scene as superheroes with no cultural hinterland, yet earning a million pounds a year and living like royalty. Perhaps most worrying are the recent images of American soldiers in Bagdad, barely seventeen years old handling lethal weapons which, as Germaine Greer observes, is real life played out like a video game.[26] Also worrying is the ubiqitous mobile phone which children of a younger and younger age insist on owning in order to mirror their peers. No longer having to smell and sense someone, they speak inanely at the touch of the electronic button, securely distant from any genuine interaction; the ultimate representation of alienation in our society.

So here we are, probably ten years into the electronic virtual world, and children are experiencing the full power of this transformation within their own cultural landscapes; they are the first generation to experience a change which is arguably as profound as the effect the Industrial Revolution had 150 years previously on the lives of ordinary children. Amongst other things that the industrial revolution brought about was statutory schooling for all children under the age of 14 to provide education and primarily to protect children from exploitation in mills and factories. Regulation followed abuse, and transformed the culture of society. When will this generation of liberals recognize the need to think long and hard about the conditions which are being created for contemporary children, as their counterparts did 150 years previously? There may be an upside to it all, but for now one can't help thinking about the downside.

As I complete this chapter, the *Manchester Guardian* headline describes a marketing campaign which uses a sophisticated range of digital techniques which are sinister in the disguised form they take. 'Revealed: how food firms target children' explains how industrial food firms are using sophisticated techniques to market to children. Referring to Kellogg's Real Fruit Winders, using mutant fruit characters, advertising agency Leo Burnett's report states that it … 'spreads the word about the brand virally', by word of mouth, following an initial underground communication campaign. In this way it has managed to 'seed' the characters created as marketing icons together with their secret language. This happened initially at concerts, in magazines and in cinemas. It also used clothing to place the characters with children's celebrities gaining exposure on TV shows and

music channels popular with children. New microsites were created on websites popular with children such as capitalfm.com and digit.co.uk. All this activity was unbranded and disguised. It should be emphasized that Kellogg's Real Fruit Winders were awarded the 'Tooth Rot' award by the Parents Jury in 2002, an independent panel of 800 parents set up by the Food Commission to look at foods marketed to children. It contains real fruit which has been processed and supplemented by sugar, hydrogenated fat and other ingredients with little nutritional value.[27] All of this so-called viral marketing has taken place without the knowledge of parents.

What then is the upside of the new electronic landscapes of childhood? The development of computer skills which comes with the potential for such intensive play can and should be recognized as a positive aspect of this new electronic environment. Beyond the sheer joy of play (for children and adults alike), cyberspace is opening all sorts of new artistic forms. For example, the ability to see and experience virtual landscapes creates spatial literacy which is immensely valuable in the realm of architecture and three-dimensional design. The very style of contemporary architecture, with its high quality of material and spatial syncopation, without doubt shows how knowing contemporary designers can be about their buildings, ahead of their construction. Animations enable buildings to be experienced in a lucid way, so that all building proposals can be described and understood as they flow spatially from one room to the next. This was one of the defining qualities great architects of the Modern Movement were able to handle without the benefit of computer technology. Now, all architects can control this aspect of architecture and as a consequence can concentrate on other matters.

There is some evidence that the new generation of younger architects who grew up immersed in computer gaming culture has a far more enhanced understanding of architectural space than those who did not have such a background. We carried out a brief survey of 40 university architecture graduates and concluded that the top ten per cent of students surveyed were highly immersed throughout their childhood years in gaming culture. Of cource it is early days relatively speaking to fully assess this, and it will be interesting to return to this in a decade to assess how far this spatial dexterity has been carried through into the design of the new generation of buildings. However (as someone of the older generation), one can only marvel at how communicative of spatial and architectural intentions the new computer animations have become. It excites a whole range of understanding which places architecture on the same plain as art and drama, in that it can be experienced as a complex three-dimensional form; its uses can be rehearsed prior to construction.

> *Let's try something bold. Let's start from the assumption that games are an important form of contemporary art. What kind of art are they? Most often critics discuss games as a narrative art, as interactive cinema or participatory storytelling. But perhaps we should consider another starting point, viewing games as a spatial art with its roots in architecture, landscape painting, sculpture, gardening or amusement-park design.*[28]

To create a sense of place, many computer games describe space as a continuum. These graphic sequences are becoming more and more sophisticated, and provide the potential for real place making in the future. In his essay *The Virtual Reality of the Tea Ceremony*, Michael Heim[29] observes that some website designers are now trying to create a sense of continuity as a foil to the usual disconnected nature of most Internet sites. The search for wholeness, he believes, is the way in which artists will make sense of cyberspace and create more harmonious, musical places in which people may come to feel more comfortable. However, he adds that computers currently have a tendency to isolate us as individuals. Because of the instantaneous nature of these new space networks, time barriers drop and we lose a sense of distance from one another when entering cyberspace for any extended time periods. This he believes is where the danger lies; respect seems to require

distance and if we lose this interior distance, what he describes as *'the vastness of our spiritual landscapes'*, then we risk losing respect.

Within realms of real space, digital technology has enabled the worlds of work to become fluid. Our living and working places increasingly are used in flexible ways. By changing software, the use of a place is transformed. We no longer need an office, as previously determined; today an office can be a home, or a place for leisure. Work can take place on a train or in a car. Our places are therefore more generic and may no longer need to have a predetermined identity. One of the challenges of contemporary design is to adjust to this lack of identity in a place. One of the most difficult and exciting identities we have to grapple with, and move on conceptually, is the school.

Notes

1 Eisenman, P. (1996). Visions Unfolding – Architecture in the Age of Electronic Media. In *Theorising Architecture – a New Agenda for an Anthology of Architectural Theory* (K. Nesbitt, ed.) p. 557, Princeton Architectural Press, New York.
2 Benton Foundation in association with the National Urban League 1968.
3 Kitchen, R. (1998). *Cyberspace*. Chichester: John Wiley and Sons.
4 Quoted from *Antipode – a Radical Journal of Geography*, Vol. 34, No. 2, March 2002, Blackwell, London.
5 McLuhan, M. (1964). *Understanding Medie: Extensions of Man*. New York: McGraw Hill.
6 In September 2003 Microsoft UK closed down all of their chat rooms as a result of concerns regarding the welfare of young people involved in this. 27 children have been raped or seriously assaulted as a result of meetings with fellow users over the past year.
7 Bakewell, J. (2003). *The Centre of the Bed*. p. 28. London: Hodder & Stoughton.
8 Philip French book on film.
9 *Reading Digital Culture* (David Trent, ed.) Oxford: Blackwells.

10 Spufford, F. (2003). *Backroom Boys: The Secret Return of The British Boffin*, p. 20. Faber.

11 Jenkins, H. and Squire, K. (2002). The Art of Contested Spaces. In *Game On – The History and Culture of Videogames* (King, L. ed.) p. 66, Laurence King Publishing Ltd in association with the exhibition 'Game On,' 16 May–15 September 2002, Barbican Gallery London.

12 See Note 10, p. 56.

13 The TV sci-fi soap *Star Trek* set on the *Star Ship Enterprise* was introduced to British TV viewers in 1972 and became an instant hit. It was often described as 'cowboys and indians in space'.

14 Le Dibidier Bros.

15 Turkle, S. (2001). Who Am We. In *Reading Digital Culture* (David Trent, ed.), pp. 240–241 Oxford: Blackwells.

16 Bakewell, J. (2003). *The Centre of the Bed*. pp. 45–60. London: Hodder & Stoughton.

17 Game On, Pokemon as Japanese Culture by Masuyama.

18 Heft, H. (1988). 'Affordances of Children's Environments: a functional approach to environmental description'. Children's Environment Quarterly, Vol. 5, No. 3, pp. 29–37.

19 Turkle, S. (2001). Who Am We. In *Reading Digital Culture* (David Trent, ed.) p. 243. Oxford: Blackwell.

20 The UK Government launched a research project to develop exemplar solutions to the new secondary schools. Alsop architects along with six other teams were invited to develop new projects to streamline the reconstruction of schools within the UK in July 2003.

21 Laurie Peake talking to the Alsop exemplar scheme as contained in the brochure accompanying their design, October 2003.

22 A number of the interviews regarding the use of educational software are taken from the *Guardian Classroom of the Future* supplement, December 3, 2003.

23 The word 'cyberspace' was originally coined by science fiction writer William Gibson and was referenced by Neil Spiller on the *Late Show*, BBC 2, 26 September, 1990.

24 Ackroyd, P. (2000). *London The Biography*. London: Catto and Windus.

25 Virilio, P. (2001). Speed and Information: Cyberspace Alarm. In *Reading Digital Culture* (David Trent, ed.) p. 24, Oxford: Blackwells.

26 Germaine Greer publicizing her book *The Boy*, Thames and Hudson, London, 2003.

27 The *Guardian*, International Edition, Thursday May 27, 2004, front page. The article refers to a detailed submission by advertising agency Leo Burnett to the Institute of Practitioners in Advertising for one of its 'effectiveness' awards in 2002.

28 Game On Page 65.

29 Heim, M. The Virtual Reality of the Tea Ceremony. In *Cyber Reader – Critical writings for the digital era* (N. Spiller, ed.), Phaidon.

9

Spaces without children

Helen Penn

Editor's introduction

In this chapter Professor Helen Penn discusses the issue of children and their presence within the public domain. What is the public domain?

In this context it can be defined as the shops, restaurants, airports, railway stations and other public areas which are distinct from the private territory of the family, the home, the motor car or dedicated institutions for children such as the school or the daycare centre where children are supervised and become the responsibility of adult carers, parents and relatives.

Here she makes the point that many of what might be termed the new public domain are places which are predicated upon commercial expediency. She recognizes that there is also a non-commercial, more traditional public domain. In this we might include public parks, streets, sports centres, the countryside which is accessible, the National

Figure 9.1
Organized childcare groups after school can stifle the natural inquisitive nature of children. (Photo: Mark Dudek.)

Parks within the UK and perhaps most interesting, left over wasteland in and around our cities heartlands.

She raises concerns about the limited opportunities that children have to spend time without the immediate controlling presence of adult relatives or paid carers. She compares the contemporary condition of children, confined and restricted in an anti-social environment, with historical accounts of children's play in the public domain. In the past children appear to be active outdoor creatures engrossed in collective and group activities play and socialization which is self-generated, relying on imagination and inventiveness. In contrast, a contemporary view of childhood groups within the public domain is one where children are anti-social criminals. It is only when children are supervised and properly controlled that they are acceptable.

These two views are perhaps extreme, however one suspects that the author's view is one which genuinely laments the lack of children to be seen in the public domain. They are, as she says, becoming an endangered species like the skylark. As for interaction with them, fear of strangers and abduction makes this virtually impossible.

In some senses her view is harking back to a simpler time, but she raises some important issues about how we should design our urban spaces. Her's is a radical view which encourages the mingling of adults and children in public places as essentially civilizing. She asks us to consider the

Figure 9.2
A skateboard park in west London, one of the few public spaces for older boys which combines aspirational peer group cool with a degree of physical risk for the participants. Some might question the label 'art' when referring to the work of the graffitiists, however there is no doubting its authenticity within contemporary youth culture. (Photo: Michele Oberdieck.)

places we design for children's unsupervised activities, such as parks and streets, to be more child orientated. Safety, she believes, should not be the only criteria, rather a more balanced view about the public domain should be struck which respects the aspirations of children to be independent.

Introduction

One of the most significant changes in the urban landscape over the last century has been the disappearance of children. In industrialized societies children are literally disappearing. Families are much smaller and, except amongst certain minority groups, the birth rate has fallen to below replacement levels. But children have also disappeared from public view. Pictures, postcards and photos of urban life a century ago invariably included children of all ages. Now they have vanished from public spaces. Like the skylark – perhaps not so far-fetched an analogy – they have become endangered. The pleasure in watching their unselfconscious and exuberant games, or even the annoyance caused by their chasing, taunting and throwing balls, is no longer to be had. Children are literally perceived to be 'in danger' outside of their immediate domestic space; and to 'be dangerous' to others if they roam unattended. Compare this with the account by John Muir of his childhood in a small industrial Scottish town outside Edinburgh in the 1840s:

> Among our best games were running, jumping, wrestling and scrambling ... our most exciting sport however was playing with gunpowder. We made guns out of gas pipe, mounted them on sticks of any shape, clubbed our pennies together for powder, gleaned pieces of lead here and there, cut them into slugs, and, while one aimed, another applied a match to the touch-hole. With these awful weapons we fired at the gulls and solan-geese as they passed us. Fortunately we never hurt any of them that we knew of. We also dug holes in the ground, put in a handful or two of powder, tamped it well down around a fuse made

> of a wheat-stalk, and reaching cautiously forward, touched a match to the straw. This we called making earthquakes ... Another favourite sport was climbing trees and scaling garden walls. Boys eight or ten years of age could get over almost any wall by standing on each others' shoulders, thus making living ladders. To make walls secure against marauders, many of them were finished on top with broken bottles imbedded in lime, leaving the cutting edges sticking up; but with bunches of grass and weeds we could sit or stand in comfort on top of the jaggedest of them. In the winter, when there was but little doing ... we organized running-matches. A dozen or so of us would start out on races that were simply tests of endurance, running on and on along a public road over the breezy hills like hounds, without stopping or getting tired ... we thought nothing of running right ahead ten or a dozen miles before turning back.[1]

John Muir, who became a great American naturalist, is reckoned to be a reliable observer, despite his Arcadian leanings. He probably did not exaggerate his childhood overmuch in the retelling. Such childhoods are unimaginable and intolerable now. We do not expect children to be so adventurous or imaginative or expose themselves to danger in this way. If they did, we would consider them disturbed and seriously in need of correction and restraint, over and above the occasional thrashing that John Muir endured. We cannot conceive of such levels of activity in relatively young children, unless they were being cruelly trained as part of a relentlessly ambitious sports programme. Gangs of young boys, or any kind of voluntary and adultless association of children are also perceived to be subversive, a threat of trouble and disturbance to the social order. John Muir and his friends would have no place whatsoever in a contemporary urban setting.

Children as a danger to others

> packs of feral children roaming our streets ... this terrifying generation of murderous, morally blank wolf-children, fatherless, undisciplined, indulged

one minute then brutalized the next...we need to lock up more of these thugs and punish them.[2]

This quotation is one of many lamenting the breakdown of law and order, for which children are being held partly or wholly responsible. We monitored articles about children in one suburban local newspaper, and one national paper in July–August 2002. The popular press exaggerates, trivializes and sensationalizes everyday events, but even allowing for common distortions, the comments expressed hostility to children (or else alerted parents to the sometimes quite minor dangers that children faced outside and inside the home – see below). The articles included:

- residents opposition to a local youth club '*homes and cars had been vandalized and they had been verbally abused by the youngsters*'
- dangers of teenage pregnancy
- boys hurt by plastic pellets in a 'shootout' between boys using fake weapons
- the substantial costs of keeping children amused in the summer holidays and the waste of money and self-indulgence involved
- the eviction from a council house of a large single-parent family whose children were out of control
- children with weight problems
- young children buying crack cocaine
- noisy children lowering property prices
- noisy children spoiling holidays
- residents wanting soundproof fences around a school to screen the noises of children playing
- truanting children
- children shoplifting
- anti-social behaviour orders versus locking up and '*leathering*' offenders
- under-age children working
- prosecution of children who attack teachers
- under-age drinking
- gangs of joyriders
- gangs of railway vandals
- '*vandals as young as five*' causing damage to housing estate
- children watching pornographic films and videos
- children's litter causing problems for dogs!

In some ways this hostility is nothing new. A trawl of similar papers 20 or 200 years ago would have also revealed fear and hostility towards children on the streets. But one would have expected more sympathetic contemporary attitudes, if only because the UK is a signatory of the United Nations Convention on the Rights of the Child.[3] The *New Statesman*, commenting on the hostility to children, remarked that whilst middle-class parents can purchase activities for children, and arrange the transport to get to them, poor families do not have this manoeuvrability. Their children, already at a disadvantage for space, and without the consumer goods that have become a 'normal' aspect of childhood, play out, and in playing out become still more exposed to contempt. Being on the streets *per se* labels children as coming from poor and uncaring families.

> *Middle class parents deal with the absence of public play-space for their children through expensive hobbies and clubs, by buying houses with big gardens, or – increasingly – drugging their kids with Ritalin. These are not options open to poor children ... It would seem that this is our approach across Britain; we treat poor children with fear and contempt.*[4]

This point is also made by Colin Ward in his classic book *The Child in the City*.[5] He details ways in which children have in the past used city spaces as venues, hideyholes and for sports as various as fishing and ferreting. The book was originally written in 1978. In an afterword in the 1990 edition he suggests that poor children are now more disadvantaged in their access to urban spaces, disadvantaged both by their poverty and by public attitudes towards it. The recent report *The State of London's Children* emphasizes that in London there is a higher proportion of children than in other parts of the country, but that poor children, especially children from migrant communities, have less access to goods and services, even those supplied by the state such as education or leisure services. Not only are children restricted in their use of public spaces, but also there are considerable gender and ethnic differences in children's access to public space.[6]

Dangers and strangers

Is the world a more dangerous place for children, or is it increasingly the convention to represent it that way? It always was dangerous – a century ago accidents with horses, spillages of noxious fluids, the intermingling of workplaces with living spaces, open fires and gas lighting meant that child deaths through accidents in the UK were about 50 000 per annum, very high indeed. Now we have one of the lowest rates of child accidents of any industrialized country. The accident rates have been reduced so dramatically partly through progressive health and safety legislation. Yet it is not societal concern that continues to keep accidents low. Rather, it is the insistence that keeping children accident free is a personal, parental concern, an individualization of responsibility.

Road traffic, for example, is far more dangerous, pervasive and polluting than it was even fifty years ago. It is proportionately more dangerous for poorer children, whose accident rates are significantly higher than those of middleclass children.[7] Yet protection against road accidents is

Figure 9.3
(a) Princess Diana Memorial Park safety signage. An environment where children's freedom is limited by the possibility of litigation in the event of accidents. (b) The ease and safety of car transport at a personal level far outweighs considerations of the greater good. (Photo: Michele Oberdieck.)

regarded as an individual, parental, matter rather than as a societal matter. Hence the irony of car advertisements which stress how they offer protection and safe conveyance to the children whose parents can afford the car; although the increase in cars that would come through such purchases represent a danger to all children, and contribute to increased levels of lead in the atmosphere. Parents who take their children to school by car are castigated, but the ease and safety of car transport at a personal level far outweighs considerations of the greater good. Road traffic presents a real danger to children. A societal solution – traffic control and restricted car use – is the most effective way of addressing it. Instead we teach children the highway code or offer them limited protection by providing lollipop ladies at school crossings.

However, in another area, in the interpretation of health and safety legislation towards children who are looked after by people other than their parents, there is arguably an excess of zeal. Such zealousness has also become individualized, an anxiety on the part of childcare workers that they may be held personally responsible for the normal bumps and bruises of childhood.

The 1989 Children Act required all children outside of their homes and looked after by others for more than two hours a day to be closely surveilled by adults. Young children spending their days in nurseries are often very restricted in their movement, and protected against every possible – and impossible – contingency. I have described how, in one daycare nursery I visited, the only exercise children had was to go to a carpeted exercise room, where they were allowed to walk on a beam six inches off the floor, provided they held the hand of a childcare worker whilst doing so.[8] In another 'model' training nursery, the very small outside yard was rubber coated and completely bare. There were no non-rubberized surfaces, no nooks or crannies, no unsurveilled spaces. The manager explained to me that 15 years ago her daughter had fallen in a schoolyard and damaged her front teeth, and she never wanted another child to go through the same experience. Because of a freak accident a long time ago, a

generation of children were being forbidden any physical activity or challenges.

These incidents are unfortunately typical of the childcare in the UK. The childcare system has its historic roots in the child welfare movement, catering for vulnerable children. The training of childcare workers, and the health and safety legislation that governs daycare nurseries, emphasize children's vulnerability and negate children's capacities and in particular their ability to negotiate the physical world. It is above all a surveillance system.[9]

The Government's most recent green paper on children at the time of writing, *Every Child Matters* (2003)[10], is almost entirely about child protection and control. The Government states that it aims to reduce levels of educational failure, ill-health, substance misuse, teenage pregnancy, abuse and neglect, crime and anti-social behaviour. The tenor of the paper is that the nuisance children cause must be addressed. There is very little in it that sees children as a resource, as fellow citizens, as potentially willing contributors and participants in society.

The monitoring of the press over the two-month period also produced a series of concerns about the dangers posed to children, including pigeon droppings, dogs, foxes, babywalkers, dehydration, a syringe in a toy medical kit, broken fences, and above all fears of children being molested or abducted. This letter to a national paper sums it up:

> The answer about why today's children cannot have fun without parental supervision is simple. We had one quality missing in the life of children today, freedom. Provided we returned to the nest at the agreed time, we could go where we wished and thereby develop our creative and imaginative skills without the need of adult help/or sophisticated toys. Now we are obsessed with protecting our children against traffic, abductions, molestations, mishaps on school trips, drugs – the list is endless.[11]

Parents in the UK are typically cautious and safety conscious, perhaps unwisely so, about their children's physical prowess. In other countries, particularly in the Third World children are routinely expected to demonstrate more energy, more stamina and more robustness and expose themselves to risk – as John Muir did. We have coined the expression 'hyperactive' to describe children whose levels of physicality might once have been taken as normal.

Perhaps the greatest exaggerations of risk are in what is called 'stranger danger'. The incidence of children who are molested or abducted in public spaces, shocking as it is, is very small, and has not increased significantly over the last century. Children are much more likely to suffer abuse and trauma at home, closed off from public view. However such incidents of strangers molesting children are greatly inflated and become national news. Prurience and voyeurism are stoked up by the press, and pursued by vigilante groups. At the time the research described below was being carried out, two girls had been abducted. The public hysteria and headlining was so great, that it became impractical to finish the research, since the answers became affected by what was seen as a monstrous danger lurking in the background for all unattended children.

The perceptions of children's exposure to danger in turn reflect a public understanding of young children as passive, vulnerable and incapable (except for gangs of poor children who cause havoc on the streets). International and historical comparisons of childhood suggest that the UK in the twenty-first century represents an extreme view of the need to protect children.[12] In Norway for example, it is common practice to expect young children in nurseries and schools to camp out in winter, in order to accustom themselves to harsh winters.[13] Young children routinely undertake work and contribute to income maintenance and family well-being in or out of the home in the Third World. Children in many other places are viewed as more resilient, more able to fend for themselves and defend themselves, more capable of contributing to family welfare than we allow.[14]

Consuming children

On the one hand, children are perceived to be in a state of continuous exposure to unacceptable risk, to themselves and to and from others. On the other hand, we express serious concern that they will become couch potatoes, overweight, under-exercised and solitary. Children now consume passively through TV, video and computer games, the thrills, dangers and subversion that John Muir created for himself first hand.

> *(Children's cartoons and commercials) portray an abundance of the things most prized by children – food and toys; their musical themes and fast action are breathtakingly energetic, they enact a rebellion against adult restriction; they present a version of the world in which good and evil, male and female, are unmistakably coded in ways easily comprehended by a young child; they celebrate a community of peers.*[15]

Adults' expectations of children and children's expectations of themselves are necessarily related. It is possible for adults to confine and regulate children partly because of the escape hatch offered to children by the products of consumer culture. In turn, consumer culture creates for children a hyper-reality, with which they willingly engage. A recent Australian study suggested that although children, even as young as three, were knowledgeable and capable of exercising some scepticism about the claims to reality of what they saw on TV, videos, and computer games, they did not question at all the market culture that gives rise to such advertising and promotion. They took it as normal that such goods would be provided for them, and that they would have endless opportunity to choose amongst them.[16]

Children's consumer culture, and the ways in which it is promulgated, are now well-researched areas.[17] It is the flip-side of children's disappearance from public spaces. Children are not merely being protected, confined and contained; they are also offered alternatives and distractions.

Parents are very uneasy about consumer culture, and the breakdown of values it seems to imply.

> *Parents express a range of concerns to do with the welfare, whereabouts and well-being of their children. Because they are time-poor, they worry that their children receive too little of their*

Figure 9.4
(a) Advertising is almost everywhere within the modern urban environment encouraging children to demand and challenge in order to get what they want. (b) By comparison children in more traditional rural communities, such as these Thai children on a school field trip, are more physically active and connected to the sensory pleasures of the natural environment. Their public spaces are far less commercially orientated. (Photos: Michele Oberdieck.)

time and energy. They thus involve them in more and more supervised activities. They also worry that their children need more protection from a world that is losing a sense of belonging and increasingly seen as hostile as a result of drugs, heightened violence and abuse ... Because they have raised their children on the principles of child-centredness, they worry that they have been perhaps too open, too permissive, and somehow

contributed to difficult-to-deal-with behaviour ... They fear that they have over-indulged their children, over-compensated for their own parental deficiencies through consumer goods, overexposed them to the more adult themes of life.[18]

Some researchers consider that the media exploit and exacerbate these fears. Certainly there is good

Figure 9.5
The Kindertagesstatte, Neukolln, Berlin. One of the new generation of daycare facilities for children which are high cost, dawn till dusk, highly institutionalized 'child parks', which reassure parents that their young children are well looked after. Parents can work or play for the whole day whilst their children are educated. (Photo: Ulrich Schwarz.)

evidence to illustrate the enormous sophistication, complexity and reach of market campaigns aimed at children and their parents. Advertisers of commercial products encourage children to demand and challenge in order to obtain what they want (or what is being promoted) and at the same time play on the guilt feelings of their parents. Cartoons, commercial TV, film and advertising simultaneously promote, and offer opportunities to resolve, inter-generational conflict.[19]

Young children have proved a lucrative market for the exploitation of parental inadequacy. All

manner of toys are marketed as 'educational'. '*Our mission is to provide families with a HUGE selection of creative and stimulating products in a customer-friendly entertaining and interactive shopping environment because we believe kids learn best when they're having fun.*'[20]

Parents and childcare workers alike have come to believe that nurseries should resemble shopping malls, in their reproduction of continuous multiple choice. Writing about American preschools, Tobin comments that:

> *Customer desire is reproduced by the material reality of our preschools. The variety of things and choices offered by middle-class preschools is overwhelming to many children. We create over-stimulating environments modelled on the excess of the shopping mall and amusement park ... We have become so used to the hyper-materiality of our early childhood care settings that we are oblivious to the clutter; settings that provide more structure and are less distracting seem stark or bleak.*[21]

Harry McKendrik carried out an analysis of privately provided play settings; private out-of-school clubs but also at leisure centres, shopping malls, pubs, and other entertainment centres. He concluded that children had relatively no say or control in determining their access and use of such places; they were 'parked' there by adults who had other agendas – to shop or to socialize or to exercise. These playspaces were marketed as an opportunity to provide parents with free time, whilst their children were 'educatively' and safely cared for.[22]

Childlore and childplay

The distinguished environmentalist Roger Hart summed up the changing nature of children's lives in the cities of the industrialized world like this:

> *their diminished freedom in space and time, the growth of mass media as an acculturating force at the expense of peer culture and local culture,*

a reduced contact with the natural world, the private and more exclusive provision of spaces for play and recreation at the expense of more inclusive public space, an erosion of community in the geographic sense of the word, an increase in social class segregation, the loss of meaningful work opportunities and a growth of violence.[23]

If this seems a bleak picture, there are also contra-indications that children continue to create and pursue their own interests and identities independently from those of adults when time and space permits. In 1969 Peter and Iona Opie recorded children's games in close-to-home spaces – driveways, pavements, streets, carparks. They identified more than 3000 games played by children. They argued that this rich children's culture was carried on in the interstices of everyday spaces, the *'child-to-child complex ... of people going about their own business within their own society ... fully capable of occupying themselves under the jurisdiction of their own code.'*[24] Indeed, they were dismissive of the idea that this children's culture could be shaped or controlled by adults in any way.

Although it is now much less likely that children would be allowed to play out and find spaces for their own use, recent evidence suggests that 'schoolyard lore' or 'childlore' is still vibrant in school playgrounds.[25] Despite the overwhelming contemporary pressures to which they are subject, children, as they have done since time immemorial, have their own games, rhymes, chants and crazes, their own ways of amusing themselves. As Iona Opie comments:

Amidst the bustle and noise of the playground can be seen remarkable skills of organization, quick agreements and decisions, and instant adaptability. The basic games demonstrate the pleasures of strategy and movement that probably predate language itself. We can begin to understand what constitutes fun, what humour is thought cleverest, what noises are most satisfactory to make, what prowess is admired. Simply by examining which songs and rhymes are the most popular, we can see that the mental attitude found most useful in an uncaring world

is insouciant, defiant, offhand, pretending not to care. The important thing in a playground or other gathering is to protect one's ego.[26]

This 'childlore' is still the daily currency of the playground for most children.[27,28] It has been charted in Australia, Britain, Continental Europe and north America, and in ethnographic studies in the Third World. Childlore and childplay reveal dimensions of creativity, artistry, musicality and complexity. Some of it, such as ball and skipping games, is highly active and requires dexterity and physical coordination. It is performative, carnivalesque, subversive and parodic – including elements of parody of the very features of advertising that seems so threatening. It includes narratives, epithets, jeers, taunts, riddles and jokes. It is fun, but not necessarily all the time for all of the children taking part, and it sometimes veers on bullying (although bullying, too, is subject to interpretation). Much of this childlore is scatalogical or subversive, e.g.:

Mary had a little lamb,
She fed it on cream crackers,
And every time it dropped a crumb,
She kicked it in the knackers.[29]

The persistence of such childlore, despite all the concerns to the contrary, suggests that there are overwhelming reasons for its continuance. Brian Sutton Smith, the guru of children's play, argues that *'childlore deals with behaviour that has traditionally been regarded as non-serious, but as this behaviour appears to be a systematic part of the human repertoire, to think, therefore, it is unimportant might be a mistake.'*[30]

Marc Armitage claims that layout of playground space inadvertently affects the nature of the games that are played in it. He carried out 90 play audits of school playgrounds over a 5-year period. He pointed out that designating an area as a particular kind of playspace is no guarantee that it will be used in that fashion; on the contrary, the most unlikely – or to adults unsuitable – places will be commandeered for games. Playgrounds have shrunk, as land has proved more profitable for other uses; and playtime has shrunk as teachers

Figure 9.6
(a) Child in the daycare centre, protected from the threat of stranger danger. Project: the Portman Centre garden designed by Mark Dudek. (b) Child in the supermarket, often given the freedom to select any item from the shelves, perhaps a counter to their lack of freedom elsewhere. (Photos: Michele Oberdieck.)

have become more obsessed with curricular and supervised activities. Neither self-directed play nor the playground itself are accorded the priority they had in earlier times.

Boys playing football, typically a minority of the school population, now claim a great deal of space – typically more than half of the hard surface area, to the detriment of girls, younger children, and other games. Playgrounds with nooks and crannies – round the back of steps, in corners, are commandeered for games, e.g. marbles on drain covers, cops and robbers games by metal grilles or fences. (Gaol games and imprisonment games were a feature which occurred in all the play audits. Frequently witches prepared potions in gaol-like places!) Armitage comments that:

The primary school children of today can quite easily be left alone on the playground and their spontaneity will do the rest. This is in fact what already happens. But for them to be able to make use of this spontaneity to the best of their ability, and to do so without the need for direct adult intervention in their play, the

environment provided for them as a place to play must respect the finding that children themselves are informally organizing their available spaces and features to meet their own needs. As adults, our role should be to support this and provide an environment that caters for what children actually play as opposed to what they should or could play, or even what we think they play.[31]

This childlore is created wherever children gather, in streets, in parks, in playgrounds. They still gather in the playground, although less than previously, but they have effectively been deterred from using other public spaces.

Children in the UK and elsewhere

The trends that isolate children, re-create them as vulnerable, accident prone and in need of protection, and simultaneously exploit their market potential, are widespread, an inevitable off-shoot of contemporary consumerist societies. But these trends can nevertheless be questioned and challenged. Certain countries have always been more pro-natalist and more proactive in favour of children. One key indicator of societal attitudes towards children is toleration of child poverty. If children live in poverty, one can either blame the parents for being so unwise as to reproduce without being able to guarantee financial security for their children, and thus dooming their children to suffer poverty in their turn; or else one can take the view that all children are entitled to an equal chance, whatever their parents' circumstances, and income maintenance, and other measures to combat poverty should be redistributive and targeted towards children. In most European countries child poverty rates are very low, typically 5–10 per cent. In the UK they are at least 30 per cent. Despite Government claims to the contrary they show little sign of falling. UNICEF has criticized the UK (and the USA which is still worse) for their position about child poverty.[32]

Another indicator is the level of early education and childcare services, and the extent to which they are publicly provided. How early should the state accept responsibility towards young children or intervene as little as possible? In France, publicly provided childcare services for working parents were first introduced in 1848. In the UK, in 2002, there is still no commitment to public childcare provision. Generally the UK compares poorly with other European countries.[33]

There are many other ways in which Government, locally and nationally, could be more proactive towards children, and take children's views into account. There have been some recent changes in the UK, but they fall a long way short of what is currently on offer in other countries. In France, for example, most children take part in 'Sejours des Vacances', residential holiday playschemes that enable them to experience environments different from the ones they normally live in; they swop between urban, rural and seaside settings.

Norway has a Children's Fund, to which any child or group of children aged between 5 and 16 may apply *directly*, and without adult intervention, for funding of projects. An evaluation of the funding suggested that whilst children applied for a wide variety of projects, the majority of bids were from children who wanted to build their own huts or cabins! Both the Children's Fund, and the uses to which it appears to be put are beyond our experience in the UK.

In design-conscious Italy, it is assumed that children are as discerning aesthetically as adults. Leila Gandini, writing about the famous group of nurseries in Reggio Emilia comments that:

> There is attention to detail everywhere – in the colour of the walls, the shape of the furniture, the arrangement of simple objects on shelves and tables … it conveys the message that this is a place where adults have thought about the quality and instructive power of space.[34]

In Holland and Denmark most children are able to cycle to school because of carefully regulated off-road cycling paths, which offer complete protection from car traffic.

In Sweden, advertising to children is carefully controlled. Children's TV programmes are advertisement free and advertisers are limited in the way in which they can target children – restrictions which have been suggested as a useful model by the EU.

Public perceptions of children: interviews with adults

The relative paucity of children's experiences in the UK, and the limitations they experience, suggest that, by default rather than by intention, we are hostile to children. This attitude is compounded by beliefs that children are a nuisance, an encumbrance, and above all the personal property and private responsibility of their parents. This sombre perception was confirmed by the newspaper cuttings described above. For this chapter, we also undertook a small pilot study.[35] We carried out semi-structured interviews with over 100 adults, parents and non-parents from a variety of ethnic and class backgrounds. The interviews were carried out in various public and semi-public settings – in supermarkets, in parks, waiting outside schools, in restaurants – to ascertain views about the presence of children in those spaces.

We included supermarkets because they encapsulate many of the dilemmas described above. They constitute a semi-public space where parents and children regularly come in their hundreds of thousands. Yet they are a place of extreme consumer stress. There is a plethora of goods which to a young child may appear overwhelmingly tempting, but present a very different value to the parent who shops. Conversely, many of the goods over which parents deliberate are mystifying to children. How do parents and children behave in such circumstances; and how do the staff in the shops negotiate 'the whine factor' – the deliberate ploy by advertisers to get children to influence their parents over purchases.[36]

The three stores we visited, all from well-known chains, had policies on children. These policies included control of displays at checkouts – no or few sweets; keeping dangerous items on higher shelves; posting safety notices and instructions on trolleys; offering play cars to children, attached to trolleys; and having procedures for dealing with lost children. The respondents almost all noticed the strains that occurred, but tended to blame parents for not controlling or admonishing their children sufficiently. The manager of one store went so far as to describe it as a class issue:

> There is a 50/50 balance (in this store) between affluent and non-affluent parents and the difference between the two is very noticeable. Affluent parents generally keep an eye on their kids at all times and are polite when there are any problems with their children are pointed out to them. Non-affluent parents tend not to be so observant and are often rude to staff if any comments are made with regard to their children.

Almost all the staff in the stores said that whilst some children were well behaved, they had noticed children behaving badly: eating stock (especially pick and mix); having tantrums; screaming; running around and pulling items off shelves; or even getting into open freezers in search of ice-cream! Parents

tended to try to act responsibly about their children's behaviour, although there were some unfortunate lapses. He gave two examples: two mothers fighting over their children's behaviour; and a mother refusing to control her child who was throwing oranges 'what do you expect, he's only a child'. There was a consensus that even if supermarkets had child-friendly policies, they were difficult places for children. Children influence family purchases, and are commercially welcome because they do, but many of our respondents considered that the best way to deal with shopping was to avoid bringing children. This may be wise, but hard to arrange.

In parks, traditionally a refuge for children, dogs reigned supreme. Although the council in the parks in this study had provided dog bins, they were often disregarded and dog mess was common. There were also many dogs out with their owners, but running free. Respondents, including park managers, thought that the main users of parks were dog owners rather than children. One park was described as 'a relaxing friendly place for dog owners to meet'. Dog owners seemed to think dogs and children could share space; non dog owners were more sceptical, and some thought dogs were a hazard, especially to children, 'Dogs are a bloody pest'.

But all respondents, parents and non-parents alike, were clear that the park was a dangerous place for unaccompanied children: 'its not right, its dangerous, they might be kidnapped or raped or murdered ... dogs are not the problem, animals aren't wicked, it's the human beings that are the problem.' 'kids need to play, vent their feelings, but its not practical ... there is nothing wrong with the world, it is the people in it.' 'Children should be able to run around and explore. But it's not safe these days. What if an accident happened? There are child snatchers, dodgy perverts. You have to be very careful. Children are easy targets.'

No one thought that children should visit the park on their own, or even as a group, but considered that adult supervision was essential at all times. Children were more likely to be secure in enclosed or specially designated playground areas. The parks were used by organized groups – schools, keep fit clubs, football clubs – but not children on their own.

The Government's task force on urban green spaces suggested that parks are barometers of the state of the area in which they are located. Only 18 per cent of parks are in good condition (including one of the three in our survey). Parks are disregarded because, paradoxically they are free: '*While other forms of recreation, from indoor sports and leisure to computer games, are aggressively marketed to urban populations, a visit to the local parks can seem a less exciting option.*'

The solution of the task force was that parks should have more designated places within them, for specific activities and games. The parks we visited had park rangers, whose job was partly educative. They produced pamphlets for children identifying birds and plants, laid nature trails and put on events. But this was all adult directed and adult led. Two of the parks also had very busy 'one-o-clock clubs', separate playspace where carers could come with young children, with indoor and outdoor facilities. But these playspaces were locked and guarded outside of their short periods of weekday use.

School playgrounds are one of the few remaining spaces where children can congregate and play freely. We interviewed mothers waiting outside a school, about their views on their children's use of school playgrounds in and out of school hours. The school was a Victorian building with enclosed asphalt yards and a small picnic area with benches. There was an additional closed off play space with outdoor equipment for nursery age children. Parents criticized the space for having no shade and no green space, no quiet corners for reflective games, and no proper football pitch, but recognized that it gave children opportunities to play with one another. When we asked whether (as in some countries) the schoolyards should be open to children outside school hours, not everyone agreed. One parent argued that '*This is a school, its for learning!*' Another took the view that children left alone would destroy everything: '*This is a country of young yobs*'. The majority welcomed the idea of the playground being used after hours, but **only** with adult supervision and tight security,

otherwise there would be accidents, vandalism, and worse.

We were interested too in spaces for eating. Eating is an intimate and social event – is it possible to eat in public with children? MacDonalds make a speciality of catering for children, but many eating places exclude children. We spoke to five restaurant managers, two of them from well-rated restaurants. One of the latter claimed that children were welcome at all times. Children were provided with crayons and paper, and at weekends they ran videos in the downstairs bar area for children. They did not consider children difficult – although their parents could be: '*Often it is more effective to talk directly to a child if there is a problem, because in a public place like a restaurant children are more likely to listen to staff than to their parents.*'

The other well-rated restaurant also welcomed children and provided activities. The manageress felt that '*you need to have a specific awareness of children and their needs in order to create a child-friendly environment, e.g. carrying hot food and liquids around the restaurant, parents and staff have to be aware of the danger.*'

A third restaurant, a Turkish firm, accepted as normal that children would come in with their parents. But the remaining two restaurants were more hostile: '*Children can run around and get in the way of staff, they can also be very demanding and noisy. This ruins your enjoyment of the meal. You go out for dinner to enjoy yourself, not to listen to screaming.*'

Apart from McDonald's and similar chains, however, there was no place where children could eat on their own, or hang out. It may be that many small, individually owned cafes are more tolerant of children and young adults. Most children have a very limited income. They could not afford to buy much food; consumption of food ties them to home. However, there are many take-away food outlets, and if children eat out, they often do so on the move, or hanging around. For adults, eating is a collective pleasure. For children, it may be a more solitary affair. Children's access to food, the spaces where they consume it, and who they eat with would make an interesting study.

Conclusion

The evidence suggests, and our own small survey confirmed, that children have a hard time in accessing public spaces. They are subject to constant surveillance when they do. Children's resilience, creativity, need for activity, and their friendships with one another are constantly underrated. At the same time they are subjected to overwhelming consumer pressures. The preferred solution for most adults, if not children themselves, is not to make existing public spaces more accessible to children, but to create separate spaces and institutions for them. But even these separate spaces are controlled and surveilled. The health and safety legislation, and the requirements of the 1989 Children Act for adult surveillance of children's activities means that all spaces where children spend time must be surveilled and controlled by adults. Building on Danish examples, the Adventure Playground movement from the 1950s, initiated by Lady Allen of Hurtwood, tried to create spaces for children that minimized adult intervention and tried to cede as much control of the environment as possible to children themselves.[37] The kind of spaces and the kinds of attitudes described by the playworker Jack Lambert in 1974 have mostly vanished:

> Our job is simply to allow (children) the space and scope they need to play … I feel it is dangerous to go around talking about the significance of children's play … it is down to this, I am not a leader but a servant to the children.[38]

If the situation for children is to change, then action needs to be taken on many fronts. The public view of children as vulnerable, threatening and in need of constant surveillance and control by adults, needs to be challenged.

The sociologist Berry Mayall has argued that schooling is a central arena where childhood can – and must be – rethought. At present, children are taught prescribed knowledge in formalized settings. Children at school are generally assumed to be immature, untrustworthy and incompetent, and schooling is literally and metaphorically designed around these assumptions. The new discipline of the sociology of childhood is providing a conceptual basis for challenging schooling and curriculum:

> In the sociology of children, data collected with children and by children, is teaching us adults that children are knowledgeable, constructively critical social agents, competent, able to cope, resilient.
>
> The social construction of childhood leads us adults to question our assumptions, by recognizing that they are tied into our social and political systems and goals.
>
> The structural sociology of childhood tells us that children are contributing to the social order. They do socially useful and indeed necessary things, including active engagement with learning, contributions to household and more general economies, and participation in building and promoting good social relations.[39]

The United Nation Convention on the Rights of the Child provides an accessible charter for taking children seriously. The Convention stresses children's rights to protection, provision and participation in the daily happenings of their lives. Various organizations have used the Convention as an opportunity to provide an advocacy platform for children themselves.[40] Children's own views about their circumstances, even the views of very young children, can help shape their environments.[41]

Robin Moore carried out scholarly research in three settings – in inner London, in a new town, and in a decaying northern industrial town. He asked local children to map the areas where they played, showing him where they went and what they did.[42] In this study, carried out 20 years ago, children freely mentioned playgrounds, streets, footpaths, fences, parks and open spaces as sites for their play. Moore concluded that there were a number of policy initiatives to support children's play and use of public space. Firstly, by ensuring their participation in the planning, design and management of their surroundings. Secondly, by making the streets liveable – by controlling traffic. Thirdly, by recognizing and conserving special childhood places, acknowledging where children play and respecting it in any kind of planning and redevelopment. Fourthly, by 'roughing up' urban parks and greens because spaces used by children are often 'overdesigned and highly manicured'. Fifthly, by providing 'animateurs' – people whose job, like that of playworkers, or in Scandinavia 'pedagogues', is to support children in using their environment. If these kinds of planning initiatives were needed in the 1970s and 1980s, they are needed even more now.

But as well as children gaining more independent access to public spaces, i.e. parks, streets, and schoolyards, where they can congregate and play, more attention needs to be paid to the spaces provided exclusively for children. As Shier writes:

> We should be concerned that children cannot be properly integrated into society and can only play freely in a special preserve behind a high fence. It has been suggested that our priority should not be the building of playgrounds but the redesigning of the environment as a whole, and indeed the restructuring of society so that the needs of children are recognized and provided for in every aspect of community life ... (but) even in some future society which accepts and values its children, the children will want special places for themselves where they can pursue their own interests.[43]

How those places might look, what they might contain, how children themselves might influence their design and content and ongoing activities are the subjects of this book. But paradoxically such initiatives are taking place at a time when the rhetoric of child protection is overwhelming and the consumerization of childhood is ferocious. In many ways children are marginalized, isolated, exploited, belittled and confined as never before.

Notes

1 Muir, J. (1913). *Story of My Boyhood and Youth.* Reprinted by Canongate Classics, Edinburgh. 1996. p. 22.
2 Peter Hitchens, quoted in the *New Statesman*, 23.9.2002, p. 24.
3 The UK has recently been criticized by the United Nations Committee on the Rights of the Child, (Session 31, Oct. 2002, Concluding Observations) for failing to uphold children's rights in a number of key areas.
4 ibid, p. 25.
5 Ward, C. (1990). *The Child in the City.* London: Bedford Press.
6 O'Brien, M., Jones, D., Sloan, D. and Ruskin, M. (2000). Children's Independent Spatial Mobility in the Urban Public Realm. *Childhood*, **7** (3), 357–277.
7 IPPR. (2002). *Streets Ahead: Safe and Liveable Streets for Children.* London: IPPR.
8 Penn, H. (2000). Policy and Practice in Childcare and Nursery Education. *Journal of Social Policy*, **29** (1), 37–54.
9 Penn, H. (1997). *Comparing Nurseries.* London: Paul Chapman.
10 DfES. (2003). *Every Child Matters.* Green paper on the future of Children's Services. www.dfes.gov.uk/everychildmatters.
11 Letter to the *Daily Express*, July 10, 2002. p. 29.
12 Alanen, L. and Mayall, B. (2001). *Negotiating Childhood.* London: Falmer.
13 OECD. (2000). Country report on Norway. Paris: OECD.
14 Woodhead, M. (1999). *Working Children.* Stockholm/London: Raada Barnen/Save the Children.
15 Seiter, E. (1995). *Sold Separately: Children and Parents in Consumer Culture.* NJ: Rutgers University Press. pp. 11–12.
16 Kenway, J. and Bullen, E. (2001). *Consuming Children.* Bucks: Open University Press.
17 Kline, S. (1993). *Out of the Garden: Toys, TV and Children's Culture in the Age of Marketing.* London: Verso.
18 13 ibid. p. 80.
19 Buckingham, D. (1995). The Commercialization of Childhood? The place of the Market in Children's Media Culture. *Changing English*, **2** (2), 17–20.
20 Toyshop brochure, quoted in Kenway and Bullen (2001), p. 82. (See note 16.)
21 Tobin, J. (1997). *Making a Place for Pleasure in Early Childhood Education.* New Haven: Yale University Press, p. 16.

22 McKendrik, H. (2000). KID CUSTOMER? Commercialization of playspace and the commodification of childhood. *Childhood*, **7** (3), 295–314.

23 Hart, R. (1995). *Children as the makers of a new geography*. In *Building Identities: Gender Perspectives on Children and Urban Space* (L. Karsten *et al.*, eds) Amsterdam: Institute for Social Geography, University of Amsterdam.

24 Opie, P. and Opie, I. (1969) quoted in Moore, R. (1986). *Childhood Domains*. Berkeley, California: MIG Communications, p. xiv.

25 Opie, P. and Opie, I. (1959). *The Lore and Language of Schoolchildren*. Oxford: Oxford University Press.

26 Opie, I. (2001). *Foreword*. In *Play Today in the Primary School Playground* (J. Bishop and M. Curtis, eds) p. xii, Bucks: Open University Press.

27 Blatchford, P., Creeser, R. and Mooney, A. (1990). Playground games and playtime. The Children's View. *Educational research*, **32** (3), 163–74.

28 Bishop and Curtis, ibid.

29 Bishop and Curtis, ibid. p. 15.

30 Sutton Smith, B. (1970). Psychology of childlore: the triviality barrier. *Western Folklore*, **29**, 1–8. p. 4.

31 Armitage, M. (2001). *The ins and outs of school playground play: children's use of 'play spaces'*. In Bishop and Curtis ibid. p. 55–56.

32 UNICEF. (2000). *Child Poverty in Rich Countries*. Florence: UNICEF.

33 OECD (2001). *Starting Strong: Early Education and Care in Twelve Countries*. Paris. OECD.

34 Gandini, L. (2002). *The History of Reggio Emilia*. In *Lessons from Reggio Emilia* (V. Fu *et al.*, eds), p. 17, NY: Pearson.

35 These interviews were carried out by Eleanor Snow.

36 Kline, ibid.

37 Shier, H. (1984). *Adventure Playgrounds*. London: NPFA.

38 Lambert, J. and Pearson, J. (eds) (1974). *Adventure Playgrounds*. London: Penguin, p. 157.

39 Mayall, B. (2003). *Sociologies of childhood and educational thinking*. Professorial lecture. London: Institute of Education.

40 For instance the Office of Children's Rights for London has worked with groups of young people to try to influence the Greater London Authority strategy on children.

41 Mayall, B. and Hood, S. (2001). Breaking Barriers: Provision and Participation in an out of school centre. *Children and Society*, 15, pp. 70–81.

42 Moore, R. (1986). *Childhood Domains*. Berkeley, California: MIG Communications, p. xiv.

43 See note 37.

Helen Penn is Professor of Early Childhood in the School of Education at the University of East London. She acts as consultant to various international organizations including the EU, the OECD, UNICEF and UNESCO. She has worked all over the world, most recently in Central Asia and Southern Africa. She has written many books and articles on the position of young children and services provided for them.

10

Razor blades and teddy bears – the health and safety protocol

Judith and John Hicks

Editor's introduction

For many working fathers living in urban areas, large parts of the weekend are spent standing in the municipal children's playground watching over their young children. These places provide a physical and social outlet for their children, an escape. This is especially important when they are living in confined home environments, such as a flat which has no outside play area for children to let off steam.

This was certainly my experience as the father of young boys. How many hours it seemed I spent following my kids around the local playground. For all but the most nervous, the child's natural inclination will be to go for the most challenging, even dangerous, piece of play equipment. They will do the things which feel dangerous and Dad must be around to catch them if they fall. Now my growing children will hardly go near children's play parks and I look back to those times with a certain degree of nostalgia.

Recently, as I passed a previously well-used play area with my youngest son (now aged 9), I asked him why he no longer wanted to go there. It's boring, he replied. He likes the high monkey bars and particularly enjoys climbing on top of the bars, he confided. He also likes pipes which he can crawl

through. But that, as far as purpose designed play equipment is concerned, is about as far as his interest goes. He likes the 'really high stuff'. The environment in the old playground is simply not challenging enough. It does not meet his aspirations.

It is a widely held view that the health and safety agenda is subverting and diminishing the culture of contemporary childhood. Here, one of the foremost experts in this area will argue that rather than being the negative phenomena that it is generally considered to be, children's health and safety legislation is largely a good thing. John Hicks believes that contemporary culture demands safe accessible environments for children. It is an important cultural process of socialization. Furthermore, if designers understand the rules that apply, they can still design imaginative play parks which continue to challenge the physical boundaries for our children.

In this chapter he describes the evolving history of children's play parks, and explains the basic rules for evaluating safety and developing good design strategies for children's play parks. He goes some way to defining exactly what 'child friendly' actually means and sets out the rules which ensure that the environment complies with modern health and safety legislation.

Figure 10.1
A three-year-old boy from a hill tribe in rural northern Thailand wanders away from the family group; his adventure into the wilderness is only temporarily delayed by the high fence and the barbed wire at the bottom of the slope. This is designed not to keep him in, but to restrict the entry of goats. He soon negotiates his way through and is found wandering happily down towards the river valley below. (Photo: Michele Oberdieck.)

A recent news item which in bold print declared that 'Compensation culture turns our parks into dreary, fun-free deserts'[1] is all too typical of the way things are portrayed. He argues that, whilst children's safety must always be paramount, this is by no means incompatible with the provision of well-designed, imaginative play spaces that encourage both independence and collaboration. In fact, it is in his view axiomatic that the two go hand in hand.

Introduction

Play conferences commonly warm up members by inviting them to identify key words and activities relating to their own childhood play experiences. Plainly these relate to the age of the participants and in recent years the customs and practices of the 1950s and 1960s have predominated. Key phrases, words and attitudes that generally emerge include 'freedom to roam', 'absence of traffic', 'street games' and 'bullying', while the fears of child abduction or molestation are generally raised as more recent issues. There is seldom reference to the incidence of accidental injury or death. With prompting, the group normally echoes one or other of the lately fashionable urban myths that include swings removed because they were facing the wrong way, playgrounds closed because conker gathering created an unacceptable risk, and the need to close recreation areas rather than ensure that they comply with requirements of the Disability Discrimination Act 1995.[2]

There is a puzzling certainty attaching to these criticisms which is perhaps best illustrated in relation to swings as discussed in a recent newspaper article: 'Another regular occurrence, it is said, was the removal of three-in-a row swings because the outer swings could hit the one in the middle'.[1] This is a version of the invariable practice of playground inspectors to recommend the removal of the centre swing in these cases since, following current British Standards, gaining access to the centre swing is considered hazardous. Stories such as that referred to above serve as reminders of the context within which children's play is often currently discussed; there is a depressingly familiar air to the current implicit call for the closure of conventional play areas. With the introduction of new standards in 1999, the same chorus was raised and many playgrounds were closed or else stripped of serviceable play items not judged dangerous, but non compliant with new, not retrospective, advisory notices. The two key changes of the past ten years are:

1 The replacement of British Standard (BS) 5696 Playground Equipment intended for Permanent Installation Outdoors (amended 1986) by a new European standard BS EN 1176 1988, and
2 the Disability Discrimination Act 1995 (DDA).

These changes can be seen within a substantial historical context.

Playgrounds in Britain – a brief history

Towards the end of the nineteenth and throughout the twentieth century five successive and distinct phases or fashions in playground design can be recognized within the UK:

1 *Monumental, 1880s–1920s*. This period is characterized by twenty-foot-high massively constructed boat-shaped swings, 'Witches Hat' roundabouts and crash stop plank see-saws, all within a tasteful assemblage of formal flowerbeds, fountains, muzzle-loading cannon on plinths by the bandstand, surrounded by wrought iron gates and railings.

2 *Social and Natural*. The period 1920–49 saw, largely in southern England and the Home Counties, a brief burgeoning of aspirational sports investment, with tennis courts, pools, lidos and bowling greens. World War Two consigned much of the ironmongery and the ground staff to assist the war effort and through a process of neglect, coupled with a growth in spectator sports, fields and pitches were the major areas of provision and improvement in the 1950s, prior to selling off portions for housing and similar developments.

3 *Scrapyard, 1950–70*. As in so many other ways the Scandinavian countries drove playground fashion within this period with their development of Adventure and Craft play centres which in England largely consisted of concrete pipes under mounds, railway sleeper forts and knotted ropes hanging from trees. These were potentially high risk situations that appear to have produced few injuries, while apparently justifying the next phase. An absence of playleaders in British playgrounds effectively removed a major element from the best European practice, but the development of 'urban farms' in some centres partially compensated for this.

4 *Supersafe, 1970 and after*. From the 1970s onwards there has been a major development of interest in inspection services and safety surfaces. Some part of this priority change was a natural and justified response to campaigning on behalf of children who had sustained quite devastating injuries due to neglect or negligence, but these developments can otherwise be seen as being driven by what is often described as a litigious society seeking substantial compensation for minor injuries.

5 *Play for all*. Inclusive Play – the pattern was set by the development of special playgrounds

Figure 10.2
A very large ship's mast and roped crosspiece roundabout/swing structure constructed from recovered timber (telegraph poles). This item was constructed by a former master mariner in the 1940s and fails all relevant standards. It has, however, an accident free record.

When the ropes supporting the crosspiece are wound around the central post and released the 'riders' fly out in a way that is potentially hazardous to onlookers. This is judged to be a high risk item and removal has been advised. If the item is to remain in use then minimum measures to be adopted should include:

1 A secure fenced and gated entry system should be put in place enclosing an area equal to the maximum extent of the 'riders' in motion plus two metres in all directions.

2 The safety surface should be restored and extended by at least a metre to all sides.

3 Safety inspections on ropes and fastening points should be undertaken daily and a close inspection should be made each week.

for disabled children in London which, with discretion, admitted siblings and others without impairments. The Disability Discrimination Act 1995 (DDA) endorsed and carried forward this philosophy while encouraging bolder and more ambitious provision of services for all upon an integrated basis. Currently the move is against specific provision for any minority interests and there are substantial funds in place to improve facilities overall.

From the Empire-sustaining challenges of Victoria's Jubilee parks to the Sputnik and moon rocket inspired play equipment of more recent times, community values and priorities have shaped play provision. The same considerations apply today and, whether starting from scratch, adding a new item or embarking on a full refurbishment and improvement programme, the first step should be to consult the community as a whole and seek to identify and reflect community values while, where necessary, reconciling diverse or contradictory aspirations.[3]

Child development and the importance of outdoor play

Children develop socially, intellectually, physically and emotionally in every aspect of their lives. It is axiomatic for early years practitioners and other professionals that play is a powerful medium for developing and expressing self-awareness, social learning, imagination, awareness of the world and physical skills. Play is, as Janet Moyles expresses it, a natural tool for learning, fun and a powerful motivator.[4] For Moyles, the key element in play is children's ownership of their actions and, indeed, independent activity is, to some degree, central to most definitions of play. Other important and frequently cited features of 'real' play include enjoyment, spontaneity, involvement, persistence and concentration. Play cannot be taught, although it may be modelled by others, and it cannot be imposed, as Miss Haversham found in Dickens' *Great Expectations*.

Almost all situations provide some opportunities for play. It has, however, been shown that for some children there is a fundamental difference between their behaviour and preferences inside and their outdoor play, even in the context of nurseries and playgroups where there are usually rich opportunities for indoor play. The literature suggests that outdoor play may be particularly liberating for less advantaged children and for boys, who may find a greater freedom to talk, to develop dramatic scenarios, to organize cooperative play and to engage in vigorous, sometimes noisy, physical activity without inhibition.[5]

Differences also exist between the relatively highly structured and supervised activities of groups in the outdoor areas of nurseries and primary schools and the generally more open-ended, less structured opportunities provided by public parks, playgrounds and recreation areas. Here, the extent of supervision by carers varies considerably and children may consequently have a greater or lesser degree of freedom to do as they choose, explore and experiment. Public playgrounds invariably provide large fixed play equipment, that is immovable and cannot readily cater for different or changing needs. The onus is, then, on the children to make the best of what is provided, sometimes in ways that are unintended. As often as not, for example, we see children attempting to climb up a slide rather than descending in conventional fashion, deliberately colliding with others, or testing the speed at which various objects will slide down the chute. Older youths may even attempt to ride their bicycles up the slide. It can be persuasively argued that children playing in this fashion are exercising more imagination and initiative – and hence learning more – than the solitary individual being pushed on a swing. Indeed, one of the paradoxes about the notion of safe play is that equipment that provides insufficient challenge for the target age-group is more likely to be misused, often in a hazardous manner.

Traditionally, fixed play apparatus has been designed with an emphasis on developing physical skill and gross movement, especially climbing, balancing and swinging. In some circumstances this tends to encourage competitive rather than cooperative behaviour, creating a play environment that can be intimidatory for younger children and especially for those with a variety of impairments. At worst, such equipment provides few, if any opportunities for modification or for utilizing the apparatus in different ways. Sand and water play are obvious exceptions, but climatic conditions in Britain are not favourable, and there is only limited provision in public parks. Some conventional play apparatus, see-saws for example, require interaction and cooperative behaviour – these are the beneficial exceptions.

Fixed play apparatus generally allows for letting off steam, but sometimes fails to address other key benefits of play, in particular:

1   opportunities for imaginative role play;
2   quiet and contemplative play;
3   the development of manipulative and fine motor skills;
4   discovery and experimentation.

These critical comparisons have less application in reserved toddler play areas that are equipped with multi-play units offering low level, small-scale play items such as Tic Tac Toe, abacus, shape sorting and chime bells, together with play shops, 'living areas' and kitchens. However, the general argument remains persuasive.

Writing about the design of preschools in Reggio Emilia, John Bishop gives a powerful description of flexible and infinitely adaptable play spaces that children can 'appropriate for themselves', reflecting the free and independent social interaction of the street or piazza.[6] The experience of Reggio Emilia provides a welcome reminder of what the children themselves bring to any play space. Until quite recent times there was a seasonality about play, relatively uninfluenced by adults, and in part related to time of the year and to the more important cricket and football seasons. Such play might incorporate 'bows and arrows', marbles, 'fives' or jacks, conkers and – as now – skipping and yo-yos, as well as games with improvised materials of all kinds. Children still bring their own imaginative ideas to public play spaces, as well as their bikes, scooters and sporting equipment. Good design can cater for and encourage this tendency.

The current agenda

Perhaps the most interesting aspect of the present surge of interest in play and playgrounds is why this should have become an issue. Within months, two different government departments have produced closely focused reports, each related to the New Opportunities Fund (NOF), Barnardos have funded a three-year 'Better Play' programme, the National Playing Fields Association (NPFA) has issued a new report and the Commission for Architecture and the Built Environment (CABE) is developing an initiative.[7]

A number of simple answers are suggested. The Government, in the run-up to the 2001 election, pledged £200 000 000 for improving children's play opportunities and is now soliciting advice and applications for funding to enable the money to be spent wisely. Long-term neglect of play facilities nationally is evident in almost every community and so current need is plainly matched to future funding. More important, there is growing awareness of the health and social costs of an increasingly obese society, which might in part be derived from inactive 'couch potato' children.[8] Rightly or wrongly, there is a perception that better designed and safer playgrounds might help to counter this by encouraging more children to engage in active, outdoor play.

The Office of the Deputy Prime Minister's earlier report on environmental issues (ODPM 2002) also singled out play spaces, and especially play space for children with disabilities, as needing guidance and funding. The implications for children's play space of the Disability Discrimination Act, fully implemented in October 2004, has been relatively neglected until recently, so that children and carers with disabilities have had little specific consideration.

There is a need to explore ideas such as those contained in the Office of the Deputy Prime Minister's guide, notably the suggestion that play area providers might allocate staff to supervise children at fixed points in the day.[9] The case for play leaders appears to be well made here and the subsequent proposals of the Children's Play Review report *Getting Serious About Play*, which includes specific funding proposals, makes it appear realistic.[10]

The linkage between the quality of play, the frequency of accidents and the degree of supervision of young children is beyond question and so the distinction between supervised and unsupervised play space is of interest here. The age, size, condition and location of play apparatus all have a bearing on safety but only rarely can individuals or advocacy groups have a significant influence on these issues. On the other hand, effective supervision and guidance can reduce the effect of unsuitable locations or choices already made, without inhibiting children's freedom to play independently and constructively. Aggression, wilful damage and unsuitable dress or demeanour, unavoidable hazards in public space, can also be confronted by an active supervisory presence. At its simplest level, supervision provides the possibility of rescue and first aid as necessary. In Germany it is unlawful to allow unsupervised children under the age of three on playgrounds. In Britain we appear content to incorporate special elements within our version of the European standards to address the risk attached to this situation. Vandalism is always a potential issue when play areas are equipped with items less robust than well-secured multi-play units – and even they can never be wholly secure – but supervision, coupled with an active community interest, can go some way towards limiting these problems.

There is undoubtedly more to children's safety and community well-being than swings and roundabouts, since the location and management of the playground in a time when drive-by shootings, muggings, stalking and stabbing incidents are reported regularly in the press may be seen as a social order as well as a health and safety issue. The political thrust is, then, to improve the quality of life of the whole community.

Figure 10.3
This recently installed skate bowl is directly in line with the main entrance point and so presents serious risks to some potential visitors. Fencing is minimal and appears to direct vulnerable people towards points of danger.

Unguarded approach route to some facilities, notably areas with wheeled sports provision, incorporate a serious potential hazard to some categories of visitors, especially the blind and people with learning disabilities. It is recommended that the installation and/or the renewal of fencing be considered within an early review of all such locations.

Figure 10.4
This is a five element multi-play unit incorporating two tyre climbers. Unfortunately children have twisted the tyres until the ground fixing was extracted, like a rotten tooth, creating two freely swinging tyres which potentially collide with one another, the side members and passing children.

In this case safe, and dull design has been overcome by childish enterprise.

Figure 10.5
A Freestanding slide – home-made – very steep and very fast. It is described here as a freestanding slide but might be seen as a hybrid and so more difficult to fault under specific BS paragraphs such as 1:4.2. Only some of the more obvious breaches are listed as examples: there is evidence of rot in the platform; the recovered timber-linked carcinogenic and associated risks have obvious application here.

Additionally there are the following BS breaches.

1   There are numerous head and other entrapment points in the structure. Low/medium risk.
2   The ramp is at a greater angle than the maximum permitted 40°. Medium risk.
3   There is an absence of sufficient and appropriate guard rails, handrails and other support and access aiding features. Medium risk.
4   The side and bottom structural sections invite climbing and perching. Low/medium risk.
5   The item fails grip/grasp requirements. Low risk.
6   Accessible height is in excess of three metres. Medium risk.
7   The impact attenuating surface in place around the platform is inadequate. Medium/high risk.

As a part of an inspection report in 2003 a registered inspector said that 'this item has no place in or near a playground for young children since, while falling short of being dangerous, it is certainly high risk'. Remedial work has been undertaken but another inspection company was awarded the inspection contract in 2004.

Playground safety in perspective

Setting aside the common experience of trivial injury associated with scrapes, cuts and bruises which are an inescapable part of childhood, interest in safety in playgrounds has not figured largely in expressions of community concern until quite recent times. The systematic collection and analysis of playground accidents and injuries is a comparatively recent phenomenon which is ascribable to both the comparative rarity of the events and what might be seen as a predictably defensive posture adopted by the providers of play services and equipment.

Around thirty years ago Illingworth et al.[12] collected statistics over an eighteen-month period relating to 200 playground accidents requiring hospital treatment in a Sheffield hospital. This study and a number of others have been analysed in the work of Karen King and David Ball.[13] The Health and Safety Executive recently published further research from Dr David Ball which, in revisiting the same issue appears to call into question the value of any provision of impact absorbing surfaces (IAS) in relation to their effectiveness in preventing injuries to children. The report confirms earlier findings that the major risk factors in playgrounds are behaviour, equipment height and bodily orientation in falls to the ground, but takes no account of the requirements of DDA; further consideration of this issue is indicated.

In 1991, the Townswomen's Guild undertook a comprehensive survey of play opportunities and hazards in 878 playgrounds across Britain.[14] In a characteristically forthright way they identified the major hazard areas and noted the degree to which dogs and dog fouling, traffic, missing or broken ancillary items, the deliberate introduction of hazards, razor blades, absence of safety surfacing and risk of falling or collision injury all contributed to the potential for child injury. This was perhaps the first reasoned and 'official' complaint at the degree to which councils were allegedly responding to a perceived and possibly exaggerated fear of litigation by removing anything that might present a hazard:

'They (the children) surely need to be presented with some challenges and learn to respect the dangers in life! If safety's pushed too hard as the sole issue, playgrounds are simply gutted without any corresponding positive action. Or the equipment is rendered so safe that it ceases to have any point.'[15]

That said, the report clearly identifies hazards such as 'plank' swings, 'Witches Hats', crash see-saws, wood or metal swing seats and redundant machinery used as climbers. The Guild's common sense approach to risk in play is in contrast to other examples of this discussion where, through a combination of exaggerated and naive use of language, the impression is given that preventable child injury is considered tolerable.

In 1992, the Department of Education and Science published *Playground Safety Guidelines* which, while alluding to risk, skirts the problem by identifying challenge and adventure as natural aspects of children's play but stressing the need to 'experience these in a safe environment'.[16]

UK television personality Esther Rantzen probably more than any other individual raised public anxiety in relation to safety in playgrounds in *Which* reports published in June and July 1994.[17] On the basis of Department of Trade and Industry estimates of 30 000 playground accidents annually, she commissioned NPFA to lead safety audits on twenty-five playgrounds in major cities across Britain. The outcomes, predictably, identified issues arising from the toleration of known hazards, inadequate or neglected maintenance of equipment, crowded sites, unsuitable equipment, vandalism and hazards such as damaged fencing and broken bottles. Her campaign for safer playgrounds was influential in establishing the need to install appropriate safety surfaces and bringing to public attention the need for regular inspection and maintenance of play space.

Current legal requirements

The whole of the protection currently afforded to playground users in relation to civil and criminal law derives from that same legislation and relevant case law which protects us in every other aspect of our working, leisure and community lives. There is no specific 'Playground Safety Act' and this is interesting because, in contrast to the play and recreation lobby, there is no evidence of employers or the trades unions urging the benefits to be derived from knowingly entering or utilizing premises or apparatus with recognizable risk potential.

Following a landmark legal judgment, all British Standards now include a statement to the effect that compliance with a British Standard does not of itself confer immunity from legal obligations. In other words, providers of playgrounds and equipment are required to take every possible step to ensure safety; mere compliance with the relevant standard is not enough.[18] Case law has further established that providers are expected to be aware that children do not always use equipment in the anticipated way. In particular, the duty of councils to undertake or to commission regular inspections of play space and equipment is clearly embodied in legislation and established as good practice.

Councils, like other providers, are required to ensure that visitors to their premises are safe. This duty of care applies to all, including unauthorized visitors, and warning notices offer little protection against actions for negligence. Children cannot be expected either to read or to respond to notices, and are known to be less careful than adults and so require special consideration and protection. In short, playground designers and providers are expected to be aware of and address foreseeable causes of injury to any site user. Similarly, the requirement to carry out a risk assessment at specific intervals or in response to changes cannot be ignored. Various legislation concerning health and safety requires providers to ensure that people are not exposed to risks and must make a 'suitable and sufficient' assessment of risk.[19]

Playground design

The first consideration must be that of meeting or exceeding the minimum statutory requirements relating to the provision of play space, first in regard to safety and suitability but then in relation to accessibility and the inclusion of all. The second is to consult potential users and their communities. Here it needs to be borne in mind that children, when consulted, can adopt a realistic and shrewd approach to expressing needs, but are as liable to be readily persuaded as their parents to adopt either the latest trend or an entirely traditional approach to play space. Sometimes both groups may, for understandable reasons, fail to take into account wider community interests and priorities.

Playgrounds tend to serve particular groups and communities and seldom, except in holiday resorts, camping and caravan sites and commercial premises, attract significant numbers of children that are not local and commonly acquainted, if not friends and neighbours. The strategic planning for a new or improved playground must, therefore, take account of and respond to long-term local community needs. These include the current and projected age structure of the immediate locality and the proximity of the proposed site to children's homes and schools. This is of increasing importance in catering for the play needs of disabled or otherwise disadvantaged children, their parents or other carers. Land cost is a significant consideration, including alternative site usage and development potential, especially possible benefits from 'planning gain'. Local housing trends, new estates under construction and areas subject to clearance, upgrading or redevelopment need to be taken into account. Specific consideration should be given to residents who might object to a playground, the elderly or the sick, perhaps, for whom noise would be an unwelcome intrusion. On the other hand, isolated sites are rarely appropriate: for children to be discreetly overlooked is to be safe.

Other considerations are:

* Safe, well-lit access via paths, cycle tracks and roads.
* Opportunities for shared and mutually supportive roles such as neighbouring council park nurseries providing experience of growing and propagation.
* Any environmental or other hazards, i.e. standing water, railway lines, electricity sub-stations and pylons, busy roads and previous, possibly contaminating, land use.

It is worth bearing in mind that, even in small and isolated communities, the range of purposeful activities can be extended through cooperation and liaison with schools and local authorities. Play equipment and facilities can be purchased and maintained on a shared basis while there are attractive opportunities for extending play through a mobile play unit on the lines of the mobile library. This procedure is specifically commended and endorsed in *Getting Serious about Play*.[10]

Whatever the immediate local priorities, there is always a limited budget to work within and some essentials of design remain valid, regardless of fashion or finance. Natural features such as a sloping site can add to amenity use at no cost in, for example, providing a ready-made slope for a mound slide or a BMX track. Similarly, inherent

Figure 10.6
This new(ish) roundabout incorporates risk to users since either it has been incorrectly installed or else the spindle is worn/damaged to the degree that there is a tilt on the platform giving ground clearances ranging from 60–95 mm, with a consequent risk of crush injury. BS EN 1176 5: 1998: 6:2;3 permits a ground clearance of between 60–110 mm. The ground clearance here apparently conforms, but the assumption is that ground clearance is consistent at the periphery and for at least 300 mm towards the axis, otherwise there is, as here, the risk of rotation drawing body parts into a diminishing space with consequent crush or friction burn injuries resulting. Medium risk.

Figure 10.7
This small girl is demonstrating how she received neck injuries on the castellations on a newly installed multi-play unit. The gaps are wide enough to admit her neck and so, standing on tiptoe, she could put her head over the lower sections but when she tired and lowered to a normal standing position she could not pull back from the head trap.

Figure 10.8
This old playground incorporated three potential hazards which were removed in a refurbishment programme in the 1990s.

1   The self-build platform had neither handrails, guard rails or any safety surfacing, incorporated unexpected obstacles as well as head and torso traps, and so represented apparent risk to users.
2   The 'Spider climber' incorporates hard objects in the falling area and lacks a safety surface.
3   Parallel bars invariably attract children, usually girls to hang head down like bats with their legs wrapped around a bar. The absence of safety surface suggests high risk in the event of losing grip.

Figure 10.9
This user-friendly play house has safety surfacing only on the inside but the risk of climbing and falling is minimal. Either (a) no safety surfacing is required or (b) the minimum extent of surfacing required by BS, 1.5 metres, should extend from all potential fall points.

Figure 10.10
This ramp on a brand new multi-play unit has not been secured to the ground. It can be lifted and dropped like a drawbridge and so represents serious risk of injury to adventurous children.

physical features can assist in ensuring a clear separation of age-related play apparatus and amenities. The early stages of planning should always take into account the very different play needs, interests and physical capabilities of children at various ages and stages of their development. The age- and ability-based zoning of play equipment is an important issue. As an aid to supervision, high visual barriers, including trees, limiting long sight lines to all parts of the play area should be avoided. Such boundaries as low-level hedging, can, however, divide an otherwise bleak space in an imaginative way, creating small enclosures and giving children a sense of privacy without limiting opportunities for adults to oversee activities from a distance.

It is worthwhile spending a great deal of time at the planning stage since good playground design aids the development of social, creative and intellectual interaction between children, as much as physical activity, and allows younger, less robust and more timid children to share as much from observation as from active participation in play. Provision for social space, including well-planned arrangements for seating and shelter, encourages parents and other carers to stay on site, and can

constitute an important safety feature as well as helping to guard against bullying and vandalism.

As we have argued previously, every opportunity should be created for extending the concept of the playground to meet a wide range of developmental needs. This is not merely a place for exercise and amusement, but a space where every opportunity should be taken to encourage creative, exploratory learning experiences. Low cost, renewable and inclusive access to play can be developed by, for example, regarding paved areas and paths as potential mazes, hopscotch pitches, giant snakes and ladders boards and painted target areas. Sundials can be created with painted panels, designed to use children as the gnomon; this could form an entertaining, educational and entirely practical self-help community project. Surfaces prepared for use as 'graffiti boards' encourage artistic expression and perhaps focus genuine graffiti in specific, readily-cleaned locations. If the whole community is to be involved, then a 'trim track' set up with regularly updated age-related targets and achievements would be called for.

Part of a growing problem in approaching the design of play areas derives from the mistaken belief in a community-inspired need to temper boldness in concept to the mundane requirements of conventional play areas; whereas what is in fact needed is age- and ability-related, as well as accessible, play provision that also has elements of excitement and surprise for all users. The importance of drawing upon the natural environment cannot be overstated. The priority here is play mounds rather than landscaping, wild flower meadows as well as areas of close-cut grass and living willow structures designed as tunnels, arches and gathering places. Weatherproof signs and screens illustrating commonly observed local wildlife encourage learning and observation, while the display of 'archive' pictures showing the park/playground in former times might encourage a sense of community ownership and history. Whatever is decided in relation to layout, the emphasis must be on function rather than appearance.

Equipment and surfacing

Among the complaints relating to playground design and management is the fact that the play equipment industry seldom produces new or exciting variants on old ideas; the influence of the 'compensation culture' is also often blamed for this. This view does not bear close analysis. If there is an absence of originality in design and marketing, this is largely due to market leaders in possession of a comfortable market share and an absence of innovative entrants into the field. For new entrants it is all too easy to make a comfortable living from discreet versions of proven designs. There is, in any event, a limit on innovation in the mechanisms available, but in the materials field, the manufacturing industry has made spectacular changes in recent times. These changes are seldom evident in the design of play equipment, except to the degree that anti-vandal measures have encouraged the use of durable protective materials.

Some organizations have responded to this problem by providing separate areas equipped with 'big boy toys' in the form of adventure trails that would as readily serve as commando training facilities, with scaling walls and rope-assisted climbs up to and above three metres in accessible height.

More acceptable innovative designs or variations on old themes include:

- sophisticated aerial flight/runways – an acceptable variant on the traditional rope over the stream;
- the development of swing–roundabout–see-saw combinations which enliven traditional activities by providing opportunities for variation;
- pedal-driven roundabouts;
- games walls, which are a marketed version of the same walls, garage doors and fences that we kicked balls against when young;
- multi-use games areas (MUGAS) – games walls providing a mini multi-sport arena at relatively low cost.

Moving to the more esoteric end of the market, a few companies produce interactive play items which will 'talk' to children in playgrounds. At least one manufacturer markets large, heavy mobile figures that will take a good beating and will strike back at the unwary, as well as a giant boxing glove intended to direct and channel aggression. Finally, through the application of fluid dynamics a manufacturer has produced an all-age, all-size very safe hydro scale play item. These and other less common items are worth considering alongside more traditional equipment: the possibilities are very wide.

The physical location and orientation of any fixed play equipment are important. Slides should point north rather than south to reduce the effects of solar gain, while swings should not move in directions that add to risk or discomfort through dazzle from sunshine in spring and autumn. All items should be laid out in such a way as to discourage crowding around or between popular items. Equipment with moving parts, swings for example, and those that create uncontrolled or 'forced' movement such as slides, should be located on the fringes or other uncongested parts of the site so as to avoid collisions and movement clash.

Safe surfaces are an essential feature where play equipment exceeds a height of 60 cm. A full discussion of the requirements set out in the relevant British Standard and the relative merits of different impact-absorbent surfaces is set out in Hicks 2003:12. Sometimes the value of well-maintained grass as a safe surface beneath low-level items of equipment is overlooked.

The characteristics of accessible and inclusive play equipment

A very high priority in the design procedure should be that of seeking to anticipate and fully conform to the requirements of The Disability Discrimination Act 1995, fully implemented in October 2004. Unrestricted physical access is essential. In all areas of risk – which may arise from moving parts, swings, environmental hazards, unexpected obstacles, chain walks, 'stepping stones', dizzy discs or wheeled activities, skate boards, bikes and roller blades, pools and standing water, steep drops or steps – surface texture changes such as a broad gravel surrounding area or other tactile indicators should be in place to give warnings or reminders of risk to those with disabilities.

Detailed and specific advice on this topic can be found in Hicks.[20] This work enables robust and reliable judgements to be made on sites and specific facilities or services at play locations within them. It addresses the need to describe and quantify accessibility and inclusivity in relation to the whole available range of play equipment and apparatus in a way that is objective and systematic in approach. To this end there follows an initial approach to access evaluation that subsumes, but is not confined to, that limited range of 'special needs' equipment that is perhaps mainly appropriate to supervised institutional use. The importance of this emphasis on standard equipment being evaluated in relation to its degree of accessibility by all cannot be overstated. For inclusivity to be accepted as a worthwhile and achievable objective in play situations, the degree to which we make, or fail to make specific provision for those with impairments will tend to condition attitudes across the whole range of service users.

If this or some similar system is adopted, then play providers can be objectively advised or observe for themselves the degree to which specific items of equipment meet access and inclusivity priorities. This would influence purchasing decisions likely to discreetly assist and enable all, while disadvantaging none.

This proposed hierarchy of accessible and inclusive play equipment characteristics can readily be adopted and applied within the extensive public involvement in proposals to allocate funds. The required outputs and outcomes determined locally can readily inform the design, purchase and installation of new play equipment and apparatus.

5 play item short descriptors	Definitions and commentary
1. A user-friendly item	1. A subjective judgment made to indicate an absence of obstructions or specific barriers
2. A user-friendly item with low level play opportunities	2. As (1) above but with abacus, shape sorts, slider panels, pinball games or similar ground level based activities
3. A user-friendly item with low level play opportunities and aided access to some elevated sections	3. As (2) above but with ropes, handrails, grab handles or other self-help access aids in place. Ideally at least half of the elevated sections are accessible
4. A user-friendly item with low level play opportunities and good unaided access to most of the elevated sections	4. As (3) above but with transfer platforms, ramps, low-level shallow access, and/or a protective surface finish for comfortable access or return crawling. An accessible return route to original start point, ground or elevated level is presumed in this case
5. A user-friendly item with low level access and good unaided access to elevated sections that also enables and encourages cooperative play	5. As (4) above where relevant, but with dual or multiple user roles such as speaker tubes, tic-tac-toe, sand tables, water play and shop fronts. Inclusivity is a 'stand alone' concept only in part dependent upon accessibility considerations

The outcomes in this case can be simply expressed in percentage terms, with 25 per cent accessibility being given cumulatively from categories 1 to 4 with, for example, an item capable of meeting the terms of the category 4 descriptors being 'accessible'. Items meeting none of these are 'inaccessible' but others might possibly be 25, 50 or 75 per cent accessible. An item meeting the requirements of section 5 is described as being both accessible and an 'inclusive' play item. In those cases where there are no elevated items then 'accessible' status can be attached at descriptor 2 level and with this qualification the presence of dual and multiple use items also gives an 'inclusive play item' status in such cases.

Here are a few examples to follow up these descriptions:

1   Many swings and unitary climbers rate 'user-friendly' status, but high level stilt slides, climbing walls and overhead bars do not.
2   Numbers of toddler multi-play units rate descriptor 2 status (50 per cent accessible) and some also rate as inclusive play items with the inspector's discretion to rate the item 100 per cent accessible in those cases where elevated sections are of little significance.
3   Most medium-sized multi-play units with five or more play elements do, or by thoughtful or advised specification at the contract stage could, meet descriptor 3 level status (75 per cent accessible).
4   Without specific planning, specification and appropriate access route provision few medium- or large-sized multi-play unit elements would fall into the 100 per cent accessible category. In these cases we are probably looking mainly at the products of companies with a substantial US market or presence and so a degree of commitment to and experience of built-in access systems, the provision of status targeted activities and the related provision of ground as well as elevated access routes supplemented by appropriate surface treatment.
5   Very much as 4 above but with the ambiguities of 'inclusivity' evident. So a large multi-play unit could have a whole hierarchy of low-level play as well as physically testing activities, ground accessed overhead bars and rings for example, ramps, rails, rubber surfaces and built-in mobility aids as well as space to store a wheelchair or other mobility aids. But pairs of low-level speaking tubes, play activity frames and some see-saws would meet the same specification. A standard wooden play house would too.

Wicksteed Leisure in one of the first and best of a spate of recent guides to the DDA state that:

'The aspiration of those providing play facilities must be to create challenges for all and barriers for none. Where totally shared experience is not always possible, then at least opportunities can be created for similar and, if possible, qualitatively equal experience for all children.'[21]

It is difficult to quarrel with this view.

Negligence and getting risk in perspective

In startling contrast to the compensation culture referred to at the start of this chapter and from a superficial reading of the literature, it appears currently fashionable in Britain to underplay the potentially lethal or crippling aspects of risk in relation to children's play space and a single statement can be taken as being indicative of a growing mood:

Exposure to real risk in playgrounds provides beneficial learning experience and a sought after thrill.[22]

If this were a single and perhaps perverse interpretation of children's aspirations and needs then it might be dismissed as simply another mistaken minority view, but weightier authorities make much the same point. The Play Safety Forum in a policy statement in 2002 claimed that 'Children need and want to take risks where they play'. Fortunately they temper this with the risible addition 'play provision aims to manage the level of risk so that children are not exposed to unacceptable risks of death or serious injury'. The

Deputy Prime Minister's report (ODPM 2003) sets up a man of straw when it quotes a parent as saying that risk (to their disabled child) is preferable to exclusion from play. At a later point in the same report this is linked to 'the pressure of the increasingly litigious climate in which we live'.[23]

Recalling that risk is a measure of the chances of an identified hazard causing injury, then the implications of these statements appear obvious: we are advised to tolerate known risks of injury to children. While no examples are offered, one might speculate on measures such as delaying the repair of damaged guard rails; permitting cycling and skateboarding on paths; removing restrictions on dog fouling on play space; encouraging the fixing of ropes over streams; perhaps even bringing back the 'Witch's Hat' (an exciting piece of vintage play equipment associated with many accidents).

Contrasting these views with those of the Townswomen's Guild quoted earlier, it is clear that for some, an explanation of the degree to which they underrate risk as an issue in children's play might be their life experience and occupations. To draw an analogy from another field, some studies of risk in employment have demonstrated 'attitude problems' in relation to safe practice. In a study of measures to encourage the use of protective clothing, helmets, gloves and boots in welding it was found that management saw the safety conscious and conforming operatives as being 'half witted, slow but reliable people who gave very little trouble'.[24] Other operatives did not necessarily share the 'cissy' judgement but said that that was how such people would be seen by many of their colleagues. Close parallels might be drawn between this situation and wheeled sports where, even within a macho environment, the best advice available recommends the use of protective clothing including helmets as well as gloves, knee and elbow guards:

People get injured on BMX tracks and it is essential that all site users are made aware of the dangers associated with wheeled sports. They need to wear a BS EN 1078 quality helmet, gloves, elbow, wrist and shin protectors and should at all times have their arms and legs

covered to reduce the severity of the cuts, bruises and friction burns that inevitably go with the sport. (21)

The acceptance here of risk of injury is implicit and inevitable – it goes with the territory of wheeled sports generally; it is in the anticipation and mitigation of risk elements that service providers have a proper role.

If this is not seen as a contradiction in terms it might be claimed that the ability to take risks safely is a function of skill and experience, rather than of early onset 'rites of passage', necessity, ignorance or taking opportunities for the display of bravado. The skilled skater can achieve total weightlessness in spectacular exhibitions on full size half pipe ramps, 'verts', at a height of 4 metres, but this is not a sport for novices, poseurs or the nervous. The ability to complete the move is invariably accompanied by the committed use of the required protective clothing.

It may be helpful to distinguish between risk, the managed experience of risk and the appearance of risk:

- Risk is merely the chance or possibility of injury occurring, usually within identified and specific contexts. Since it is impossible to wholly exclude risk, the unhelpful phrase 'we tolerate risk' has some limited validity.

- There are in place well-documented and agreed risk assessment procedures to address the hazards with which risks are associated. Thus measures are taken to engineer out the hazard; to substitute less hazardous parts or materials; or else to introduce procedures which minimize risk.

- Within other contexts children, tense with fear, are guided up the ladder, or rocked while held on the see-saw and so experience all of the terror of danger without suffering the slightest chance of concomitant injury.

Similarly, we can distinguish between making the play space safe and using the play space safely:

- Making the place safe involves removal of, or otherwise countering, specific known or presumed risks;

- Using the place safely might require confidence in the skill of the rider or skateboarder to overcome whatever hazard is perceived.

An informed appreciation of risk is necessary for survival in all sentient creatures and is an essential element in many real-life contexts. We do not, however, make it a practice to expose troops in training to live ammunition or train fire and rescue personnel in genuinely hazardous blazing buildings. What possible purpose can there then be in asserting a need for 'real' risk in children's playgrounds? Most people do not tolerate genuine risk of injury any more than they expect to find real ghosts in the ghost train. This is not to deny that the appearance or pretence of danger may have some value in enabling children to develop the means of coping with potentially dangerous real-life situations as they grow up.

From the first, a well-established safety policy should commit site owners to providing a safe place and means of delivering play services and experience, while using their best endeavours to maintain safety and to require safe practices and behaviour. There is of course in playgrounds, as elsewhere, a dissonance between what is required and what is actually tolerated, and so:

- We sometimes tolerate poorly designed and even dangerous play equipment. The simplest solution to this aspect of a greater problem lies in planned programmes of public education and the spreading of good practice through partnership, with the play equipment industry leading the way.
- Economic considerations and mistaken social attitudes are sometimes allowed to influence the location of play equipment and play space. So the play area goes where the developer can't build a house or the land is poor or at a considerable distance from the houses of people who don't like the noise of children at play. 'The road isn't really dangerous', some say, 'It's just that the cars go too fast.'
- We are sometimes reluctant or unable to insist that play equipment is adequately maintained throughout its life and to recognize

when its usefulness is at an end. After all, it all costs money and the rates are high enough already.
- We may fail to recognize incorrect installation of equipment and so allow it to remain. Since in Britain we have had national standards on construction, installation and maintenance play equipment since 1959, it is difficult to explain this or any of the other points without recourse to words like 'incompetent' and 'indifferent'.
- Sometimes, but perhaps not as often as we defensively suggest, child misbehaviour or inappropriate use of apparatus contributes to accidents or exacerbates the outcomes. It is a pity that we have to discuss this issue in the context of the majority or serious injuries to children and especially fatalities occurring in domestic situations or on the roads.

King and Ball (1989) make the startling claim that on a conservative reappraisal of the Illingworth accident data, they can identify more than 99 out of 200 accidents that could have been prevented *'by a combination of design...layout...active supervision and teaching children better use of the equipment.'* Nevertheless, it appears certain that the introduction of British Standard (BS) 5696 in 1979 provided a considerable boost to safety through its clear and supportive references to unsafe surfaces, procedures and product design. Statistically it is made clear in all relevant studies that playgrounds are, comparatively speaking 'safe' places, but the public perception is one of danger and the need for constant vigilance on the part of responsible authorities. This is variously represented as either the outcome or the cause of what is described as 'an increasingly litigious society'.

Conclusion

There is reason to suppose that the fifty or so 'hits' achieved in any search engine when key words such as 'play' and 'injury' are fed into the computer demonstrates the presence of an active and enterprising legal profession, but it is questionable whether this represents a genuine problem. Search for 'car', 'pavement' or 'work', again with 'injury', and the same firms appear and offer the same 'no win – no fee' services. This is the tone and tenor of the times, and while deploring its worst 'ambulance chasing' attitudes, there is little evidence of a specific problem in relation to children's play. Evidence of actual litigation is relatively slim and it would clearly be wrong to deny children compensation if they do suffer loss or pain as a result of the neglect of others. Perhaps, for whatever reasons, some providers merely fear the cost of their neglect, rejecting the reforming and innovative powers of the litigation process.

In more recent times, the passing of The Disability Discrimination Act 1995 left a lead in time of nine years before implementation, and it appears perverse to complain of a litigious community spirit if some disadvantaged people complain that to date nothing has been done to meet the minimum terms of the Act.[2]

Whatever merit there is in the 'litigious society' claim generally, some evidence of abuse of the system is provided in the manifesto issued in March 2004 by the Commission for Architecture and the Built Environment (CABE) which estimates that £117 million is paid out annually in bogus or excessive compensation claims for injury and urges that '*we should challenge the assumptions of some local authorities who take a safety first approach.*'[25] But this 'evidence' is flatly contradicted by The Better Regulation Task Force (BRTF), a government agency set up to monitor and scrutinize matters of public concern. In a report dated May 27, 2004 it shows that there were 60 000 fewer personal injury claims registered in 2003/04 than in the previous reporting period: '*You don't get money for nothing. It doesn't happen in the way that television advertisements suggest: someone has to be negligent*' said Teresa Graham, who carried out the study. She also points out that more than half of the awards for damages made in county courts in 2002 were for sums less than £3000 (BRTF 2004). It is perhaps in appreciation of these simple truths that four firms specializing in this area of work ceased trading over the period 2003/04.

The way ahead is clear in Britain now:

- There is legislation in place that requires, rather than encourages, play providers to seek to address and cater for the needs of all clients and service users regardless of their abilities.
- There is encouragement and support for community action in play and leisure provision.
- Funds have been earmarked for specific areas of social and community-based play needs and is conditional upon local consultation outcomes.
- There is a shift away from the 'compensation culture' that for a brief time seemed so pervasive and damaging.

We should not create spaces which will be unusable in five years' time due to the risks they expose children to. Designing with the child in mind is about understanding the age ranges which apply. Supervision is particularly important, particularly after parents lose contact with the play patterns of their older children. Today children's aspirations are so high. They visit state-of-the-art supervised play parks such as Disneyland where equipment is of such an advanced nature that no municipal play facility can expect to meet those aspirations. Perhaps a more modest agenda needs to be accepted which encourages older children to hang out, feeling relaxed and uninhibited within a space which is 'cool'.

Notes

1 Clover, C. (2004). Compensation Culture turns our parks into dreary, fun-free deserts. *Daily Telegraph*, 25 March.
2 The Disability Discrimination Act 1995. London: The Stationery Office.
3 Hicks, J. (2003). *Guide to the Design and Management of Children's Playspace*. www.orston.org
4 Moyles, J. (1998). To play or not to play. That is the question. In *The Early Years* (Smidt, ed.), London: Routledge.
5 Bilton, H. (2002). *Outdoor Play in the Early Years*. 2nd edn. London: David Fulton.

6 Bishop, J. (2001). Creating Places for Living and Learning. In *Experiencing Reggio Emilia* (Abbot, L. and Nutbrown, C., eds), Buckingham: Open University Press.

7 John, A. and Wheway, R. (2003). *Can Play Will Play*. National Playing Fields Association (NPFA).

8 Dietz, W. (2002). The obesity epidemic in young children, *British Medical Journal*, **322**, No. 7282, pp. 313–314; cited in Department for Culture Media and Sport (2004) *Getting Serious About Play*.

9 Office of the Deputy Prime Minister (2002). *Living Places; Cleaner; Safer; Greener*. London: ODPM, p. 49.

10 Department for Culture, Media and Sport (2004). *Getting Serious About Play: a review of children's play*. London: Department for Culture, Media and Sport.

11 British Standards Institute (1998). British Standard BS EN 1176.

12 Illingworth, C. (1975). Two hundred injuries caused by playground equipment. *British Medical Journal*, **4**, pp. 332–334, 8 November 1975. Cited in King, K. and Ball, D. (1989). *A holistic approach to accident and injury prevention in children's playgrounds*. LSS.

13 King, K. and Ball, D. (1989). *A holistic approach to accident and injury prevention in children's playgrounds*. LSS.

14 Townswomen's Guild (1991). *Danger Children at Play*. A further report from this group, now known as 'Townswomen', is to be published in 2007.

15 Ibid p. 10.

16 Department of Education and Science (1992). *Playground Safety Guidelines*. London: The Stationery Office.

17 Consumers Association (1994). *Which*, June and July 1994. Some of these studies also drew upon an earlier *Which* Report (1976) which by extrapolation of a limited study claimed that there might be 150 000 playground accidents in UK each year.

18 British Standards Institute (1986): British Standard (BS) 5696 Playground Equipment intended for Permanent Installation Outdoors (amended 1986).

19 The National Playing Fields Association Guide *Legislation and Children's Play* (NPFA 1998) explains fully and clearly the legislative basis of the obligations and duties owed by councils to site users and visitors.

20 Hicks, J. (2004). *Accessible and Inclusive Playspace*. 2nd edn. www.orston.org

21 Ibid p. 13 and Wicksteed Leisure (2003). *A Guide to the Disability Discrimination Act 1995*.

22 Oxfordshire Playing Fields Association Play Safety Forum (2003). Managing risk in play provision. In *The Playing Field*, Winter 2002/2003. cpc@ncb.org.uk

23 Office of the Deputy Prime Minister (2003). *Developing Accessible Play Space*. London: ODPM, p. 39.

24 Pirani, M. and Reynolds, J. (1976) 'Gearing up for Safety' in *Personnel Management*, June 1976.

25 Commission for Architecture and the Built Environment (2004). *The Value of Public Space*.

Judith Hicks is a tutor in the School of Education at the University of Birmingham. With a background in nursery and infant teaching, she held primary headships in the north-east of England and Midlands before spending five years as the early years adviser for the City of Birmingham. Her current research interests are in early years education and the inspection of primary schools.

John Hicks served a traditional craft apprenticeship in mechanical and electrical engineering, won a scholarship to Ruskin College, Oxford and then went on to Trinity College. He spent thirty years in further and higher education and for the past fourteen years has operated a small consultancy and playground inspection business whilst publishing extensively on playgrounds and disability issues.

11

The sustainable landscape

Susan Herrington

Editor's introduction

In the spring of 2000, Susan Herrington received funding to study how the schoolyard could serve as a community resource. As part of her work as a landscape designer and as an academic deeply involved in developing theories of children's environmental awareness, she decided to run an international competition to encourage new ideas about the design of schoolyards as 'green knowledge' sites for children, teachers and the surrounding community. '13-acres' asked designers to step outside conventional thinking and design to more naturalized schoolyards that incorporate both play and learning. In addition she asked that designers employ green infrastructure and sustainable design techniques for the competition site in a new community, East Clayton, British Columbia.

Susan invited me to become one of the judges for the final entries the following year, and during a sometimes stormy period of adjudicating upon some 250 entries, I began to realize how important this all was. In our discussions, many new and exciting concepts were unfolding to me, particularly in relation to education and the sustainability agenda. Susan's concept of a landscape for learning provoked the publication you are now reading.

Here she expands on many of the important themes which have emerged in her understanding,

partly through the competition, but also through the design of numerous children's parks and school play spaces in which she has personally been involved. Professor Herrington shows how a garden can be shaped to enhance the empathy children have with their natural surroundings. Natural processes within the creation of organic landscapes, such as hydrological cycles of water, the growth of plants, and the erosion and deposition of soil, can be brought into play in many imaginative ways, through the radical design of the garden. Equally, this understanding can be encouraged in simpler ways such as a wild corner, which transforms simply if left unmown, or stepping stones across a flower bed – small interventions (or lack of intervention), which encourage thoughts and attitudes which are sustainable. Simply digging up a wild protected corner of a schoolyard and planting a mini herb garden can be a marvellous antidote to urban squalor which often seems to be engulfing us, simply because adults have no education in sustainability.

Introduction

Scientific evidence of pollution and subsequent ecological degradation throughout the world has spurred a number of global initiatives that have sought to define the term 'sustainability', a concept that is key to addressing these problems. The Rio

Declaration on Environment and Development established a set of twenty-seven principles on sustainable development. Many of these principles concern the health of natural systems in landscapes or the economic productivity of landscapes. Likewise, landscapes play a key role in geographer Anne Buttimer's insights into creating a sustainable livelihood in Europe. She notes that landscapes of transformation are important avenues to reflect and study sustainability.[1] The creation of landscapes, the outdoor physical environment of a culture, is an important dimension of the sustainability issue. Landscape design typically involves natural processes, such as the hydrological cycles of water, the growth of plants, and the erosion and deposition of soil. Thus, the creation of landscapes that work with these processes in a way that does not damage or degrade them is key to sustainability. Landscape architect Robert Thayer uses the following definition to describe sustainable landscapes when he states that they are 'those landscapes which tend toward ideal conditions by conserving resources (i.e. soil, energy, water, air quality, wildlife diversity, etc.) as well as those which actually achieve a long-term regenerative capacity.'[2]

But what do these global negotiations and definitions concerning sustainability have to do with a landscape that surrounds a school or childcare centre? Education theorist, C. A. Bowers notes that 'it is at the level of public school education that the most basic schemata of the culture are systematically presented and reinforced.'[3] The landscapes we create for children in their learning environments are powerful testaments to how we as a culture treat the natural world. If we asphalt the entire play yard, surround it with a chain link fence, and fill it with plastic toys and organized sports, where winning is everything and only the strongest and fastest do so, what does that tell children? Conversely, if the schoolyard is designed to treat living organisms with sensitivity and provides opportunities for a diversity of aptitudes, doesn't this send a better message to children who inhabit it on a daily basis? The idea of designing children's outdoor spaces as places where ecological processes are made integral to the learning and developmental process is not new. It can be found in one of the oldest educational systems, the kindergarten.

German educator Friedrich Fröbel understood the importance of the external environment to education when he developed the first kindergartens in the early nineteenth century. Fröbel was one of the first educators to value play and he promoted self-initiated activities, spontaneous exploration, and experimentation with the outdoor physical environment. Gardens and excursions outdoors played a central role in his kindergarten pedagogy.[4] Another important aspect of his work was that he encouraged children to 'read' and interpret their physical environment. Hence students would follow streams to their sources and reason where the water came from, or they would discover a pattern in time when a certain bird appeared in spring. While children living in contemporary western societies increasingly spend less time outdoors, this same use of the external environment is available to us today. This understanding is echoed in contemporary times. Bill Lucas of *Learning through Landscapes* notes that, 'children read school grounds as they read any external environment. They see a set of symbols from which they deduce what it is they are supposed to be doing and feeling.'[5] If we know that the schoolyard does reveal our cultural attitudes to children, then why not create schoolyard landscapes that are sustainable?

Yet, sustainability in the schoolyard cannot be a one-way form of communication. Children and their actions are also part of the dialogue, and the larger sustainability equation. This was illuminated to me a few years ago while I was working with a kindergarten play yard in the United States. The project involved making subtle changes to the play yard itself and observing how these changes influenced the location and ways that the children interacted with the yard. Not mowing a corner of the yard was one of these changes. The children's realization of the unmown corner was gradual, and they began to notice that the yard was not a static space but a changing place. They often talked about how high the grass might grow. How high might it be when they grew up? They also became aware of maintenance people who had previously been invisible actors in the yard. Why did they mow the remaining yard? After two months the grass was up to their shoulders and there were numerous bugs that regularly ventured into this untamed part of the yard. The children made patterns by flattening down the grass, played hide-and-seek, or simply looked for things within its wild tresses. When May arrived, the project at the kindergarten was over, and the maintenance people were scheduled to start mowing the entire yard again. We had not anticipated the human blockade that the children created when the mowers headed for the unmown grass. After all, this was their part of the yard. The incident was brought to the director's attention and the grass was 'let go' until the conclusion of the school year. This experience was revelatory in showing me that children live in the immediacy of their surroundings, and that relationships forged with these external environments are key to understanding sustainable landscapes for children.

Think of the yard as a landscape

The following sections describe five projects that I have been involved with that concern landscapes created for children at childcare centres and schools. Each project is an experiment and a discovery for myself and the people involved in their own landscapes. What I describe here reflects only one perspective of the process required to create landscapes for children, and this is the view of the designer. There are other voices that are vital to the design process that include the children, parents, collaborating designers, administrators, maintenance staff, unions, and school boards. I am greatly indebted to the individuals and groups that have made and are making these landscapes possible.

In North America, elementary school-aged children spend up to two hundred days per year at school, and approximately two hours of the school day are spent outdoors in the playground or play fields.[6] With the increased use of childcare centres (often located next to or inside the school) for supervision after school, the playgrounds at schools and child centres have become a substitute for the backyards of a previous generation. This situation places an unprecedented importance on the nature of the schoolyard and what it has to offer children.

Historically, most outdoor play environments at schools and childcare centres have been assigned

Figure 11.1
Typical play yard at a school in California.
(Photo: Susan Herrington.)

217

(a)

(b)

Figure 11.2
(a) Previous infant play yard at UC Davis.
(b) Infant Garden at UC Davis. (Photos: Susan Herrington.)

the role of providing a space for physical exercise. This tendency to associate playgrounds with physical development can be traced back to nineteenth-century social programmes in Europe and North America. The yards that surrounded nineteenth-century urban schools provided not only open space for calisthenics, outdoor gymnasium structures, and formalized games, but an important remedy for physical and mental degradation: sunlight and fresh air. The gymnastic

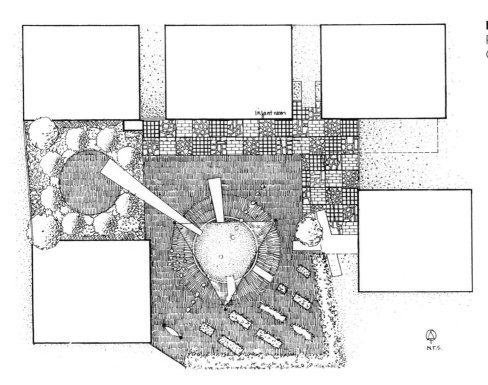

Figure 11.3
Plan view of Infant
Garden.

structures would prove to be pervasive in symbolizing play in the outdoor environment. The fabrication of these structures coincided with the development of production-line industries. The prefabricated slide could be manufactured as readily as the average domestic appliance. By the twentieth century, outdoor play spaces for children in North America meant spaces that contained prefabricated play equipment.

But what else might external play environments, the landscapes designed for children, offer besides play equipment and sports fields? The material qualities of landscape offer a rich source for imaginative events. Animals live in the landscape, it is rained upon, it floods, big winds blow through it, the sun rises and sets, and snow falls. Small changes can help illuminate the idea that the landscape is a dynamic living system. Another dynamic aspect of landscapes found at schools and childcare centres are the children themselves. In one school setting you might find children ranging in age from infanthood to pre-teens. How can outdoor play spaces at schools begin to address the needs of such a wide range of age groups? How can

landscapes that were originally designed for school-aged children begin to address the developmental milestones of the newest users of the schoolyard, namely infants?

These questions are at the heart of the Infant Garden project in Davis, California. The Infant Garden was created for ten infants enrolled in the Child and Family Study Center at the University of California. The project involved the retrofit of the centre's existing 4000 square feet infant play yard. Like the exterior play spaces found at many childcare centres for infants and toddlers, the existing yard was viewed as an outdoor floor space where play structures and play equipment were brought outdoors from the inside. The primary goal of the Infant Garden was to create an outdoor play landscape that would support the sensorimotor and socio-emotional development of *infants* as it occurred in spontaneous exploration.[7]

The University Child and Family Study Center is a laboratory where university students and teachers study the enrolled children and analyse their developmental progress. The various age groups (infant, toddler, preschool) were allocated spaces in a series of one-storey modular buildings in a campus-like setting. The university students were encouraged to manipulate the physical arrangements of the interior spaces to see how these changes influenced specific developmental abilities of the children. Furniture was moved, lights changed, or colours were added to surfaces by the university students; thus, the students and staff were very accustomed to changing their space. The design team involved myself, the director, assistant director, and other child development specialists and staff members. After my first meeting with the team, I quickly realized that infants were a unique subculture among adults and older children. When we began to consider modifying the infant's outdoor environment as an extension to the experimental setting found inside, the idea of designing the yard as a space to observe specific developmental milestones emerged. Like the requirements that might serve to organize and shape the space of an adult landscape (such as sitting and eating lunch, waiting for a bus) the developmental markers of the infants guided the creation of spaces and surfaces in the Infant Garden.

This approach opened a wide range of design considerations that went beyond the usual design requirements for playgrounds which typically involve the placement of a chain link fence, equipment and rubber matting. We thought of the yard as a garden where simple landscape elements such as earth, plants, stones, and sand would provide a rich source of loose parts and an ever-changing space for experimentation by the students and children. The primary features of the Infant Garden included a central earthen ring that contained a sand area at its centre and was shaded by an adjustable parachute canopy; a trail of stepping stones that enticed infants out into the yard; a pine circle that was planted with a variety of plantings where the infants could explore on their own; and a maze area comprised of five different plant species, all edible.

Our project became part of a comparative research project by Sarah Jane Neville, Dr Carol Rodning, Kay Jeanne Gaedeke, and Dr Larry Harper. They studied the play yard prior to construction and four weeks after construction

Figure 11.4
Plant parts as play props at the Infant Garden.
(Photo: Susan Herrington.)

of the Infant Garden to observe if the infants' use of the same site with two different physical environments was quantitatively different. The researchers found statistically significant differences between the use of the previous play yard and the garden. In the Infant Garden, the extent of spatial exploration increased, meaning that the children explored more of the yard, an action connected to cognitive and physical growth. The types of motor manipulations were more complex and varied, indicating that the infants were challenged to do more physical actions. The amount of associative play with student care givers became more intense, meaning that their social and emotional skills were engaged in the use of the garden. Finally, the number of times infants played with natural loose parts, namely leaves, twigs and flower heads, increased, augmenting the opportunity for fine

Figure 11.5
Pine circle at the Infant Garden. (Photo: Susan Herrington.)

motor development (the use of the fingers, hands and mouth).

The Infant Garden prompted me to ask how we might design children's outdoor play environments that address the breadth of developmental milestones, i.e. social, emotional, physical, and cognitive. Additionally, a major component of the Infant Garden was the introduction of plant material to the play space. This also raised questions about the potential of plant material and other landscape elements. Plant material and other standard landscape items are relatively cheap when compared to the price of play structures and rubber matting. Could the use of plant material alone begin to add to the variety of developmental opportunities a play yard provides?

Think big, act small

It is precisely these questions that we sought to answer in the Yard to Garden intervention project at the Child Development Laboratory at Iowa State University. This project involved child development specialists from the laboratory who collaborated with me to design landscape situations that would fulfil specific developmental milestones of the children (two to six years old) attending the

laboratory school. A significant difference between Yard to Garden and the Infant Garden, was the 'intervention' nature of the installation. Unlike the complete redesign of the play space at the Infant Garden, the Yard to Garden research project involved the placement of temporary and permanent landscape elements in the existing play yards of the laboratory. This entailed 23 permanent plant installations, stonework, boulders, and temporary play props such as wind chimes and giant ice blocks. This method of installation was significantly less expensive than the total redesign of the Infant Garden. Hence, we attempted to mimic what a daycare facility or school might actually be able to afford and execute. It also allowed us to assess the effects that the interventions had on the use of the existing play structures.

We hypothesized that the introduction of natural material into the existing yards would offer additional types of developmental opportunities to the children. The existing yards of the school contained several play structures, grass, trees, and an enclosing chain link fence. Observation of the children using the yards demonstrated to us that the play equipment did foster physical

Figure 11.6a
Previous preschool yard at Iowa State.

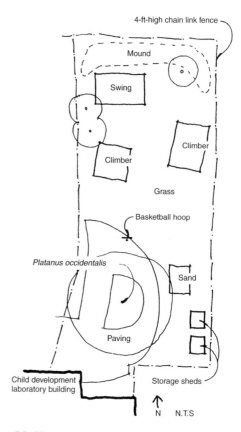

Figure 11.6b
Previous kindergarten yard at Iowa State.

4 Plantings in the asphalt area.
5 Unmown grass area.
6 Stepping stones.
7 Boulders.
8 Two vegetative rooms. Two 1.5 m × 1.5 m plant enclosures of *Euonymus alata* and *Thuja occidentalis* were installed in an open grassy area of the kindergarten yard.

Temporary interventions:

1 Ice blocks.
2 Wind chimes.
3 Overhead canopy.
4 Water troughs.
5 Movement of playhouse.
6 Sand buckets.

development. Physical competence was gained as the equipment was used and abused by children. The play structures were gravitational forces in the yard for the children as they were sites where children gathered to socialize. Consequently, the physical prowess of a child established his or her order in the social hierarchy of the class. The child who could climb the highest and the fastest was the leader. Some children, many of them kindergarten girls, who were not drawn to the play equipment, did not venture into the yard at all, but stood against the school wall to socialize.

The hypothesis of this research contended that interventions of temporary and permanent landscape elements would offer different and more varied types of developmental opportunities than those provided through the existing yards. We compared children playing in the existing yards that contained primarily equipment and a chain link fence with the same children playing in the same yard with the interventions. The interventions are as follows:

Permanent interventions:

1 Sensorimotor planting circle.
2 Plantings at the arch climber.
3 Plantings at the bridge of the main play structure.

The results suggested that when simple landscape elements were introduced into these yards,

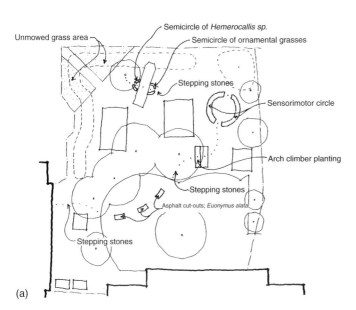

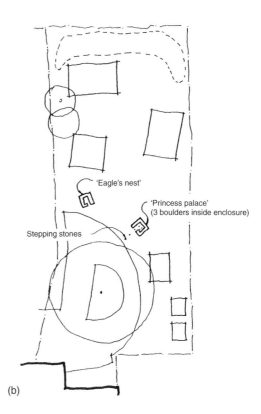

Figure 11.7a, b
Interventions at the Iowa State play yard.

different types of development were encouraged.[8] For example, we found that the vegetative rooms referred to in Figure 11.7b above inspired a wide range of fantasy play that was not witnessed prior to their installation. The use of these vegetative rooms changed the existing social hierarchy of the class because some children were more attracted to the rooms, and unlike the play structures these spaces became sites for fantasy play and socialization. Children tended to use these rooms more frequently and for longer durations than the equipment. The social hierarchy in the vegetative rooms was based on a child's command of language and the imagination that he or she brought to that space. The child who could be the most creative and inventive was the leader. Hence, the social hierarchy of the play yard was now linked to the cognitive and emotional prowess of the children. The children who were dominant in the play structure social setting were not always the dominant children in the vegetative rooms. These

soft 'living' rooms and many of the other plants also accentuated the seasonal changes taking place in the outdoor play space, and encouraged children to observe their environment more closely. For example, the leaves of the *Euonymus alata* shrub turn brilliant red in autumn and the children noticed this as well as their unusual winged branches.

Other examples are the stepping stone pathway and boulders. As part of the intervention project, we imbedded approximately twenty stepping stones, evenly spaced apart, into the play yard. The stepping stones travelled in a meandering path from the school's exit door to the yard, to the major play equipment structures, and through a part of the yard that was not usually used by the children. We found that children followed these stepping stones, and they began to play in previously under-used parts of the yard. We don't typically think of children following paths; however, paths are landscape elements that help structure our

223

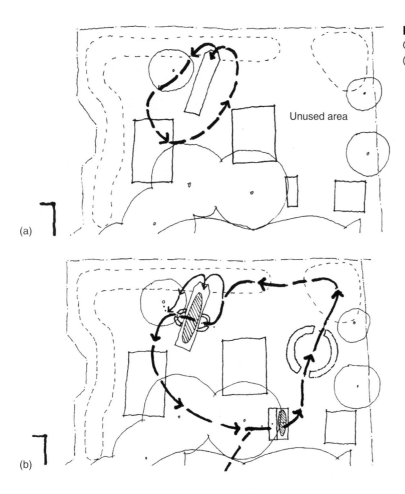

Unused area

Figure 11.8
Circulation before (a) and after (b) interventions.

understanding of the environment. When travelled upon, they are both a physical experience and a cognitive measurement of the space. We also placed approximately four boulders throughout the yard thinking that they would be climbed on or serve as markers in outdoor games of tag. However, much to our surprise, the children began moving the boulders. This task often took two or three children, and this activity provoked planning, cooperation and coordination. Another dimension of boulder moving was that the children became keenly aware of the other children using the yard. During our study, two different groups (morning and afternoon) used the yard. Typically, toys and other items used by the previous group were put away at the end of their playtime in the yard; however, the staff didn't move the heavy boulders. As a result, the morning group would move a boulder to a certain place in the yard, and then the

afternoon group would move it somewhere else. The boulders became memory markers between the children in the different groups.

This project provided tremendous insight into how designers and people who work with children can fine-tune the design of existing outdoor play spaces to match the specific developmental goals of their programmes. It also illustrated how the detailed nuances of the outdoor play environment matter in the daily life of children. Unlike the Yard to Garden project which intervened on an existing play yard or the Infant Garden project that involved the total redesign of an existing play yard, there may also be opportunities where the school or childcare centre and its accompanying outdoor play space is an entirely new construction. This was the case at Bright Horizons childcare centre planned for eighty-six children ranging in age from infanthood to pre-teen, in Ames, Iowa.

Figure 11.9
Unmown grass at the Iowa State play yard. (Photo: Susan Herrington.)

Figure 11.10
Eagle's Nest at the Iowa State play yard. (Photo: Susan Herrington.)

Multi-tasking

The Bright Horizons childcare centre was developed as a prototype for four centres planned for property owned by Iowa State University. The centre included twelve infants, eighteen toddlers, twenty-four pre-schoolers and thirty school-aged children. The design of the exterior play spaces involved myself, architects and landscape architects of record, university students, child development specialists, and staff from the Iowa State

Department of Facilities Planning, and Planning and Design.

The project site was the southern slope of a grassy hillside, typical of the undulating landforms of a till plain landscape. The site also contained a substantial stand of mature trees, and an active drainage swale that cut diagonally across the slope. The initial design for the outdoor play space included an 8000 square feet play area off one exit door of the childcare building. This proposed play

225

space contained a small open grass area, a large multi-level play structure, rubber matting, and a four-foot-high chain link fence that enclosed the space. Our first impressions of this proposal noted that this design failed to take advantage of the existing site conditions; the trees, the slope, the swale, or the southeast exposure that would serve as an ideal setting for a garden.

Iowa State University landscape architecture students created models that re-envisioned the outdoor play area using the existing conditions of the site. Students were encouraged to refrain from relying on play structures for the sole content of play. When we reported back with our models to the designers of record and the university, we were informed that the student designs were too costly, and that they must adhere to the budget allocated to the play yard. This budget was itemized as 'equipment' and constituted less than 3 per cent of the overall budget. After further negotiation, we realized that we needed to consider the budget of the play yard as part of the construction for the entire building process, and not simply as a piece of equipment. Fortunately, the University Design and Planning staff worked with Child Care Resources to redistribute the yard as part of the drainage and grading plan, which was 24 per cent of the overall budget; thus folding the landscape design into the construction tasks.

Hence, the yard emerged as part of the construction process. Numerous earthen mounds that helped to separate children's diverse activities were made from the spoil piles created by the building excavation. The existing swale was preserved as part of the drainage system for the building run-off, and stones and trees that were removed during demolition were placed in the play yard for children to climb upon. 'Landscaping plants' that were originally planned in the front of the building for decorative purposes were placed within the children's play areas at the rear of the building, and the equipment budget was used for small bridges that crossed the drainage swale and for moveable objects like sleds, bikes, wagons, and gardening tools.

The final design for the Bright Horizons play yard was organized into three exterior play spaces (the infant/toddler, the preschool and kindergarten, and

Figure 11.11
Veterinary school childcare yard swale. (Photo: Susan Herrington.)

the school age space) which more than doubled the size of the previous proposal for the yard. Each age-specific yard was directly related to the use of the interior space of the building, so that the infant/toddler room extended out to the infant/toddler yard, the preschool and kindergarten room extended out to the preschool yard, and the school age room extended out to the school age yard. Fieldstones from a local farm were placed throughout the site. Each yard contained these stones, some forming council rings while others were spread out to climb upon and view out from.

The exterior play spaces were separated by a forty-eight-inch-high fence, but gates were installed that allowed movement through each yard, and the drainage swale that took run-off from the building served as a unifying element that passed through all three play spaces. In the warm weather months this

Figure 11.12
Veterinary school
childcare yard sub-space.
(Photo: Susan Herrington.)

Figure 11.13
Veterinary school
childcare yard slide
mound. (Photo: Susan
Herrington.)

swale is a place to dig and watch for bugs, in the rainy season it carries running water. During the winter months it is a snow-packed conduit for navigating through the play yard. The channel also reveals to the children that the play yard is not a static picture of play outdoors, but an ephemeral event that is linked to the weather, natural processes, and human manipulation. Additionally, because the perimeter fence meandered into the established wooded area, this shady naturalistic area where bugs could be caught and children could play became part of the yard.

While much of the work I've described deals with the small-scale nuances of a singular site, I wanted to know how the design of children's outdoor play spaces might relate to larger environmental issues relative to planned communities. Could these children's spaces that were becoming increasingly 'green' in my own work be valued not only by children, but by the entire community as an ecological resource? The following two projects, the Los Altos Schools and the 13-acres international design competition, have begun to answer these questions.

Zoom out

The Los Altos School District, located south of San Francisco in Northwest Santa Clara County, has one of the highest ranked Academic Performance Index (API) records and the highest Scholastic Aptitude Test (SAT) scores in the state of California. With a population of 3950 students and an anticipated population that will exceed 4500 students by 2008, Los Altos is in the process of upgrading its school facilities as one of its five major long-term goals. Gelfand RNP Architects of San Francisco began work in 1999 to update the District's eight campuses. These are six elementary (kindergarten to sixth grade) schools which include Almond, Bullis-Purissima, Loyola, Oak, Santa Rita, and Springer; and two intermediate (seventh and eighth grade) schools, Blach and Egan. Two schools per year were modernized over three years. The original campuses were all prototypical California 'finger plan' schools with rows of one-storey stucco classroom barracks connected by exterior covered walkways and separated by undifferentiated paved spaces. Little regard was given to the inherent qualities of the dry hill and valley landscape and coastal climate of Los Altos. In the schoolyards, bright green grass, which indicates irrigation, contrasts with the existing landscape.

In developing the Master Plan for the Los Altos schools, functional aspects concerning access and parking were addressed, but there was also an emphasis on realizing that each school exists in a particular context. The Master Plan was prepared with the goal of not only updating all existing buildings, but redesigning the site infrastructure, outdoor play areas and sports fields so that these external environments were more diverse for developing children and more ecologically

Figure 11.14
Veterinary school childcare yard tree grove. (Photo: Susan Herrington.)

sensitive to the surrounding environment. Thus, the Master Plan not only sought to address the identified site 'problems' (for example drainage), but also used the mending of these problems as an opportunity to create a landscape that would lend itself to experiential learning and imaginative play.

The original outdoor spaces of the schools typically consisted of paved asphalt areas, grass playing fields, and manufactured play structures in bark chip, soft fall zones. Water run-off on the site was handled through piping underground. One of the first tasks was to daylight the site water by exposing it to the surface in planted swales. This was done in response to new water quality requirements for the filtration of roof and paving run-off through planted areas before entering the storm water system. However, it was also designed to enhance students' awareness of natural phenomena as a means of enriching the experiential and learning qualities of the site.

For example, the plan for Bullis School (the initial school under study) has third to seventh grade classrooms terraced up a steep hill where the landscape is not irrigated, and indigenous plants have been installed. To access these classrooms, students must cross a seasonal swale that will be developed to support the life and earth science areas of the curriculum, as well as the cultural study of California and its agricultural and horticultural history. By daylighting the previously piped site run-off and planting the swale banks, this schoolyard landscape becomes a didactic setting for the study of ecological relationships between the intermittent water flow, and the plants and other organisms that flourish or die as an outcome of the presence of water. Likewise, the setting of the classrooms in an unirrigated environment highlights seasonal changes typically masked by manicured lawns that are kept green year around, and will hopefully prompt teachers to adopt it as a base for exploration. In developing the Bullis school site, we were responding to a site with drainage problems and a fifty-feet elevation drop from the top of the site to the street. The possibilities that grew out of this school site caused us to re-examine the other Los Altos sites, all relatively flat, to see how

standard school plans could provide some of the qualities suggested by the Bullis site.

Interconnected with the ecological goals of the Los Altos Master Plan are the social, cognitive, and emotional needs of the children, and the educational potential of the outdoor spaces. Each of the eight school campuses was designed to be quite different in order to reflect their different communities in Los Altos; however, in working with parent and facilities committees, basic needs regarding outdoor social spaces became evident at all schools. All school campuses were zoned for easy community use of libraries, sport, and multi-purpose facilities. Each fully-developed campus has an exterior space that is identified by an academic spatial typology, for example a quad, which is for the exclusive use of and cared for by the children in the upper grades. It is anticipated that children can look forward to achieving ownership of this space during their last years at the school. A larger, unirrigated space is also planned for each campus, usually on the margin of large open areas, where it can be easily supervised. This area is a less architecturally defined space where the nature of the play area can accommodate the changing social needs of the students, and the objectives of teachers who wish to use the space as a learning site for environmental curricula. During the elementary years tremendous growth and development occurs for the students. The kindergarten area is close to the front of each school, facilitating parent interaction, and providing safe and secure play areas that are distinct from the play areas of older children. A Parent Teacher Association servery adjoins seating so that parents can more easily socialize while waiting to pick their kids up, or after dropping them off.

Another important dimension of the Master Plan is the physical and visual relationship between the school buildings and their adjacent outdoor spaces. Each classroom has its own outdoor project area accessible and visually evident from inside the classroom. These project areas are loosely designed with the intention that they will be shaped in large part by the students and their teacher. Newly added north windows and skylights will increase the light quality in the classrooms and allow for the changes in the outdoor environment to inform indoor schooling. On the south side classroom walls, which originally contained only clerestory windows, project display windows were installed along with message centres at classroom doors, increasing awareness of the children's activities.

The challenge in developing these schools was to accommodate the traditional uses of outdoor space: parking, playing fields, play structures, and the buildings, while providing places for the less quantifiable needs of growing children. Children construct many of their ideas of the world at school, and traditional schoolyards privilege hierarchical and conformist representations – lines, rules, groups, teams, and competition. Children whose skills are imaginative and dramatic need to be supported and challenged and the landscape is an ideal setting for this development. Children who excel at finding bugs under rocks need rocks to turn over, or a forest to enchant. In developing the various sites, we have been making spaces in between classrooms, on the margins of fields, and within new intermediate spaces to broaden the diversity of activities and kids that will be welcomed by the schools. Another project that looks at schoolyards as expansive learning sites where a number of developmental needs are met is the 13-acres international design competition.

Healthy competition

In the spring of 2000, I received funding from the Hampton Foundation, the University of British Columbia's James Taylor Chair, and the Real Estate Foundation of British Columbia to study how the schoolyard could serve as a community resource. This research resulted in orchestrating the 13-acres international design competition. This competition involved the design of schoolyards as 'green knowledge' sites for children, teachers, and the surrounding community. One of the primary goals of the competition was to inspire people who design children's environments to explore the schoolyard as an untapped site for ecological rejuvenation and

environmental education. This competition asked designers to step outside conventional thinking and combine two paradigm shifts emerging in the development of landscapes in North America. The first shift is from the design and use of schoolyards for primarily organized sports and play equipment to more naturalized schoolyards that incorporate both play and learning as a community resource.[9] The second shift is from the design and planning of communities that are detrimental to the ecological environment, to communities that are planned to employ green infrastructure and sustainable design techniques.[10]

In the past decade there has been a rising concern among parents, educators, and designers to reinterpret the schoolyard to address community needs. Currently, schoolyards are typified by expanses of pavement, prefabricated play structures, and chain link fence. Schoolyards of the twentieth century rarely exhibit any sensitivity to the site's ecological conditions, the school's cultural setting, or the children and neighbours who use it on a daily basis. A key dimension of the competition was to grapple with this very notion of the schoolyard as a site for cultural communication. While a competition may not be a familiar tool to all people, it is a well-known method for opening up new possibilities in physical design.[11] The design competition is a proven way to inspire changes in practice and perception, both by professional designers, and by the general public. For example, the design for the Vietnam War Veteran's memorial often comes to mind when the word 'competition' is used. This project reinvented the way memorials were designed and treated in North America.

The competition sites were two proposed schoolyard and park sites (each approximately 13 acres) planned for the District of East Clayton in Surrey, British Columbia, Canada. Surrey is British Columbia's second largest and fastest growing school district. The East Clayton sites were selected because the plans for this new district have been nationally recognized as a demonstration site for sustainable practices.[12] Since the early 1990s, the city of Surrey, and the University of British Columbia's James Taylor Chair of Livable Communities have collaborated to envision a sustainability plan for the development in East Clayton, Surrey. In 1998, the Headwaters Project was conceived as a partnership that would demonstrate sustainable urban development in lower mainland communities in British Columbia. The Headwaters Partnership is an advisory committee supported by the Real Estate Foundation of British Columbia, Environment Canada, the Ministry of Municipal Affairs, Affordability and Choice Today (ACT), Greater Vancouver Regional District, and the Federal Department of Fisheries and Oceans. Together, the key players involved in the Headwaters Project coordinated the efforts of Surrey planners, engineers, developers, environmental consultants, and a community advisory committee to formulate a Neighbourhood Concept Plan for the East Clayton community of Surrey. The Neighbourhood Concept Plan was based on seven principles of sustainability:

1   Increase density and conserve energy by designing compact walkable neighbourhoods. This will encourage pedestrian activities where basic services (e.g., schools, parks, transit, shop, etc.) are within a five- to six-minute walk of their homes.
2   Provide different dwelling types (a mix of housing types, including a broad range of densities from single-family homes to apartment buildings) in the same neighborhood and even on the same street.
3   Communities are designed for people; therefore, all dwellings should present a friendly face to the street in order to promote social interaction.
4   Ensure that car storage and services are handled at the rear of dwellings.
5   Provide an interconnected street network in a grid or modified grid pattern, to ensure a variety of itineraries and to disperse traffic congestion and provide public transit to connect East Clayton with the surrounding region.
6   Provide narrow streets shaded by rows of trees in order to save costs and to provide a greener, friendlier environment.
7   Preserve the natural environment and promote natural drainage systems (in which storm water

is held on the surface and permitted to seep naturally into the ground).

(East Clayton NCP, 1999.)

The Neighborhood Concept Plan also identified the two schoolyard park sites as locations for storm water filtration, habitat preservation, and community communication in East Clayton. Members of the Headwaters Project were keenly aware of the important roles that these two sites played in reflecting the sustainability principles of the concept plan. The idea of a competition emerged as a way of extending and strengthening the plan's mission by providing an array of design solutions that envision the schoolyards. Representatives from the Headwaters Project, the city of Surrey Engineering Department, School Facility, and Parks and Recreation Department, the University of British Columbia, and the Evergreen Foundation played an integral role in the creation of the competition's design programme. Surrey representatives insured that the nature of the competition was applicable to the city's regulatory policies as well as its visions for sustainable, yet economically viable development. Headwater representatives ensured conformance to the principles set out in the Neighborhood Concept Plan as a demonstration site for sustainability in the lower mainland of British Columbia. Landscape architecture and education students from the University of British Columbia, and Dr Rita Irwin with UBC Curriculum Studies, also participated in the development of the competition design programme.

After two half-day workshops and many electronic communications, we determined the design programme in August 2000. The 13-acres design programme described the competition criteria and specified that competitors should explore and envision designs that use ecological systems as educational and community resources. Design entries were requested that employed multiple uses of the schoolyard, and layered natural systems, play spaces, and community outreach programmes in one dynamic site. It was not an intention of the design programme team that the winning scheme should be the exact solution for

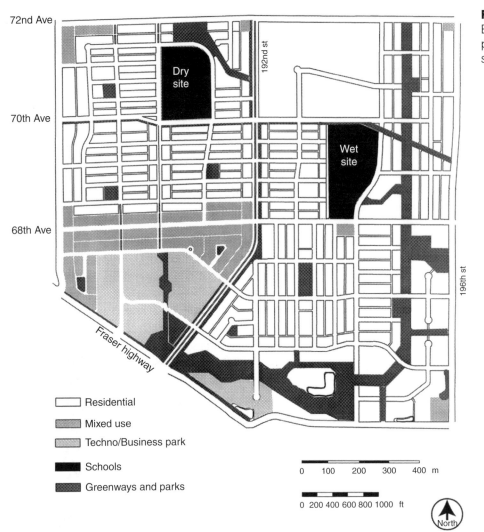

Figure 11.15
East Clayton land use plan with competition sites.

the site. Rather, the built solution would evolve as the East Clayton Community developed and moved into the neighbourhood. The competition was a means of getting people to think early on in the building process about what the schoolyard parks sites could be, other than the standard yards witnessed in most communities in North America.

The two combined park and school parcels were called 'dry site' and 'wet site'. School and community gardens were the dominant site programmes for the dry site, and water retention was the primary programme for the wet site. The school architecture was based on a modular system designed by Erno Goldfinger in England during the 1930s, and was given to all registrants for

modification. In the design programme, entrants were encouraged to treat the material of landscape, earth, water, walks, wind, etc. as sources for play and learning. Four frameworks were defined as criteria for submission:

1   The cultural endeavour – how can we produce schoolyard/parks that dislodge conventional thinking about these spaces?

2   The public programme – how can we organize on one site the multiple uses that are required of schoolyard/parks today?

3   The landscape of childhood – how can we design schoolyards as landscapes, landscapes that support learning and imaginative play?

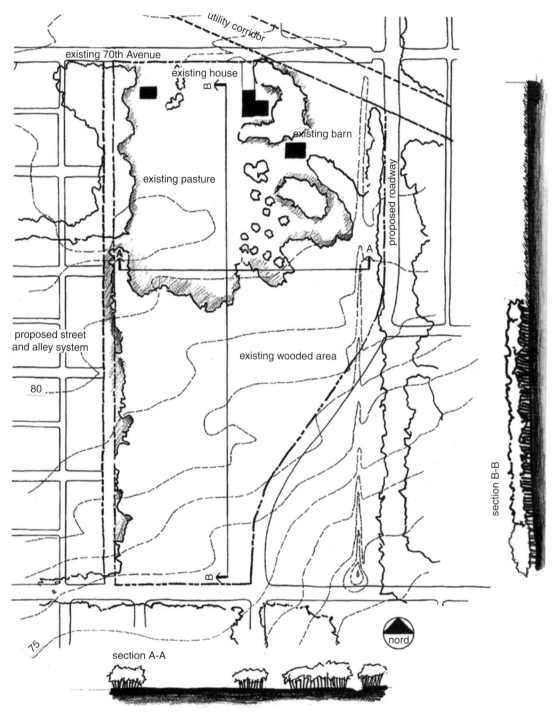

utility corridor

existing 70th Avenue

existing house

B

existing barn

existing pasture

proposed roadway

A

A

proposed street
and alley system

existing wooded area

80

section B-B

B

nord

75

section A-A

Figure 11.16a
East Clayton wet site plan.

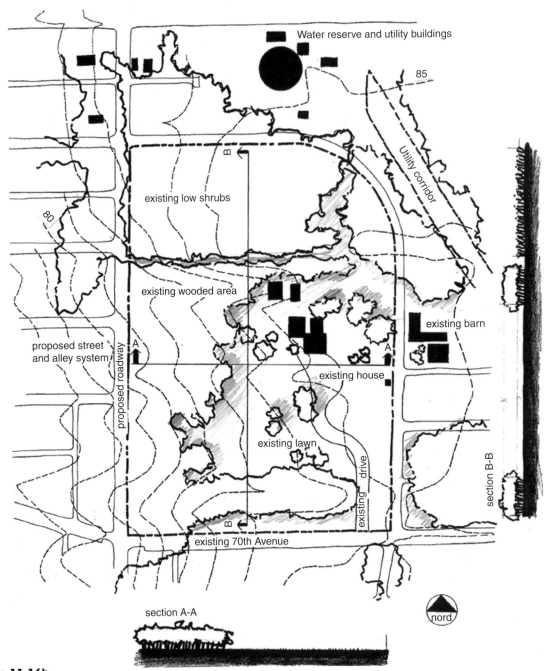

Water reserve and utility buildings

85

Utility corridor

existing low shrubs

80

existing wooded area

existing barn

proposed street
and alley system

proposed roadway

existing house

existing lawn

existing drive

section B-B

existing 70th Avenue

section A-A

nord

Figure 11.16b
East Clayton dry site plan.

4   The ecological plan – how can we design
    natural systems as a tool for learning in the
    schoolyard/park?[13]

In May 2001 we received 258 entries from
32 countries ranging from Europe, North America,

the Middle East, Asia, New Zealand, and
Australia. A jury of six internationally-recognized
professionals and three Surrey Representatives
evaluated these entries. The jury included Irene
Cinq-Mars (Montreal), Gina Crandell (Boston),
Mark Dudek (London), Mark Francis (Norway),

Figure 11.17
The 13-acres competition jury process. (Photo: Susan Herrington.)

Lorna Fraser (Surrey Parent Organization), Peter Latz (Munich), Francisco Molina (Surrey Senior Planner and Urban Designer), Cornelia Hahn Oberlander (Vancouver) and Umer Olcay (Surrey School Board Facilities Manager).

The jury deliberated for three days. First prize was awarded to Nicholas Gilsoul of Brussels, Belgium; second prize was awarded to Claudia Illanes Barrera with Andrew Harris Diez and Loles Herrero Canela of Barcelona, Spain; and third prize was awarded to Kamni Gill of Massachusetts, United States. The jury also gave nine honourable mentions. First honourable mention was awarded to Peter O'Shea with Sara Wilson of Charlottesville, Virginia, United States; second was awarded to Joel Agacki and Michael Striegel of Milwaukee, Wisconsin, United States; and third honourable mention went to Barbara Le Strat of Versailles, France. Honorable mentions were also given to Franck Jarosz of Strasbourg, France; Dave Hutch and Jean Kindratsky of Vancouver, Canada; Robert Dorgan of Las Vegas, Nevada, United States; Philippe Luc Barman and Gabriela Barman at Nonlinear Architecture in New York City, United States; Robert Kastelic and Carina Rose at Ultrapolis of Toronto, Canada; and Herve Meyer and Angela Morague of Rotterdam, the Netherlands. As noted by the judges, the competition generated many provocative ideas from a broad spectrum of geographies. An important theme that emerged from the review of the proposed design solutions was the significance of linking community and educational programmes with natural processes occurring on the schoolyard site.

The ability to feel empathy towards other living creatures is one of the most fundamental steps towards attaining sustainable landscapes. If the daily life of the schoolyard is filled with natural objects (plants, animals, water, etc.) it is anticipated that an enriched awareness will be developed in children towards these living elements and the empathy they engender. Dynamic natural environments and the types of experiential learning opportunities that they furnish, such as fostering an understanding of life cycles, may also encourage an appreciation toward these changing environments.[14] Many positive experiences are to be gained by incorporating natural processes into the outdoor school environment.[15] These include life-long skills such as a greater empathy towards living things, and more immediate and tangible benefits such as improved academic performance in some subject areas.[16]

Studies that compare exposure to natural settings in the educational environment and improved academic performance are rare in the research of children's environments. However, a study by Hoody and Lieberman in the United States compared the academic performance of children attending schools that used their schoolyard primarily for physical fitness with children in schools that used their external environments as places for 'general and disciplinary knowledge, thinking and problem-solving skills; and basic life skills, such as cooperation and interpersonal communications'.[17] The researchers observed and interviewed children attending 40 different schools and found that 92 per cent of the children who attended schools that considered the schoolyard an integrated context for learning performed better in the areas of reading, writing, math, science and social studies than the children enrolled in conventional schools.

The following identifies competition entries that linked community and educational programmes with natural processes occurring on the schoolyard site. While they all addressed the four frameworks identified by the design programme, each had particular strengths. Hence, the design proposals are placed in three categories: water conveyance and nature study, forest and agricultural management; and design as play.

Water conveyance for gardening and nature study

Experiencing the schoolyard site as a dynamic setting was a key dimension of the winning solutions in the 13-acres competition. The lower mainland of British Columbia receives on average 200 mm of rainfall per year. This abundant waterfall is typically captured at the surface and then piped underground where it is discharged at locations remote from where it once fell. In particular, the jury was interested in finding solutions that would use this rainfall as a source of learning and community activity. In Nicholas Gilsouls's *Les Jardins D'East Clayton,* Gilsoul modifies the rooftops of the school buildings so that they collect and transport water to the community gardens, intended for local residential and school use. The community gardens, which he calls 'breathing gardens', serve several

functions. Firstly, they help filtrate the water running off the roof, secondly they provide irrigation to the gardens and thirdly, because the gardens are so intimately connected with the architecture of the school it is anticipated that this new system can provide numerous opportunities for learning about water, food, and land life cycles. In Gilsoul's proposal the north light illuminates the interior of the classroom and he has arranged the children's desks and chairs to augment views out to the garden.

This careful manipulation of the windows links the interior learning space with the exterior garden area and aids in showing the children the importance of the community gardening programme. Another aspect of Gilsoul's proposal is the rooftops that are planted with species that rely on wind for dispersal and propagation. Downwind from the school the community gardens are subject to these meadow seeds that will move with the patterns of the wind. Gilsoul also anticipates the fact that community gardens will not always be kept as a designer envisions. There will be times when people are unable to garden and the meadow seeds will grow from these plots. When the community plots are being used they become gardens; when they are left unattended, the meadow species will take over.

Gilsoul also left a large portion of the site untouched and this also contributed to the sustainability dimension of his proposal. A wooded area on the western edge of the site was left 'as is' so that children could play and create in the forest. During the jury deliberations, Cornelia Hahn Oberlander remarked that Gilsoul's proposal anticipated the future impact of the fully-built East Clayton community, noting that 'this scheme allows breathing room, because the land surrounding the school site will be built up.'

The second prize entry submitted by Claudia Illanes Barrera with Andrew Harris Diez, and Loles Herrero Canela also used water, but on the wet site and with an emphasis on attracting wildlife. Their 'wet site' proposal takes the water that enters the north end of the site and brings it through a series of filtration ponds and streams that eventually lead to a larger irregularly shaped

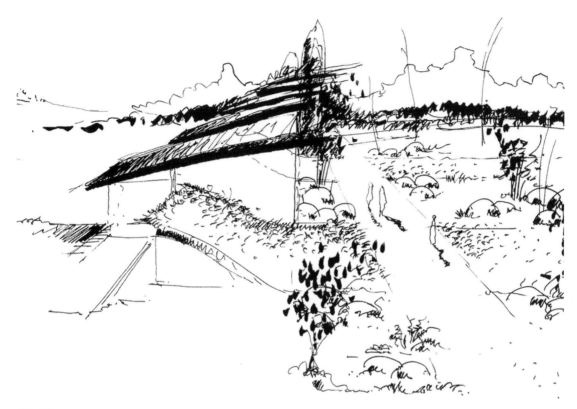

Figure 11.18
First prize sketch of planted school roof.

retention wetland. The designers used the sloping ground of the site to separate the site into three different functional areas. The north end contains buildings and sports fields, the mid-section of the site contains specific spaces for community congregation, such as garden, enclosed field, amphitheatre, and open air classroom, and the south end of the site contains long boardwalks that stretch out over the wetland, allowing neighbours and children to observe the wildlife that it will attract. The jury was impressed with the organization of the site as it relates to programmes for diverse interactions, and to the detailed attention given to the grading and planting of the wetland to optimize use by animals and children.

Kamni Gill's third placed entry entitled 'Ditches' addressed the dry site and used irrigation and drainage ditches to structure play and the movement of water. The ditches both collect and filter water, and provide places for plants and animals, as well as spaces for exploration by children during the dry months. Gill proposes three main drainage areas in her submission. A long drainage channel, with a width that ranges from 4 to 9 metres and a depth that varies from 0.5 to 2 metres, runs north to south the entire length of the site. During the rainy months, this channel receives ample run-off from the athletic fields. During the drier months, Gill proposes a number of interventions using large wood members, canopy fabric, and wooden blocks. These big loose parts allow children to change and build within the dry channel, allowing for numerous creative endeavours. Gill locates an amphitheatre at the centre of this channel on the upper slopes. This space provides a theatre for free play and formal plays.

A second ditch system is a shallow swale that circumnavigates the edges of the site and picks up storm water from adjacent streets and sidewalks in East Clayton. This open swale is key

Figure 11.19
Second prize plan view by Claudia Illanes Barrera
with Andrew Harris Diez, and Loles Herrero Canela.
(Photo: Kenneth Studtmann and Lisa McNiven.)

to the sustainability mission of the East Clayton Neighborhood Concept Plan that calls for natural drainage systems. Swales reduce the velocity of water flow and increase the filtration and absorption of storm water into the soil. The third ditch system takes run-off from the school and community buildings, and directs this water to the gardens. Here, garden plots and drainage channels are places where Gill proposes plant installations such as arbours and climber structures. The implementation of these structures during the drier months adds another important function to the ditch because children can play underneath these elements.

Honourable mentions Robert Kastelic and Carina Rose in their proposal entitled 'Wet', envision a series of seven pods (small spaces), throughout the wet site. Each pod has varying degrees of depth and soil wetness and a different educational community use planned. The varying degrees of wetness and depth create a variety of wetland types on one site, i.e. bogs, swamps, marshes and ponds. These areas will each attract similar as well as different types of living organisms and they will each evolve with variation depending on proximity to the water source, exposure to wind and sun, and their use by children, adults, and other animals. A network of pedestrian pathways and narrow watercourses connects people with the pods to form a narrative about these different wetland types. The distinct types of pods provide a living vocabulary of wetland types and the variety of different animals that these landscapes attract.

In the schoolyard/park design by Brian Vermeulen, Graeme Little, Carolyn Roy, and Cith Skelcher of England, they propose a very intimate relationship between the school's architecture and the natural processes occurring on the wet site. This is done in order to heighten the children's awareness of the connection between the rituals in their daily lives and the natural processes that are essential to a sustainable schoolyard. They propose an integrated series of wetland types and school buildings where large reed bed areas (composed of gravel and plants), marshes, and ponds actually flow under the structures. The school buildings are raised on columns, and windows are located to heighten the ecological connection between human use and natural process. For example, low windows are placed at the children's sinks so they might discover a relationship between washing their hands and the water filtration function of the wetland immediately in view.

Forest management and community events

Cultivating and harvesting food are significant programmes for understanding the external environment as a dynamic system and inculcating a respect for other living things.[18] The jury noted that many of the design proposals included programmes that used forest or agricultural

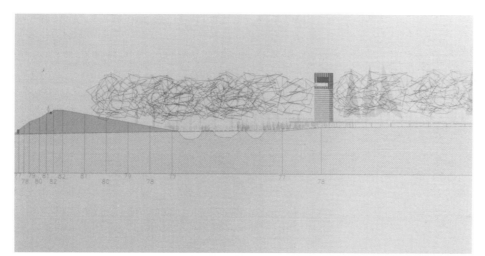

Figure 11.20
Second prize drawing by
Claudia Illanes Barrera
with Andrew Harris Diez,
and Loles Herrero Canela.
(Photo: Susan Herrington.)

management as an educational and community building event. Honourable mention Dave Hutch and Jean Kindratsky's 'Threads of Relationship' proposes a schoolyard where children and neighbours are the agents of change as they are encouraged to participate in specific events that help maintain the forest proposed for the wet site. These events occur daily, weekly, monthly, and guide the seasonal use of the site. They include the burning of underbrush, the planting and monitoring of conifers, the construction of earth shelters, or the coppicing of willow branches. Over time they

will witness directly the impact of their actions, leading to a deeper understanding of ecological and cultural processes. By proposing a schoolyard that addresses the longevity of the site over the time span of an evolving forest, the learning benefits of the site are sustained over generations.

Pierre Belanger, Mazereeuw, and Wright of Canada propose that the schoolyard/park design embrace a term borrowed from forest management: the test patch. In their plan for the wet site they locate a series of patches that are each dedicated to a specific ecological condition,

239

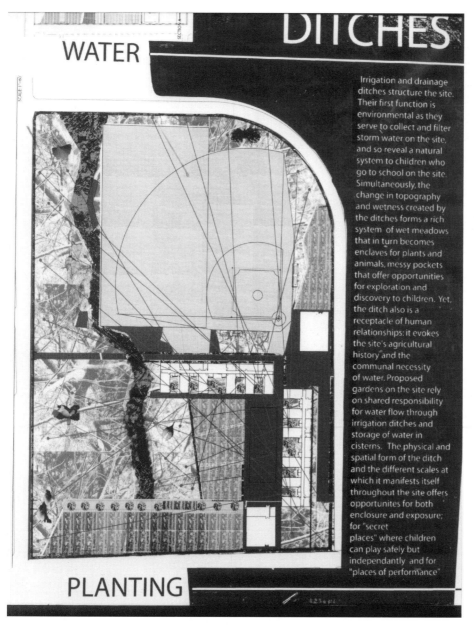

WATER

DITCHES

Figure 11.21
Third prize plan view by
Kamni Gill. (Photo:
Kenneth Studtmann.)

Irrigation and drainage ditches structure the site. Their first function is environmental as they serve to collect and filter storm water on the site, and so reveal a natural system to children who go to school on the site. Simultaneously, the change in topography and wetness created by the ditches forms a rich system of wet meadows that in turn becomes enclaves for plants and animals, messy pockets that offer opportunities for exploration and discovery to children. Yet, the ditch also is a receptacle of human relationships: it evokes the site's agricultural history and the communal necessity of water. Proposed gardens on the site rely on shared responsibility for water flow through irrigation ditches and storage of water in cisterns. The physical and spatial form of the ditch and the different scales at which it manifests itself throughout the site offers opportunites for both enclosure and exposure; for "secret places" where children can play safely but independantly and for "places of performance"

PLANTING

such as wetland patch or forest patch, and each patch is assigned a specific management treatment to be performed over time by the children and residents of East Clayton. The school building is located on the highest ground but allows for direct access to each of these patches. It is anticipated by the designers that each class and a group of residents will take responsibility for a test patch. These groups can use the patch area as an experimental ground where children and adults can study how natural systems grow, change, and die, and how human nurturing affects this cycle.

Site design and play

Children's participation in the design process is a valuable way to teach them about the multitude of problems and opportunities that must be addressed in the creation of school environments.

Figure 11.22
Third prize perspective by Kamni Gill. (Photo: Lisa McNiven.)

As 'players' in the design process, children will be able to more readily connect their own actions and decisions with environmental change, a key to sustainability. Honourable mention Robert Dorgan of the United States, uses a landscape spatial typology, represented in Fröbelian-like blocks, to involve children and neighbours in the process of designing their own environment. Vacant lots, crossroads, marshes, forests, allées and cloisters, for example, are represented by different block assemblages. Each block piece measures a quarter-acre because it was hypothesized by Dorgan that this size parcel, equivalent to a small residential lot, would be most familiar and comprehensible to children: 'The block helps introduce these "types" to a wider audience, and encourages a playful, yet studied, recombination and rearrangement of

blocks to create landscape conditions at scales far greater than the individual block.' Children and the community can actively create their landscape by assembling these modules in different combinations.

Chris Reed of Stosis in Cambridge, Massachusetts, proposes a series of site modifications, such as clearing, staking, forming, and filling, that help establish the schoolyard/park at the wet site. These modifications are done gradually as the community moves into East Clayton, and they influence natural systems in the schoolyard to create a chronology of changing site conditions. Reed first proposes 'clearing' pathways into the site. These pathways cut through the woods and meadow to encourage people to use the site. He then proposes 'staking', where seven-metre-high poles are placed at locations of the site that are most suitable for building in an ecologically sound way. These stakes are markers indicating potential building sites and are to be used as part of community discussions. Reed proposes 'forming' where walls are built across current drainage swales to divert run-off to a part of the site where over time a wetland will emerge due to successive flooding during the rainy months. Next is 'filling' where a large earthen platform is established on the site for outdoor social interactions among the growing East Clayton community. Lastly, he proposes that the existing two houses on the site are used as temporary meeting places where the school building is designed by the community.

Honourable mention Franc Jarosz of France divides the dry site into two spaces divided by the school building. To the east of the school Jarosz proposes programmes and structures invented and organized by the adult world: sports fields, outdoor classrooms, and community gardens. To the west of the school where the doors of the classroom open onto gardens and a wooded area, the children run things. This more private side of the site is the world created for and by children. It contains wild spaces where children can create their own worlds out of vegetative parts, mud, concrete tunnels, and building supplies, infusing the landscape with wonder and improbability. By delineating a children's zone within the schoolyard context, Jarosz hopes to nourish a sense of responsibility as well as creative ability.

Ulate of Costa Rica, proposes a schoolyard/park of moveable objects as a way to rotate uses throughout the yard, so as not to degrade the ecological conditions of the site's natural systems. Standard landscape's elements, such as fences and walkways, that are stationary items in most parks and schoolyards are moveable in Ulate's plans. For example, the fencing system can be moved to a number of different locations in order to allow the rejuvenation of trampled vegetated areas. These fences can also be used for social purposes by creating sub-spaces within the yard for younger children. Walkways are also movable so that they lead children and residents of East Clayton to different parts of the site during the changing seasons. Ulate also proposes that these movable pathways can end abruptly and start somewhere else in the schoolyard so that the children are left to their own volition to find the connections. Ideally, children will begin to move the pathways to places where they would like to lead others.

James Tichenor, Sean Salmon and Devyn Osborne of the United States use Geographical Positioning Systems (GPS) to create a schoolyard/park at the wet site that expresses the environmental conditions that are occurring in other schoolyards throughout the world. They selected elementary schools in Africa, China, England, France, California and Greece that would be connected via telecommunication and GPS systems. These schools would have similar features in their outdoor play environments. These features, such as pond areas, rubber-filled bladders for jumping, and large sand play areas would register specific conditions of a schoolyard in another country so as to heighten the children's awareness of the interconnectedness of the world. For example, in East Clayton the water pipes that fill the pond are regulated by incoming data from the school in England; hence, rain levels in London would determine the water depth in the East Clayton pond. By using the site as a display of changing data, the schoolyard will not only reflect changing natural conditions, but the conditions elsewhere in the world.

In November 2001, an exhibit of approximately 50 submitted designs were put on display at Robson Square in Vancouver, Canada. Nicholas Gilsoul was present at the opening to give a lecture on the ideas that generated his 13-acres submission. A panel discussion followed Gilsoul's lecture and included Nicholas Gilsoul, Patrick Condon of the University of British Columbia James Taylor Chair, and three jury members – Lorna Fraser of the Surrey Parent Organization, Umer Olcay of the Surrey School Board Facilities Manager, and Landscape Architect Cornelia Hahn Oberlander. The goal of the panel discussion was to begin the critical discussion of the design of the actual schoolyard in East Clayton. In April 2002 another exhibit of entries and a panel discussion were held at City Hall in Surrey.

13-acres helped identify important programming needs that are cogent to many communities concerned with the sustainable role of schoolyards, particularly where these communities face depleting open spaces, endangered aquatic environments, and threatened habitat areas. Because the competition resulted in so many design responses, a rich selection of creative design solutions and issues has been brought to the professional and public eye. We anticipate that the competition will provide benefits in several different ways and at different levels of local, provincial, national, and international action. Most immediately, the design proposals of the

competition have provided numerous examples of sustainable design solutions. These solutions will help the new East Clayton community to work with the city of Surrey to physically build a schoolyard as part of the sustainable demonstration site. A long-term initiative is to secure funding for the longitudinal monitoring and quantitative evaluation of the benefits of a sustainable schoolyard design, monitoring how well it functions socially and physically as a learning and community resource. Longitudinal outcomes can potentially cause shifts in the way individuals and groups envision the physical environment of the schoolyard and potentially inform incentives and guidance for emerging standards regarding sustainable development and relevant policies concerning the educational curriculum.

Figure 11.23
Robson Square exhibit. (Photo: Susan Herrington.)

Notes

1 Buttimer, A. (2001). *Sustainable Landscapes and Lifeways: scale and appropriateness.* Cork University Press.

2 Thayer, R. L. (1994). *Grey World Green Heart: Technology, Nature, Sustainable Landscape.* John Wiley.

3 Bowers, C. A. (1995). *Educating for an Ecologically Sustainable Culture: Rethinking Moral Education, Creativity, Intelligence, and Other Modern Orthodoxies.* State University of New York.

4 Rivkin, M. S. (1995). *The Great Outdoors: Restoring Children's Rights to Play Outside.* National Association for the Education of Young Children.

5 Ibid, p. 40.

6 Cunningham, C. J. and Jones, M. (1999). The Playground: A Confession or Failure. *Built Environment*, **25** (1), 11–17.

7 Herrington, S. (1997). The Infant Garden: The Subculture of Infants and the Received View of Play. *Landscape Journal*, **16**, 2.

8 Herrington, S. (1999). Playgrounds as Community Landscapes. *Built Environment: Playgrounds in the Built Environment*, **25** (1), 25–34.

9 Francis (1984/5), Olds (1989), Rivkin (1995), Neperud (1995), Birt, *et al.* (1997), Herrington (1999), Irwin Kindler (1999) – see Bibliography for details.

10 Steiner, F. and Thompson, G. F. (eds). (1996). *Ecological Planning and Design.* John Wiley. And Coffey, A. (1996). Transforming School Grounds. *Green Teacher*, **47**, April–May, 7–10.

11 Spreiregen, P. D. (1979). *Design Competition.* McGraw Hill.

12 Condon, P. (1996). *Sustainable Urban Landscapes: The Surrey Design Charrette.* University of British Columbia, The James Taylor Chair in Landscape & Livable Environments.

13 Herrington, S. (2002). *Schoolyard Park.* Vancouver: University of British Columbia Center for Landscape Research.

14 Coffey, 1994 p. 11, Orr 1994 p. 142.

15 Cunningham and Jones 1999, Herrington 1997, Maxley (1999) – see Bibliography.

16 Hoody and Lieberman, (1998), p. 22 – see Bibliography.

17 Hoody and Lieberman (1998), p. i.

18 Alexander, J., North, M. W. and Hendron, D. K. (1995). Master Gardener Classroom Garden Project: An Evaluation of the Benefits to Children. *Children's Environments*, **12** (2), 256–263.

Bibliography

Birt, D., King, D. H. and Sheridan, M. (1997). Earthly Matters: Learning Occurs When You Hear the Grass Sing. *The Journal of the National Art Education Association*, **50** (6), 7–13.

Francis, M. (1989). Children's Use of Open Space in Village Homes. *Children's Environment Quarterly*, 1.

Herrington, S. (2000). Garden Pedagogy: Romanticism to Reform. *Landscape Journal: Design, Planning, and Management of the Land.* **19** (1), 30–47.

Kindler, A. M. and Irwin, R. (1999). Art Education Outside School Boundaries: Identifying Resources, exploring possibilities. R. Irwin and A. M. Kindler (eds) *Beyond the School: Community and institutional partnerships in art education.* National Art Education Association.

Kuwabara, B. (1998). Interview. *Competitions Magazine*, **8** (4), 34–46.

Hoody, L. L. and Liberman, G. A. (1998). *Closing the Achievement Gap: Using the Environment as an Integrating Context for Learning.*

Maxley, I. (1999). Playgrounds: from Oppressive Spaces to Sustainable Places? *Built Environment*, **25** (1), 18–24.

Neperud, R. (1995). Texture of Community: An Environmental Design Education. In *Context, content, and community in art education, beyond Postmodernism* (R. Neperud, ed.). Teachers College Press.

Olds, A. R. (1989). Nature as Healer. *Children's Environment Quarterly*, **6**.

Orr, D. (1992). *Ecological Literacy: Education and the Transition to a Postmodern World.* State University of New York.

Susan Herrington is a landscape architect who is currently Associate Professor in the School of Architecture and Landscape Architecture at The University of British Columbia. She has contributed papers to numerous conferences and academic journals around the theme of children's play and has published the proceedings of her sustainable design competition, Schoolyard Park: 13-acres International Design Competition. She continues to practice as a landscape architect and has won a number of awards for her built work.

12

The edible landscape of school

Catherine Burke

One of my earliest memories of school is associated with fear of the school dinner hall. One day, during the school meal, I felt sick and discovered an escape route from the daily hazard of dinner time. I was allowed to lie down on a camp bed inside the reception class room and was left. I found great comfort there with no one to worry me. Somehow I managed to escape each dinner time for a few days as I found myself experiencing the same symptoms as soon as midday approached. A sympathetic teacher led me once more to the little camp bed and I was left alone. Like so many children, it was perhaps the fear of losing control and becoming ill which caused the anxiety and actual symptoms. This may have been magnified by the strange regimentation of large numbers eating together according to rules and orders set down in what was to me, as a newcomer in the autumn of 1962, the alien environment of the English primary school.

The school meal at that time, when the school kitchen was far from universal, was often delivered each day in large lorries, the hot food contained in metal vats. It smelled and tasted like no other food consumed anywhere and nothing about it was fresh or newly harvested. Growing up in an urban environment in Britain during the 1960s, children were far removed from horticulture and were accustomed to highly processed foods which were pouring on to the newly fashionable supermarket shelves. Few of our mothers preserved their own jams and marmalades. Tinned peas and carrots and packaged powdered potatoes, as well as factory-produced white sliced bread were our every day reality. The school meal merely magnified this reality further. Food, or its absence, structured our days and accompanied our play. We skipped to rhymes about food, we chanted in the playground, creatively playing with the sounds of the contents of school dinners. Salad became 'rabbit food', macaroni became 'drainpipes' and currant cakes 'dead flies cemetery'. Stew was 'spew' and we 'washed it all down with a bucket of sick'.

Iona and Peter Opie trailed the country during the 1950s and published their famous book *The Lore and Language of School Children,* in which they documented the cultural landscape of school children at play. In it they noted:

> *The possessors of young and healthy appetites are lyrical about their food. School dinners are 'muck', 'pig swill', 'poison', 'slops', 'S.O.S.' (Same Old Slush), and 'Y.M.C.A. (Yesterday's Muck Cooked Again').*[1]

Once a week we carried with us to school our packed breakfasts. This was to allow us to take Holy Communion at the school mass, sometimes held in our classrooms. As Catholic school children, we were not permitted to eat or drink anything for twelve hours before the school mass. Cold buttered toast consumed with friends in the classroom on a totally empty stomach tasted heavenly. I noticed for the first time, through the contents of these breakfasts, that my classmates

Figure 12.1
Serving the school dinner: 1950.

came from homes and backgrounds which differed from my own as revealed in the strange and fascinating toppings and fillings of their sandwiches. School gardens, where they existed, were tended by the school caretaker and contained rocks and flowers. We were to keep away from them. Occasionally children would get into trouble for picking the flowers. The idea that children should learn to garden was out of fashion in an 'enlightened' era that was striving to embrace the educational challenge of 'the white heat of technology.'[2]

Today, as my children attend school, the school meal and its environment has taken a different shape after two decades of deregulation and privatization. At one time the school kitchens and dining spaces were regarded as symbols of modernization and progress. Now, the space most usually associated with progress and quality is the ubiquitous computer lab. Technologies servicing large-scale food preparation and consumption are seemingly of less importance than technologies serving up web pages from around the world. At the same time the preparation of food has been 'raised' to the status of a technology itself through

a re-branding exercise. As specified by the UK National Curriculum, children and young people no longer merely learn to cook; they practise 'food technology'.[3] Food consumed in school, whether purchased in the canteen or tuck shop, or whether brought to school as a packed lunch is generally highly processed, resembling little of its original source. Drink consumed is likely to be canned and branded. In some quarters, as children become physically less active and nutritionally more wanting, concerns are being voiced about the health consequences of heavy reliance on processed foods in their diets. The 'McDonaldization of diet' is a shorthand for rising levels of obesity and associated disease in school-aged children and the spread across Europe of American-style eating habits.[4]

Children and young people today are widely considered to be out of touch with the origins of the food they consume and have little awareness of the nutritional value of what they eat. The parent or grandparent who traditionally passed on essential wisdom about food and survival can no longer be taken as given in many families. The industrialization and commodification of food has supplanted the family as a site of learning and the food industry has profited massively from the expectation that women will structure their lives around the workplace rather than the kitchen. However, it has been recognized since the inception of mass schooling that school was a means of equipping those out of touch with such wisdom with the tools of survival. During the second half of the twentieth century, however, the association of manual work with low paid occupations encouraged the mainstream educational establishment in Europe and the United States to place more value on academic knowledge and competencies. This continues today as literacy, numeracy and the development of skills in Information and Communication Technologies are compulsory subjects in schools. Gardening, once an established part of the curriculum, is sidelined as an after school activity if it exists at all and cooking would have disappeared entirely from the curriculum were it not re-branded as a 'technology'.[5]

But there are exceptions. Schools outside the mainstream, such as Steiner or Waldorf schools, have maintained work with the hands as of equal value to work with the mind. This is not usually the case in mainstream schooling. However, a renewed appreciation of the edible landscape of school is currently generating cutting edge projects advancing curriculum design and architectural planning within schools. Some of these examples will be explored in this chapter. The 'edible schoolyard', part of an international 'growing schools' movement is evidence of a reassertion of the maxim, 'We Learn by Doing'. Initiatives such as these have the potential for changing schools and the experience of learning just as much as e-learning projects which attract so much attention and sponsorship. The evidence presented in this chapter argues the case that for children, the edible landscape matters just as much as the electronic landscape which they embrace. Food is fundamental and despite official and professional preoccupation with pedagogy that embraces the revolutionary potential of computer-supported learning and teaching, for children and young people the edible landscape represents an essential part of survival in the modern school.

It has long been regarded as essential that children should learn how to prepare and produce food for the domestic table. For most of the twentieth century, this was a prescribed activity for girls. It was considered to be so important – indeed for many the principal reason for allowing girls to be educated at all – that often a flat or apartment was attached to the school where older girls could practice their 'house craft' skills in a realistic setting. Girls educated in the 1950s and 1960s may well remember the task of making their cookery overall during several weeks of instruction before commencing cookery lessons. Today, the homely pinafore is rarely seen and pupils are more likely to be clad in industrial apparel such as a white overall and hat. These are significant contextual changes which reflect a fundamental shift in the perceived purpose of education about food. There has developed over recent years a change of focus from the domestic table to the commercial outlet. Indeed, the contemporary emphasis on learning

about the technology of food production, particularly in commercial or market contexts constitutes a form of 'Industrial Pedagogy' which carries with it serious implications in terms of the quality of education and feeds straight into the hands of the 'fast food' giants.

> *The site for cooking (or food processing) has transferred: from the home and the school; to the factory and catering outlets – and it is this transfer which the national curriculum aims to facilitate and encourage.*[6]

Accordingly, children in the UK spend time designing marketing formats and considering mass production within a technological and industrial approach to knowledge and learning that leaves out much of value in the human understanding of food and its production and consumption. Thirteen- and fourteen-year-old boys and girls in state schools now learn bread making together but they are instructed to conceive of this activity in terms of producing an industrial and commercial product. A worksheet entitled 'Control Systems for Bread Making' advises *'When you make a loaf of bread, you need to check that you have made it properly'*.[7] One might have in previous generations carried out such a check by simply eating and enjoying the newly baked bread. However, the pupil today is conceived of as the future manager of a production line and the instruction is in keeping with this projection. The pupils are required to behave in the context of *'a factory system for controlling the bread making process to make sure that the end product is safe and reaches their quality standards'*.[7] None of the test procedures involve eating or even tasting the bread.

This shift in the culture of food production and consumption in educational environments mirrors the de-domestication of food in the industrialized world. As the processed foodstuffs market continues to expand according to demand for ever-faster, convenient and cheaper foods, these products increasingly dominate the dietaries of households. The Commission of the European Union recently published *Nutrition Education in Schools: Europe Against Cancer* in which it acknowledged the centrality of educational environments in long-term strategies for improving the health and well-being of the community and in raising levels of self-esteem among youth.[8] This awareness is beginning to bear fruit.

The UK Government Department for Education and Skills (DfES) has introduced the 'Growing

Figure 12.2
The Schools Organic Network: Findern School, Derbyshire, UK.

Schools' initiative, designed among other things to challenge the knowledge gap that has arisen among recent generations of children and young people between what they eat and the origins of food. A primary outcome of this initiative is the envisaged spread of school gardening projects as an integrated part of the curriculum.[9] A separate ongoing project is 'The Schools Organic Network', an initiative of the Henry Doubleday Research Association which distributes free organic vegetable seeds in the spring to schools with an interest in food gardening. A website promotes activity through publicizing the achievements of the network of schools.[10]

These projects are radical initiatives that challenge many contemporary ways of seeing children and manual labour. The labouring child is an image associated in the modern mind with exploitation, oppression, the antipathy of freedom to learn. This was not always the case. The early Kindergarten movement, especially that part influenced by Friedrich Froebel (1782–1852), recognized in gardening the possibilities for young

Figure 12.3
Children's Garden, unidentified kindergarten, Los Angeles, c.1900.

children of working with the fundamental structures of life. As a platform for learning, the garden environment, especially if landscaped in a style that mirrored fundamental life forms, would take on the role of teacher.

Foebel designed his own children's garden, which shows the integration of flowers, herbs and vegetables and the individual and communal plots he regarded as fundamental for the spiritual and social development of young children.[11]

For many in the United States, working the land is associated in popular memory with images of slavery. On both sides of the Atlantic, farming is associated with a precarious lifestyle and rarely with good standards of living. Images of child labour and child slavery are generally employed to argue the case for universal schooling as an essential feature of 'development'. In Britain, images of the labouring child are read in conjunction with a progressive view of educational history which sees the gradual emergence of an academic education as an entitlement for all children. Already, in the early twentieth century, the relative demotion of gardening in the school curriculum was apparent when teachers were forced to argue its case. But

the benefits of cross-curricular integration were fully appreciated by commentators. *'Gardening as a school subject…should not be regarded as a training for industry, but should lead to an interest in nature. It should not be treated as an isolated subject, but every opportunity should be taken to use it to add reality to the ordinary work, and the ordinary work should assist the gardening'*.[12]

For a short period, during the war years, schools in England developed garden plots to help supply the food for the midday meal. In November 1941, one school noted in its log book: *'Dinner cooked in the school – meat and four vegetables, pudding and custard – costs 3d. per day. All vegetables except potatoes from the school garden'*.[13]

The selective system of secondary education which was adopted by the majority of Local Education Authorities in England following the 1944 Education Act helped to further undermine gardening, horticulture and animal husbandry. Those children, tested at eleven years, who were considered academic, would be protected from getting their hands dirty in the grammar school environment where they would be nurtured towards a professional career. Children considered

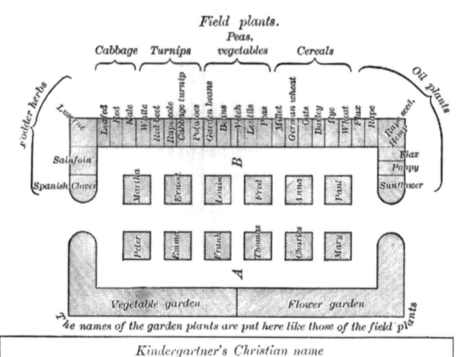

Figure 12.4
'The Garden for the Children is the Kindergarten' from Friedrich Froebel's *Education by Development*, New York, 1899.

Figure 12.5
The Labouring child: 1950s.
Featherstone School,
South Yorkshire, England.

less bright would be channelled to schools where manual work on the land, particularly for boys, was a necessary part of the curriculum. The relegation of garden work and its association within the educational context with lower levels of intelligence has continued until today and has contributed to the negative or demeaning association of horticulture and husbandry with learning.

So how do children and young people themselves view the edible landscape of school? How has this changed over time? How important to them is food and drink in everyday life in school and what does the association with certain kinds of foods signify in the culturally diverse environments of schools today? What is the nature of the forces acting on children within the edible landscape of school, shaping their bodies and minds as they develop their tastes, knowledge, value systems and market power as young citizens? How do they respond to initiatives to integrate the growing and preparation of food into the curriculum?

What follows is an exploration of the edible landscape of school from the points of view of various contemporary players. These are:

- Children themselves, explored through their ideas and designs for change in the school environment.

- Teachers and others who are working towards the integration of the edible landscape within the curriculum of school.
- Food companies who are seeking to expand their marketing activities via corporate sponsorship within schools.

An historical perspective or long view of the edible landscape of school is taken to explore and reveal continuities and patterns of change over time. But to begin with, we look at this landscape through the eyes of the child or young person captured at two different points of time in the UK.

'The School I'd Like': envisioned edible landscapes, 1967 and 2001

The school I'd Like
Would be so fun
With no strict teachers
And in the shape of a big bun

(Sarah, age 11, Edinburgh.)[14]

In 1967 the *Observer* newspaper hosted a competition which provided the opportunity for secondary school children in the UK to describe and design their preferred or ideal school. Nine hundred and forty-three entries were received amounting to some half a million words, innumerable charts, collages, architectural or pseudo-architectural drawings. In the words of Edward Blishen, who later edited the collection into a small volume, *The School That I'd Like*, 'it amounted to an enormous, remarkably good humoured, earnest, frequently passionate and, at its best, highly intelligent plea for a new order in our schools.'[15] Critical appraisal of the edible landscape, in particular of the school meal, became a section of the book entitled 'One of the Main Grumbles'. Here, Blishen remarked:

> If schools are ever widely improved, children will lose one of their best jokes and most beloved grouches. But it is clear from the evidence of these essays that they would endure the loss gladly. Given their attachment to the joke, there can't be any doubt that in a great many schools the meals are still badly cooked and indifferently served. The chief pleas come again and again, and are all represented here: not only for good cooking, but for varied menus; some say in the size of the meal on any particular occasion; the avoidance of banal or eccentric combinations of dishes; an opportunity to choose among alternatives; and a pleasant environment in which to eat.[16]

A generation later, the question has been put once again to children and young people in the UK, this time from the age of five to eighteen. The Educational Supplement of the *Guardian* newspaper was invited to host a competition. As in the original competition, the newspaper covers the whole of the British Isles and is read in countries across the world. Corporate sponsorship of the competition secured ICT equipment to be given to the schools from which winning entries were received. The competition was held between January and March 2001.[17] But unlike the original 'School I'd Like' 'competition, this time there was a fundamental commitment to archive each and every one of the entries which amounted to some 20 000 pieces. Invited to choose any format, submissions took the form of essays, poems, photo essays, letters to the prime minister, project files,

video, paintings, three-dimensional models, power point presentations and interactive CD-Roms. Some schools produced entries from all pupils, some came in the form of class or group entries, some were individual entries and many were from individual children who used their own initiative supported by other family members outside of school.

The edible landscape features strongly in the majority of entries and it is possible to see within them the impact of the enormous changes that have taken place in the provision of school meals in the UK and the commodification of food more generally. It is possible to read the way that changes in the general edible landscape, the widespread privatization of the school meals service coupled with the 'McDonaldization' of diet, has altered the culture of consumption and has influenced the expectations of children and young people.[18] However, it is also possible to identify a strong continuity with the past in the desires of children and young people to 'have a say' in the edible landscape of school. There is much evidence of continued dissatisfaction with the quality and quantity of food, the environment in which food is prepared, served and consumed, as well as with the contextual organization of discipline, surveillance and control around pupils' consumption. But these are not mere grumbles. Children are keenly interested in food and there is here a considerable body of inventive and creative thought given to ways in which food production, processing and consumption can be improved and form a rich and satisfying platform for learning.

One of the winning entries of the competition came from a 'Special' school situated in the north west of England. Longley Special School renamed itself 'Longley Dream School' for the purposes of the competition. This state mainstream school cares for and educates 130 children aged five to sixteen with 'complex special needs' and has two autistic units. The older children surveyed the whole school under the guidance of their teachers and produced a report, a significant part of which discusses the edible landscape of the school. They described the kind of space for eating they would prefer, emphasizing the need for adequate space in

We need more heating because every day in the winter it is too cold in the dining hall and it is too hot in the summer so we need to cool it down.

Figure 12.6
Longley Dream School canteen.

We Want A Dinner Place Like This

Cafe

We need a new burger bar in the hall for people who can buy food. We also need a new sandwich bar for children who can eat egg, cheese, and tuna.

People who are a Muslims can't eat ham, hot dogs, chicken, or turkey, because only original people can eat this food.

general and for intimate smaller social eating spaces in particular. Choice of where to sit, whether in a large or small space is important. The need for better furnishing to create a warm, quieter and calmer atmosphere is mentioned.

The preferred setting for eating was photographed to help illustrate the kind of environment envisaged in an ideal or 'dream' school. Some of the requirements are basic.

The report indicates a strong awareness of the importance of nutrition to support a lively educational experience. No token offering but a 'good breakfast' would be ideal in a 'dream school'. The needs of school staff and pupils are recognized equally.

Dining areas, since they usually occupy large open spaces, are noisy and hectic. For many children, this represents a particular area of discomfort. In spite of the tendency towards ever-faster consumption of food on the move, young children often crave a space of calmness within which to take their time to digest their food. The school dinner hall or canteen suggests otherwise.

> *I would like a school with kind and quiet people and a teacher who would help me whenever I got stuck and at dinner time, when I walk into the dinner hall, it would be quiet and not loud. (Jessica, age 9, London.)*

Edible landscapes are in evolutionary terms, original landscapes. Food and drink is fundamental to survival and in the compulsory, largely controlled and increasingly scrutinized territory of the school, children recognize the importance of this landscape. School meals, served up in noisy halls or canteens are associated with heaviness, dullness, grey colours and dismal moods. Both in 1967 and today, children readily associated the serving of school food with the institutional, such as the prison, with reference to the traditional emphasis on control and regulation of bodies.

School meals are ghastly affairs, which always cause disturbance among pupils and adults. (Angela, age 15, Blishen, 1969, p. 150.)

At the present time in the UK, school meals in primary schools are often served within an atmosphere of distrust and compulsion, sometimes within enforced silence. This goes a long way to explain the prevailing dislike of the school meals assistant or supervisor whose job it is to ensure that the meal is taken with the minimum of fuss and waste. This person, usually a low paid contracted worker with little professional status, can sometimes be seen to make up for their lack of professional authority in the school by displaying rather autocratic tendencies. These in turn can be adopted by older children in the role of prefects or school meals monitors. For a child who is feeling a little unwell, is simply not hungry, or who needs to visit the toilet during the meal time, the dining area can become a forbidding and threatening place.

In 1967, secondary school age children commented on the regimentation of school meals which was so disliked:

In my school nobody will force the pupils to eat if they don't want to. (Girl, age 14, Blishen, 1969 p. 150.)

These systems are wrong because, particularly in boys school where senior boys have the power to beat younger boys, having power over others can give pupils an overbearing or even sadistic disposition. (Alexandra, age 13, Blishen 1969, p. 159.)

It was felt that the civility and sociability essential to enjoyable collective eating was missing or neglected in school. In an ideal environment '*We would not be thrown out at lunch time but would be allowed to go*

somewhere to sit and talk.' (Janet, age 14, Blishen, 1969, p. 156.)

A generation later, it is clear from some of the commentary that accompanies competition entries that compulsion and discipline are still felt as oppressive by young children in school canteens as is made clear by such comments as '*The school I would like is a school where you can go crazy in the canteen and get out of your seats all of the time*'. (Kealan, age 6, Derry.)

A generation ago, the food itself, traditionally a meat and two vegetables dish, was considered to be dull, dead or lacking life. Dreams, schemes, fantasies and suggestions about how the school environment might be made ideal were coloured with metaphors of food and drink in light or weightless contexts. Interestingly, the food itself remains unchanged despite the technological packaging and other inventions envisaged.

Down to the feeding hall by mono-rail they speed, a sunlit room floating in space …
Boys stand before vast shining machines;
Press-button feeding is the rule of the day.
This one gives shepherd's pie, this treacle stodge,
Eaten from paper plates, disposable.
Then to the gym, for trampolines in space or
Half an hour's horseplay in the low gravity chamber.
This is the school I'd like to go to … I think?
(C. (boy), age 13, Blishen, 1969, p. 32.)

The lightness associated with sophisticated technologies in relation to school dinners is a theme repeated thirty years on:

My ideal school would be a hovercraft. There would be lots of schools, each covering a small area. The hover-school will be powered by solar power. The large roof will be made of solar panels. At night the hover school will have to land to conserve its spare energy for an early morning. When the schools land for lunch break, next to the landing site will be four small canteens, one for each year. (Katherine, age 9.)

Natural metaphors have long been associated with educational environments. The Ancient Egyptian hieroglyphic for education was an image of dew falling from the sky. These ancient resonances reflect a spiritual, transforming and regenerative concept of education, something which is expressed fully in many of the metaphorical allusions used by modern children and young people in the 'School I'd Like' collection. For example, the school is envisaged in the shape of a flower, the classrooms as petals, altogether a symbol of life, growth and nourishment.

The centre of the flower is a big glass dome and that is the main hall; the heart of the school. It would be much more lighter than electric lights. I would also like some of the older children in the school to climb on ladders and make stained glass designs on the dome. This would mean that when the light shines through it will make lovely patterns on the floor. The stalk of the flower would be the main corridor from the leaves at the bottom and the flower head at the top. It would be extremely long and would have toilets, lost property, shops to buy your dinner, a library, and a quiet room. (Sarah, age 10, Sheffield.)

This child, new to schooling, lets the metaphor flow with soothing effect:

I wish my school would be a flower school. I would have flower tables and chairs. I wear flower clothes. I would wear little flowers in my hair ... I eat flower sandwiches. I drink Ribena. I have flower shaped crisps and flower shaped sweets and biscuits. (Ellie, age 5, Cheshire.)

Other recent research initiatives that have explored the ways in which children conceptualize school spaces in northern European countries show that edible metaphors are often readily used to describe school itself. In these accounts, school can be likened to 'a nightmare', 'being buried alive', a 'bitter lemon' or a 'rotten apple'.[19]

Avoidance of contact with adults – and especially the lunchtime supervisor or kitchen worker – is indicated in the desires of schoolchildren. The robotic dinner operative is an attractive option for many. And in general, the application of technology to the harsh environment of the dining room or dual or triple use school hall, with its rules and associated punishments, is echoed in these voices of children and young people. The tedium of queuing is recognized by many school pupils and once more, technology is considered to offer a possible solution:

Each pupil would have a computer with all the necessary things that you would need to get through the school day. If you put money in the slot school dinners would pop out of a hatch in the middle of the pack, saving time on queues for them.'(Andrew, age 13, Bristol.)

Dinner isn't served by dinner ladies. As a matter of fact they are not served by anyone at all. They come hurtling towards us on a huge spinning wheel and it's pot luck what we get, because as soon as we decide what we want, our pick is probably on its way round again. (Jade, age 9, London.)

Many schools habitually utilize the school hall for a multitude of purposes; the most common combination being the canteen and the gym. This is discussed as an enduring problem by children in describing their ideal school environments. 'We need a separate dining hall because some of the little children drop bits of food and when we do PE some of the food gets in our feet.' (Thomas, age 11, Yorkshire.)

But there is thoughtful consideration given to the economic use of space:

Instead of eating our dinner in our assembly hall, and having to rush our food because it is not big enough for us all, I think we should have a proper canteen for our main hot dinners and a cafeteria for snacks, drinks and to sit on rainy days and have a chat.

The cafe should be open at breaks too, so that we can get extra drinks and snacks if we need them. At the moment we have to go all afternoon without a drink, unless we save some from lunch. This is bad on hot days. This would be good for us socially, and the rooms could be used for the after school clubs as well, so the space won't ever be wasted. (Kimberley, age 10, Derbyshire.)

At the same time, the sheer dullness of spaces for eating was commented on: 'Our canteen needs decorating because at the moment it's very dull. I'd like

Figure 12.7
Tool shed and tool and boot racks: the edible schoolyard, Berkeley, California.

to have new dinner ladies, because the ones we have are a bit grumpy.' (Serena, age 8, London.)

The 'School I'd Like' competition 2001 revealed a yearning among children for the potential of an integrated curriculum, combining the indoors with the outdoors, and with the production of food at its centre:

> *At the side or front of the drama block there should be a large shaped pond. The pond will be at the side of a fenced in allotment with a green house. All fenced in with a hedge to prevent children from falling in and it could be part of the students' curriculum to look after it. We would need a shed to keep all the tools in.* (Carl, age 15, Sheffield.)

'Learning by doing' has long been the maxim of critical pedagogy from John Dewey to John Holt. For Dewey, the school garden was regarded as a central part of the curriculum, its produce serving the school and wider community. In spite of the industrialization of the countryside and the commodification of nature, it is not often recognized that young children can still perceive the value of such an approach to learning.

> *There would be a big cafeteria overlooking the river and lots of choices of healthy food. I think we should have a small farm so we can learn to plant and grow our food and look after animals. We could have a small snack bar in the grounds and take it in turns to make and sell things like bread, sandwiches and biscuits.... We could have a special classroom in the trees to help us study nature really close up. We could have a ladder and walkway in the treetops.* (Hannah, age 8, Barrow Hill.)

In such a school, there is fun and fairness and children will 'have a say', even taking an active part in food production and preparation. In this envisaged school...

> *... we have really nice school dinners, which if you have any comments or complaints about there are some forms by the till which can be filled in.... We have monitors that help the dinner ladies cook. We only have chips once a week because they are junk food. Sometimes we have chicken nuggets, but they often cook tasty dishes with vegetables and we eat a lot of fruit. Some of the food is grown in the garden like herbs and*

vegetables. We have cookery lessons where we learn how to make cakes and biscuits and eat them for our lunch. My friend Gary once found a penny in his biscuit. (Max, age 9, Birkenhead.)

Lack of formality, or at least irregularity of sitting arrangements in dining areas is appealing to the school child past and present. It seems to go hand in hand with increased choice of food, as illustrated in the following extracts from the 1969 collection:

… A choice of dish only if it is from stringy beans to cannonball peas. The actual room could be bright and airy and the tables arranged in an orderly but not regular pattern. (Anne, age 14, Blishen, 1969, p. 151.)

'Whoever compiles the menus cannot have much of an idea of catering. A particular example of this is: green salad, fish, chips and peas. Ugh! I know that if it was left to me or others that will remain anonymous, such a combination would not dare to cross the mind.

All this would be stopped in my ideal school, and pupils would have a menu of several dishes to choose from. I realise the possibility of unnecessary waste, but we could combat that by ordering the meal several days beforehand.' (Valerie, age 14, Blishen, 1969. p. 150.)

What is most often expressed is the desire for a decent social context for eating. Rather than the regular, rectilinear arrangements of bodies around tables and chairs, with the implied head of table and authoritarian regime mirroring that found in the classroom and the rest of the school, an alternative is envisaged. What then becomes challenged is the formality and associated meanings of control in spaces which are, from the point of view of the young person, predominantly for enjoyment and social interaction. Limited choice of food and little freedom to socialize implies a regular or linear arrangement of furniture; greater choice and freedom to socialize implies irregular arrangements and smaller groupings to facilitate interaction.

School break times usually imply a certain freedom from control but this is increasingly tempered by adult supervision and increasing levels of technologically enhanced surveillance. Children desire more private spaces free from observation and control.

Interestingly, when asked if they had any spaces to call their own in school, young people in a recent study did not locate the dining area as one such space, but rather the locker or the desk among very few such spaces, explaining 'The school feels like a public space belonging to the whole world.'[20]

Given the opportunity to reflect on the whole school, its organization and built environment, there were few children in the UK in 2001 who had nothing to say about food and the edible landscape. Quite the contrary, and most were delighted to have the opportunity to comment.

My head bursts with ideas that could be changed on food. Like more choices such as Indian food for the Indian children, Chinese food for the Chinese children and so on or you could just have more choices for children who wanted to try out different foods … Sometimes I wish that lunchtimes were longer, there are times when I feel I have hardly sat down to eat and three tables have gone out to break already. (Isobel, age 9, Birmingham.)

The edible landscape, according to children and young people across the UK, should reflect the cultural landscape of difference and diversity and should be inclusive of all tastes and types. There is a clear line of thought reflected here that tells of young people's awareness of the different needs of their peers. The recognition and promotion of such diversity, if embraced, would improve school meals.

The meals should be better and we should have an Indian cook, an Italian cook, a Chinese cook for a good variety of food. (Thomas, age 11, Cardiff.)

Meals will be well cooked and healthy. They will be made from organic food and there will be a wide variety of vegetarian food and meals for different religious groups. It will be cheap and those who can't afford it have free meals. (Isobel, age 14, Ipswich.)

At each end of the corridor there would be a nice water cooler which everyone could drink out of and … the canteen would have to sell nice new and exciting food which is healthy, but you don't notice that it is. In the lunch break, I would enjoy a different meal from the one the day before. (Valerie, age 12, Glasgow.)

Even in the most unlikely scenarios and futuristic contexts, the dining room is still awarded pride of place.

My ideal school would be on top of a volcano so it would always be warm even in the winter … Inside there would be swimming pools, science labs, computer rooms and rooms to chill out in but most importantly, a dinner hall. But just because the dinner hall is inside, it doesn't mean that the pupils can't eat outside, maybe on the edge of the volcano! (Patrick, age 10) (See Plate 18.)

Fast food culture is certainly reflected in hundreds of entries to the 'School I'd Like' competition, 2001. But often, the emphasis is tempered by an acknowledgement that such food can be dull and uninspiring. Once more, variety, difference and diversity reflecting the community of the school are valued highly within these idealized environments. (See Plate 19.) 'The canteen would have several different parts, one part would be McDonald's, Burger King, Pizza Hut and a fancy restaurant which serves food from all over the world.' (Aimee, age 12, Glasgow.)

Resistance to highly processed food is plentiful and it is clear that children are at least as aware as their parents of the poor nutritional value of the fast food market. These accounts betray an understanding of the primary function of food, but fun and fairness are paramount.

It just isn't fair! Just because we are juniors it doesn't mean we can't have milk!!! Why can't we have it, is it because we don't need calcium? Or are our bones strong enough already, I don't think so, or should we behave like infants to get it? Furthermore, we should have a fruit stall for when we have our break, instead of crisps and

chocolate bars and what not, to help our immune system. (Bonnie Louise, age 10, Cardiff.)

The ideal edible landscape would not be institutional. Rather it should resemble the adult world where 'the customer is always right' and respect and care is taken as given.

In the school I'd like, we should be able to go for our dinner at any time that we want during the whole hour and ten minutes lunch break. They should also keep all the food hot. Grown ups wouldn't stand for eating cold food so why should we! (Sarah, age 10, Sheffield.)

For a large number of children, the most exciting prospect of changing the edible landscape of school is to incorporate more of the patterns of consumption they associate with a good time outside of school. The incorporation of such features means that school resembles something other than a place of learning and becomes a place of fun. Choice translates into a choice between brands.

In the hall there will be a McDonald's in a corner, a Burger King in a corner and a KFC in a corner. In the classrooms it will be like chocolate land, that means you can eat the tables and chairs. You're only allowed two pieces a lesson. (Amelia, age 10, Mytholmroyd.)

For breakfast, we will have a McDonald's breakfast bar. The menu would be Egg muffin, sausages, hash browns and for drink we will have milkshake, milk and orange juice. (Anthony, age 10, Romford.)

I would have a McDonald's in my ideal school because you absolutely have to eat, and I would have a canteen for those who do not like chips etc. (Lucy, age 10, Lichfield.)

Inherited edible school spaces

The children commenting on their idealized or imagined school environments, both in 1967 and today, did so within an inherited school design and tradition. The edible landscape, and particularly the school meal, is immediately recognizable as a fundamental feature of schooling, particularly in the UK where the school day was established early in its history as lasting late into the afternoon. Some European countries established early a system whereby the school day terminates around lunchtime, children returning to their homes to eat. In Germany, from the early twentieth century it became customary to freely provide warm milk and a roll to school children. Here, as in Scandinavia, children today carry a snack to school, consumed together with their peers mid morning (see below). In the United States, the midday school meal became common practice in the early decades of the twentieth century as concern grew about the health of the growing population. On 'The Vital Question of School Lunches', Mary Josephine Mayer noted in 1911

> *That large numbers of school children are undernourished is a statement which no longer admits of dispute. The fact has been recognized and dealt with in Europe, and now we of the United States are waking up to conditions that cry aloud for action ... How much longer shall we ignore the plain fact that education can come only after bread?*[21]

That children's cognitive capacities were limited through undernourishment was recognized at this time by commentators who were campaigning for free and compulsory school meal provision as a fundamental feature of state (or public) education.

> *Mental disability is not only preventable but in many cases curable. In a large number of instances, after the careful attention and midday dinner of the special schools, the children are returned to the elementary schools with a new lease of mental vigour.*[22]

By 1931, one third of school children in the United States were receiving a midday meal. But already, the cafeteria system which facilitated some choice was leading to concerns surrounding the nutritional value of what was consumed. It was suggested that teachers should always eat with the children and exhibit model behaviour in their choice of foods

and that menus should be posted in classrooms 'so that the child, guided by his teacher, may dwell upon his purchases in advance'.[23]

The school meal service in England and Wales, with its origins in the 1906 Education (School Meals) Act, was associated with notions of progress, advancement, improvement of the health and well-being of the nations' children and of the 'race'. Indeed, it was regarded as an educational and 'civilizing process' in itself. *The school dinner may ... be made to serve as a valuable object lesson and used to reinforce the practical instruction in hygiene, cookery and domestic economy.*[24]

With its roots in philanthropy and voluntary welfare provision for undernourished children, by 1906 the state's provision of school meals was argued for as 'not a work of relief, but of education.' The link between nourishment of body and mind was established.[25]

This was also the case in the United States where the school canteen was seen by educational experts as a key area of social education. The lunch room was regarded as a 'social behaviour laboratory and school health centre'. It provided opportunity and practice for responsibility, consideration and courtesy. It opened opportunities for the teaching of 'proper health habits, personal hygiene, good conduct, selfcontrol, promptness, unselfishness, and thoughtfulness'.[26] The education of children about food was considered vital for the well-being of society on both sides of the Atlantic.

> *The lunch work should be a vital part of the health teaching in every school. The children who stay at school for lunch need hot food at the noon hour, but that is not all. An excellent opportunity is offered for instruction and training in right food habits, and teachers should take advantage of this to the fullest extent possible. The lunch at school should never become a perfunctory matter. It is not just a question of providing food, but is a means of teaching the boys and girls to eat in the right way the foods that are good for them.*[27]

It is clear from early accounts that the association of school children with food and drink was also

Figure 12.8
School children eating on a roof top, New York, 1911.

seen as potentially chaotic. It served to remind those seeking to 'improve' the morals and behaviour of the 'lower' classes, of the chasm of difference that existed between the social classes. One detects a sense of fear and revulsion in these early accounts of collective consumption. It was noted that in many cases dinner was eaten in 'a perfect pandemonium of noise' and such 'disorderly conduct' as the throwing of food was reported by the Parliamentary Committee looking into the working of the Education (School Meals) Act in 1910.[28] Thus from its inception, the edible landscape of the school can be seen to have been a territory of contested desires and intentions, a battleground between the perceived needs of the adult and the child and a exhibition space for the product of educational endeavour.

From the early days of the implementation of the Education (School Meals) Act in 1906, schools in England and Wales experienced great difficulties in finding adequate and appropriate space to prepare food and to serve it to children. Schools were providing hot food and drink in classrooms, halls, cellars and outhouses. When the pupil's desk was turned into a table for the purpose of eating, teachers were concerned to hasten the dining period in order that desks could be cleaned of debris. In the early 1900s, especially in the USA, it

was becoming common for separate dining areas to be located in the basement or roof space of some of the larger schools. The use of the top floor of a building for dining was considered advantageous since ventilation and the removal of odours from the rest of the school was desirable.

Ideally, spaces devoted to the preparation and consumption of food should be cut off from the rest of the school building. The use of the school roof, with fabric canopy, is evident from the above photograph from a New York site taken during the first decade of the twentieth century.

Schools in France at this time sometimes went to great trouble in ridding the school of the vestiges of food preparation and consumption. According to one account:

The boys ate at little marble tables. As soon as they had finished, a relay of servants carried off plates and dishes; the windows were thrown wide open; a mighty hydrant was opened, and a deluge was sent flying over tables, floor, and walls; and in a moment, crusts, crumbs, smells and foul air disappeared in one gush.[29]

The specified dining area and kitchens of schools designed during the 1920s symbolized modernization, progress and quality in educational provision. Partly, this was a practical necessity as schools were drawing pupils from ever-larger catchment areas and returning home for the midday break was an impossibility for many. On the development of 'The Urban School' in 1920s London, it was noted *'The secondary schools of the time are noteworthy for the provision of a full kitchen and dining service evidencing the fact that they were intended as centres of excellence drawing their pupils from a wide catchment area'.*[30]

The school hall is at the heart of the traditional school. This rectangular space was originally, at least for the poor, the school room in its entirety. The hall, whether central or adjacent in relation to classrooms and other facilities, served in the majority of schools built in the twentieth century as the principal gathering space for assembly, celebration, physical exercise, public examination, performance and the consumption of food. In addition, the hall in the state school took on a symbolic function to suggest the school's unity, ethos and essential hierarchical nature. In the English public school and in the majority of grammar schools, which attempted to emulate the public school, the hall typically could seat the whole school, with masters assembled on a raised platform, the headmaster seated centrally. In the public schools of Great Britain, these arrangements were continued when the hall was turned over to its dining function, masters and prefects having special seating arrangements emphasizing their relative power and status in the school.

This large communal space was conceived of by planners of state schools as multi-purpose for reasons of economics.

This space can be used perhaps for only two hours a day and does not earn its keep. Architects therefore looked for other areas in the building which, if suitably designed, could be used for dining as well as for their primary purpose ... Occasionally classrooms have been used by providing sliding or folding partitions which can be removed to open up a large common area in which the midday meal can be taken. It must be admitted that some arrangements for dual use of dining space involve

an element of inconvenience, (however) ... it represents the common sense compromise which, as householders, we are prepared to make in our own homes in order to ensure value for money.[31]

As a consequence, the utilization of the school hall and even the classroom for dining purposes has become ubiquitous in the experience of children and their teachers over generations. Unlike the essentially adult landscape of the work place, where communal eating in canteens is set apart from spaces devoted to production or manufacturing, and other forms of recreation, the edible landscape of the school has historically overlaid its other functions. However, the demand by children for separate and specialized eating areas, like those which have become expected in the adult world of work have been over time and remain today as the dual use of spaces – especially the school hall – still cause misery for many children.

The corporate edible landscape of school

It's back to school and kids aren't the only ones heading for the classroom. Marketers are taking more and more products from the boardroom to the homeroom and lunchroom through innovative partnerships.[32]

A 1995 report by the US-based Consumers Union divides corporate involvement in schools into four categories. First is in-school advertising, such as advertising or corporate logos on buses, walls, scoreboards, and book covers. Second is commercialism in classroom magazines and television programmes. Third are corporate sponsored educational materials and programmes, including multimedia teaching kits, workbooks, posters, and other teaching aids. Fourth are corporate sponsored contests and incentive programmes, such as a programme with Pizza Hut restaurants that rewards reading with free pizza or deals with McDonald's which donates vouchers as school prizes.[33] In addition there is the exclusive contract with beverage companies and other firms that supply vending machines.

Corporate involvement in schools as an attempt to shape and influence children and young people's drinking habits has a long history. Milk products have long been associated with health and growth in children and there is a strong tradition in the UK and Europe of providing milk products to children without charge. Usually, cocoa was provided, but occasionally other milky warm drinks were marketed as 'healthy' for growing children. During the 1930s Horlicks, a malted milk drink was served as a hot mid-morning drink in over 6000 schools every day. All the necessary equipment was lent free to schools by the suppliers as is suggested here in a school log entry dating from 1932, '*The Horlicks rep. has called for the urn, cups etc. loaned by Horlicks, as it has been decided by vote of the children to discontinue providing the Horlicks milk each morning during the winter months.*'[34]

The 'Horlicks School Scheme' appears to be an early example of corporate marketing in schools using the persuasive educational argument for choosing the product.

Horlicks is made from pure, fresh, full-cream cow's milk and the nutritive extracts of wheat and malted barley. It is easily and quickly prepared – with water only – and served hot or cold. All the necessary equipment is lent free to schools. Reports show that in these schools the children are brighter, more alert. They have increased energy and they are more regular in their attendance than before the introduction of the Horlicks School Scheme.[35]

This practice of providing free milk was terminated as an entitlement in England and Wales during the 1970s in government cost-cutting measures. However, the tradition continues in Scandinavian countries where companies vigorously pursue schools as immediate customers for their products and recognize children and young people as customers of the future. Iceland's largest dairy company has, over years, sponsored school activities and secured contracts through a child- and family-friendly marketing strategy. Rather like the milk drink company Horlicks, in the 1930s, the Icelandic Dairy Company today provides equipment free to schools to enable easier access

to the product. '*We supply the schools with refrigerators for this milk stock. The newest on the market is a refrigerator for 10-litre bags of milk and the children bring their own glasses to get the milk directly from the tap, ice-cold.*'[36]

Today in the USA, soft-drink bottlers and distributors are among the leading supporters of school sports activities. In 2000, Sacramento City Unified School District agreed an exclusive 'pouring contract' with Pepsi, receiving $2 m in a five-year deal. This resulted in the entire district's seventy-seven schools offering Pepsi as the only drink, the school authority earning twice the income available from local deals.[37] In the UK, many secondary schools have come to rely on large chunks of income from contracts with companies who supply canned drink and vending machines, while primary schools have become plied with free exercise books carrying subtle advertising for a drinks manufacturer.

Deregulation and privatization of the school meals service in the UK and the USA have provided the opening for the fast food industry. But a crucially additional factor is the wider process of 'McDonaldization' which, according to recent critical commentary voiced in Europe, can be recognized in the demotion and the narrowing down of food within the curriculum alongside the Americanization of European eating patterns and habits.

De-skilling and 'McDonaldization' are parallel developments, both interacting and feeding off each other. One could not flower (or de-flower, as the case might be) without the other. We are invited to ponder on the possibility that the de-skilling experience in food education might generate another type of product – the 'McChild'.

Since the movement to invite private companies to tender for school meals contracts began in the USA and the UK in the early 1980s, rather than a widening of choice, an increase in diversity and a raising of quality what has occurred is a rendering of stereotypical fast and cheap food as a substitute for a nutritious midday meal. Ultimately, eating environments resemble one another – a Burger King interior is more or less identical whether you are eating your burger in Paris or New York. The disciplinarian regime of the school meal service is becoming, in many places, supplanted by the uniformity of logo-laden, market-driven carbohydrates. The 'McDonaldization' of the school lunch is well underway and meals can now be taken without the awkward clutter and clatter of plates and cutlery.

In contrast to the clear desire for quality and choice voiced by children recently in their entries to the 'School I'd Like' competition, surveys of what children and young people prefer to eat at lunch times in school environments regularly report what we are not surprised to hear. When faced with the restricted range of products on offer the result is predictable in underlining what we are assumed to believe is true. *'Now it's official: this most recent survey found that a plate of chips is the most popular savoury lunch, followed by pizza, sausage or hot dog, spaghetti and burger.'*[39]

'Kids will be kids' is the resigned message that is conveyed, one that seems to suggest that although worrying, there is little that can be done about it in spite of the growing incidence of childhood obesity and associated ill health. The old and traditional has become replaced by the new and familiar and with it a new way of calculating the cost, value and efficiency of the school meal.

It could be argued that it is the wider contextual landscape of branded packaging that is the most insidious and powerful in the long term. Some schools in South Yorkshire, England, have done away with cutlery and plates altogether and the lunchtime meal is consumed with the help of paper cones, plastics, polystyrene and of course aluminium cans. Paradoxically, this is partly conceived of as a form of waste management – the waste being the 'left-over' foodstuff that in the past would have been substantial since children had little choice but to take what was offered. This 'waste' was often recycled and made its way to the local piggery. However, strangely, the waste products of the minimalist school canteen do not appear to count as waste at all. The disposal of polystyrene cups and plates, papers and card, sometimes sporting logos of corporate sponsors, mimic the practice outside of school in the local

McDonald's or Pizza Hut. The acceptance of such materials and the management of their disposal within educational environments speak volumes for the neglect of any ecologically-driven curriculum and indeed the toleration, if not the promotion, of an individualistic 'me-first' culture.

McDonald's sees the school landscape as fertile ground for their advertising campaigns. During the spring of 2002, a film crew were shooting a commercial for McDonald's inside a High School in Vancouver. The commercial features a friendless boy clutching his fries and sauce hiding in the school bathroom. Here he smears his face with fries and sauce in front of a mirror. When he returns to the school corridor, his peers pursue him as the most popular boy in school!

In the USA the privatization of school meals programmes has increased in recent years with some unfortunate consequences for public health. The edible landscape of public schools in the Chicago Schools District, which privatized its school meals in 1997, is reported to be one of infestation, dirt, debris and grime. Such is the state of repair of some of these school buildings that chips of an inedible kind are turning up in the food. The *Chicago Tribune* recently reported that *'School kitchens and cafeterias are infested with insects and rodents. Chips of paint were observed floating in cooking pans and cafeteria walls were coated with accumulated grime'.*[40]

Not surprisingly cases of food poisoning have risen among children in the district.

Some of the most determined and aggressive examples of 'philanthropic' marketing of products within schools are that of the Burger King Empire in the USA. Founded in 1997 in memory of its founder, James W McLamore, the Burger King/ McLamore Foundation is:

a public, non-profit organization which works to coordinate the entire BURGER KING® system in a philanthropic effort dedicated to providing educational opportunities for deserving youth in the United States, Canada and Puerto Rico.[41]

Burger King loses no opportunity to remind its customers in the wider community of its worthy intentions 'to contribute to the development of a more skilled workforce for the future'. Eating a burger in one of its thousands of restaurants in the USA, the customer is reassured that the bill for the food will include a donation to the foundation, thus enabling worthy individuals to receive scholarships. Such finance also contributes to the programme of nationwide 'Burger King Academies'. At this time, twenty-four such 'academies' have been established in the United States. Burger King presents itself as a concerned company, so alarmed at the dropout rate in high schools that it has joined together with Communities in Schools, Inc. in forming a national network of twenty-four academies supported via corporate contributions and foundation funds.

Exploitation of what has been called 'cradle to grave marketing' can operate on parental anxieties around the learning experience of very young children. Burger King has recently collaborated with Sassy, manufacturer of 'educational' toys, to promote its meals. Customers are encouraged to imagine that the Burger King restaurant is indeed a landscape of learning, as while they eat their burger they have the opportunity to read about child development. Families with children under the age of three were, in January 2001, offered not simply a toy but peace of mind in the form of a Sassy premium. Ever more sophisticated in the presentation of marketing ploys, parents were assured that the choice of sixteen different designs introduced each year had been carefully chosen to match 'four critical stages of a child's mental development: moving and exploring, interacting and feeling, communicating and talking, and thinking and learning'.[42]

Food companies are quick to see the opportunities offered by government policies that insist on computer-supported teaching and learning in all schools while resources are not put in place to provide the infrastructure, hardware and training. Anxious to present a benign face to consumers, supermarket chains supply customers with vouchers to buy computers for schools and snack food companies take on the role of hosting websites for schools. A case in point is the activity over the past decade of snack food company Walkers, a UK subsidiary of PepsiCo. Walkers' 'free

books to schools' campaign is estimated to have distributed 2.3 million books, with 98 per cent of UK schools taking part. This was welcomed by the government as a means of helping stretch limited school budgets. More recently, Walkers has established a school website hosting function in collaboration with the UK Government body, the National Grid for Learning. Walkers has a long history of marketing with the school pupil and their parent in mind, with particular use of football heroes of the moment.

In some parts of the UK, McDonald's already provides textbooks, Pepsi provides 'Jazzy' exercise books sporting subtle advertising, Cadburys has a 'World of Chocolate' resource pack for children, the Meat and Livestock Commission provides a recipe book and Nestlé, Pringles and McVities all offer books and equipment in return for vouchers. The edible landscape of school is coming to resemble the high street and competition for this captive market is intense.[43]

Edible spaces: designing for choice

The exercise of choice matters for children. In spite of Human Rights legislation and increased awareness of the importance of agency in childhood, the economic or market imperative is today the more powerful force. Early examples of initiatives in furnishing an element of choice in school meals can be found. A New York high school cafeteria in 1934 introduced suggestion boxes, soliciting from the girls 'what they would like and how they would like it'. The same school offered the following 'conveyor belt' feature:

> *The students passing in line, help to make their own sandwiches ... The student chooses her filling and the kind of bread she wants; the worker spreads the filling on the top slice of bread and hands the girl that slice and the one beneath it, on waxed paper. Then, as she goes down the line, the girl can put her sandwich together.*[44]

The 1960s was a decade which encouraged a new look at edible landscapes. The Space Exploration Programmes of the USA and USSR stimulated technological developments in the reconstitution of foodstuffs. Experiments using frozen foods in school meals programmes began and there was a sense that the problems of transporting meals cooked in centralized kitchens might soon be overcome by advances in technology. These developments in turn encouraged new concepts of design in the management of food in educational environments. *'The ultimate may be an electronic belt, with an overhead infrared generator heating pre-packaged frozen foods as they roll down the serving line. They will mean savings in refrigeration costs, a transformation of kitchen equipment and new approaches to storage and warehousing.'*[45]

The management of choice and freedom in edible landscapes does have design implications. Different arrangements of the design and management of space express choice or lack of it. This was recognized within the experimental era of the 1960s when regimented rows of tables and chairs began to be replaced by more social arrangements, mirroring what was happening in the open plan classroom where adult control was marginalized.

The results were remarked upon by the Superintendent of Schools at Ridgewood High School in Norridge, Illinois where the cafeteria was divided four ways with movable doors to make separate dining areas. The doors, which created areas of increased intimacy, could be removed to make open spaces when required:

> *It provides an entirely different type of atmosphere ... we don't have gang feeding anymore; it's not a military type operation. The students behave and act much differently when sitting at a table with only three or four from when they're in the midst of a group of two hundred and fifty. The noise level is down and there are fewer discipline problems. We find we've been able to run our dining room without faculty supervision. The only adults in the area are two general aides whose job it is to clear up the tables.*[46]

This expressed preference for small social eating areas within a large open space is a recurring theme over time, especially when young people themselves are consulted. A recent example can be found in the consultation process which accompanied the School Works programme of building improvement of the inner city London school, Kingsdale in the UK.[47] At this school, where 67 per cent of children have free school meals, it was noticed that few children actually sat down to eat, making the atmosphere rather threatening for the younger or smaller children. When asked what changes they would make to the built environment, the children's major concern was to reduce the size of the dining space, making smaller spaces for groups of children to eat together. 'Girls and boys did not seem to experience this differently as they all seemed to dislike the ordeal of dining at the school.'[48]

Children and young people today crave to be treated with trust, and desire that the built learning environment might not resemble a school at all. Many have known little else than the fast food 'McDonaldized' fare on offer. The argument often put today by managers of school meals contracts is that reverting to the traditional school meal would result in total lack of uptake and the consequent haemorrhaging of the school community during lunch breaks to the local shops and cafés. This was noted as a problem in previous generations when 'Pupils were going down-town for a hamburger and soda or coming to school with a couple of candy bars for lunch.'[49] More attention to the ideas for changing the environmental context of eating, and especially to the ideas of children and young people, would arguably remove this barrier to change.

Resistance to the commercialization of the edible landscape in schools has been consistent since the introduction of the first vending machines in the late 1950s. When vending machines were installed at Redondo High School, California in 1958, students protested, carrying banners through the cafeteria with slogans such as 'Iron Monsters' and 'One-Armed Bandits'. Later, the machines were sabotaged when students in metalwork classes fashioned 'special slugs to knock the machines out of commission'.[50] More recently in the USA, the State of California has pioneered anti-corporate campaigns with some success. Alex Molnar, professor of Education at the University of

Figure 12.9
Cool Fuel water carrier provided by Yorkshire Water and designed by primary school children.

Wisconsin-Milwaukee and director of the Centre for the Analysis of Commercialism in Education, has reminded us that the landscape of the school is popularly and traditionally believed to be benign. Therefore, he argues *'in a school, everything that's going on is supposed to be good for you. When you take that venue and you exploit it for a particular special interest, you do a lot of damage to children'.*[51]

Designing for choice means allowing children and young people some freedom from over-marketed brands and promoting exposure to more healthy options. Children need to drink during the school day and it is clear from the 'School I'd Like' evidence that many simply want to be able to drink water when they need it. Bottled water is becoming 'cool' and schools in the UK have begun to experiment with water distributors and dispensers.

In the autumn of 2002, all 1400 primary schools in the city of Leeds were provided with water coolers free of charge by Yorkshire Water, the local service provider. The initiative was generated by concerns that children were not drinking sufficient water during the school day and that drinking water was accessed, if at all, via taps inside toilet blocks.

Such changes in the edible landscape of school resist the fast food fix that seems for many to be an inevitable feature of modern childhood and adolescence. Indeed, speed has more generally come to be an expectation of contemporary life.

Portable edible landscapes

In the United Kingdom, an estimated 50 per cent of school children bring packed lunches for their midday meal, a far lower proportion than elsewhere in Europe. An unknown number of children take food to school in the form of snacks of variable nutritional value. A packet of crisps can be consumed on the way to school, as a substitute for breakfast. According to a recent survey, 40 per cent of children have, by way of breakfast, a chocolate bar or a packet of crisps on the way to school.[52] Crisp packets turn up again as plastic pencil cases and holdalls. Certainly in Britain, where packet crisps were invented during the 1940s, the primary school classroom and wider environment can almost not be envisaged without the ubiquitous crisp packet.

Often, the crisp packet accompanies the lunch box which often, in the UK at least, is a contested and emotive object in a child's life. In the territory of the lunch box, conformity and competition are powerfully combined. Never merely a container, the latest fashions, trends, TV heroes, 'must have' toys or status symbols are coated in plastic on the boxes designed for the younger child. Not only the shape and outer design of the box, but its contents, usually express conformity. In the UK, it has been noted that a child may suffer bullying as the result of a non-conformist lunch box.

> *There's a lot of pressure from other kids to have the right kind of ready-prepared food, and anything homemade is terrible. I've seen shocking teasing when other kids see what one child has in a carefully prepared lunch box: they show no mercy!*[53]

Official concern over the content of lunch boxes was evident in the early years of the twentieth century. Children who walked long distances to school often carried food for the midday meal with them, since they were not able easily to return home. In 1905, the Inter-Departmental Committee on Medical Inspection and Feeding noted 'The lunches brought by the children were generally of a most unsatisfactory nature'[54] and suggested these should be supplemented by hot soup or cocoa.

Almost a century later, official concern with the contents of lunch boxes is, outside of the Scandinavian countries, nonexistent. However, there are local initiatives that have attempted to influence the content of packed lunch boxes and raise awareness in general of the importance of the portable edible landscape. Teachers at Edgware Infant and Nursery school near London decided to intervene and attempt to raise awareness of the poor nutritional contents of food brought to school by very young children. There were cultural issues identified, as some of the diverse backgrounds of the children did not contain any tradition of packed food. The starting point in raising awareness was an exercise of drawing the contents of the lunch box and labelling the items. After a series of community workshops and

practical sessions, the pupils were asked again to draw the contents of their boxes. The differences were reported to be 'staggering'.[55]

In Iceland, food skills and home economics are high status subjects in the National Curriculum from the age of six. Here also, the school building is sometimes used on a shift basis to host early years education in the morning and later years in the afternoon. The younger children bring with them a box or food bag containing a mid-morning snack. Without any official policy or statement there is a universal understanding among the school community and parents about what is acceptable content. This practice is strengthened by the sponsorship of a dairy company who supplies children with the food containers. '*For many years all 6-year-old children get a plastic box for their provisions from home, along with a ruler, eraser and a timetable when they start at school in August. A letter is included to parents where we use an official propaganda to point out the necessity of healthy eating.*'[56]

Here, conformity is 'cool' and seems to be generally accepted. Usually children will bring a sandwich and it is expected that the bread will be wholesome. Any drink will either be water or milk and a piece of fruit is most usual. Strictly frowned upon is any sweet, chocolate or fatty food such as crisps and a child who brought such content to school would be looked on by his or her peers as an unfortunate – quite the opposite of what happens in the UK. Parents expect schools to be places where good food is consumed within a pleasant environment.

Where children do stay at school to eat a hot meal, the cost is subsidized so that parents pay only thirty per cent of the cost. A traditional family type meal is served consisting of meat or fish with vegetables and a drink of milk or water. No sweet or desert follows. Teachers always eat the same food alongside the children on a rota basis and this is a valued and paid activity within the educational system.

Children and young people have traditionally carried food with them from home to school for lessons in cookery. Now labelled 'Food Technology' in the UK National Curriculum, the word 'cooking' does not get a mention. This explains partly the

Figure 12.10
Children enjoying their mid-morning food break at a school in Iceland.

Figure 12.11
The Cooking Bus.

emphasis on 'cooking' and 'making' food rather than its design, production and marketing that fuels the 'Focus on Food' campaign which was initiated in 1998.

Not every school has space or equipment enough to teach food preparation and cooking skills and often, especially in primary schools, the general classroom is used with the aid of microwave ovens. The Royal Society for the Arts' Focus on Food campaign has recognized this and a portable kitchen, or Cooking Bus, is a design feature of this initiative which works to encourage interest and pleasure in cooking and to have the subject made a compulsory part of the national curriculum. The Cooking Bus is sponsored by Waitrose supermarket and travels the length and breadth of Britain stopping at schools or supermarkets for a week at a time. It comes supplied with experienced teachers, 'state-of-the-art' equipment and food supplied by Waitrose. When opened up the bus becomes an impressive teaching kitchen for up to sixteen children who are, in stages, all shown how to make a meal or a range of dishes, usually representative of a particular culture or region. After cooking the food, the children then sometimes sit down together and eat it.[57]

The Cooking Bus, unlike most children's home kitchens, is a highly serviced, pristine environment. Food ingredients appear, as if by magic, often still packaged from the supermarket and otherwise arranged already weighed out in attractive containers. There is an air of the TV cookery show about the space. Although basic skills are taught, for older children at least, little emphasis is placed on the slow work of acquiring, preparing and assembling ingredients. This is done by others before the children enter the bus. Washing up is done by adult assistants and the pupils have a rare experience of cooking at ease. It is fast and effective. Vegetables, fruits and herbs are presented as beautiful objects, the lighting and wall mirrors seem to enhance the natural colours of the ingredients rather as they do in supermarket outlets. The teacher emphasizes the quality of equipment as necessary in order to cook well. The utensils are provided by the John Lewis partnership of which Waitrose is the principal food branch.

After cooking in Waitrose-branded plastic overalls, at the end of the session the pupils are supplied with branded foldable cardboard containers in which to carry their produce home within a branded plastic carrier bag. The teacher's plastic overall is branded 'Savoy Educational Trust', a branch of the well-known, high quality London hotel which provides funding for the teachers' salaries. But will cooking at school ever be the same again? The Focus on Food campaign hopes so and does its best towards this aim by means of in-service teacher training held in the bus and by

leaving behind its colourful, glossy *Food Education Magazine,* free to all registered schools. Inside the magazine, celebrity cook Gary Rhodes demonstrates how to make pastry and the reader is directed to the Waitrose website for more 'curriculum connections'. The Cooking Bus is on the road for forty-eight weeks of the year and the project relies totally on large amounts of corporate sponsorship which are secure for the immediate future. The UK supermarkets are in intense competition with one another and each must find its marketing niche in relation to education in the pursuit of brand loyalty. Research carried out by academics at the University of Reading in England will report on the effects on children of sustained education around food. Clearly, the effect of sustained educational activity on the wider community is something that the supermarkets are prepared to gamble will pay off.

Growing schools and edible school yards

> ... the outdoor clay oven is full of flame, stoked with dry sticks collected in the woods; next to it the bread made from the wheat from our 'field' in the garden is rising. In the classroom the jam made from the hedgerow blackberries in September is being brought out; and butter made from cream from the local farm, is being salted and put into dishes. Bottles of apple juice made in September and stored in the freezer are being defrosted. Class three will celebrate the end of the term's farming work with a jam sandwich and a glass of juice, won by the sweat of their brows....[58]

In contrast to the approach taken by 'Focus on Food' in the UK, the growing schools and edible school yard movements are conscious of the importance of teaching, through experience, that food does not originate in the supermarket, but in the soil through labour and care. The schoolyard projects discussed here position themselves as part of a wider movement towards building sustainable communities. There is an important difference between learning to cook dishes from different parts of the world from recipes provided and learning the cultural significance of food from and alongside members of the local community. Until recent times, the skills and knowledge about the production, preparation and presentation of food were learnt within an oral culture, primarily in the home or wider community. To replicate and rescue some of that traditional understanding around food in schools, the emphasis is placed on learning through experience. The land and the local community provide inspiration and resources in an approach which prioritizes respect, tenureship and collective endeavour.

'From working to learn to learning to work', the outdoor classroom is an extension of the 'main lesson' in a Steiner school. The philosophy which underpins the educational landscape of the Steiner or Waldorf school is one that views the child in its early stage of development in becoming human as the embodiment of an early stage in the general evolution of humanity. From this perspective, the young child might be viewed as a natural 'hunter-gatherer' within a primeval landscape. Within such a philosophical framework, work with the brain is viewed as inseparable and of equal value to work with the heart and work with the hand. This has not been the case within the dominant paradigm of school which has come to regard the academic as superior to the practical and the pursuit of intellectual knowledge and skill as more valuable than the passing on of traditional wisdom about domestic husbandry.

Recognition of the circle of the year through its changing seasons requires a flexibility of human response if the natural powers of sun, wind, earth and water are to be orchestrated to fulfil human needs. Teaching and learning according to the circularity of the turning seasons brings those involved face to face with the consequences of their previous endeavours. In contrast, the dominant ideology of mainstream schooling is linear; children and young people move on and away from their previous work. Once complete, the work may or may not be celebrated. Most likely it will be measured according to values and standards externally derived and enforced. Most significantly, the child learns in school that work carried out rapidly takes its place in the past; to revisit the very same site of work represents failure, the danger of falling behind, or enforced punishment. Some would argue that the lesson taught is 'detachment' from the content of learning.[59]

Such a 'seasonal pedagogy' contrasts and clashes with an 'industrial pedagogy' in many ways. A 'seasonal pedagogy' challenges expectations about the landscape and ecology of school. The urban school building and environment took on an established form in the industrial era, rising from its roots in the workhouse and the factory.[60] The concept of progress accompanying the establishment of mass education in European countries and the United States led to the establishment of a uniformly bounded environment, an urban 'island' of childhood even in a rural location.[61] It was an avowed part of the project of national mass education to frame the school alongside the church as the only sites of generating and transferring valuable knowledge within a community and particularly to disassociate wisdom from the domestic arena. Even in the inter-war period in England, while gardening was part of the curriculum, it was forced to take place outside of the school boundary within which was built the ubiquitous asphalt schoolyard.[62] In the mainstream, schools generally became hard environments, the outside spaces conducive to ball play, drill and physical exercise. The rise of competitive school sports in the grammar and high schools helped preserve some green areas but even these have in recent years been sold off by many schools struggling to survive under restricted budgets. Strongly established in the popular concept of school is the familiar building situated within a neatly kept, bounded territory which speaks of academic rather than agricultural labour and achievement.

A 'seasonal pedagogy' contests the traditional management of time and the organization of the school day, week, month and year. The growing season presents the opportunity and the necessity for a great deal of active engagement with the land in the spring and summer while there is much less activity during the winter months. Although the turn of the year is predictable, the weather and conditions are not and activity needs to be flexible in response. At peak growing times, the growing plants dictate what activity is needed where and when. The same tasks need to be repeated throughout the seasons; the efforts of one year are recognized in the next and the effect in reality is cumulative. 'The picture varies from year to year; it evolves and changes'.[63]

The transformation of schoolyards in the Berkeley school district of California has its origins in the efforts of Robin Moore who led the landscape architecture school at the University of Berkeley.[64] In 1980, Moore saw the potential for using the outdoor environment of schools to enliven children's learning experience, teach sustainability and encourage community involvement.

The space was a desert of asphalt, so typical of many school yards. But by asking people what they liked about the yard, and what they wanted to change, ... the yard is becoming a place where community and school can meet.[65]

Washington School yard, a one and a half acre site within a high density urban neighbourhood became the best known example of school ground revitalization in North America and inspired other projects. The food garden was one of a number of features that included a natural play area. This project established what could be achieved and inspired others. Two decades later, it is still a vibrant, living and utilized feature of the landscape of the school (see Plate 20).

The district of Berkeley is a short distance across the bay from San Francisco. It has a lively, young, diverse population with the University of California campus at its heart. The movement for organic and whole foods took root here during the 1970s and 1980s and it is possible to find the widest possible choice of high quality, fresh local produce in the regular farmers' markets or the vast food stores. Cafés, restaurants and bistros serve foods in the traditions of every part of the globe. But most children who attend the public schools are accustomed to fast foods such as TV dinners

and are used to a poor or non-existent diet. Nevertheless, the cultural climate in Berkeley has motivated the community to support initiatives around transforming the edible landscape of school. In August 1999, Berkeley School Board in California set in motion a revolution in the place of food within schools. After a decade of anxiety fuelled by scientific speculation about the impact of pesticide residues on fruits and vegetables consumed, together with the introduction of genetically altered foods, and the ever increasing fast food market, the pressure was on for a change. Parents and teachers, and some food specialists including Alice Waters, a well-known local chef and restaurant owner, campaigned for change. A three-year campaign in association with the Food Systems Project of the Centre for Ecoliteracy, including fundraising, finally brought success. As well as the introduction of organic produce, the Berkeley school district plan has banned the use of genetically engineered or irradiated foods and dairy products from cows injected with the recombinant bovine growth hormone. Other goals of the district's plan include establishing a child nutrition advisory committee and eliminating food additives and high-fat, high-sugar snacks available in school. Schools are directed to serve tasty, fresh, local and organic foods in ways that reflected the districts' ethnic diversity.

It is intended that all sixteen public schools in the district will have gardens used by teachers and pupils as open air classrooms and sources of food for the school lunch, and the whole philosophy is to have food become a central part of education. An integrated curriculum which promotes awareness of the way food is grown, the environment, and health is the central plank of the policy. The further development of the policy is managed by The Berkeley Food Policy Council, a coalition of residents, non-profit agencies, community groups, school district and city agencies formed in May 1999. It is pledged 'to build a local food system based on sustainable regional agriculture that fosters the local economy and assures all people of Berkeley have access to healthy, affordable and culturally appropriate food from non-emergency sources.'[66]

The edible school yard is an organic garden and kitchen non profit-making-project that integrates the curriculum and lunch programme at Martin Luther King Junior Middle School in Berkeley, California. The school serves a very diverse community – the majority of the 820 children are of non-European origin. A large proportion are from impoverished backgrounds. Most parents work and children rely heavily on ready-prepared fast food. Few have garden plots of their own at home. From the start, the project had the backing of celebrity chef Waters whose prominence in the project helped to secure financial support which now amounts to some $400 000 annually, most of which pays for the salaries of six full-time workers. It also pays for half of the time of a science teacher in school who works on the project. One hundred tons of compost from the City of Berkeley helped to start the one acre plot in a raised area above the main asphalt yard of the school. Started in 1995, pupils, parents and teachers together transformed the playground area into a beautiful vegetable, herb and flower garden. The style is organic: a wide variety of vegetables and fruits complemented by

flowers and herbs. The children have constructed the boundaries, the fences and scaffolding out of natural materials. There is no fence surrounding the garden which is open at all times for the community to visit and admire (see Plate 21).

Very little vandalism has occurred as the entire garden is cared for by all pupils and their sense of ownership is strong. Involvement in the garden begins with the youngest grade six children who enjoy harvesting, roasting and eating corn using the garden oven. This establishes the principle of the garden landscape, that food comes from the ground and working with it is fun and satisfying. A 'scavenger hunt' follows and children are encouraged to experience for themselves the sights, smells, textures and sounds of the garden. Thereafter, each ninety-minute 'lesson' starts at the centre of the garden in the open air classroom, a circular arrangement of branches woven together to form a kind of dome.

On a rotational basis, each grade works in the garden or the kitchen over three-week intensive ninety-minute periods, a total of three hundred children each week throughout the year. After

Figure 12.12
The outdoor classroom, the edible schoolyard, Berkeley, California.

school classes are available and a summer programme, free of charge, is also provided covering garden and kitchen work.

During six days of annual statutory testing, the edible school kitchen prepares and serves a nutritious and delicious breakfast to children free of charge. Out of the full number of 820 pupils currently registered, the breakfast is voluntarily taken by around 300, a few minutes before their tests begin. The idea behind the breakfast is that the children are likely to perform better in the tests on a satisfied stomach. The 300 who take the offer of the breakfast could be an indication of the approximate number regularly coming to school on an empty stomach. The breakfast consists of something hot, for example, on a particular day that might be oatmeal, macaroni cheese, or scrambled eggs, served with a chunk of wholesome organic bread (provided as a donation by a local bakery), a full piece of fruit and milk. Everything is prepared fresh on the morning and is served in an informal atmosphere of respect, enjoyment and celebration.

Children relish these breakfasts and are overheard to say they regret the end of the testing period. If funds allowed, the project would like to provide such breakfasts during the whole school year. More generally, classes are held in the edible school kitchen. As many ingredients as possible are harvested straight from the school garden, the rest provided by local organic farmers' markets. Some of the ingredients such as lentils or rice may be prepared in advance so that the children can work with the raw foods, preparing and cooking them in the short time period available. Any brand labels are removed as children are led to focus on the value of working with locally harvested foods. After the cooking is complete, the tables are set by the children and they sit to eat their meal together.

One thousand miles north of Berkeley, just over the border into Canada is Vancouver, with a distinctly cooler climate but an equal passion for schoolyard revitalization. Here, Gary Pennington, while Professor of Education at the University of British Columbia, started the first school food garden in Vancouver. Built in 1989, the food garden was part of a larger project at Lord Roberts Elementary School in the West End of the City, Canada's highest density neighbourhood. The predominant type of residence is high rise and

Figure 12.13
Lunch is prepared and served: the edible schoolyard kitchen.

consequently there is very little garden space available to the community. In its early days, Pennington said of the children 'the food garden increases their sense of wonder. It's pretty magical, but at the same time, it demystifies the concept of food production'.[67]

The garden at Lord Roberts Elementary still exists and has laid the foundations of other schoolyard revitalization projects. Evergreen, a Canadian national non-profit environmental organization sponsors and promotes through its 'Learning Grounds' programme the transformation of barren school grounds into dynamic natural outdoor learning environments. A special emphasis is placed on participative and democratic planning. The design process starts off in the classroom where children are encouraged to dream up their imagined ideal schoolyard. The next stage involves the children and teachers surveying the land and drawing up practical possibilities. An important part of the learning process is around negotiating possibilities within the boundaries dictated by physical, legal and customary features.

One of the most adventurous projects carried out through a participative design process is found in a disadvantaged multicultural inner city community in Vancouver.

Grandview Uuqinak'uuh is an inner city elementary school in Vancouver's East End. Built in the 1920s, the school accommodates a culturally diverse community. More than half of the children who attend and a core of teachers and learning assistants are of 'first nations' ancestry. This strong cultural context is supported by several first nation housing projects in the neighbourhood. Communities from Eastern Europe, China and Vietnam are also served by the school. Over 90 per cent of households are headed by single mothers. This rich cultural heritage is embraced in a school community which is determined to challenge the deprivation and associated levels of crime and disaffection in this neighbourhood. The school gardens were designed to be the 'backyard of the community' since so many of this community living on the margins do not have access to garden space.

Three years ago, the grounds were dirty and dangerous as some members of the community used them for recreational purposes leaving litter behind. A vast open space was transformed into 'a more beautiful, useable and sustainable space where children and the community can learn.'[68] The design emerged out of a process of gathering ideas from workshops and open houses with staff, students, parents and other members of the community. Many of the original ideas came through to the final design and parents, teachers and children together constructed the garden beds and helped to construct and decorate the outdoor classroom.

The school has been renamed in the Nuuchahnulth language, Uuqinak'uuh meaning 'beautiful view' and the school day begins with the beating of a drum. The design of the school garden is reflective of the character of the school and the 'voice' of the community and there was, from the start, good support for aboriginal design elements among the teachers.

This diverse community is invited directly in to the school ground by means of renting a small garden plot within a larger space of raised beds. The layout is formal and contrasts with the organic, informal style found in Berkeley. This was a design requirement of the community, a direct response to the fear voiced by the community that the gardens would look messy in winter.[69] It seems, from the final design, that the needs of the adult members of the community, teachers, staff, parents and others overruled some of the most popular ideas for the garden voiced by the children. The most favoured design idea of the children was for a waterfall followed by a stream or creek, and growing flowers and vegetables was prioritized. In the final gardens there is no water feature as adults feared that this might encourage drug use.

Cooking 'fun for family' classes are held on a weekly basis. First nations and Vietnamese parents and children enjoy learning and eating together during these classes. Several times a year, cultural social events featuring food and dance are held. Hot breakfast and hot lunch programmes are used by the majority of children.[70] The children's food garden is also set out in wooden framed raised beds constructed by the children with the help of parents and teachers. Corn, tomatoes, radishes, carrots and lettuces are grown but the size of the vegetable gardens is inevitably limited by the commitment of parents and others in the community to share their labour freely. The original idea of growing ample food for the lunch programme in at least one season has been compromised. However, the butterfly and bird habitat has been planted with edible fruits and berries that can be grazed by children in season. Once an area prey to drug trafficking and prostitution, the school has transformed a recreation field into a vibrant open air inter generational classroom.

'Seeds of the future'

Starting a garden is like planting seeds of hope for future generations to have better lives.... Our school grounds are going to be transformed into something fertile and fruitful.[71]

On a global scale, school feeding programmes are perceived by agencies such as the World Food Programme to be the key to ending global hunger and associated inequalities. Drought and associated famine which strike areas such as Kenya immediately impact upon schools where children, especially girls, are withdrawn while their families cope with the short- or long-term crisis. UNICEF has reported a drop in school attendance of between 5 and 10 per cent in such areas at these times.

Poverty, hunger or malnutrition are usually associated with the non-industrialized majority world. But the incidence of child poverty is on the increase in many Western countries and providing nutrition in the school environment is regarded as a key to tackling wider problems of inequalities and related issues.[72]

In spite of major changes in the type and origins of food consumed in school there are important continuities over time which the historical perspective allows us to recognize. These continuities in children's experience and culture underline the fundamental importance of the edible school landscape for children. They draw

from it in ways that allow their creative impulse to become active. Food becomes a language of communication, a coded language that children know how to interpret from their collective play. Food represents survival which goes a long way to explain why it features so strongly when children of all ages are invited to describe or design their ideal school environment. This creative outlet is important to recognize and what the historical record testifies is that, in spite of the 'McDonaldization' factor, the evidence shows that young children will respond to the edible landscape in creative ways as long as they are allowed free time together to play or socialize in the school or schoolyard.

Food gardens mature over a growing season. Inspiring change in children's appreciation of food takes time and the school projects where they exist are set against gigantic competition from the fast food industry and commercial food companies. Designing edible landscapes is an important part of the future of school, and listening to what children say they want, beyond hearing what is expected, is key to transforming, through design, the next generation's attitude towards food and consumption.

Notes

1 Opie, I. and Opie, P. (1977). *The Lore and Language of School Children*. Frogmore, St Albans: Paladin. pp. 182–184.

Today, it is still possible to observe in any primary school playground the length and breadth of the UK, children chanting rhymes to accompany skipping and other games. Many of these feature food. Some contemporary examples might include:

Oh I wish I was a little round orange
Oh I wish I was a little round orange
I'd go squirty, squirty, squirty
Over everybody's shirty
Oh I wish I was a little round orange!

North, South, East, West,
Cadbury's chocolate is the best.

Jelly on a plate,
Jelly on a plate,
Wibble wobble, wibble wobble,
Jelly on a plate.

Milk, milk, lemonade,
'round the corner, chocolate's made! (A chant to accompany picking someone to be 'on' in a game of chase.)

Apple, strawberry, treacle tart,
I know the name of your sweetheart,
A, B, C, …. (skipping rhyme)

The rhythms are the same although the words signify a changed context,

A Pizza Hut, a Pizza Hut,
Kentucky Fried Chicken and a Pizza Hut.
McDonald's, McDonald's,
Kentucky Fried Chicken and a Pizza Hut.
(skipping rhyme).

2 The phrase 'the white heat of technology' was used by Prime Minister Harold Wilson after winning the UK General Election in 1964.

3 See for example 'Enterprise guide, case study *Cocktails and Canapes,* UK National Curriculum, Design and Technology key stage 3 support materials.' Food Technology pupils in Year 10 undertook a design and technology enterprise, working with local businesses, providing food for a large-scale event and then producing a recipe book for sale. The enterprise provided an insight into the food industry, illustrated the commercial value of food production, encouraged the pupils to find out about local food and required them to mass produce quality food products.

4 See for example Winterton, J. (2002) Multinationals, ready meals and malnutrition – why fat is a socialist issue. *The Guardian,* 26 February.

5 Although the school curriculum was never prescribed in Britain until the introduction of the National Curriculum in 1988, pre-war manuals for teachers such as *Handbook of Suggestions for Teachers,* published in 1927 by the Board of Education, devoted a whole chapter to gardening.

6 Stitt, S., Jepson, M., Paulson-Box, E. and Prisk, E. *Food Skills in the National Curriculum: An International Perspective.* Paper presented at BERA Annual Conference September 1996.

7 Worksheet 'Control Systems for Bread making'. Ridgwell Press. Accessed March 2002 in use at key stage 3, 13–14-year-old children, UK.

8 Arnhold, W., Dixey, R., Heindl, I., Loureiro, I., Perez, C. and Snel, J. (1995). *The European Guide to Nutrition Education in Schools: Europe Against Cancer.* Holstein: European Commission.

9 In the UK, The Growing Schools Garden project is part of a wider government initiative, The Growing Schools Programme, launched by the Department for Education and Skills (DfES) in September 2001. The project aims to increase schools' interest and involvement in outdoor education, using school grounds, farm visits and growing as a resource.

A key objective is 'to help children understand where their food comes from, so they can make informed consumer choices and understand the benefits of a healthy diet and active lifestyle'.

10 The Henry Doubleday Research Association. Schools Organic Network. http://www.hdra.org.uk/ schools_organic_network/index.htm

11 See Brosterman, N. (1997). *Inventing Kindergarten.* New York: Abrams Books.

12 *Handbook of Suggestions for Teachers* (1927), Board of Education, London. H.M.S.O. p. 385.

13 Log book entry, Shurdington School, accessed via www.shurdington.org/oldschool.htm. During the Second World War in the United States, the Victory Gardens similarly employed children in growing food.

14 A full discussion of 'The School I'd Like' archive can be found in Burke, C. and Grosvenor, I. (2003) *The School I'd Like. Children and Young People's Reflection on an Education for the 21st Century.* London: Routledge.

15 Blishen, E. (1969). *The School That I'd Like.* London: Penguin. p. 9.

16 ibid, p. 149.

17 The *Guardian, Education Supplement,* 16 January and 5 May, 2001, p.

18 The term 'McDonaldization' from Ritzer, G. (2000). *The McDonaldization of Society.* Pine Forge Press.

19 Gordon, T., Holland, J. and Lahelma, E. (2000). *Making Spaces. Citizenship and Difference in Schools.* New York: Palgrave McMillan Ltd.

20 ibid. p. 144.

21 From *The Review of Reviews*, April 1911. I am grateful to Kate Rousmaniere of the University of Miami in Ohio for references to early school meals provision in the United States.

22 L. A. Selby, 31 March 1909, quoted in Buckley, M. E. (1914). *The Feeding of School Children.* London: Bell and Sons Ltd. p. 83.

23 Latimer, R. (1935). Problems of Public School Cafeterias. *Practical Home Economics,* Vol **13**, no. 6, p. 178.

24 Selby-Bigge, L. A. *Report on the Working of the Education (Provision of Meals) Act up to 31st March 1909.* p. 83.

25 *Hansard*, March 2, 1906.

26 Craddock, M. E. 'The School Lunch' Texas State College for Women. College of Industrial Arts. Bulletin no 156. July 1, 1931.

27 The Lunch Hour at School. (1920) *Evening Post,* New York, July 10,

28 Buckley, M. E. (1914). *The Feeding of School Children.* London: Bell and Sons Ltd.

29 'The Builder', 4/1/1890 cited in Clay, F. (1902). *Modern School Buildings.* London: B. T. Batsford. p. 160.

30 Ringshall, R., Miles, M. and Kelsall, F. (1983). *The Urban School. Buildings for Education in London, 1870–1980.* G.L.C. London: The Architectural Press.

31 Ministry of Education Pamphlet no. 33, (1957). *The story of post-war school building.* p. 38. London: Her Majesty's Stationery Office.

32 For a full analysis of the scale of corporate involvement in schools in the USA, a good place to start is the Center for the Analysis of Commercialism in Education, School of Education, University of Wisconsin-Milwaukee.

33 *Captive kids: a Report on Commercial Pressures on Kids at School*, Consumers Union, 1995. See http://www.igc.org/consunion/other/captivekids/pressures.htm

34 Shurdington school log, www.shurdington.org/oldschool.htm#COCOA%20versus%20HORLICKS

35 I am grateful to Ian Grosvenor for this reference discovered among papers at Birmingham City Council Education Library.

36 Information supplied by South Iceland Dairy.

37 BBC News 30 June 2000. In one school a pupil was suspended for wearing a Pepsi t-shirt on Coca-Cola day. Noble, M. 'The Branding of Education' in Global Social Justice. 30/01/2002. www.globaljustice.co.uk

38 Stitt *et al.,* 1996.

39 The *Guardian,* 23 July, p.

40 Jackson, D. (2002). *Chicago Tribune*, 1, May, p.

41 Information taken from Burger King's website, accessed March 2002. www.burgerking.com

42 www.burgerking.com. In 1999, Burger King was forced to recall an estimated quarter of a million Pokemon balls given away free to toddlers after a baby suffocated and died in California as a result of receiving one. BBC Online. Tuesday, 28 December, 1999, 19:43 GMT 'Burger King in Pokemon recall'

43 Walkers' website: www.walkers.co.uk. See also Geoff Rayner, Chair of the UK Public Health Association. 'Today's Lesson, Get Munching' in Health Matters, issue 44, spring 2001. The Walkers' showcase website is a National Grid for learning (NGfL) badged site. This means that the website applied to be included in the NGfL portal via the NGfL content registration form which can be accessed at: http://challenge.ngfl.gov.uk/gridreg

44 Brannigan, E. The School Lunch. A New York High School Cafeteria. *Practical Home Economics,* Vol **12**, no. 11, pp.

45 Bard, B. (1968). *The School Lunchroom: Time of Trial.* New York: Wiley. p. 48.

46 Bard, op. cit., p. 103.

47 See www.schoolworks.org.uk

48 Notes from workshops coordinated by School Works, summer 2000.

49 Bard, op. cit., p. 30.

50 Bard, op. cit., pp. 53–59.

51 Alex Molnar, 'Corporate Involvement In Schools: Time For A More Critical Look'. Center for the Analysis of Commercialism in Education, School of Education, University of Wisconsin-Milwaukee.Winter, 2001.

52 *The Guardian,* 23 July, p.

53 Mary Whiting, quoted in the *Guardian* 5 September, 2001.

54 Inter-Departmental Committee on Medical Inspection and Feeding cited in Buckley, op.cit. p. 37–38.

55 *Focus:* Healthy Eating. **11**, pp.

56 Information supplied by South Iceland Dairy.

57 Focus on Food. www.rsa.org.uk RSA's 'Focus on Food' Campaign is led and managed by the Design Dimension Educational Trust. The Campaign's principal supporter is Waitrose, food shops of the John Lewis Partnership. See *RSA Journal,* June 2002, pp. 22–23.

58 *Steiner Education Journal,* November, 2001.

59 The term is taken from John Taylor Gatto (1992) *Dumbing Us Down: The Hidden Curriculum of Compulsory Schooling.* Philadelphia: New Society Publishers.

60 The first secular schooling supported through state funding in England was established in the heart of the workhouse.

61 I am grateful to John R. Gillis for the reference to 'Islanding' taken from his paper presented at the Designing Modern Childhoods Conference, Berkeley, California, May 2002.

62 The author's mother has recounted how in her elementary school, a local landowner donated a plot of land for use by the school. This was in walking distance of the school situated in the north east of England.

63 *Steiner Education Journal,* November, 2001.

64 Moore is currently Director of The Natural Learning Initiative and Professor of Landscape Architecture in the School of Design, North Carolina State University. For information about the Natural Learning Initiative, see www.naturalearning.org

65 Moore, R. cited in Penner, T (1999) Grandview Community Schoolyard. School Ground Revitalization Project, Graduation Project. U.B.C. Department of Landscape Architecture

66 Jed Lawson, Coordinator of Berkeley Schools Food Project.

67 Pennington, G. cited in *School Garden Guidelines* (1989). Published by City Farmer and Imperial Oil Limited. p. 5.

68 Penner, T. (1999). *Grandview Community Schoolyard.* School Ground Revitalization Project, Graduation Project. U.B.C. Department of Landscape Architecture. p. 4. The project coordinator was Illene Pevec.

69 Penner, T. ibid. p. 45.

70 The breakfast programme is sponsored by a local bank.

71 Sam Fillipoff in Knickerbocker, N. Community spirit blooms in Grandview garden. *Teacher Newsmagazine,* Volume 13, Number 1, September 2000.

72 The School Children's Food Foundation of Newfoundland and Labrador was formed in 1994 to provide information and funding required to establish and sustain breakfast, lunch and snack programmes in schools and community centres throughout the province.

Illustrations

All photographs by C. Burke apart from:

Figure 12.1 Serving the School Dinner, from Armfelt, R. (1950). *Our Changing Schools. A Picture for Parents.* Prepared for the Ministry of Education by the Central Office of Information, London: HMSO, p. 34.

Figure 12.2 Findern School, from HDRA Organic Schools Network website.

Figure 12.3 Children's Garden, from Bosterman, N. (1997). *Inventing Kindergarten.* New York: Abrams, p. 37, credited to Zindman/Freemont New York.

Figure 12.4 ibid, p. 31.

Figure 12.5 Featherstone School Collection.

Figure 12.6 By Jamie Proud.

Figure 12.8 Roof top, New York, from *The Review of Reviews*, New York, April 1911.

Index